The Two Irelands and the Diaspora

Anne Groutel

The Two Irelands and the Diaspora

The Politics and Economics of a Self-Serving Attachment

palgrave
macmillan

Anne Groutel
Université de Rouen Normandie
Rouen, France

ISBN 978-3-032-12354-1 ISBN 978-3-032-12355-8 (eBook)
https://doi.org/10.1007/978-3-032-12355-8

Les deux Irlandes et la diaspora: un attachement intéressé

Translation from the French language edition: "Les deux Irlandes et la diaspora: un attachement intéressé" by Anne Groutel, © Anne Groutel 2021. Published by Presses universitaires de Caen. All Rights Reserved.

This Palgrave Macmillan imprint is published by the registered company Springer Nature Switzerland AG.
The registered company address is: Gewerbestrasse 11, 6330 Cham, Switzerland

To Corentin and Florian

Foreword 1

Every year in the month of March, Irish politicians and leading figures in business, culture, and academia leave the country to celebrate St Patrick's Day in cities throughout the world. Ireland's national holiday is the focus of a series of events highlighting Ireland's economic and cultural global reach and its extensive diaspora. Ireland increasingly deploys the term "diaspora" in a fluid manner to those who are Irish by birth and ancestry, and others with strong economic or emotional ties to Ireland. This extensive St Patrick's Day demonstration of "soft power" is relatively recent. It was initiated by the government in Dublin, but leading figures in Northern Ireland now participate, both in shared events and in gatherings that concentrate on the Northern Ireland diaspora.

The important role that many diasporic communities now play in global businesses and politics is well recognised. As Anne Groutel describes so well, in 2009 when the Irish economy was undergoing a major recession, the government convened the Global Irish Economic Forum to brainstorm how to revive the economy. That event was attended by one-hundred and eighty leaders in business, the arts, and communications. And in the spring of 2025, when US President Donald Trump announced his plans to impose swingeing tariffs on imports into the USA and singled out Ireland because of its dominant role in pharmaceutical imports, the Irish government responded by setting up a Strategic Economic Advisory Panel, drawn from US business leaders with strong connections to Ireland.

The history of the Irish diaspora, and the role of Irish-American politicians in securing a political settlement in Northern Ireland, has been comprehensively covered in numerous books and articles. Anne Groutel gives due recognition to these aspects over the past century. But the significance of this book lies in her detailed investigation of the role that this diaspora has played in transforming the Irish economy by attracting significant foreign direct investment. She is the first scholar to this. Her book fills a major gap in the economic and social history of Ireland over the past century, and this story is also of interest to other countries who are now trying to follow the Irish model of economic development. Investment by diasporic communities in their home country is increasing seen as a significant force in the contemporary global economy.

Groutel has adopted an all-island focus, writing about developments both in Ireland and in Northern Ireland. The Irish diaspora was and is an all-island phenomenon, and both parts of Ireland have been seeking foreign direct investment for many decades and continue to do so. The history of twentieth-century Ireland and Ireland's economic development has generally been written in a partitionist manner. By breaking with that tradition her work fits admirably into the increasing number of studies that are underway under the Irish government's Shared Ireland initiative and the parallel research being carried out by ARINS—a joint project between the Royal Irish Academy, Notre Dame University, and the *Irish Times.*

This book concentrates on North America—the USA and Canada. The more complex story of Ireland's diaspora in Britain and whether it impacted on economic development is a matter for another day. Northern Ireland retains strong ties with Canada, and in the 1950s and 1960s the leading businessmen in the USA with an Irish ancestry were more likely to come from Ulster-Scots or Anglo-Irish Protestant family backgrounds. With a more industrial economy, and political leaders who were often businessmen (in contrast to the political leadership in Ireland), Northern Ireland was the first part of Ireland to engage with diasporic networks for economic reasons. The fact that US and Canadian troops were based in Northern Ireland, during World War II whereas Ireland was neutral, served to strengthen trans-Atlantic ties. In 1956 DuPont, a major US textile firm, established a large plant in Derry/Londonderry, which was significant, not just as a major employer, but a company that hired workers regardless of their religion; this was uncommon in Northern Ireland at the time. During the 1950s Northern Ireland businessmen travelled to the USA seeking markets for their products, and learning about modern production methods, as did their counterparts in Ireland. The US consultancy firm Arthur D. Little wrote a report on industry in Northern Ireland, several years before it was commissioned to write a similar report for the Irish government.

By contrast the Irish government was rather hesitant about engaging the economic heft of Irish-America, in part because reports from Irish consulates in the late 1950s suggested that the Irish communities in most American cities carried little weight in corporate USA. The election in 1960 of John F. Kennedy, the first US President from an Irish Catholic background and a member of an affluent business family, marked a turning point, but at the time the Irish government was quite uncertain how to gain economic leverage from Kennedy's presidency. Indeed, the Irish ambassador to the USA was tasked with trying to persuade Kennedy to make a statement expressing support for Irish unification; he was not asked to assist in promoting Irish–US business connections. Nevertheless, Kennedy's 1963 visit to Ireland was significant. When Seán Lemass the Taoiseach (head of government) visited the USA shortly afterwards, and shortly before Kennedy was assassinated, he concentrated on extending American-Irish business relations. As Groutel shows, he was hosted by a number of prominent US businessmen with investments in Ireland. She highlights the critical role played by some early Irish-American businessmen, whose names have been largely forgotten—notably John Mulcahy who brought Pfizer to Ringaskiddy, county Cork. This plant, still thriving, inaugurated Ireland's now dominant place in the global pharmaceutical industry. During Lemass' visit the Irish-American Council for Industry and Commerce was inaugurated with a membership drawn from elite Irish-American business leaders, especially those with economic links to Ireland. This was not the first Irish-American business association; but unlike the others, the 1963 network survived, probably because Ireland's more open economy and aspiring membership of the EEC provided a strong economic rationale for its existence, and it was endorsed by the Irish government. In the following decades, the members visited Ireland regularly, generally travelling to Killarney, playing golf, and meeting leading political and business leaders. Most of these activities were low key, rarely reported in the Irish media, but they were nonetheless significant in establishing closer relationships and a better knowledge of the modern Ireland.

Although US and international investment in Ireland grew during the 1960s, until the 1970s Northern Ireland was much more successful at attracting foreign direct investment, and many of the incentives that the Irish government introduced during the 1960s, such as providing advance factories, were already on offer in Northern Ireland. The outbreak of violence in the late 1960s, which continued until the 1990s, made it much more difficult to woo overseas investors to both parts of Ireland, but its impact was much greater in Northern Ireland. It was only after the signing of the 1998 Good Friday/Belfast Agreement that Northern Ireland could again mount an effective drive to attract foreign investment. It was assisted by the support that successive US administrations have shown for the Northern Ireland Peace Process, and their justifiable belief that a prospering economy would help to strengthen that peace. Between 1998 and 2002, seventy US trade missions visited Northern Ireland. Historic links with Canada were renewed; groups such as the Friend of Belfast in Boston were established, and substantial investments followed. Some were offshoots of businesses already established south of the border. Northern Ireland has also emerged as an important location for films and TV series.

Most accounts of the Irish economic success story emphasise that it was a very slow process. It was only in the 1990s that the Irish economy began to catch up with and overtake other European countries. Ireland's success in attracting FDI is now widely recognised, and Ireland is seen as a model for other countries to follow. Groutel shows that this belated, sometimes uncertain development is mirrored in the story of the business diaspora, and how it was leveraged by the Irish government. The Irish economy has now evolved taking on all the major features of an advanced globally connected economy. Likewise, the diaspora has become a more complex phenomenon. There are more than seven hundred Irish companies, operating in the USA, employing over 100,000 people; US businesses in Ireland employ roughly twice that number. On a per capita basis Ireland is the largest source of foreign direct investment in the USA. Groutel poses the interesting question: "Diaspora Business Elites: an overly pervasive influence?" She suggests that the 2010s brought a change in that relationship. The interaction between government and business, in Ireland, as elsewhere has become much more complex. Ireland is a major location for US pharma companies and leading firms in IT and the digital economy. It is their most important base in the EU. The Irish government is increasingly being lobbied by these businesses on issues such as EU regulations. Irish businesses operating in the USA are yet another critical voice that the Irish government must heed.

Groutel's impressive research into this important and neglected story shows that although diasporic connections may prompt investors with diasporic connections to consider Ireland or Northern Ireland as business partners, or investment locations, ultimately economic interests are decisive. But that does not detract from the value of deploying emotional ties to an Irish heritage or Irish connections as a tool of economic policy.

University College, Dublin, Ireland
Mary E. Daly

Foreword 2

The Irish diaspora numbers seventy million people worldwide, almost half of whom (thirty-three million) live in the United States.[1] Some were born in Ireland; others claim to be "native Irish". From my point of view as an Irish citizen living in France for more than twenty years and as co-director of the diaspora strand of research of the scientific interest grouping Irish Studies: Networks and Issues (GIS EIRE), this book, which makes a significant contribution to the field of research on the diaspora, is timely.

From independence in 1921 to the 1980s, successive Irish leaders sought to stem the tide of emigration. The departure of young Irish men and women for other countries was draining the country of its lifeblood and hampering the country's economic development. In the 1980s, the political discourse began to change and emigration became a valued experience for the younger generation, a way of travelling and gaining experience that could be put to good use once back in Ireland.

The widespread use of the term "diaspora" in relation to Irish emigration in the 1990s owes much to the President of the Irish Republic, Mary Robinson. Her presidency was marked by openness to the emigrant populations for whom Ireland was the home territory. Exchanges and connections with those who wished to maintain a link with Ireland were encouraged. These relationships were to become vitally important in the period following the financial crisis of 2007. The huge Irish diaspora had the capacity to help the country out of its rut, and this was not lost on the authorities. A strategy to tap into the potential of the Irish diaspora population was therefore formally implemented and Dublin called upon the elite of the diaspora. This enabled Irish leaders to build a global network of high-profile Irish people (the Global Irish Network) and to establish business links that could help Ireland emerge from the crisis. Prominent Irish-Americans were an important part of this strategy.

In this monograph, Anne Groutel examines the relationship between Ireland and these Irish-American figures. For the first time, a diachronic study presents a comprehensive analysis of the relationship that successive Irish governments and Northern Ireland authorities have had with Irish-American business elites since the late 1950s. While much research has been conducted on the post-financial crisis period of 2007 and the diasporic strategy that was implemented in its wake, the author highlights, with the support of numerous original primary sources, the existence of a burgeoning diasporic strategy focused on Irish-America as early as the 1920s.

Although the use of diaspora is generally seen in a positive light for home countries, Anne Groutel points to the potential risks inherent in this approach. Indeed, giving too much influence to diaspora tycoons may lead them to want to interfere in the formulation of public policies in the country of origin with the far-reaching consequences that this may have.

This book concludes by asking what the future holds for Ireland at a time when the United States seems to be losing interest in it, as evidenced by the recent work of Liam Kennedy.[2] New paradigms will likely need to be considered and formulated to ensure the continuation of future relations between Ireland and its diaspora in the United States.

Université Rennes 2, France Grainne O'Keeffe-Vigneron

Notes

1. Data from the American Community Survey 2010–2014, published by the United States Census Bureau, online: https://www.census.gov/content/dam/Census/newsroom/facts-for-features/2016/cb16-ff04_stpatricks_day_2016.pdf.
2. Liam Kennedy. 2019. A Sense of an Ending: Late-Generation Ethnicity and Irish America. Irish Studies Review, 27, 1.

Acknowledgements

First of all, I would like to sincerely thank the two anonymous reviewers for their insightful and constructive suggestions, which have significantly strengthened the arguments and overall quality of the English version of this book.

I would also like to express my deep gratitude to the Economic Life Unit (formerly CERVEPAS), my former research team, within the Center for Research on the English-Speaking World (CREW, Université Sorbonne Nouvelle), which provided a stimulating, dynamic, and warm framework for discussion and reflection over the years. I would like to express my warmest thanks to Professor Martine Azuelos, founder of CERVEPAS, for her wise and benevolent eye and the help she gave me in the final stages of preparing the original version of this book.

I am also grateful to the scientific interest grouping Études Irlandaises: Réseaux et Enjeux (GIS EIRE) for their financial contribution to the publication of the French version of this book to the Presses Universitaires de Caen (2021). I would like to thank Professor Christophe Gillissen and the Interdisciplinary Research Team on the British Isles, Ireland, and North America (ERIBIA) of the University of Caen Normandie.

I am also indebted to my colleague and friend Dr Grainne O'Keeffe-Vigneron who shares my scholarly interest in the Irish diaspora and who kindly agreed to write one of the forewords of this monograph.

My thoughts are also with my dear friends in the huge Irish diaspora who have made me feel the complexity of their intimate relationship with the land of their ancestors.

I will not forget to thank my friend Christine Baldy, who has given me unstinting support over the years during my research visits to Northern Ireland.

Finally, nothing would have been possible without the patience and understanding of my sons Corentin and Florian to whom this book is dedicated.

Contents

About the Author

Anne Groutel began her career in the private sector in Belfast, Northern Ireland, where she lived from 1986 to 1994, before returning to France and changing her career path. An associate professor at Paris 1 Panthéon-Sorbonne University for 24 years, she was appointed Full Professor of English-Speaking World Studies (specialising in Irish Studies) at University of Rouen Normandy in September 2024.She is a member of the Équipe de Recherche Interdisciplinaire sur les Aires Culturelles (ERIAC UR 4705), the French Society of Irish Studies (SOFEIR), and the European Federation of Associations and Centres of Irish Studies (EFACIS).She currently directs the academic research group *GIS EIRE: Études Irlandaises, Réseaux et Enjeux*, where she also co-leads the research strand "Repositioning Ireland in the World: Old Configurations, New Realities", in collaboration with Dr Gráinne O'Keeffe-Vigneron.Her research has appeared in numerous academic publications and focuses on the economic and diplomatic history of both Northern Ireland and the Republic of Ireland, from the time of partition to the present day, with a particular interest in strategies of the Irish state regarding economic development; political and economic relations between the two Irelands; influence of the United States and the Irish-American diaspora on the Irish economy; Ireland's strategy for developing soft power.She is the author of two monographs: *La coopération économique entre les deux Irlande* (Presses Universitaires de Caen, 2003) and *Les deux Irlandes et la Diaspora* (Presses Universitaires de Caen, 2021). She also co-edited *Revisiting the UK and Ireland's Transatlantic Economic Relationship with the United States in the 21st Century* (Palgrave Macmillan, 2017), and a forthcoming volume co-edited with Dr Gráinne O'Keeffe-Vigneron, *Ireland and Soft Power: Roots, Reach, Realities*, will be published in 2026.

Abbreviations

AOH	Ancient Order of Hibernians
BCC	Belfast City Council
BIDO	British Industrial Development Office
CI	ConnectIreland
DFA	Department of Foreign Affairs
ECA	Economic Cooperation Administration (US government agency)
FDI	Foreign Direct Investments
IMF	International Monetary Fund
GAA	Gaelic Athletic Association
GDP	Gross Domestic Product
GIEF	Global Irish Economic Forum
GIN	Global Irish Network
IAEAB	Ireland-America Economic Advisory Board
IDA	Industrial Development Authority (1949–1993)/Industrial Development Agency (1993–)
IFI	International Fund for Ireland
IFSC	International Financial Services Centre
IRA	Irish Republican Army
ITLG	Irish Technology Leadership Group
IUSCICI	Ireland-United States Council for Industry and Commerce Incorporated
LIT	Limerick Institute of Technology
NAI	National Archives of Ireland
NAMA	National Asset Management Agency
NARA	National Archives and Records Administration
NICRA	Northern Ireland Civil Rights Association
NIDC	Northern Ireland Development Council

NISP	Northern Ireland Science Park
NORAID	Irish Northern Aid Committee
PRONI	Public Record Office of Northern Ireland
PRTLI	Programme for Research in Third-Level Institutions
RG	Record Group
SDLP	Social Democratic and Labour Party
UCDA	University College Dublin Archives
UDA	Ulster Defence Association
UVF	Ulster Volunteer Force

Preliminary Remarks on the Concept of Diaspora and the Irish Context

While the primary objective of this book is not to theorise the concept of diaspora, it is nonetheless essential—particularly as a prelude to our empirical investigation of the two Irelands, the diaspora, and economic development—to clarify what differentiates diasporas from other ethnic communities residing outside their country of origin. It is also pertinent to assess the extent to which Irish communities in North America align with these defining characteristics. As Jacques Barou aptly notes, "[N]ot all migrations result in the formation of diasporas. Many migrant groups eventually assimilate into the host society and lose any meaningful connection to their country of origin".[1] In contrast, diasporas typically display a greater degree of cohesion than ordinary expatriate or ethnic communities, and their enduring attachment to their ancestral homeland is a defining feature. These traits—among others—constitute a valuable resource for states aiming to mobilise the economic potential of their overseas nationals or descendants.

Historically, the term "diaspora" was most closely associated with the Jewish experience and remained narrowly defined until the 1990s. During this period, it gained considerable traction in media and academic discourse, eventually becoming part of everyday vocabulary. Traditionally, the concept has evoked not only spatial dispersion but also themes of exile, displacement, and a traumatic or catastrophic origin. Interest in the concept was significantly renewed in the 1990s, leading to its development as a distinct field of inquiry—diaspora studies—particularly within the Anglophone academic world.

However, rather than leading to a consensus among scholars, the definition of the diaspora remains contested,[2] with the criteria emphasised varying significantly across disciplines. For geographers, as Chantal Bordes-Benayoun and Dominique Schnapper observe, the memory of the territory is a foundational element.[3] In contrast, Yves Lacoste prioritises demographic considerations, suggesting that a diaspora exists primarily when a significant portion of a population has left its territory of origin.[4] In his view, dispersion on a large scale is the defining criterion.

Within the social sciences, other parameters take precedence. William Safran was among the first to propose a conceptual framework comprising six defining features.[5] According to his model, diasporas are communities of people exiled en masse and dispersed from a central homeland to at least two peripheral foreign regions.[6] These communities preserve a collective memory of their place of origin and maintain, whether symbolically or materially, a real or imagined connection to it.[7] They often perceive themselves as permanently marginalised within host societies and consider return—alongside the protection or restoration of their ancestral homeland's security—a core objective.

In an effort to clarify and delimit the use of the term, Robin Cohen developed a typology that identifies five categories of diasporas: labour, victim, cultural, imperial, and commercial.[8] He broadens Safran's definition by incorporating voluntary migration and emphasising the enduring nature of ethnic consciousness, framing diasporas as long-term historical phenomena. In a similar vein, Michel Bruneau highlights the individual's conscious desire to identify with and participate in the diaspora:

> A sense of belonging, an identity, must be maintained over time by a conscious decision and even by virtue of a certain persistence. […] Members of a diaspora can be perfectly integrated and acculturated in the host country like the Jews, the Armenians in France or the Greeks in Australia, but they are not assimilated otherwise they would have lost all sense of identity and would no longer belong to a diaspora.[9]

For Gabriel Sheffer, however, ethnic identity awareness can "go dormant" for a time and be reawakened at any time, despite the effects of acculturation.[10]

In reaction to the "narrow" view of the concept of diaspora, another conceptual approach which is based on completely different criteria was constructed through the paradigmatic example of the black people of the

Americas for Paul Gilroy[11] and that of the Afro-Caribbean people for Stuart Hall.[12] The key words are no longer "continuity of the link with the territory of origin", but "cultural hybridity", "fluidity of identities", "attachment to several places", "noncentre", and "attachment to a culture rather than a territory", because for James Clifford a diaspora may very well be a group of individuals linked by "[...] a shared, ongoing history of displacement, suffering, adaptation, or resistance [which] may be as important as the projection of a specific origin".[13] There is therefore no single definition of "diaspora" that is unanimously accepted.

Furthermore, the case of Irish immigration over a period of several centuries illustrates perfectly what Bruneau writes about the difficulty to fit a diaspora into a particular category:

> [...] It is often not possible to make a strict distinction between those who migrate for political reasons and those who do so for economic reasons. There are more or less forced departures as a result of oppression, famine or living conditions deemed unbearable by those who take the decision to migrate. Apart from extreme cases, political or economic motives are often mixed or concomitant. On the other hand, long-term diasporas are the result of several waves of migration, some of which were more politically motivated, others more economically motivated.[14]

Indeed, in the sixteenth and seventeenth centuries, the persecution of Irish Catholics by the British Crown forced leading Gaelic earls, clergymen, seminarians, and landless peasants to flee Ireland. They went to France, Spain, Italy, Germany, or the Caribbean. However, the reasons why many Ulster Scots[15] left Ulster in the eighteenth century were both political and economic. Faced with poverty, high rents, and discrimination by Anglicans,[16] some migrated to Britain, where industrialisation was beginning to take root, while others pursued opportunities across the Atlantic. This emigration proved historically significant, as by the nineteenth century, no fewer than nine individuals of Ulster-Scots descent had held the office of President of the United States.

The economic consequences of the Act of Union of 1800,[17] which established the United Kingdom of Great Britain and Ireland, were disastrous for Irish industry[18] and the entire island's economy declined from the 1820s onwards. In the period 1800–1845 alone, an estimated one million people left Ireland for North America and half a million for Britain.[19] During the first part of the nineteenth century, the island experienced several periods of famine, but these were nothing compared to the Great Famine from 1845 onwards.[20] More than two million people fled Ireland because of hunger.[21] One and a half million headed for the United States, which was a favoured destination until the 1920s.[22] A report published in the early 2000s suggests a steady decline in the Irish population from 8.2 million in 1841 to 4.2 million in 1961.[23] The Great Famine, one of the darkest episodes in Irish history, has left a lasting mark on the collective memory of the populations forced to leave and their descendants. For Cohen, this traumatic event that caused the exodus of millions of Irish justifies the Irish diaspora being classified as a victim diaspora.[24]

These Irish immigrants, often stereotyped as prone to violence and excessive alcohol consumption, were met with hostility by segments of American society, particularly the Protestant bourgeoisie and middle class. As a result, Protestant Irish who had previously settled in the United States tended to distance themselves from the newly arrived Catholic immigrants.[25] The term "Scotch-Irish" became widely used to distinguish those who had previously been referred to simply as "Irish" from the refugees of the Great Famine. The latter were also targeted by the Know Nothing Party, a nativist movement that advocated a discriminatory policy against Catholics. Mostly unskilled, Great Famine immigrants rarely managed to improve their living conditions.[26]

That said, some Irish immigrants succeeded in amassing considerable wealth in the United States. Despite occupying the lowest social strata in Ireland, many possessed a basic level of education[27] and were English-speaking, which facilitated their integration. Their upward mobility was particularly noteworthy given that the American business sphere at the time remained largely dominated by the descendants of the original English settlers—the White Anglo-Saxon Protestants (WASPs)—and that social advancement for individuals outside this elite was exceptionally difficult.[28] In *Real Lace*,[29] Stephen Birmingham tells the story of the first Irish Catholic millionaires in the United States. They had large villas built for themselves in Southampton,[30] which became one of the most exclusive resorts in the early twentieth century. Some of their children formed the Murray-McDonnell-Cuddihy "clan". Later, the circle widened to include the Ford and Vanderbilt families, among others.[31] But this dynasty was one of the exceptions. In 1900, 14% of the Irish-American community was lower middle class and only 6% was upper middle class or elite.[32]

Irish-Americans did, however, experience a meteoric rise through the twentieth century.[33] Some of them became prominent in sports, politics, and entertainment. By the end of this century, they were widely represented on the boards of many American multinational companies.[34] In the early 1970s, a number of affluent Irish-Americans chose to retire in Ireland. By 1970, the American Embassy was issuing approximately six thousand pension cheques to Irish-American retirees residing in the country. Returning to Ireland at this stage in life had come to signify social achievement, marking a reversal of earlier perceptions in which return migration was often associated with failure.[35]

For Cohen, one of the characteristics of diasporas is the maintenance of real or symbolic links with the land of origin. Indeed, people from Ireland continued to keep in touch with their families back home by mail. They often sent them money (remittances) and kept up to date with the news from the island. The existence of political, religious, and/or cultural organisations is an integral part of the diasporic fact and contributes to the perpetuation of these links. However, the decision to join these diasporic organisations or networks is a matter of individual choice. Dale B. Light attributes a very important role to these organisations in the context of Irish communities in the United States. He argues that in the nineteenth century, only a small minority of immigrants from Ireland who settled in urban areas arrived with a constructed and coherent Irish ethnic identity. Their religious beliefs were varied and few were active in advocating for an independent Irish State.[36] In Light's view, the proliferation of organisations in several major American cities in the second half of the nineteenth century contributed to the emergence of a sense of identity, the contours of which became clear after the American Civil War.[37]

The Catholic Church, which was well established in the United States and well organised, was a central player in the development of these organisations. Similarly, the nationalist organisations militating for the Irish cause,[38] which from the 1860s onwards sought to recruit members from among the newly arrived emigrants from Ireland, played an essential role in the construction of the identity of the Catholic community of Irish origin in the United States: "Initially antagonistic to each other the Church and nationalist organisations gradually reached an accommodation".[39]

From the beginning of the nineteenth century, Irish nationalists understood the financial and political value of enlisting the support of people of Irish descent living abroad.[40] Their financial contributions[41] went both to organisations that advocated constitutional nationalism and peaceful methods and to those that advocated the use of force to achieve their aims. In the latter part of the nineteenth century in the United States[42] and Australia,[43] supporters of constitutional nationalism were predominantly middle-class and affluent members of the Irish Catholic community. The harder line of nationalism tended to attract the urban working class. Constitutional nationalism was most prevalent in both the United States and Ireland.[44] However, the repression that followed the Easter Rising of 1916, a landmark chapter in Irish history, reversed this trend. The execution of the rebels by the British authorities was so striking that it caused a massive turnaround in Irish public opinion and that of the Irish Catholic community in the United States[45] and Australia.[46] Nationalism, which advocated the hard way, was the main beneficiary. Between 1916 and 1921, the Irish-American Catholic community contributed ten million dollars to the independence cause.[47]

Éamon de Valera (1882–1975)[48] was one of the leaders of the Easter Rising of 1916. An American citizen, he was not sentenced to death like some of his comrades. At the end of 1918, he was elected as a Sinn Féin member of parliament (MP) along with seventy-three others, many of whom, like him, had been taken prisoner. In January 1919, these MPs proclaimed the Irish Parliament, Dáil Éireann. De Valera escaped from prison in February 1919 with his comrade in arms, Michael Collins, and stayed in the United States from June 1919 to December 1920. During this period, he sought to have his legitimacy and that of the Irish Parliament recognised. During his long journey, he managed to raise five million dollars in exchange for bonds. These funds were to be used to establish an Irish republic.[49] While a small number of very large subscriptions, coming from wealthy Irish-Americans business people and politicians, attracted much public attention, the vast majority of the bond certificates were purchased by lower-class immigrants.[50] Some Irish sympathisers, employed in the media, also tried to draw international attention to Irish nationalist claims.[51]

On the Protestant side, the Orange Order,[52] founded in County Armagh,[53] moved to the North of England and Scotland in 1807, and a few years later to the United States, Canada, Australia, and New Zealand. Its activities had a religious, political, cultural, and social dimension. Faced with the rise of the Home Rule movement in Ireland, Edward Carson[54] (1854–1935) and James Craig[55] (1871–1940) organised Unionist resistance[56] in Ulster. Together they created the Ulster Volunteer Force (UVF), a militia ready to take up arms in the event of a Home Rule victory. Contributions to the Carson Defense Fund, which supported the militia's arms requirements, came mainly from the United Kingdom. But the movement also received financial support[57] from the Ulster Protestant community in Canada.[58] In Australia, although the Irish community was predominantly Catholic, the UVF had powerful allies, including Sir Samuel McCaughey,[59] one of the country's wealthiest men, who contributed twenty-five thousand pounds to the fund. Donald M. MacRaild points out, however, that in the United States the Orange Order did not have a unifying function and failed to form a sufficient critical mass to truly cement this community.[60] In addition, it is important to note that after the political partition of the island, the interest of diasporic communities in the political cause, both nationalist[61] and unionist,[62] declined until the traumatic events that took place in Northern Ireland in the 1960s and 1970s.

Although the term "diaspora" appeared as early as 1953 in John Anthony O'Brien's *The Vanishing Irish*,[63] it did not enter common usage in Ireland until the mid-1990s. Prior to this period, Irish nationals who had emigrated were typically referred to simply as emigrants, collectively identified as the Irish abroad—a designation that remains in use today. The hyphen has traditionally served, and continues to serve, as a linguistic marker of the hybrid identity of the descendants of Irish emigrants living overseas, as in the case of "Irish-American". The Irish President Mary Robinson's[64] strong homage to the "Irish diaspora",[65] which emphasised the multi-generational nature of the phenomenon,[66] significantly contributed to the popularisation of the term, particularly in political discourse. Since the 1990s, the concept of the diaspora as a community has received increasing attention from researchers studying Ireland.[67]

Paradoxically, in the 1980s, the Irish emigrants to the United States exhibited fewer characteristics of the "narrow" definition of a diaspora. Indeed, O'Brien highlights the sharp contrast between Irish-Americans and the wave of Irish immigrants to the United States in the 1980s. These "new Irish" were much more highly skilled, ambitious, and dynamic. These were the people who returned to Ireland in large numbers from the mid-1990s onwards, when the Irish economy took off and the country needed them for white-collar jobs.[68] For many Irish people, going to work in the United States nowadays is no longer an economic necessity. Rather, it is an experience designed to enhance their career path. Feargal Cochrane notes that the vast majority of those who go to the United States today are young and highly mobile.[69] They do not necessarily aim to settle there permanently. They stay in touch with their relatives through new communication technologies and can visit them easily since it has become cheaper to travel. As a result, once in the United States, they are less likely than previous waves of emigrants to seek out other Irish people in "ethnic" cultural and sporting organisations. For Cochrane, the "narrow" view of diasporas, with its emphasis on group cohesion and the notion of forced departure, no longer corresponds at all to the reality of Irish immigrants in the United States. Liam Kennedy's more recent study of Irish-Americans and Irish immigrants in Chicago confirms this trend.[70] Furthermore, the dramatic intensity of the Famine-era immigration narrative may therefore be fading: "[...] Irish identity is no longer associated with immigrant trauma or oppression, but [represents] pride, honour, and this is less directly associated with the country of origin".[71] Finally, there is a widening gap between an ageing and conservative Irish-American community and an Ireland that is, by contrast, becoming increasingly open and tolerant.[72]

For a long time, researchers working on the Irish diaspora were divided on whether to include the Irish Protestant population in the diaspora. Protestants have a different ethnic background, political aspirations, culture, history, and religion from the Gaelic Catholic populations. Furthermore, Piaras Mac Éinrí and Brian Lambkin argue:

> Scots-Irish ethnicity has virtually disappeared, whereas 'Irishness' has been replenished by ongoing immigration and the mediatisation, even popularisation, of Irish ethnic identity.[73]

For Wesley Hutchinson, the Irish imaginary has benefited the nationalist cause at the expense of unionism, whose image is not as attractive.[74] It is worth adding that the Protestant emigrants from Northern Ireland and their descendants are not the target of the discourse of the authorities of the Republic of Ireland when they call for the assistance of "the diaspora". This diaspora, whose Gaelic origin is emphasised, is now sometimes referred to as "the Global Irish".

Yet, recent years have seen the emergence in intellectual circles of an inclusive vision of a plural, hybrid, multi-ethnic, and global Irish diaspora.[75] The particularities of the Irish case and the issues at the heart of this book have thus led us to take Nicholas Van Hear's broad definition of the concept of diaspora as a point of reference: "the dispersion of the population from the land of origin into two or more territories; the persistence of the presence abroad although the exile is not necessarily permanent, as movements between the land of origin and new countries of residence may develop; the existence of exchanges—social, economic or cultural—between and among the spatially separated populations making up the diaspora".[76] Van Hear's definition acknowledges the importance of home territory and, insofar as it is free of overly rigid criteria, allows for an inclusive use of the term "diaspora" to refer to all populations originating from the island of Ireland that have been dispersed around the world for several generations.[77]

Given the diversity of realities that the term "the diaspora" encompasses in the Irish context, its use could be confusing. It is therefore necessary to emphasise that in those parts of this study that deal with the Republic of Ireland, the word refers to people of the Catholic faith, of Gaelic descent. Indeed, that is how its inhabitants understand it. However, it is important to note that the term "The diaspora" is commonly used by Irish politicians to refer to the senior Irish-American businessmen with whom the leadership works, not the diaspora as a whole. We have distinguished the subset represented by the "Northern Irish diaspora", that is, people of Protestant or Catholic faith from Northern Ireland, and specified whether we were referring only to one or the other community where this made sense.

Notes

1. Jacques Barou. 2007. La planète des migrants: circulations migratoires et constitution de diasporas à l'aube du XXIe siècle. Grenoble: Presses universitaires de Grenoble, 151, quoted in Chantal Bordes-Benayoun. 2012. La diaspora ou l'ethnique en mouvement. Revue européenne des migrations internationales 28, 1: 27. https://doi.org/10.4000/remi.5700
2. Stéphane Dufoix. 2011. La dispersion: une histoire des usages du mot diaspora. Paris: Éditions Amsterdam, 389.
3. Chantal Bordes-Benayoun, Dominique Schnapper. 2006. Diasporas et nations, Paris: O. Jacob, 177.
4. Yves Lacoste. 1989. Éditorial: géopolitique des diasporas. Hérodote 53: 3–12.
5. William Safran. 1991. Diasporas in Modern Societies: Myths of Homeland and Return. *Diaspora: A Journal of Transnational Studies* 1, 1: 83–99. https://doi.org/10.1353/dsp.1991.0004

6. It should be noted that Safran, in his attempt at creating a typology, makes no reference to the case of Ireland.
7. For Tölölyan, this is what differentiates the ethnic community from a diaspora. Khachig Tölölyan. 1996. Rethinking Diaspora(s): Stateless Power in the Transnational Moment. *Diaspora: A Journal of Transnational Studies* 5, 1:16. https://doi.org/10.1353/dsp.1996.0000.
8. Robin Cohen. 1997. Global Diasporas: An Introduction. Londres: UCL Press.
9. Michel Bruneau. 2004. Diasporas et espaces transnationaux. Paris: Anthropos, 22, 24.
10. Gabriel Sheffer. 2003. Diaspora Politics: At Home and Abroad. Cambridge: Cambridge University Press, 75.
11. Paul Gilroy. 1993. The Black Atlantic: Modernity and Double Consciousness. London - New York: Verso.
12. Stuart Hall. 1994. Cultural Identity and Diaspora. In Colonial Discourse and Post-Colonial Theory. A Reader, eds Patrick Williams, Laura Chrisman, 392–401. New York: Columbia University Press.
13. James Clifford. 1994. Diasporas. *Cultural Anthropology* 9, 3: 306.
14. Michel Bruneau, Diasporas et espaces transnationaux, 21.
15. The Ulster Scots are an ethnic group which descended mainly from Lowland Scots who came to Ireland as part of the Ulster Plantation (the term used to describe the settlement of this historic province in the north of the island of Ireland) which began in the seventeenth century.
16. These Ulster Scots were of the Presbyterian faith.
17. The Act of Union of 1800 is also called the Act of Union of 1801. The act itself was passed on 2 July 1800 and the union became effective on 1 January 1801.
18. E. R. R. Green. 1976. Industrial Decline in the Nineteenth Century. In The Formation of the Irish Economy, ed. Louis M. Cullen, 89–100. Cork: Mercier Press.
19. Patrick Fitzgerald, Brian Lambkin. 2008. Migration in Irish History, 1607–2007. London: Palgrave Macmillan, 161–162. The rationalisations carried out by the landowners led many Irish people employed in agriculture, and now without jobs, to leave the island, which was also going through a period of political instability. In addition, the price of the crossing to America was becoming increasingly affordable, encouraging many Irish to make the move. Lawrence McCaffrey, Ellen Skerrett, Michael F. Funchion, Charles Fanning. 1987. The Irish in Chicago (Ethnic History of Chicago). Urbana: University of Illinois Press, 64–65.
20. This was caused by a shortage of potatoes. Mildew caused a sharp drop in the production of this foodstuff for several years in a row.
21. Fitzgerald, Lambkin. Migration, 172.

22. Canada, Great Britain, Australia, New Zealand, Argentina, and South Africa also received refugees from the Great Famine, but in smaller numbers.
23. Government of Ireland, Department of Foreign Affairs. August 2002. Ireland and the Irish Abroad. Report of the Taskforce on Policy Regarding Emigrants to the Minister for Foreign Affairs Mr. Brian Cowen, 6.
24. Cohen, Global Diasporas, 67, 69–70, 181.
25. Whereas in the eighteenth century the majority of those leaving Ireland were Ulster Presbyterians, the proportion reversed in the following century and Catholics became the most numerous to emigrate. Fitzgerald, Lambkin, Migration, 159, 163. Blessing estimates that by 1840 Protestants were down to 10% of the total. Patrick J. Blessing. 1985. Irish Emigration to the United States, 1800–1920: An Overview. In The Irish in America: Emigration, Assimilation and Impact, ed. P. J. Drudy. Cambridge: Cambridge University Press, Irish Studies 4: 19.
26. Laurence A. Glasco. 1975. The Life Cycles and Household Structure of American Ethnic Groups: Irish, Germans, and Native-Born Whites in Buffalo, New York, 1855. *Journal of Urban History*, 1, 3: 351. https://doi.org/10.1177/009614427500100305.
27. A national education system was inaugurated in 1831. In 1850, two hundred and fifty thousand Irish young people were attending school. Half a century later, this number had risen to 1.25 million. Patrick Fitzgerald, Brian Lambkin, Migration, 194.
28. Frances W. Gregory, Irene D. Neu. 1952. The American Industrial Elite in the 1870s. In Men in Business: Essays in the History of Entrepreneurship, ed. William Miller. Cambridge: Harvard University Press: 197–199; William Miller. The Business Elite in Business Bureaucracies: Careers of Top Executives in the Early Twentieth Century. In Men in Business, ed. William Miller: 286–305.
29. Stephen Birmingham. 1987. Real Lace. London: Futura.
30. Southampton is located on Long Island, New York.
31. Birmingham, Real Lace, 6.
32. At that time, a number of second- and third-generation Irish-Americans had skilled jobs, particularly in construction. Dennis Clark. The Irish in the American Economy. In The Irish in America: Emigration, Assimilation and Impact, ed. P. J. Drudy: 237; Lawrence McCaffrey. 1997. The Irish Catholic Diaspora in America. Washington: The Catholic University of America Press, 85.
33. See: Jay P. Dolan. 2008. The Irish Americans: A History. New York: Bloomsbury Press, 209–307.
34. The Servicemen's Readjustment Act of 1944 or GI Bill (1944) provided funding for university education or vocational training for many demobil-

ised World War II veterans, which helped improve the career prospects of many Irish-Americans. Dolan, The Irish Americans, 226.

35. John MacCarthy. 1970. Now the Yanks Are Coming Back and Staying. *The Irish Times*, 23 May.
36. Dale B. Light. 1985. The Role of Irish-American Organisations in Assimilation and Community Formation, In The Irish in America: Emigration, Assimilation and Impact, ed. P. J. Drudy: 112–114.
37. Light, The Role of Irish-American Organisations, 129.
38. On the rise of nationalist sentiment among Irish immigrants, see: John Belchem. 1995. Nationalism, Republicanism and Exile: Irish Emigrants and the Revolutions of 1848. Past and Present 146: 103–135. https://doi.org/10.1093/past/146.1.103.
39. Belchem, Nationalism, 131.
40. People of Irish descent could use their influence with the authorities in the host country, in this case the United States, which it was hoped would intercede with London on their behalf.
41. See: Joseph P. Finnan. 2004. John Redmond and Irish Unity, 1912–1918. Syracuse: Syracuse University Press, 155–192.
42. R. J. C. Adams. 2022. Shadow of a Taxman. Oxford: Oxford University Press, 119–126. Kevin Kenny. 2006. American-Irish Nationalism. In Making the Irish American: History and Heritage of the Irish in the United States, eds Joseph J. Lee, Marion R. Casey, 290–292. New York – London: New York University Press.
43. Malcolm Campbell. 2008. *Ireland's New Worlds: Immigrants, Politics, and Society in the United States and Australia, 1815–1922.* Madison: The University of Wisconsin Press, 147.
44. Kenny, American-Irish Nationalism, 294.
45. Kenny, American-Irish Nationalism, 294–295.
46. Campbell, Ireland's New Worlds, 169.
47. Kenny, American-Irish Nationalism, 295.
48. During the 1916 Easter Rising, Éamon de Valera commanded the Irish Volunteers at Boland's Mill. Captured and sentenced to death, he was ultimately released due to factors such as his American citizenship and the public outcry following the British execution of other Rising leaders. After his imprisonment in England, de Valera returned to Ireland and emerged as a key figure in the War of Independence. Following the Anglo-Irish Treaty, he led the Anti-Treaty faction of Sinn Féin until 1926, when he and his supporters founded Fianna Fáil, a new political party. De Valera remained a central figure in Irish politics into the early 1960s. He succeeded W. T. Cosgrave as president of the Executive Council and later became Taoiseach after the enactment of the 1937 Constitution of Ireland. He served as head of state and held the office of Taoiseach three times:

from 1937 to 1948, from 1951 to 1954, and from 1957 to 1959. *Dictionary of Irish Biography*. Éamon de Valera. https://www.dib.ie/biography/de-valera-eamon-dev-a2472. Accessed 9 June 2025.
49. Dave Hannigan. 2008. De Valera in America. The Rebel President's 1919 Campaign. Dublin: The O'Brien Press. In fact, only half of this sum was used for this purpose, but it allowed de Valera, among other things, to create the *Irish Press*, a daily newspaper that unwaveringly supported Fianna Fáil, the party he founded in 1926. For a detailed account of de Valera's stay in the United-States, see also: Adams, Shadow of a Taxman, 134–165, 210–235.
50. Adams, Shadow of a Taxman, 217–224.
51. Mary E. Daly. 2008. *The Irish State and the Diaspora*. 33rd O'Donnell Lecture, University College Dublin, Dublin, National University of Ireland, 18 November, PL-497–25, 2008, 7 Adams, Shadow of a Taxman, 165–171.
52. The order is a Protestant fraternal organisation founded in 1795. It was named the Orange Order after William III, Prince of Orange, who defeated the armies of the Catholic King James II at the Battle of the Boyne in 1690. From its inception, it was opposed to Catholic emancipation and later to Irish independence.
53. Armagh is a town in what is now Northern Ireland.
54. Dictionary of Irish Biography. Edward Carson. https://www.dib.ie/biography/carson-edward-henry-a1514. Accessed 10 June 2025.
55. Dictionary of Irish Biography. James Craig. https://www.dib.ie/biography/craig-james-a2144. Accessed 10 June 2025.
56. The noun and adjective "Unionist" refers to those who support maintaining the union with Britain.
57. For the financial contribution to the Home Rule movement in Canada, see: D. C. Lyne. 1967. Irish-Canadian Financial Contributions to the Home Rule Movement in the 1890s. Studia Hibernica 7: 182–206. http://www.jstor.org/stable/20495870.
58. A. T. Q. Stewart. 1969. The Ulster Crisis, Resistance to Home Rule, 1912–1914. London - Boston, Faber and Faber, 138–139.
59. Samuel McCaughey was originally from Ballymena (County Antrim) in Northern Ireland.
60. Donald M. MacRaild. 2002. Wherever Orange is Worn: Orangeism and Irish Migration in the 19th and Early 20th Centuries. *Canadian Journal ofIrishStudies*28–29,1–2:101–102.https://doi.org/10.2307/25515430.
61. Dolan, The Irish Americans, 204–205.
62. Maldwyn A. Jones. 1980. Scotch-Irish. In Harvard Encyclopedia of American Ethnic Groups, ed. Stephan Thernstrom, 907. Cambridge – London: Belknap Press of Harvard University Press.

63. John Anthony O'Brien. 1953. The Vanishing Irish: The Enigma of the Modern World. New York: McGraw-Hill, 4, 6, 103.
64. Mary Robinson served as the president of Ireland from December 1990 to September 1997. She was the country's first female president.
65. Ireland. Houses of the Oireachtas parliamentary debates Dáil Éireann, 2 February 1995, 448–5 (Mary Robinson).
66. Piaras Mac Éinrí, Brian Lambkin. 2002. Whose Diaspora? Whose Migration? Whose Identity? Some Current Issues in Migration Studies. *The Irish Journal of Psychology*, 23, 3–4: 134–135.
67. Feargal Cochrane. 2010. The End of Irish-America: Globalisation and the Irish Diaspora. Dublin: Irish Academic Press. Mary P. Corcoran. 2003. Global Cosmopolites: Issues of Self-Identity among the Transnational Elite. Études irlandaises 28, 2: 135–150, special issue: L'Irlande et les États-Unis au 20e siècle, eds Carle Bonafous-Murat, Wesley Hutchinson; Enda Delaney. 2006. The Irish Diaspora. Irish Economic and Social History 33: 35–45. https://doi.org/10.1177/033248930603300103; Breda Gray. 2002. The Irish Diaspora: Globalised Belonging(s). *Irish Journal of Sociology* 11, 2: 123–144. https://doi.org/10.1177/079160350201100207; Breda Gray. 2013. Towards the Neo-Institutionalisation of Irish State-Diaspora Relations in the Twenty-First Century. In Emigration Nations: Policies and Ideologies of Emigrant Engagement, ed. Michael Collyer, 100–125. London: Palgrave Macmillan; Katy Hayward, Kevin Howard. 2007. Cherry-Picking the Diaspora. In Immigration and Social Change in the Republic of Ireland, ed. Bryan Fanning, 47–62. Manchester: Manchester University Press; Aoileann Ní Éigeartaigh, Kevin Howard, David Getty (eds). 2007. Rethinking Diasporas: Hidden Narratives and Imagined Borders. Newcastle: Cambridge Scholars.
68. Matthew J. O'Brien. 2003. Ethnic Legacy and Immigrant Mobility: The New Irish and Irish America in the 1990s. Études irlandaises 28, 2: 119–133.
69. Cochrane, The End of Irish-America, 22.
70. Liam Kennedy. 2019. A Sense of an Ending: Late-Generation Ethnicity and Irish America. *Irish Studies Review*, 27, 1: 26–27.
71. Kennedy, Sense of an Ending, 34.
72. Kennedy, Sense of an Ending, 31.
73. Mac Éinrí, Lambkin, Whose Diaspora?, 137.
74. Wesley Hutchinson. 2000. Espaces de l'imaginaire unioniste nord-irlandais, Caen: Presses universitaires de Caen, 27, https://doi.org/10.4000/books.puc.490.
75. Mac Éinrí, Lambkin, Whose Diaspora?

76. Nicholas Van Hear. 1998. New Diasporas: The Mass Exodus, Dispersal and Regrouping of Migrant Communities. London: UCL Press.
77. The Irish diaspora is estimated at seventy million people worldwide. Kingsley Aikins, Anita Sands, Nicola White. 2009. The Global Irish Making a Difference Together: A Comparative Review of International Diaspora Strategies. Dublin: The Ireland Funds, 3.

CHAPTER 1

Introduction

Ireland's[1] complex relationship with its diaspora has gone through different phases since the country gained independence in 1922. Once it was achieved at the cost of the political partition of the island, the young State aimed, firstly, to secure its political sovereignty. In the second phase,[2] the protectionist policy implemented from 1932 onwards was aimed at achieving economic independence from Britain as well as protecting its nascent industry from foreign competition. In the years following partition, the links between Ireland and what were then known as "the Irish abroad" seemed to loosen. The late 1950s was a pivotal time, as Irish leaders decided to move away from protectionism and towards a market economy. To this end, they began to enlist the help of some Irish-American captains of industry to attract foreign investment.

Inward-looking until the late 1950s, the Irish economy has since become one of the most open[3] in the world. The relative speed of the transition from one stage to the other has been surprising.[4] The reasons for this dramatic expansion from the mid-1990s onwards have been extensively studied by economists, political scientists, sociologists, and by economic historians of Ireland who have identified a number of factors as possible explanations for this phenomenon.[5] However, the influence of highly placed Irish-American businessmen is hardly ever mentioned among them. Some of these tycoons have been instrumental in bringing foreign direct investment (FDI) to Ireland and, more recently, to Northern

A. Groutel, *The Two Irelands and the Diaspora*,
https://doi.org/10.1007/978-3-032-12355-8_1

Ireland. These have contributed significantly to the globalisation of the Irish economy.[6]

The participation of diasporas in the economic development of their home territories is generally seen as very positive and therefore desirable. For Kevin Kenny, engaging their diaspora can help nation-states escape their programmed "death" in the age of globalisation[7]:

> For all the talk of the demise of nation states in the age of globalization, governments that reach out to 'their' diasporas are clearly augmenting their economic power. They are even beginning to extend their sovereignty by offering concessions on citizenship or voting rights to overseas populations in return for political or economic support. Diaspora can therefore serve to strengthen rather than undermine nation states.[8]

Among the researchers who have looked at the economic potential of diasporas and how it is, or could be, used to the benefit of home countries,[9] some have focused on the philanthropic function of diasporas[10] in economic and social development, others on the importance of diaspora networks in international trade,[11] or on the assistance diasporas provide to their home countries in attracting FDI.[12] This contribution is considered as a trump card in a world where states compete for investors. Although in the past diasporas were associated with exclusion and rejection, today they enjoy a very positive image.[13]

Michel Bruneau underscores the fundamental tension between diasporas—transnational in nature, organised through diffuse networks, and lacking a clearly defined territorial base—and the nation-state, whose authority is territorially bounded and exercised within fixed borders. According to Bruneau, several responses to this contradiction are possible: diasporas may exist independently of nation-states; states may choose to disregard their diaspora populations; or, alternatively, states may develop strategies to engage with their diaspora, seeking to harness their potential for economic development or to encourage the formation of lobbying groups within the political and economic spheres of host countries.[14] Ireland adopted the latter approach as early as the 1960s.

Although the economic influence of prominent Irish-American individuals on both the Republic of Ireland and Northern Ireland remained largely unacknowledged for some time, it has become increasingly significant since the early 1960s. This book aims to contextualise and analyse their contributions to economic development and public policymaking in Ireland—dimensions that align with a broader diasporic framework:

> Relationships between diasporas and their homelands are an integral component of a diaspora framework analysis. To what degree does the diaspora participate in the affairs of the homeland? What is the flow of political and policy influence in both directions between diasporas and homelands? How do changes in power and resources affect homeland/hostland relationships? These questions underscore the need to consider relationships between diasporas and homelands diachronically, as their dynamics are subject to change over time. In addition, the homeland relationship may differ from one segment of the diaspora to another.[15]

Recent research on the economic potential of the Irish diaspora has largely adopted a synchronic perspective. This study, by contrast, takes a diachronic approach that is unprecedented in scope. Spanning nearly a century—from the political partition of the island to the mid-2010s—it draws on a wide and diverse range of sources, including a substantial body of unpublished archival material, parliamentary debates, interviews, press excerpts from both Irish and international media, as well as secondary literature.

Part I examines the growing distance between Ireland and its diaspora in the aftermath of independence, a gap that persisted due to the absence of sustained political will to reverse the trend. It also explores the reasons why early efforts to mobilise the Irish-American market in support of national development largely failed. By the late 1950s, the Irish economy was in a state of crisis. The protectionist policies implemented since 1932 had reached their limits, prompting the government to shift course and open the country to foreign investment. Yet Ireland faced significant structural challenges: a lack of natural resources, a small domestic market, and a peripheral geographical position within Europe.

Part II traces how, in the early 1960s, prominent Irish-American business figures began to engage with the Irish state, playing a critical role in Ireland's transition from economic protectionism to a liberal, outward-looking model. Shortly before, Northern Ireland's political leaders made a comparable attempt to solicit the support of US-based entrepreneurs with ties to the province.[16]

This parallel analysis of Northern Ireland allows for a comparative assessment of the initiatives undertaken by both jurisdictions during the

1950s and 1960s to mobilise diaspora-linked or diaspora-sympathetic actors in the United States to attract American investment.

It is important to clarify, however, why Northern Ireland is largely absent from Part I and why the treatment of the region throughout the book is less extensive than that of the Republic. There is little archival or press evidence to suggest that Northern Irish authorities actively sought to engage their diaspora for economic purposes prior to the 1950s. Furthermore, economic and trade policymaking did not fall fully within the competence of the devolved Northern Irish government. While informal or personal transatlantic connections may well have existed between businessmen and politicians from the province and their American counterparts, no official record of such ties has been identified. Additionally, from the late 1960s onward, Northern Ireland was governed directly from London until the Good Friday Agreement of 1998, a period during which building relationships with diaspora businessmen was not among the priorities of the British authorities. In any case, no sources currently available suggest that such efforts were pursued.

Part III focuses on the growing political and economic influence of prominent Irish-Americans on both parts of the island, particularly during key moments in their recent histories. In the late 1980s, the Irish government discreetly renewed its engagement with the entrepreneurial elite of the diaspora. The quiet support of these actors was instrumental in helping Ireland recover from economic stagnation and transform into one of the most globalised economies in the world—an evolution that brought both opportunities and vulnerabilities. During the financial crisis of 2009, several high-profile diaspora figures once again responded to appeals from the Irish government.

Northern Ireland, for its part, endured several decades of political instability and violence during the period known as the Troubles. In the early 1990s, a small group of Irish-American business leaders spontaneously entered the political arena in Northern Ireland with the aim of fostering peace and reconciliation. Since the signing of the Good Friday Agreement in 1998, some of these individuals have continued to support the region economically, whether through direct investment or by promoting Northern Ireland in the United States.

Part IV turns to the 2010s, a period during which several leading diaspora figures became increasingly prominent in Irish public and economic life. They played a significant role in promoting entrepreneurship and encouraging a shift towards a model of economic development that appeared, at least superficially, to be less dependent on multinational corporations. Nevertheless, their attempts to deepen their involvement in Irish affairs encountered various constraints. While the contribution of diasporas to their countries of origin is typically framed in positive terms—as a desirable and valuable resource—this book also considers the unintended consequences of such involvement. In particular, it explores the tensions that can arise when informal diaspora influence challenges the authority and legitimacy of domestic political elites.

This book also looks at the nature of the relationship between the authorities of the two Irelands and the diaspora, their respective motivations and the way in which political leaders have managed to secure the active support of the diaspora. At the end of the 1960s, Yair Aharoni[17] argued that traditional economic models, which assume investors act rationally to maximise profits and have access to perfect, free information, oversimplify how investors really behave, and suggested a social or behavioral approach to understanding investor decisions. They often have to decide without knowing everything and try to reduce this uncertainty as much as possible. Cultural ties can help lower this barrier by improving trust and the circulation of information on markets, even if he concluded that emotional ties did not directly lead to investment after interviewing Jewish American businessmen. Building on Aharoni's work, John J. Teeling's[18] findings are especially valuable. He conducted interviews with directors of foreign companies operating in Ireland in the mid-1970s and with staff from the Industrial Development Authority (IDA), Ireland's development agency. These interviews showed that Ireland had built a strong informational advantage, which helped make the country more appealing to offshore investors by reducing the uncertainty and risks of investing abroad. This advantage partly came from the presence of a large Irish-American population. Indeed, Irish-American business elites were seen as more open to hearing and trusting investment-related information about Ireland. In other words, personal and cultural connections to Ireland could make someone more willing to consider opportunities there.[19] Teeling reported: "I.D.A. officials felt very strongly that cultural ties were responsible for many projects in Ireland. When questioned as to whether the cultural ties rather than the profitable opportunities were the primary cause of investment there was generally a concensus [sic] that such ties caused the businessman to see the opportunities which in turn resulted in the investment".[20]

Nielsen and Riddle believe that the reasons why diaspora members invest in their home country is an issue that has not been fully explored.[21] They also point to the shortcomings of the international finance literature, which tends to reduce investor motivations to financial self-interest. Borrowing theoretical elements from economics, finance, psychology, and sociology, Nielsen and Riddle set out to develop a model that takes into account other factors that may influence diaspora members' decision to invest in their country of origin. Without denying the importance of financial interest, they suggest that their choice to invest in their country of origin is partly the result of a need for social recognition within the diaspora group and/or a kind of moral obligation towards the land of origin, or a desire for emotional satisfaction.[22] Tjai M. Nielsen and Liesl Riddle admit, however, that their model needs empirical testing for validation. This book therefore seeks to enlighten the reader on the complexity of Irish-American business high-flyers' motivations for investing directly in Ireland or facilitating investment there. Their relationship with the Irish authorities, while fond and nostalgic in discourse, is nonetheless ambiguous and self-serving.

The Irish authorities have indeed successfully engaged the diaspora's entrepreneurial elite and forged increasingly close ties with some of its members. Political discourse is particularly instructive, as it highlights the methods used by Irish leaders to awaken and sustain the diasporic consciousness—or at least the ethnic identity—of Irish-American business figures. The positive and negative aspects of the influence some Irish-American tycoons have exerted on the authorities on both sides of the Irish border will be brought to the fore.

Notes

1. In this book, the term Ireland is used to refer to the Irish Free State (the official name of the state from 1922 to 1937) and then the Republic of Ireland (since 1949).
2. As Barry points out, in June 1923, the Executive Council of the Free State's Cumann na nGaedheal administration appointed a Fiscal Inquiry Committee to assess the impact of both existing and proposed tariffs. While republican parties (Sinn Féin and later Fianna Fáil) and some small industrialists supported protectionist measures, major exporting firms, along with key sectors such as transport, banking, and agriculture, advocated for free trade. According to Barry, the Cumann na nGaedheal gov-

ernments of the 1920s were "pragmatists rather than ideologues". Prioritising stability, they refrained from implementing a broad system of tariffs. Frank Barry. 2023. Industry and Policy in Independent Ireland, 1922–1972. Oxford: Oxford University Press, 71, 80.

3. An open economy is one in which international trade flows freely and accounts for a significant share of the country's gross domestic product (GDP).
4. See: Andy Bielenberg, Raymond Ryan. 2016. An Economic History of Ireland since Independence. London - New York: Routledge; Graham Brownlow. 2010. Fabricating Economic Development. The Economic and Social Review, 41, 3: 301–324; Kieran A. Kennedy, and Brendan R. Dowling. 1975. Economic Growth in Ireland: The Experience since 1947, Dublin: Gill & Macmillan; Cormac Ó Gráda. 1997. A Rocky Road: The Irish Economy since the 1920s, Manchester: Manchester University Press; Eoin O'Malley. 1989. Industry and Economic Development: The Challenge for the Latecomer, Dublin: Gill & Macmillan.
5. Kieran Allen. 2000. The Celtic Tiger: The Myth of Social Partnership in Ireland, Manchester: Manchester University Press, 21–34; Proinnsias Breathnach. 1998. Exploring the 'Celtic Tiger' Phenomenon: Causes and Consequences of Ireland's Economic Miracle.

   European Urban and Regional Studies 5, 4: 305–316. https://doi.org/10.1177/096977649800500402; Brian Nolan, Philip J. O'Connell, and Christopher T. Whelan (eds). 2000. Bust to Boom? The Irish Experience of Growth and Inequality, Dublin: Institute of Public Administration; Peadar Kirby. 2002. The Celtic Tiger in Distress: Growth and Inequality in Ireland. Basingstoke: Palgrave; Paul Sweeney. 1999. The Celtic Tiger: Ireland's Continuing Economic Miracle, Dublin: Oak Tree Press.
6. The degree of globalisation of an economy is measured in a broad sense through cross-country comparisons based on the relative importance of FDI financial flows, income flows and FDI positions as a percentage of GDP. Organisation for Economic Co-operation and Development (OECD). 2005. Measuring Globalisation. OECD Handbook on Economic Globalisation Indicators, Paris: OECD, 24.
7. See: Kenichi Ohmae. 1995. The End of the Nation State: The Rise of Regional Economies, New York: Free Press.
8. Kevin Kenny. 2013. Diaspora: A Very Short Introduction, Oxford: Oxford University Press, 107.
9. See for example: Jennifer M. Brinkerhoff (ed.). 2008. Diasporas and Development: Exploring the Potential, Boulder: Lynne Rienner Publishers; Yevgeni Kuznetsov (ed.). 2006. Diaspora Networks and the International Migration of Skills: How Countries Can Draw on Their Talent Abroad,

Washington, D.C.: The World Bank, WBI Development Studies; Yevgeni Kuznetsov. 2011. Why is Diaspora Potential So Elusive? Towards a New Generation of Initiatives to Leverage Countries' Talent Abroad. In Realizing the Development Potential of Diasporas, Krishnan Sharma, Arun Kashyap, Manuel F. Montes, and Paul Ladd, eds. 171–187. New York: United Nations University Press. https://doi.org/10.18356/7cdd951b-en. In the Irish context, Kingsley Aikins, Anita Sands, and Nicola White have recently focused their work on how to develop a diaspora strategy, one of the ambitions of which is to help governments make the most of the economic potential of diasporas. Kingsley Aikins, Anita Sands, and Nicola White. 2009. The Global Irish Making a Difference Together: A Comparative Review of International Diaspora Strategies, Dublin: The Ireland Funds.

10. Anne Groutel. 2024. Irish Diaspora Business Elite philanthropy: Boon or Bane? Revue Lisa/Lisa e-journal, 22, 57, special issue: Diasporas, States and Economic Development in the English-speaking World: Opportunities and Threats, Ondine Aza, Anne Groutel, and Caixia Tan, eds. https://doi.org/10.4000/lisa.15866; Paula D. Johnson. May 2007. Diaspora Philanthropy: Influences, Initiatives, and Issues, Boston – Cambridge: The Philanthropic Initiative, Inc - The Global Equity Initiative, https://tpi.org/resource/diaspora-philanthropy-influences-initiatives-and-issues/ accessed 4 June 2025.
11. David M. Gould. 1994. Immigrant Links to the Home Country: Empirical Implications for U.S. Bilateral Trade Flows. The Review of Economics and Statistics, 76, 2: 302–316. https://doi.org/10.2307/2109884; Keith Head, John Ries. 1998. Immigration and Trade Creation: Econometric Evidence from Canada. Canadian Journal of Economics 31,1: 4762. https://doi.org/10.2307/136376.
12. Beata S. Javorcik, Çağlar Özden, Mariana Spatareanu, and Cristina Neagu. 2006. Migrant Networks and Foreign Direct Investment. World Bank Policy Research Working Paper 4046. Washington: The World Bank.
13. Chantal Bordes-Benayoun. 2012. La diaspora ou l'ethnique en mouvement. Revue européenne des migrations internationales 28, 1: 13–31. https://doi.org/10.4000/remi.5700.
14. Michel Bruneau. 2004. Diasporas et espaces transnationaux. Paris: Anthropos, 98–99.
15. Kim D. Butler. 2001. Defining Diaspora, Refining a Discourse. Diaspora: A Journal of Transnational Studies, 10, 2: 204. https://doi.org/10.1353/dsp.2011.0014.
16. We will sometimes use the term "the province" to refer to Northern Ireland.

17. Yair, Aharoni. 1967. The Foreign Investment Decision Process. Boston: Division of Research, Harvard Business School.
18. John J. Teeling. 1975. The Evolution of Offshore Investment. DBA unpublished thesis. Harvard University. Quoted in Frank Barry. 2023. Industry and Policy in Independent Ireland, 1922–1972, 141. Oxford: Oxford University Press. I am deeply thankful to the anonymous reviewers for pointing out this reference.
19. Teeling, The Evolution of Offshore Investment, 56–57.
20. Teeling, The Evolution of Offshore Investment, 58.
21. Tjai M. Nielsen, Liesl Riddle. 2007. Why Diasporas Invest in the Homeland: A Conceptual Model of Motivation. https://doi.org/10.2139/ssrn.987725.
22. Nielsen, Riddle, Why Diasporas, 8–16. Dominique Schnapper notes that in the United States it has even become a social handicap not to be able to identify as a member of a diaspora. Like ethnic origins, belonging to a diaspora is a source of prestige and satisfaction. Dominique Schnapper. 2001. De l'État-nation au monde transnational. Du sens et de l'utilité du concept de diaspora. Revue européenne des migrations internationales17, 2: 29. https://doi.org/10.3406/remi.2001.1777.

PART I

Ireland and Its Diaspora: The Distance Is Widening (1921–1955)

In January 1919, political violence broke out in the South of Ireland. It led to the Irish War of Independence which lasted until 1921. During the conflict, the Government of Ireland Act 1920, an act passed by the British Parliament, organised the partition of the island of Ireland, creating two separate political entities, Northern Ireland and Southern Ireland. Both were to have autonomous parliaments, but would remain regions of the United Kingdom. In June 1921, Éamon de Valera agreed to a ceasefire with the British and talks were held. This led to the Treaty of London, ratified by Dáil Éireann[1] in December 1921. This treaty established Ireland as a dominion, known as the Irish Free State, within the British Empire. Northern Ireland, consisting of the six counties of the province of Ulster, which was part of this new state, was given the opportunity by the treaty to remain a member of the Union with Great Britain within the United Kingdom. The Northern Ireland Parliament decided that Northern Ireland would indeed remain within the United Kingdom. Subsequently, the Boundary Commission (1924–1925) was given the task of drawing the border.

Dominion status meant that the British sovereign remained the head of state. He would be represented by a Governor-General. In addition, the members of Dáil Éireann had to swear allegiance to the British Crown.[2] The majority of Irish people supported Arthur Griffith[3] and Michael Collins[4] who led the Irish delegation at the negotiations that produced the 1921 Anglo-Irish Treaty. However, some, including de Valera, could not bring themselves to accept the terms of the Treaty of London and continued to defend the Republican cause. A civil war broke out on 18 June 1922, the day after the treaty supporters won the election. Nearly four thousand Irishmen lost their lives in the fighting, which ended on 30 April 1923, when de Valera ordered a ceasefire, followed by an order to lay down arms on 24 May.[5] William T. Cosgrave,[6] leading a new party, Cumann na nGaedheal, served as the head of the Free State's Executive Council from 1923 to 1932.

Notes

1. Dáil Éireann is the lower house of the Irish Parliament, Houses of the Oireachtas.
2. It was not until 1948 that the Irish Parliament passed the Republic of Ireland Act, which took effect on 18 April 1949. The Executive Authority (External Relations) Act 1936 was repealed by The Republic of Ireland Act 1948, and Ireland subsequently became an independent republic outside the Commonwealth of Nations. The new Act vested the powers formerly possessed by the King in the President of Ireland.
3. Dictionary of Irish Biography. Arthur Griffith. https://www.dib.ie/biography/griffith-arthur-joseph-a3644. Accessed 10 June 2025.
4. Dictionary of Irish Biography. Michael Collings. https://www.dib.ie/biography/collins-michael-a1860. Accessed 16 June 2025.
5. Joseph J. Lee. 1989. Ireland, 1912–1985: Politics and Society. Cambridge - New York: Cambridge University Press, 56–69.
6. Dictionary of Irish Biography. W. T. Cosgrave. https://www.dib.ie/biography/cosgrave-william-thomas-a2077 Accessed 9 June 2025.

CHAPTER 2

Emigration and the Diaspora: Ireland's Complex Attitude in the 1920s and 1930s

The idea of the revival of the Tailteann Games was first proposed in the 1880s by Michael Davitt, a socialist, trade unionist, and advocate of Home Rule. His initiative reflected a broader cultural movement of the time, led by intellectuals seeking to promote a Gaelic identity free from English influence and rooted in rural traditions. This cultural nationalism was expressed through several key organisations: the Gaelic League worked to reinvigorate the Irish language; the Irish Literary Revival sought to rejuvenate native literary forms; and the Gaelic Athletic Association (GAA) aimed to preserve traditional Irish sports. Together, they embodied a collective effort to reassert Irish cultural identity.[1] In 1919, Sinn Féin, a prominent republican party, also showed renewed interest in reintroducing the Tailteann Games in a modern form,[2] but the outbreak of the Irish War of Independence put an end to these plans.

Plans to hold the Games resurfaced in 1922, but the outbreak of the Civil War put the project at risk. D. McCullough, who had attended a meeting of the organising committee the day before, warned the Provisional Government's Minister for Finance that cancelling the event would be a mistake, given the high level of anticipation among Irish communities in North America:

> No matter what the financial consequences are I think the Games should be proceeded with as I found in America that they were the one thing our people all needed. The Americans themselves take an interest in Ireland at

A. Groutel, *The Two Irelands and the Diaspora*,
https://doi.org/10.1007/978-3-032-12355-8_2

present as they absolutely fail to understand the various other happenings, but the Tailteann Games appeal directly to their imagination and create a great deal of kudos to our Nation and the magnitude of the event appealed to America very much. The carrying out of the Tailteann Games in my opinion would be the very best propaganda that could be done [sic], and I hope that the Government will in every way assist in having them carried out fully and with as much éclat as possible.[3]

However, due to the political instability of the period and the strain on public finances,[4] the decision was ultimately made to cancel the Games. In the aftermath of the Civil War, the Irish government sought to promote reconciliation between former opponents. Reviving the Tailteann Games was seen as a means of supporting this effort. It also served as a symbolic assertion of Irish nationhood—one that included the diaspora, who were expected to take part. As the next section will demonstrate, the initiative was also driven by financial considerations.

2.1 The Irish Diaspora Invited to Tailteann Games

The first modern version of the Tailteann Games was finally held from 2 to 17 August 1924, following the Paris Olympics, which facilitated the coming to Dublin of a number of medal winners. Their presence was to help draw crowds and contribute to the success of the games, but only Irish or ethnic Irish athletes were invited to take part.[5] The Irish diaspora travelled from England, Scotland, Wales, the United States, Canada, Australia, New Zealand, and South Africa to compete.[6]

For James J. Walsh, Postmaster General, who was responsible for organising the games, the Tailteann Games offered an ideal opportunity to "glorify" Irish culture, intended to serve as the cohesive force binding the Irish people together following their liberation from British rule:

> The games provide neutral ground and an arena outside the contentious scope of politics. Through that channel we are hoping that our race[7] will be more effective for the general good. In other words, it will bring harmony amongst the Irish race.[8]

Walsh further believed that this event would be a model that could be replicated elsewhere in the world and would provide an opportunity for people of Irish descent abroad to reconcile:

I think, that some such organisation as the Tailteann Games should exist in all those countries where the Irish people are pretty numerous, if only for the purpose of giving them some neutral ground on which they can cooperate for the general upliftment of their race.[9]

In 1929, in the same vein, Walsh wrote about the games:

It will show those of other lands that this Island of ours is not a colony, but the home of a Race [sic] of historic lineage unsurpassed elsewhere.[10]

The content here is overtly nationalistic.[11] Moreover, according to Reynolds, the games:

[...] pointed to the ideal of racial purity embedded in Celticism and the Pan-Celtic movement and to strains of nationalism that regarded the Irish as demeaned by any association with non-white colonial subjects [...].[12]

Thirty-two sub-committees were given responsibility for organising the games throughout the island. The Belfast authorities, however, informed James J. Walsh in November 1923 that they preferred "to push their part of the Country as a separate entity and for their own ends".[13] Given the spirit of the games and the strained relations between Belfast and Dublin, this decision was to be expected. James Craig,[14] the Prime Minister of Northern Ireland, was formally invited to attend the opening but declined.[15] While the games were greeted with great enthusiasm by the Irish population, as the deadline approached, the authorities were increasingly alarmed by the large number of tourists who were expected to come for this occasion. Kevin O'Higgins, Vice-President of the Executive and Minister for Justice, was concerned about maintaining law and order. What would happen if the available accommodation ran out?[16]

According to information received by O'Higgins, at least one hundred thousand Irish-Americans were expected to make the trip that summer. Indeed, every year since 1914, they had had to postpone their coming because of the political instability in the country.[17] Although this figure was only an estimate, as it was difficult to predict the exact number of people who would make the trip, there was cause for concern. In Athens and Antwerp, tourists had been reduced to sleeping in public gardens during major events. Walsh was well aware of the disastrous effect this had on the image of both countries.[18] Furthermore, it was also risky to allow tourists to venture into certain parts of the island as they could potentially become targets of individuals with malicious intent:

> During the month of August the Railway Companies [sic] will run a daily express to such places as Glendalough, Killarney, Connemara, and Belfast and the North, but we have no guarantee whatever that Tourists [sic] will not be fleeced in these places, though all possible steps have been taken to impress hotel managers of their responsibility in the matter. Yet, as I say, it will be extremely difficult for us to guarantee that in any stage of a tourist's trip through the Country [sic] will he be free from an imposition of some kind or another, and I am satisfied myself that whilst a visitor would find little fault with the fact that he had to put up with certain inconveniences in regard to accommodation, and that the difficulty would be readily understood and appreciated, let him once be bled by a jarvey, or somebody of that type, and his memory of the event will be of a more lasting character.[19]

Wash was therefore concerned that hoteliers and taxi or jaunting car drivers would take the opportunity to raise their prices unreasonably. Although he had been assured by the Hotel and Restaurant Association that this would not happen, he still felt that particular vigilance was required and suggested that the government should control price increases during the games.[20]

2.2 Beyond Culture: The Economic Ambitions of the Tailteann Games

Although the main purpose of the games was not to make a large financial profit,[21] it was not lost on Walsh that there were economic benefits to holding such an event. Responding to criticism from some Teachtaí Dála (TD)[22] that the sums allocated to the event were too high, Walsh argued, firstly, that the Tailteann Games could be a real boon to tourism. At that time, 43% of the Irish-born population lived abroad.[23] Convincing them to attend the event and, why not, to visit the rest of the island[24] could be a significant source of revenue for the young state. Publicity brochures informing visitors of the island's tourist attractions were published for this purpose.[25]

Walsh also insisted that those of their compatriots who had become wealthy abroad represented a potential that should not be overlooked. Indeed, the primary target audience was Irish-American tourists, not the average Irish citizen.[26] He also brought to the attention of Irish parliamentarians the economic benefits that the country could gain from the event in the longer term:

> It is of some importance to have foreigners coming here and spending money. We do not want to turn this country into a Switzerland. At the same time, we feel we are justified because there are many Irish-Americans who, having made money, desire to return to the old land, settle down here, buy property, and help this country. That is actually what is occurring. Irish-Americans have come back to this country and are buying property. [...] that is a very desirable development. I do not suppose anyone wishes to do anything to discourage that.[27]

Secondly, Walsh highlighted the fact that the efforts made over a number of years to increase shipping links between America and the Irish port of Cobh had met with little success. However, since the announcement of the Tailteann Games, four companies had decided to call at the port, since it was expected, according to the Minister, that twenty-five thousand people would travel from North America for the occasion. He was confident that the shipping links would continue thereafter.

The organisation of this event was an opportunity to gauge the strength of the diaspora's attachment to the land of origin. Feeling a sense of belonging, attachment, or nostalgia for Ireland was one thing, making the journey was another. It required a personal and financial investment.[28] In 1922, D. McCullough had argued for the continuation of the Tailteann Games on the basis of strong American enthusiasm for the event. But, against all expectations, F. O'Hanlon, the emissary responsible for coordinating the organising committees in the United States, was not greeted by a cheering crowd when he arrived in New York:

> I arrived by S. S. Olympic in New York on the night of Tuesday 16th October [1923]. No representative of the American Committee or its Chairman met me on landing, and neither did any representative of the Irish Societies [sic], Clubs or Organisations. The Press passed me over, unnoticed, and altogether my reception was not encouraging [...]. On reaching my hotel I learned by telephonic communication that the American Committee of Aonach Tailteann had not met in more than two years, and that its Chairman, through pressure of other business, would be unable to meet me for a week.[29]

O'Hanlon admitted that "[…] the division of the Irish Race in America […]"[30]and the cancellation of the Tailteann Games in 1922 had made his task difficult, but by dint of hard work he had managed to mobilise enough people in the Irish community abroad to carry out the selection of athletes and the organisation of the logistics and funding of their arrival:

> It became evident to me at once that interest had to be revived. […] It meant work and lots of it, but the co-operation and assistance of those in a position to help was readily forthcoming, and now on leaving U.S.A. temporarily I am happy to say that the position has changed, any prejudices which existed have been substantially removed and the prospects are now bright indeed.[31]

Walsh was not the only one with ulterior motives, for among the Irish-Americans who planned to make the trip to Ireland, some had ambitious plans. Thus O'Hanlon found that, after a lukewarm reception, interest in Ireland began to grow rapidly among business-minded individuals within that community:

> The people here are again beginning to look for something really big [sic] to Ireland. In commercial circles they see possibilities of big trade developments with Ireland and even within the last few weeks the first real attempt has been made to open up trade relations in a big way and on a sound basis with Ireland. Within these few weeks the 'Irish Enterprise Corporation' has been brought into being by a group of keen, patriotic Irish-Americans. […] Some of America's leading business-men are now taking an interest in this question of trade development with Ireland and many of them will be found in Ireland next summer, so a wonderful opportunity may be knocking at our doors if we are only willing and fit ourselves to take it.[32]

However, this renewed interest did not translate into a significant rise in trade between the two countries in the years that followed. Moreover, the early 1930s marked a shift towards protectionist policies on both sides of the Atlantic: the United States adopted trade barriers, while the newly elected Fianna Fáil government in Ireland introduced similar measures to support the growth of its nascent industrial sector.

2.3 The Tailteann Games: A Symbolic Success, a Short-Lived Legacy

A large number of traditional sports were included in the programme of the games.[33] In addition to sports competitions, poetry and literature competitions and performances of traditional theatre and dance were also held.

Although the celebration of Irish culture in the broadest sense was the essence of the event, modernity was also present. There were car races, speedboat races, and air shows, as well as a large parade where Irish companies, seeking publicity, could showcase their products. The event was a great achievement.[34] The Irish press was very positive about the outcome of the 1924 Tailteann Games.[35] The Organising Committee also considered it to be a success.[36] However, it is difficult to determine the size of the event, as there are only estimates of the number of spectators. Paul Rouse[37] put the total number of spectators at two hundred thousand for the entire duration of the games, without giving the source of this information. As for the Americans, *The New York Times*[38] reported that they were "numerous" in the opening parade of the games, without giving any further details. The archive records do not contain any estimates of the number of Irish-Americans who travelled to Ireland specifically for the occasion. One thing is certain: no one was forced to sleep in the city's parks and the organisation was considered satisfactory.[39]

Although the Irish government recognised the potential prestige the event could bring, it remained cautious about becoming too closely associated with it, fearing a financial failure. Walsh struggled to secure even the modest subsidies he had been promised.[40] In reality, the Games proved neither financially viable nor particularly successful in enhancing Ireland's international image.[41]

Nonetheless, the initiative was repeated following the same model in 1928 and 1932, but not thereafter.[42] In 1924 and 1928, the Tailteann Games benefited from the presence of Olympic medalists, as the Olympic Games were held in Paris and Amsterdam, respectively. This advantage disappeared in 1932, when the Olympics took place in Los Angeles. That same year, the Irish Games also faced competition from the Eucharistic Congress, which was held in Dublin simultaneously. These challenges were further compounded by the economic crisis in the United States and poor weather conditions. Moreover, unlike the Olympics, the Tailteann Games attracted limited international participation, were always held at the same venue, and lacked innovation—factors that likely contributed to waning interest.

In 1932, in a speech to his countrymen in Ireland and the United States,[43] the words of Éamon de Valera, President of the Free State Executive, did not betray any animosity towards the games:

> The Tailteann Games [...] have our whole-hearted approval. The games are of very great national value, unifying our people in sentiment and giving them, no matter what land they live, a just sense of pride in the spiritual ideals, physical prowess and intellectual achievements of the games. It is our wish, therefore, that the Tailteann Games should by their success, reflect in this year something of our ancient glory and instill in our youth respect and reverence for the heroes and heroines of the past [...]. I sincerely hope that past events will no longer interfere with the popularity of the games, which I feel will add considerably to the prestige of the Irish nation.[44]

Yet, despite this enthusiasm, the Irish authorities decided not to provide the annual grant of ten thousand Irish pounds requested by the Tailteann Games Council for the next edition of the games. Sinn Féin had been enthusiastic about the project before the civil war. However, when Fianna Fáil[45] came to power, it was difficult for its leaders to support an initiative whose image was now associated with the victorious Cumann na nGaedheal.[46]

For Walsh, the opportunity to perpetuate the links between Ireland and the diaspora and to strengthen the latter's cohesion and ethnic identity awareness was abandoned for political reasons. As the process of assimilation proceeded, there was a danger that these links would become more tenuous over time.[47]

2.4 Emigration as a Necessary Burden: Political Perspectives in Early Free State Ireland

The Cumann na nGaedheal government did not prioritise tackling emigration,[48] seemingly viewing it as an intractable issue beyond its control.[49] Fianna Fáil, however, capitalised on the situation. At the party's inaugural meeting, de Valera forcefully declared that the scourge of emigration had to be eliminated:

> The best of our people - the young men and women of vigour and enterprise, the foundation on which the whole future should be built - are daily taken from us. We are being bled by an emigration worse today than almost at any time since the exodus that followed the Great Famine. That must be stopped.[50]

Emigration was not a central theme in Cumann na nGaedheal's 1932 general election campaign. In contrast, Fianna Fáil maintained that the issue could be tackled through job creation—an objective the party firmly committed to achieving.[51] But for Delaney "[...]such an assumption was at best naïve and perhaps disingenuous".[52] Yet de Valera and Seán Lemass[53] proclaimed during the campaign that Fianna Fáil would create so many jobs that Irish people who had emigrated to the United States[54] would have to be repatriated to fill all the vacancies. Some opposition TDs were quick to remind Lemass of these claims a few years later.[55]

It was clear that neither agriculture nor industry could generate enough jobs to meet the demand of the Irish population at that time, a fact that de Valera came to agree with.[56] Unemployed Irish citizens emigrated, thereby reducing the financial burden on the state and mitigating the risk of social unrest at home.[57] Emigration therefore continued to act as a safety valve.[58]

2.5 Irish Attitudes Towards the Diaspora: Between Pride, Disdain, and Ulterior Motives

In 1937, sometime after the decision was made not to renew the Tailteann Games, Joseph P. Walshe, then Secretary General of the Department of External Affairs,[59] wrote to de Valera to draw his attention to the importance of promoting Irish culture among Irish-Americans in order to maintain the link with them, otherwise Ireland would not be able to count on their support in times of need. The letter[60] is accompanied by an appendix that outlines the state of the diaspora's relationship with its country of origin. Some members of the diaspora continued to take an interest in Ireland, but if left unchecked, their numbers would decline inexorably:

> It is this class that will [...] constitute, in a few years more, whatever there will then be of the Irish empire in America. What use its existence might be to Ireland in a later emergency will depend, largely, upon what pains are taken meanwhile to make it 'Ireland conscious'. [...] There you have the picture of what is happening to the 'twenty millions [sic] of Irish blood' [...]

> they are left with a name [...]. But unless there is supplied at least 'a little leaven [that] leaveneth the whole lump' our American Irish empire will be a mirage [...] which might be just too bad. Whence is that leaven to come? I think from your side.[61]

However, this warning was not heard in Dublin. Admittedly, the attitude of political circles towards their expatriate compatriots was ambivalent. Some boasted that the Irish presence abroad gave Ireland a prestige and influence out of all proportion to its size or political and economic weight on the international scene.[62] Others claimed, with a touch of bitterness, that the Irish left the country not out of economic necessity, but for the sake of adventure or because they felt that Ireland could not offer them a future that matched their ambitions.[63] It would seem that those who remained in Ireland generally looked with both irony and condescension on their fellow emigrants to the United States, whom they nicknamed "Yanks":

> The Irish-Americans are the most sentimental of all our exiles. Indeed, we have become amused when they return at their sentiment about everything Irish, and I fear we have little sympathy with their romance.[64]

For Piaras Mac Éinrí and Brian Lambkin, the Irish attitude towards the diaspora was:

> [...] A complex mixture of resentment, begrudgery and denial, with perhaps a touch of a suggestion of betrayal, with those who were 'really' committed to the new Irish State being prepared to stay on and stick it out in spite of hardship.[65]

For his part, Seán Lemass became aware early on of the other benefits the country could derive from the diaspora. By the early 1930s, although a strong advocate of economic protectionism, he was convinced that the country could not survive in total autarky. By this time, he was already convinced that Ireland needed to start developing the tourist industry. His fellow citizens and the Irish population abroad were, in his view, a ready-made market. In 1931, a few months before his party's victory in the 1932 general election, he made a statement to this effect in a parliamentary sitting of the Dáil:

> It seems to me that we have not in this country either the climate or the facilities, or, may I say, the legislative intention of providing attractions for tourists that are provided in certain Continental countries. Nevertheless, the attempts made were of a nature that would indicate that those who are responsible for the tourist development were contemplating entering into competition with these Continental countries. [...] It seems to me that if attention were concentrated in getting the Irish people to decide upon spending their holidays in Ireland, and the Irish in America and the Irish people in foreign countries to come home for their holidays to Ireland much more beneficial results would be secured. [...] It seems to me that the most profitable field for the expenditure of energy in the matter of attracting tourist traffic to the country is being neglected by the existing association.[66]

Indeed, in 1939, Lemass, then Minister for Industry and Commerce, introduced an ambitious bill[67] which provided, among other things, for the establishment of the Irish Tourist Board, a public body which could acquire, or commission the construction of, and manage tourist establishments. Lemass was careful to emphasise that this would benefit both the Irish and tourists from outside the country, most of whom, he stressed, were not exactly foreigners:

> [...] let us provide these holiday facilities for our people and let us see that they can get not merely good and cheap holidays in this country, but holidays as good as they can get anywhere else, if we can possibly secure it. We think it will pay to do it, but, over and above that, we can attract visitors from abroad. Seventy-five per cent. of these visitors will be people with racial associations here. [...] These people are going to take holidays in any event, and if they do not come here, they will go elsewhere. Is there any reason why we should not set out systematically to organise the bringing of them here, so that whatever profit is to be got will be secured for this country, instead of leaving it to other countries, such as England, France, Switzerland, or some other country, the Governments of which have more business foresight than we have displayed here in the past?[68]

Lemass was one of the few people in government at the time who believed that the contribution of the diaspora to the national economy could go far beyond the money sent to families back home. Indeed, in Irish political circles, there was a tendency to distrust anything that came from outside. Lemass faced strong criticism from the main opposition party, Fine Gael,[69] whose members denounced the threat that foreign tourists posed to Irish language, culture, and identity.[70] Lemass sought to reassure parliamentarians when he presented his Tourist Traffic Bill (1939) to the upper house of the Irish Parliament:

They are not going to be foreigners coming in for the purpose of destroying Irish nationality and undermining the Irish language, but Irish people coming home to their own country to see their own folk and to renew their associations with the old country. That is what they will be. Will anyone deny that of the visitors who came to this country from the United States of America last year, 99 per cent were people of Irish origin or descent, who were coming to Ireland because they had herd [sic] Ireland spoken of in their homes in the United States who knew that they had originated here and who wanted to come back here for the purpose of seeing the old country? The same applies to people coming even from England and it certainly applies to people coming from other countries. These people are not coming in here to destroy the Irish language or to undermine Irish nationality. Their coming will have quite a contrary effect altogether, but, by bringing them in here, we can make a profit.[71]

However, the series of attacks by the Irish Republican Army (IRA)[72] in Britain, which began in January 1939, undermined the effects of the advertising campaign that promoted Ireland's tourist attractions to the British. The outbreak of World War II in September of the same year temporarily curtailed the development of the tourist industry in Ireland.[73] The potential contribution of the diaspora to the Irish economy through tourism was again closely examined by the first coalition government[74] in the late 1940s.

Notes

1. Cathal Brennan. 23 February 2011. The Tailteann Games, 1924–1936. https://www.theirishstory.com/2011/02/23/the-tailteann-games-1924-1936/. Accessed 3 June 2025. Mike Cronin. 2003. Projecting the Nation through Sport and Culture: Ireland, Aonach Tailteann and the Irish Free State, 1924–32. *Journal of Contemporary History* 38, 3: 399. https://doi.org/10.1177/0022009403038003004.
2. According to legend, the Tailteann Games—a festival celebrating sport and culture—originated in the late nineteenth century BC and became an annual event around 600 BC, before being abolished following the Norman invasion, with the last games held in 1169. Thomas H. Nally's book explains the origins and functions of this festival, which was once a

major event. Thomas H. Nally. 1922. The Aonaċ Tailteann and Tailteann Games: Their Origin, History and Ancient Associations. Dublin: Talbot Press. https://archive.org/stream/aonactailteannta00nalliala?ref=ol#page/n3/mode/2up. Accessed 4 June 2025.

3. D. McCullough to Michael Collins, 12 July 1922, S1592, National Archives of Ireland (hereafter NAI).

   Michael Collins probably received this letter, but was killed in an ambush a month later.
4. Cronin, Projecting the Nation, 399.
5. Paige Reynolds. 2007. Modernism, Drama and the Audience for Irish Spectacle. Cambridge: Cambridge University Press, 157.
6. Report of the Inter-Departmental Committee on the Feasibility of Organising Aonach Tailteann in 1939 or 1940, S8369, NAI.
7. The term "race" was then commonly used by Irish politicians. It should be emphasised that it referred mostly, but not always, as we shall see, to what we now refer to as an ethnic group, i.e. a population sharing the same culture, language, religion, origin, habits, and customs, rather than to race in the biological sense.
8. Ireland, parliamentary debates, Houses of the Oireachtas, Dáil Éireann (hereafter Dáil Éireann debates), 7, 20, 5 June 1924 (James J. Walsh).
9. Dáil Éireann debates, 5 June 1924.
10. Aonach Tailteann - 1928, Director's statement, presented to the General Council on the 23rd April, 1929, FIN/S200/2/28, NAI.
11. Indeed, it would appear that James J. Walsh was close to the fascist movement in Ireland during World War II. Eunan O'Halpin. 1999. Defending Ireland: The Irish State and Its Enemies since 1922. Oxford: Oxford University Press, 223.
12. Reynolds, Modernism, 173.
13. Letter signed by James J. Walsh [no addressee], 3 November 1923, S1592, NAI.
14. James Craig was Prime Minister of Northern Ireland from 7 June 1921 to 24 November 1940.
15. Ulster Premier Invited. 1924. *The New York Times*, 31 July; Reynolds, Modernism, 164.
16. Paul Rouse. 2016. When Ireland's Tailteann Games Eclipsed the Olympics. Irish Examiner, 18 November.
17. Kevin O'Higgins to James J. Walsh, 21 January 1924, S1592, NAI.
18. Letter signed by James J. Walsh [no addressee], 3 November 1923, S1592, NAI.
19. James J Walsh to Kevin O'Higgins, 22 January 1924, S1592, NAI.
20. Letter signed by James J. Walsh [no addressee], 22 January 1924, S1592, NAI.

21. "Seeing that the main object of the Games was the promotion of race cohesion, and that numbers mattered much more than financial results [...] the policy of absolute minimum charge, or no charge at all [...] proved a wise course to adopt". Aonach Tailteann - 1928, Director's statement, presented to the General Council on the 23rd April, 1929.
22. A Teachta Dála, abbreviated as TD is a member of Dáil Éireann, the lower house of the Oireachtas, the parliament of Ireland. The official English translation of the term is "Dáil Deputy".
23. Reynolds, Modernism, 161.
24. Walsh was well aware that this could be a risk for tourists.
25. Dáil Éireann Debates, 5 June 1924, 7, 20 (James J. Walsh).
26. Reynolds, Modernism, 164.
27. Dáil Éireann Debates, 5 June 1924, 7, 20 (James J. Walsh).
28. Reynolds, Modernism, 162.
29. Aonach Tailteann (American Committee), Report from Mr. F. O'Hanlon, 8 November 1923, S1592, NAI.
30. Aonach Tailteann (American Committee).
31. Aonach Tailteann (American Committee).
32. Aonach Tailteann (American Committee).
33. The programmes for the 1924, 1928, and 1932 Tailteann Games are on display in the GAA Museum in Croke Park, Dublin. See also the parliamentary debates in which Walsh provided the list of sports represented. Dáil Éireann Debates, 1 March 1922, S2, 2.
34. Cronin, Projecting the Nation, 402.
35. Cronin, Projecting the Nation, 406–407.
36. Report of the Inter-Departmental Committee on the Feasibility of Organising Aonach Tailteann in 1939 or 1940.
37. Rouse, When Ireland's Tailteann Games.
38. Tailteann Games Opened in Dublin, Thousands of Visitors, Including Many Americans, Present. 1924. *The New York Times*, 3 August.
39. Report of the Inter-Departmental Committee on the Feasibility of Organising Aonach Tailteann in 1939 or 1940.
40. Cronin, Projecting the Nation, 407.
41. Cronin, Projecting the Nation, 408.
42. Cronin, Projecting the Nation, 409–410; Brennan, The Tailteann Games; James J. Walsh. 1944. Recollections of a Rebel. Tralee: The Kerryman, 84.
43. This was de Valera's first radio broadcast in the United States.
44. Text of de Valera's Speech. 1932. *The New York Times*, 18 March.
45. Fianna Fáil was formed in 1926 under the leadership of Éamon de Valera. The party was the result of a split in Sinn Féin. While remaining opposed to the Anglo-Irish Treaty, the new party opposed Sinn Féin's strategy of clandestine action and abstentionism. The creation of a unitary republic on

the whole island of Ireland was the main objective of Fianna Fáil, which it intended to achieve by acting from within the institutions of the Irish Free State.

46. Brennan, The Tailteann Games.
47. Walsh, Recollections of a Rebel, 84–85.
48. Enda Delaney. 1998. State, Politics and Demography: The Case of Irish Emigration, 1921–71. Irish Political Studies 13, 1: 26. https://doi.org/10.1080/07907189808406582.
49. John Hanamy. 2013. Was Defeat Inevitable for Cumann na nGaedheal in the 1932 General Election? Master's thesis in History, University of Limerick, 97. https://researchrepository.ul.ie/articles/thesis/Was_defeat_inevitable_for_Cumann_na_nGaedheal_in_the_1932_general_election_/19829371?file=35253130. Accessed 4 June 2025.
50. Speech by Éamon de Valera at the inaugural meeting of Fianna Fáil at the La Scala Theatre, Dublin, 16 May 1926. Quoted in Speeches and Statements by Eamon de Valera, 1917–73, 1980, ed. Maurice Moynihan: 140–141. New York: St Martin's Press, 1980.
51. Delaney, State, 29–30.
52. Delaney, State, 30.
53. Seán Lemass, who participated in the 1916 Easter Rising, the War of Independence, and the Civil War, began his political career by winning a by-election on 18 November 1924, as a Sinn Féin a Teachta Dála (TD), member of the Irish parliament, representing Dublin South. He consistently won re-election until the constituency was dissolved in 1948, after which he represented Dublin South-Central until he retired in 1969. As one of the founders of Fianna Fáil in 1926, Lemass held several key positions in the party's governments, including Taoiseach, Tánaiste Minister for Industry and Commerce, Minister for Supplies. Dictionary of Irish Biography. Seán Lemass. https://www.dib.ie/biography/lemass-sean-a4787. Accessed 9 June 2025.
54. Fianna Fáil Campaign. 1932.*The Irish Times*, 15 February.
55. Dáil Éireann Debates, 4 March 1943, 89, 8 (Independent MP Joseph Hannigan and Labour MP Richard Corish)
56. Dáil Éireann Debates, 21 November 1951, 127, 6.
57. Delaney, State, 35.
58. Mary E. Daly. 2006. The Slow Failure: Population Decline and Independent Ireland, 1922–1973. Madison: The University of Wisconsin Press, 138–139.
59. Senior official in the Irish administration.
60. Joseph P. Walshe to President [Eamon de Valera], 5 October 1937, S9215A, NAI.

61. "Appendix - Memo on a proposed Irish-American Foundation to promote cultural relations between Irish at home and abroad by Felix E. Hackett", S9215A, NAI.
62. Mary E. Daly. 18 November 2008. The Irish State and the Diaspora, 33rd O'Donnell Lecture. University College Dublin, National University of Ireland, PL-497-25, 9.
63. Dáil Éireann Debates, 17 December 1931, 40, 24; 14 April 1937, 66, 6; 1 March 1939, 74, 9; 4 March 1943, 89, 8; 24 April 1957, 161, 3.
64. Bluebird. 1933. Round the World and Home. *The Irish Times*, 11 March.
65. Piaras Mac Éinrí, Brian Lambkin. 2002. Whose Diaspora? Whose Migration? Whose Identity? Some Current Issues in Migration Studies. *The Irish Journal of Psychology*, 23, 3–4: 136.
66. Dáil Éireann Debates, 22 April 1931, 38, 1 (Seán Lemass).
67. The bill was called the Tourist Traffic Bill. It was passed on 20 July 1939. Ireland, parliamentary debates, Houses of the Oireachtas, Seanad Éireann (hereafter Seanad Éireann Debates), 20 July 1939, 23, 7. See: Irene Furlong. 2009. Irish Tourism 1880–1980. Dublin—Portland: Irish Academic Press, 62–69.
68. Seanad Éireann Debates, 28 June 1939, 22, 23 (Seán Lemass).
69. Fine Gael was founded in 1933. It resulted from the merger of Cumann na nGaedheal, the National Centre Party, and the National Guard.
70. Furlong, Irish Tourism,113.
71. Seanad Éireann Debates, 28 June 1939, 22, 23 (Seán Lemass).
72. After 1922, the IRA brought together those who were on the losing side of the civil war and who continued to reject the legitimacy of the Free State and Northern Ireland, which the organisation believed to be the product of British imperialism. In 1969, the organisation split, creating the Official Irish Republican Army and the Provisional Irish Republican Army.
73. Furlong, Irish Tourism, 66–69.
74. This coalition government (First Inter-Party Government) which remained in power from 1948 to 1951 was composed of members of Fine Gael, the Labour Party, Clann na Poblachta, Clann na Talmhan, the National Labour Party, and an independent (James Dillon).

CHAPTER 3

Irish-American Dollars: A Coveted Source of Foreign Exchange

3.1 Ireland Faces Greenback Shortage

Having failed to obtain any agreement from the British and American authorities on the question of a possible reunification of Ireland, the Republic decided to remain neutral during World War II and did not allow the American army to use its air bases during the conflict. It should be noted that the majority of the Irish-American community was hostile to Irish neutrality.[1]

Ireland was, however, one of the countries that benefited from the Marshall Plan.[2] The Irish and British economies were so closely linked that it was deemed necessary to include Ireland in the programme, which enabled it to obtain a dollar loan.[3] Ireland was thus in a position to continue to import goods to support its agriculture, the produce of which helped to feed the British population.[4] At the time, almost all Irish exports were destined for the British market and were paid for in pounds sterling. There was a fixed parity between the two national currencies.[5] Ireland therefore had large reserves of this convertible currency which allowed it to pay for its imports from the United States in dollars. But imports from the United States increased dramatically after the war. Irish agriculture was indeed forced to adapt to meet the needs of the populations of the warring countries and concentrated on growing wheat. This was ill suited to the nature of Irish soils and had depleted them considerably. To remedy this problem, Ireland had to import large quantities of fertiliser and

A. Groutel, *The Two Irelands and the Diaspora*,
https://doi.org/10.1007/978-3-032-12355-8_3

agricultural machinery, among other things.[6] A major problem for the country arose when the United Kingdom, faced with a severe shortage of dollars in the sterling area in the summer of 1947, suspended the convertibility of its currency.[7]

In the late 1940s, Ireland exported little to the United States and Canada.[8] The Economic Cooperation Administration (ECA), the agency set up by the US authorities to manage Marshall Plan funds, therefore considered that tourism was the sector most likely to contribute to a rapid reduction in Ireland's dollar deficit.[9] This was also the conclusion of the first progress report of the Irish government's Inter-Departmental Working Party on Dollar Earnings.[10] This document noted that Ireland did feature in the offerings of American tour operators, but it was only one of the destinations offered as part of a longer tour of Europe. The stays were generally short and the tourists stopped off in luxury hotels.[11] The authors of this report drew the attention of the authorities to the fact that the shortage of high-end accommodation could become problematic if the number of such tourists suddenly increased.

The celebration of the Holy Year in 1950 could be an opportunity to attract some American pilgrims to visit Ireland. Rapidly increasing hotel capacity and improving the quality of services offered was a priority. Therefore, the Irish authorities were asked to put in place a plan of action to attract additional tourists as had been foreseen in the long-term plan drawn up by Washington.[12] However, the tone of the letter that Joseph E. Carrigan, head of the ECA in Ireland, wrote to Seán MacBride, the Irish Minister for External Affairs, on this subject clearly shows that, on the organisation's side, there was a concern about the obvious lack of goodwill on the part of Irish authorities:

> As I have discussed the matter with Government officials, I find everyone most friendly and receptive to suggestions, but little action seems to follow. I have been impressed in some instances by the lightness of concern about it, in other instances by the expressed hopelessness as to Ireland's ability to do anything substantial about it, and in still other instances by the apparent feeling that it is not Ireland's problem but that it must be solved by action entirely outside of Ireland. Some appear to feel that something is going to take care of it.[13]

3.2 Irish Administration's Reluctance to Develop Tourism

In fact, some senior Irish officials in the Department of Finance were sceptical about the wisdom of government intervention in the tourism sector solely to address the country's dollar deficit:

> Any hope of closing the dollar gap through development of the tourist industry is illusory unless there is a sharp fall in dollar outlay and this is unlikely to occur to an adequate extent without restrictive measures unless wheat and maize can again be bought for sterling as in pre-war days. Efforts to expand dollar income from tourism are nevertheless essential to strengthen our exchange position and it is desirable that the Economic Co-operation Administration should be satisfied that effective measures are, in fact, being taken.[14]

The author of this memorandum,[15] addressed to the government, advised to keep a cool head in matters of tourism policy:

> Policy regarding the tourist industry falls to be considered under two main heads, the general and the particular, and, though the particular aspect of promoting dollar earnings is of great importance, it should not dominate all thinking on the subject. A sense of proportion must be maintained.[16]

Finally, the Department of Finance considered that the large increase in the advertising budget recommended by the Tourist Board was "extravagant". The general level of the offer had to be improved first in order not to disappoint the tourist. A targeted advertising campaign could then be considered in the United States in places where the density of population of Irish origin was high.

It was becoming easier to travel by boat from the United States, so the number of Irish-American visitors could be expected to increase. They were not likely to cause a shortage of hotel rooms, as they were staying with relatives. Thus, diaspora tourists posed few problems.

3.3 Irish-American Tourists: A Profitable Clientele

These recommendations were perfectly in line with the report prepared in 1949 by the Inter-Departmental Working Party on Dollar Earnings which considered that Irish-American tourists should be the primary target market.[17] In this way, the construction of new hotels would not be necessary for these tourists, who, given their extended stay, spent more overall than ordinary tourists. In theory, any American with sufficient financial means was a potential tourist, but it seemed more realistic to focus on this market of fifteen million Irish-Americans, even if few could afford and felt the desire to holiday in Ireland. According to the Irish Consul in New York, the average Irish-American holidaymaker spent about five hundred dollars in Ireland, a figure which the authors of the report considered to be an underestimate. The reality, they believed, was closer to seven hundred dollars:

> Even if the tourists' average expenditure is only $500 and if the potential market is no greater than ten times the number who came here in 1948,[18] it is clear that this country is at present only receiving a mere trickle of the potentially enormous flow of Irish-American tourists and their dollars.[19]

Convincing this clientele to make the trip would be easier, it was thought, than attracting tourists with no ties to Ireland. Joseph E. Carrigan,[20] Colonel Pozzy,[21] and the Inter-Departmental Working Party on Dollar Earnings were all convinced that it would be easy to make Irish-Americans want to come to Ireland by playing the nostalgia card: "It is clear [...] from Colonel Pozzy's observations that sentiment alone exerts a very strong attractive force on Irish-Americans".[22] It was therefore deemed appropriate to limit the advertising budget, initially, to cities and regions, such as Boston, New York, and more generally the states on the east coast of the United States, where the Irish-American presence was strong.

However, as early as August 1949, Paul Hoffman, the ECA's Director General in Europe, expressed doubts about the Irish authorities' intention to address the dollar deficit.[23] Eight months later, there seemed to be little change in the situation.[24] The ECA's grand plans for tourism in Ireland had not materialised, but the organisation did not let up and managed to convince the Irish government to agree to the arrival of a US team to carry out a survey of the industry as part of the Marshall Plan technical assistance. In reality, for the ECA, this was a backdoor way of trying to achieve its ends,[25] even though Harry Clement[26] feared that the venture would be futile: "I feel very strongly that if Mr. Morrissey[27] gets the chance, he will pigeon hole the written report made by the survey team".[28] This letter from Harry Clement to Colonel Pozzy shows both the extent of the differences between the Irish authorities and the ECA, which would have liked the Irish government to allocate a substantial budget to tourism, and the American manoeuvres to achieve their ends. In the letter, Clement said he had spent several days in New York informing Robert K. Christenberry, head of the team that was to visit Ireland to conduct a study of the tourism sector, of the difficulties and resistance he was likely to encounter. He also told him what the ECA wanted to see accomplished. Christenberry, he said, had agreed. The team submitted its report in September 1950. Among other things, it was suggested that further study should be made of what attracted Irish-American tourists and that the focus should be on this section of the clientele.[29] For a time, the government objected to the publication of this report.[30] As Clement had feared, the recommendations it contained were not acted upon,[31] at least not immediately. One thing is certain: the pilgrims who went to Rome for the Holy Year celebrations did not flock to Ireland[32] as Carrigan had hoped.

In the early 1950s, the First Inter-Party Government thus seemed reluctant to encourage tourists to Ireland. In fact, it was a highly sensitive topic. Fine Gael had previously opposed tourism development, notably when Seán Lemass introduced the Tourist Traffic Bill in 1939. The party reiterated its objections in April 1946 during parliamentary debates on the Tourist Traffic (Amendment) Bill, with Patrick McGilligan[33] warning that a surge in tourism would lead to rising prices. On the same occasion, some Fine Gael Teachtaí Dála (TD) also claimed that it would jeopardise Irish culture and traditions.[34] Furthermore, at the time, many politicians and commentators also viewed tourism as a somewhat disreputable industry, echoing earlier concerns that it would encourage servility and obsequiousness among the Irish population.[35] Around the same period, the Irish press strongly criticised the Irish Tourist Board (ITB) for purchasing properties to transform into luxury hotels catering to American tourists, and more broadly for the excessive public spending on tourism development.[36] Yet the initiative quickly faltered; the hotels proved too small to operate profitably at a luxury level, and government funding was inadequate to maintain the standards required.[37] As a result, tourism became a politically contentious issue, increasingly seen by both public opinion and opposition parties as a financial black hole. Upon taking office, the First Inter-Party Government swiftly moved to auction off these hotels and to terminate the costly transatlantic service operated by Air Lingus since 1947.[38]

So, ECA leaders soon realised that the apparent inertia of the First Inter-Party Government also concealed a great deal of mistrust of the possible effects of increased tourist activity:

> We have urged unceasingly that more should be done to promote dollar earnings from this source [tourism]. The present Government has had a considerable mental hazard to overcome in this connection.[39]

However, both Morrissey and McGilligan came to recognise that Irish-American tourists seemed to be much more accessible, easily persuaded, less demanding, and equally willing to spend dollars when compared to other American tourists, and advised focusing on this market.[40] But this government did not accomplish anything significant in this sector during its last months in office.

Although the ECA team left Ireland with a sense of disappointment, clearly reflected in the organisation's final assessment of the programme, it maintained hope that its efforts might prove worthwhile over time: "It is doubtful whether the immediate results of Ireland's participation in this general program have been worth the expense and effort involved [...]. It is possible, however, that the long-term effects may more than justify the program". In retrospect, this cautious optimism proved well founded. The ECA's support enabled certain progressive Irish hoteliers to experience the "American way" first-hand through familiarisation trips to the United States organised under the Marshall Plan. This exposure played a crucial role in fostering innovation within the Irish tourism sector and contributed to broader economic developments. It also attracted the interest of influential Irish-American business figures, who would later work closely with the Irish government to channel strategic US investment into Ireland from the 1960s onwards.[41]

3.4 An Tóstal: A Festival Designed for Irish-Americans

Fianna Fáil won the parliamentary elections in May 1951. The post of Minister for Industry and Commerce was again given to Seán Lemass who, unlike the previous administration, had been a strong supporter of tourism development, especially Irish-American tourism. As soon as he took office, Lemass took charge of the dossier. A timely proposal was made by Juan Trippe, President of Pan American Airways.[42] It was in line with the Christenberry Report, which had, among other things, called for the development of diaspora tourism to extend the tourist season.[43] Trippe suggested that a cultural festival be organised to encourage people of Irish descent who lived abroad to visit Ireland during the low season.

The airline would benefit financially and the country could reduce its dollar deficit.[44] Lemass was won over by the idea. Sometime later, a festival called An Tóstal[45] was planned. The aim was to celebrate Irish culture, history, and language through performances, competitions, sports events, etc. In addition, the organisers hoped to use the occasion to showcase the economic and industrial progress made since independence through exhibitions and parades where industrialists could showcase their products.[46]

The entire diaspora would be invited to come to Ireland for the occasion. Conor Cruise O'Brien,[47] then an adviser to the Department of External Affairs, contacted Irish embassies, legations, and consulates abroad in August 1952 to publicise the event. It was necessary to try to get as many people of Irish descent as possible to come to the event wherever they were in the world, even if they could not be expected to show the same enthusiasm for An Tóstal as Irish-Americans:

> The populations of Irish origin in these countries, though considerable, are in general not as cohesive nor as attached to their mother country as are the Americans of Irish origin. Furthermore, there is in the cases of Argentina and Australia, the factor of the very great distances involved. However, I think the effort is worth making, and that the presence of even small contingents from these countries would add to the impressiveness of An Tóstal.[48]

However, it soon became clear that the promotion of the event had to be focused on the Irish-American community in the United States. Elsewhere, interest was at best limited and at worst non-existent, as in Argentina where, even after an article on An Tóstal appeared in *The Southern Cross*,[49] the Irish legation in Buenos Aires had not received a single enquiry.[50]

While he had rushed to the United States to promote the event,[51] by the end of October 1952, Hugh McNeill[52] had still not visited Britain, which did not seem to be a priority. Fógra Fáilte[53] had not undertaken a publicity campaign there either, and no articles about An Tóstal had appeared in the British press.

Although the target audience was the Irish diaspora in the United States as a whole, only a small proportion were likely to make the trip. Many of the Irish-Americans who usually travelled to Ireland were teachers, and these would not be able to come in the middle of the school year.[54] The same was true for families with children in school. The period was also unlikely to be suitable for the more affluent Irish-Americans who would prefer to come during the summer months. There would also be competition from the Archbishop of Boston's pilgrimage to Ireland in August 1953. In any case, Joe Shields, the Irish Consul in Boston, felt that it was best to appeal to the first and second generation of immigrants in the United States.[55]

According to the Irish press, the project was supported by several airlines that were convinced of its potential. Trans World Airlines intended to spend fifty thousand dollars to promote the festival. Pan American Airways, whose president had suggested the idea, had decided to allocate half of its North Atlantic advertising budget to it. A senior official of one of these airlines told McNeill: "We are not doing this because we like the colour of your hair, but because we think it will be good business for us. An Tóstal could be a winner, and we hope it will be, for our sake as well as yours".[56] According to McNeill, the said airline did not expect an immediate influx of tourists. It planned to carry three and a half thousand passengers for the first festival, but expected this number to rise to fifty thousand within five years.

The image of Ireland that was projected abroad was an issue that was closely monitored by the Irish Department of External Affairs, especially since the release of John Ford's film *The Quiet Man* in 1952 that featured negative stereotypes of Irish people: "Wife-beating, priest-ridden, blather talking gombeen men getting drunk standing around gossiping and then erupting into stereotypical Irish behaviour".[57]

John Patrick O'Brien[58] and Tom Sheehy of Fógra Fáilte were, therefore, concerned about the deleterious effect of an advertising campaign that presented An Tóstal as a world-class event, like the New York World's Fair, from the outset.[59] Indeed, it was deemed necessary to strike a chord with the diaspora to attract tourists,[60] but not at any cost. So both men took exception to the publicity produced by Pan American Airways and published in some newspapers aimed at the Irish-American community. Sheehy forwarded the airline's advertisement to O'Brien: "I would be glad if you would return this monstrosity to me as soon as you have seen it. I promise you I will give you a photo of the advertisement as soon as possible. As the copy so rightly says 'there's never been anything like it'".[61] O'Brien concurred: "This is a rather sickening example of the way the airlines are fulfilling their promise to publicise An Tóstal".[62] Michael Rynne, legal adviser to the Department of External Affairs, wrote to the Secretary of the Department of Industry and Commerce to ask him to ensure that all advertisements were hencefsorth cleared by the tourism agencies prior to publication, because:

> The Minister regards the illustration here as unsuitable and objectionable, particularly when associated with the Tóstal symbol. The dress, and the general appearance, of the musician in particular, is a characteristic stage-Irish stereotype.[63]

The Secretary of the Department of Industry and Commerce indicated a few days later that his minister, Seán Lemass, did not support the move.[64] Perhaps he was already aware that the vision of Ireland cherished by a section of the diaspora,[65] an idealised vision akin to that presented in *Finian's Rainbow*, a Broadway musical of the late 1940s, had to be exploited for commercial purposes, even if it meant setting aside the image of a country on the road to economic progress, the antithesis of the imaginary rural island.

3.5 Controversy Over Northern Ireland's Participation

The status of Northern Ireland as a separate jurisdiction raises the question of whether or not it remained embedded within the collective mental construct of the Irish diaspora's perception of the island of Ireland.[66] Whether or not to invite Northern Ireland to take part in the festival was a thorny issue. An Bord Fáilte,[67] which felt that the celebrations should be island-wide, referred the matter to Lemass. The Department of External Affairs was also consulted. Conor Cruise O'Brien shared An Bord Fáilte's view. After all, the two Irelands had recently managed to cooperate on three projects of common interest.[68] Indeed, Lemass had pointed out in his Bonn speech some time earlier that the practice of such cooperation was now well established.[69] O'Brien could not see how joint action in the field of tourism would be any different. However, behind this willingness to act in concert with Stormont,[70] there was a political agenda.[71] Michael Rynne[72] and William Fay[73] were in tune with O'Brien. Fay[74] believed that if this project was carried out jointly, it would improve relations with Northern Ireland and pave the way for the reunification that was deemed inevitable. But he doubted that this collaboration could take place:

> Finally, more Machiavellian perhaps, it would be well that the olive branch should be refused by the Six Co. folk, not by us, if it must be refused; I have a shrewd suspicion that when Mr. [Walter] Topping[75] for instance hears that the 'Ulster' Tourist Board is seriously proposing to collaborate with a Gaelic Republican festival we shall hear no of collaboration with them - but then the fault for non-cooperation would be theirs not ours.[76]

The Minister of External Affairs, Frank Aiken,[77] followed the advice of his advisers and made his position known to Lemass. However, the latter took a stand against it. He felt that if there was to be no collaboration at the governmental level, it was better for An Bord Fáilte not to engage with its counterpart in Northern Ireland. On the other hand, if the Northern Ireland authorities expressed a desire to participate in An Tóstal, he might reconsider[78] in the knowledge that it was highly unlikely that Belfast would come forward. Lemass apparently made this decision for purely political reasons[79] and won his case in the Cabinet. An Bord Fáilte was therefore instructed not to cooperate or liaise with the Northern Ireland authorities on An Tóstal.[80] It is certainly regrettable that Lemass missed this opportunity for a bilateral working relationship between both administrations.[81] However, despite O'Brien's contention, it must be acknowledged that collaboration in the field of tourism was indeed more than just "functional" cooperation as it had been between the two jurisdictions up to that point. Indeed, if they had decided to act together, political disagreements on how to present the two entities in advertising brochures, for example, would have arisen very quickly. It is notable that the border does not appear on the map of the island on the back of the brochure published by Fógra Fáilte.[82] This map, entitled "Ireland", must surely have caused some annoyance north of the border.

Lemass, despite his hostile attitude on this occasion, was the architect of a process of economic cooperation with Northern Ireland just over a decade later. The two Irelands collaborated on tourism in the 1960s, but archival records show how difficult it was for them to reach a compromise on advertising to international markets.[83]

3.6 The Bitter Disappointment of Seán Lemass

Despite all the hopes that Lemass had placed in the organisation of this festival, it was not really a success. In October 1953, while serving as Minister of Industry and Commerce and Tánaiste,[84] Lemass travelled to the United States. During this trip, he addressed the Commerce and Industry Association in New York. The tourism sector was booming in Ireland and the number of American tourists was increasing, he said.[85] According to Lemass, Ireland was trying to improve the quality of its offer. American experts had advised the Irish authorities in this regard and the recommendations of the Christenberry report had all been implemented.[86] He took the opportunity to advertise the An Tóstal festival, which was to be held again the following year. For those of Irish descent—and there must have been a few in the audience—this festival was to be an opportunity to return to Ireland:

> An Tóstal is primarily intended to be a time of reunion, a period during which Ireland is at home to its kinsfolk and friends from all countries. It is designed to facilitate family reunions - there are few Irish families which have not relatives in some part of the U.S.A. - as well as to fix a period during which people of Irish descent from all parts of the world may be assured that they will be very specially [sic] welcomed.[87]

Nevertheless, not only did the event fail to attract more tourists in the low season, but to make matters worse, the annual number of foreign visitors dropped.[88] An Tóstal was held annually for several consecutive years, but over time it attracted a diminishing number of foreign tourists. The festival came to a definitive end in 1958. Despite this failure, Lemass remained convinced of the enormous potential of the diaspora market for tourism:

> We have scattered throughout the world millions of people of Irish birth or parentage, in England, America, Australia and New Zealand, and in all these countries it is possible to sell the idea of coming home once in a lifetime to Ireland. I believe the greater part of our tourist publicity should be directed towards that end. [...] We have in the existence of these millions of people with sentimental attachments to this country a basis of goodwill on which to build that other countries could not create with all their expenditure on tourist trade publicity [...].[89]

At this parliamentary session, Lemass recalled that when An Tóstal was launched, it was clear to him that it would take several years to take off. He said that American tourism experts and the Irish-American organisations that were to relay information about the festival were of the same opinion. By this time Lemass was back on the opposition benches. William Norton[90] now held the dual position of Minister of Industry and Commerce and Tánaiste in the Second Inter-Party Government[91] (1954–1957). Lemass blamed his successor for not supporting An Tóstal with the energy and determination that such a long-term project required. He alleged Norton merely tolerated the event when full government support was needed.[92] Furthermore, Lemass insinuated that An Tóstal had fallen victim to political considerations. Although he had tried not to be too closely associated with it to avoid giving it a political colour, the festival was known to be one of his pet projects.

Lemass was unfair to Norton, to say the least. Indeed, if the First Inter-Party Government had shown ill will towards tourism development, Norton was probably the only one of its members who was open and aware of the economic potential of the diaspora. In 1952, he had portrayed the Irish-American tourist in terms almost identical to those used by Lemass:

> There is another type of American tourist who comes here - the Irish American who made good. He feels nostalgic, and he wants to come back and see his homeland, the friends of his childhood and of his adolescent years. He feels an urge to see how things are in the old land. He is an exceedingly good tourist, because he usually makes up his mind that if he is going to pay the fare from America to here he is going to stay for a long time and get value for his money. [...] We have all met him in the towns and villages throughout the country, and it must be said of him that he spends money very generously for two reasons, first, because he is on holiday, and, secondly, because he is consumed with a natural human emotion to let his friends know how well he has done since he left Ireland. [...] Seeing we are desirous of earning American dollars, I feel that the American tourist I have just described is the most desirable type. He is likely, too, to appreciate the desirability of bringing in American dollars to this country which others do not necessarily appreciate.[93]

It is true, however, that the support for the promotion of tourism was still far from unanimous in Irish political circles and that there were still pockets of resistance among TDs. John McQuillan,[94] noting that the total net contribution of tourism to the economy had been £1.25 million in 1954, objected to the proposal to grant the sum of £500,000 to An Bord Fáilte as excessive in relation to what the industry was bringing in. Furthermore, he pointed out that the majority of tourists from Britain were Irish, returning to see their relatives for a week or two at Christmas, Easter, or during the summer. They were the biggest spenders, he said. For McQuillan, they would come anyway, even without advertising. The same was true of the Irish-Americans:

> The suggestion is that we should induce people of Irish descent in America to visit here, in the words of Deputy Lemass, once in a lifetime. Have we reached the stage with An Tóstal, that to attract people of Irish descent in America we need to tell them that if they come to Dublin they will see something in Croke Park or some extraordinary display in Donegal? Do you think that people are going to be attracted by that type of poppycock? These people are coming here to visit their Irish friends, to renew old ties and friendships; they are coming one way or the other.[95]

Perhaps the failure of An Tóstal was due to this kind of attitude or, as Lemass thought, to political considerations. However, there were also other, less obvious reasons for the failure to attract Irish-American tourists. Indeed, within the Irish administration itself, initial enthusiasm was soon replaced by scepticism and inaction.

3.7 Circumspection Among Civil Servants

On 13 August 1952, Conor Cruise O'Brien conveyed to John J. Hearne, the Irish ambassador in Washington, Hugh McNeill's request that a board of eminent persons support the initiative and thus lend some credibility to An Tóstal in the eyes of Irish-Americans. In his reply, the Ambassador enthusiastically listed some fifteen Irish-sounding names from a variety of backgrounds. He admitted that it would be difficult to make a selection, as the list was so long. The Irish consuls in the United States had been contacted and were busy compiling the list of people, well introduced in the Irish-American community, who would take part in committees at the local level.[96] For the ambassador additional money would be needed to organise receptions, travel, etc., but the state had not set aside a specific budget for An Tóstal.[97] Therefore, An Bord Fáilte and Fógra Fáilte had to make do with the annual budget allocated to them and rely on voluntary work.

The attitude of the Irish consuls in the United States, all of whom were invited by McNeill to a meeting in New York at the end of October 1952, was much more reserved than Hearne's letter of a few weeks earlier had suggested. In their view, the creation of the board and committees to promote An Tóstal would cause all sorts of problems. Moreover, there was no guarantee that it would be possible to recruit enough prominent people to promote the event. The consuls stood together and McNeill, after a long discussion, had to abandon his plan.[98]

Indeed, within the Irish administration, enthusiasm waned over the months and was replaced by scepticism. In February 1953, O'Brien expressed his doubts to Joe Shields, the Irish Consul in Boston, in the following terms:

> To tell you the truth any anxiety I have about the Tóstal - and I have a certain amount - comes not from any fear that it has not been sufficiently publicised but from a fear that more energy has gone into publicising it abroad than into organising it at home. In short, I fear that the thing may have been oversold. Time may show that these fears are quite groundless but I feel I ought to mention them to you in case some Boston visitors may be disappointed. What it might be well to emphasize would be the 'folksy' and unpretentious friendly nature of the Tóstal: the fact that it is an experiment in what is to become an annual feature, and the idea that where other countries may have more grandiose festivals, designed primarily to impress the foreigner, the Irish idea is primarily to set aside a time for the entertainment of those of the millions of people of Irish origin abroad who are willing and able to come for a while. I think sales talk along these lines, although it might not be as immediately stimulating to tourist traffic as a more extravagantly optimistic approach would be fairer to our prospective visitors and therefore in the long run more beneficial to the country.[99]

Conor Cruise O'Brien also sent this letter to the other diplomatic missions involved in the organisation of the festival,[100] an initiative he took without first referring to his superiors, whom he did not inform until after the letters were sent. Seán Nunan[101] and Michael Rynne, respectively Secretary and Legal Adviser of the Department of External Affairs, made it clear to O'Brien that his initiative was not only unwelcome, but could also have unfortunate consequences. Indeed, if his words reached the ears of the organisers, they might hold the Department responsible. Worse still, "[…] tourists, actual or prospective, who get their 'tip-off' about the 'folksy' nature of An Tóstal may well spread the news and the source of it in the US and here".[102] On reading the final programme for An Tóstal, Tom Sheehy of Fógra Fáilte wrote to O'Brien to say that he fully agreed with his feelings about the "folksy" nature of the festival and that it was necessary to "[…] sell 'Ireland at home', a simple homecoming welcome, in which visitors are invited to join in our unpretentious customs, fun and hospitality, and this I agree should be the general note stressed by your officers in America."[103]

It is not clear to what extent the attitude of the diplomatic staff may have discouraged potential tourists from attending An Tóstal. In any case, the instructions from Dublin officials were not such as to urge them to promote the event as a major festival not to be missed.

Finally, it would seem that the goodwill of civil society actors, which was essential to the organisation of this festival, waned. According to Thomas O'Hara, Irish TD (Fine Gael), the lack of a sustained effort on the part of these volunteers explained the relative failure of An Tóstal:

> I am afraid that the enthusiasm waned to a great extent in the country and to some degree in Dublin City as well. We should appreciate that if we intend to build up a business it is only by persistent efforts and hard work that we can hope to succeed. There is no use in being enthusiastic about something for a week or two, or even a year or two for that matter, and then losing all interest in the project and forgetting about it. […] Indeed, it is a very regrettable state of affairs and it all comes back to the point I have been making that a great deal depends on individual effort. We are, perhaps, as a race inclined to look to the Government for everything. Governments can help in their own way but without the individual effort one cannot get very far.[104]

Here, O'Hara sketches the features of an unpersevering and somewhat dilettantish population. The following chapter will help refine this portrait of Irish society in the 1950s and perhaps shed light on why the diasporic market—supposedly within reach—was so underexploited.

Notes

1. Raymond J. Raymond. 1983. American Public Opinion and Neutrality, 1939–1945. Éire-Ireland, 18, 1, 38–45. http://www.jstor.org/stable/40105817.

2. John Bowman. 1982. De Valera and the Ulster Question: 1917–1973. Oxford: Oxford University Press, 218–266.
3. Ireland received a loan of $149 million and $18 million in grants. Bernadette Whelan. 1992. Ireland and the Marshall Plan. Irish Economic and Social History 19:61. https://doi.org/10.1177/033248939201900103. On this subject, see also: Ronan Fanning. 1978. The Irish Department of Finance 1922–58. Dublin: Institute of Public Administration, 411–434; and Troy Davis. 1998. Dublin's American Policy: Irish-American Diplomatic Relations, 1945–1952. Washington: The Catholic University of America Press,105–120.
4. Davis, Dublin's American Policy, 105–106.
5. Davis, Dublin's American Policy, 105. On the Irish currency and banking institutions at that time, see: John Kelly. Spring 2003. The Irish Pound: From Origins to EMU. Quarterly Bulletin of the Central Bank of Ireland, 90–94. https://www.centralbank.ie/docs/default-source/publications/quarterly-bulletins/qb-archive/2003/quarterly-bulletin-spring-2003%2D%2D-the-domestic-economy%2D%2D-real-and-financial-developments.pdf?sfvrsn=8c6a01d_8. Accessed 4 June 2025.
6. George W. Potter. [1953]. ECA and Ireland, Impact of Marshall Plan Funds, Changes over Face of Republic, UCDA P104/9054 (2), UCD Archives, University College Dublin, Ireland (hereafter UCDA).
7. George W. Potter. [1953]. ECA and Ireland, Impact of Marshall Plan Funds; Davis, Dublin's American Policy,104–105; Whelan, Ireland and the Marshall Plan, 50. This problem added to the structural weaknesses of the Irish economy. Kieran A. Kennedy and Brendan R. Dowling. 1975. Economic Growth in Ireland: The Experience since 1947. Dublin: Gill & Macmillan, 200.
8. European Recovery Program. February 1949. Ireland, Country Study. Washington: U.S. Government Printing Office, 44.
9. European Recovery Program. February, Ireland, Country Study, 4.
10. Inter-Departmental Working Party on Dollar Earnings, First interim report on tourism, 1949, 1, S14818 A, National Archives of Ireland (hereafter NAI).
11. Inter-Departmental Working Party on Dollar Earnings, 5.
12. European Recovery Program, Ireland, Country Study.
13. Joseph E. Carrigan to Seán MacBride, 7 December 1949, S14818, NAI,
14. The tourist industry, memorandum for the government, 16 February 1950, P35b/52, McGilligan Papers, UCDA.
15. The memorandum is not signed, but it is very likely that the author is Patrick McGilligan, the Finance Minister.
16. The tourist industry, memorandum for the government, 16 February 1950.

17. Inter-Departmental Working Party on Dollar Earnings, First interim report on tourism, 1949, 3.
18. According to this document, fifteen thousand tourists from the United States visited Ireland in 1948.
19. Inter-Departmental Working Party on Dollar Earnings, First interim report on tourism, 1949, 3.
20. Joseph E. Carrigan to Seán MacBride, 7 December 1949.
21. Colonel Theodore Pozzy was in charge of the ECA's tourism development section in Paris.
22. Inter-Departmental Working Party on Dollar Earnings, First interim report on tourism, 1949, 32.
23. Ernest Rowe-Dutton to James McElligott, 26 August 1949, P35c/8, McGilligan Papers, UCDA.
24. Memorandum of Conversation with Cabinet sub-committee on Dollar Earnings, 22 April 1950, RG 469, entry 1251, box 1, folder Taft III technical assistance, National Archives and Records Administration at College Park, MD, United States of America (hereafter NARA).
25. Anne Groutel. 2022. Ireland and the Marshall Plan: E.C.A.'s Manoeuvring to Promote Dollar Tourism. Irish Economic and Social History 49, 1: 116–135. https://doi.org/10.1177/03324893221080610. Drawing on previously unpublished American archival sources, this article uncovers various behind-the-scenes strategies employed by the ECA mission in Ireland to bypass opposition from segments of the Irish government. These tactics ultimately failed to overcome the resistance.
26. Harry Clement was one of those responsible for implementing the assistance programme within the ECA in Ireland. Peter Murray. 2009. Facilitating the Future? US Aid, European Integration and Irish Industrial Viability, 1948–73. Dublin: University College Dublin Press, 21.
27. Daniel Morrissey was the Minister for Industry and Commerce in the First Inter-Party Government. Dictionary of Irish Biography. Daniel Morrissey. https://www.dib.ie/biography/morrissey-daniel-a5991. Accessed 9 June 2025.
28. Harry Clement to Colonel Theodore Pozzy, 19 July 1950, RG 469, Europe Ireland Division, Deputy Director for Operations, Office of European Operations, Ireland Division, subject files 1948–1953, box 1, folder Irish aid, NARA.
29. Irene Furlong. 2009. Irish Tourism 1880–1980. Dublin – Portland: Irish Academic Press,165.
30. ECA activities in Ireland [undated document, probable date: 1953], RG 84, Classified General Records, 1953–1955, file 350.21, box 3, folder 500 ECA, NARA. This report was finally made public in July 1951.

31. Memorandum from Harry Clement to Paul E. Miller, 6 February 1951, RG 469, entry 1250, Mission to Ireland, subject files 1949–1951, box 1, folder Industry, tourism and special projects officer William Taft III, NARA.
32. Irene Furlong, Irish Tourism 1880–1980, 132.
33. Dictionary of Irish Biography. Patrick McGilligan. https://www.dib.ie/biography/mcgilligan-patrick-a5669. Accessed 9 June 2025.
34. Irene Furlong, Irish Tourism, 112–13.
35. Irene Furlong, Irish Tourism, 42.
36. Irene Furlong, Irish Tourism, 114–15.
37. Taft to Pozzy, subject: tourism in Ireland, 8 April 1949, records of the foreign assistance agencies 1942–1963, RG 469, office of European operations, Ireland division, 48–53, records of the deputy director of operations, subject file Irish aid – labor, box 3, N.A.R.A.
38. James Deegan, Donal Dineen. 1997. Tourism Policy and Performance: The Irish Experience. London and Boston: International Thomson Business Press,14–15.
39. Memorandum from Joseph E. Carrigan to the ECA and the ECA representative in Europe, 21 July 1950, 3, RG 469, Europe Ireland Division, Deputy Director for Operations, Office of European Operations, Ireland Division, subject files 1948–1953, box 1, folder Irish aid, NARA. This quote refers to the Irish government's hostility to Seán Lemass's earlier policy of promoting tourism.
40. Conversation with Morrissey, Cosgrave, McCarthy, document signed HGC [Harry Clement], 21 April 1950, RG 469, entry 1251, box 1, folder Taft III technical assistance, NARA; The tourist industry, memorandum for the government, 16 February 1950.
41. Groutel, Ireland and the Marshall Plan, 131–134.
42. Eric G. E. Zuelow. 2009. Making Ireland Irish: Tourism and National Identity since the Irish Civil War. Syracuse: Syracuse University Press, 124.
43. Furlong, Irish Tourism, 165.
44. Furlong, Irish Tourism,168; Zuelow, Making Ireland Irish,125.
45. An Tóstal is a Gaelic term. Ireland at Home, the English equivalent, was also used at the time.
46. Zuelow. 2008. An Tóstal: Ireland at Home. In Ireland and the America: Culture, Politics, and History. A Multidisciplinary Encyclopedia, eds James P. Byrne, Philip Coleman, Jason King: vol. II, 60. Santa Barbara: ABC-CLIO.
47. Dictionary of Irish Biography. Conor Cruise O'Brien. https://www.dib.ie/biography/obrien-conor-cruise-a9694. Accessed 9 June 2025.
48. Conor Cruise O'Brien to Hugh McNeill, 15 August 1952, 415/267, NAI; Hugh MacNeill was in charge of An Tóstal's organisation.

49. The Southern Cross was founded in 1875 in Buenos Aires by Dean Patrick Dillon, a well-known figure in the local political scene. The publication was aimed at a mainly Catholic readership. Its ambition was to perpetuate the sense of identity of the Irish diaspora in Argentina. Adam Farley. June/July. The Southern Cross, Irish America, 2014. http://irishamerica.com/2014/05/the-southern-cross. Accessed 4 June 2025.
50. Matthew Murphy to Conor Cruise O'Brien, 15 October 1952, 415/267, NAI.
51. Irish Embassy in London [signature illegible] to Conor Cruise O'Brien, 31 October 1952, 415/267, NAI.
52. Hugh McNeill was Bord Fáilte organiser of An Tóstal in1952–4. Dictionary of Irish Biography. Hugh McNeill. https://www.dib.ie/biography/mcneill-hugh-hyacinth-hugo-a5750. Accessed 9 June 2025.
53. Fógra Fáilte, specifically responsible for the advertising aspect of tourism, was created as part of the reorganisation of the Irish Tourist Board under the Tourist Traffic Act of 1952.
54. April was the time chosen for An Tóstal.
55. Document entitled "Memorandum for Major General McNeill on An Tóstal in the Boston Consular Area" attached to a letter from Joe Shields, Secretary of the Department of Foreign Affairs, 30 October 1952, 415/267, NAI.
56. An Interview with the Organiser. 1952. *The Irish Times*, 29 October.
57. Malachy McCourt quoted in Stephen Collins. 2016. The Quiet Man: Embassy in US Feared a False View of Ireland, *The Irish Times*, 23 November. Joseph Brennan of the Irish Embassy in Washington feared at the time that the film would provoke protests from an Irish-American community outraged by the portrayal of their idealised Ireland. This did not happen.
58. Dictionary of Irish Biography. John Patrick O'Brien. https://www.dib.ie/biography/obrien-john-patrick-jack-a9933. Accessed 9 June 2025.
59. Conor Cruise O'Brien to Joe Shields, 23 February 1953, 415/267, NAI.
60. Zuelow, Making Ireland Irish, 125.
61. Tom Sheehy to Conor Cruise O'Brien, 20 February 1953, 415/267, NAI.
62. Conor Cruise O'Brien to Tom Sheehy, 25 February 1953, 415/267, NAI.
63. Michael Rynne to the Secretary of the Department of Industry and Commerce, 2 March 1953, 415/267, NAI.
64. Secretary of the Department of Industry and Commerce to the Secretary of the Department of External Affairs, 20 March 1953, 415/267, NAI.
65. See: Stephanie Rains. 2003. Home from Home: Diasporic Images of Ireland in Film and Tourism. In Irish Tourism: Image, Culture and Identity, eds Michael Cronin, Barbara O'Connor: 196–214. Clevedon, Channel View Publications; Stephanie Rains. 2004.

Celtic Kitsch: Irish-America and Irish Material Culture. Circa 107: 5257; Helena Wulff. 2007. Longing for the Land: Emotions, Memory, and Nature in Irish Travel Advertisements. Identities14, 4: 527–544.

66. Clare O'Halloran highlights that the representation of the island as an indivisible whole was central to the discourse of Irish irredentism. Clare O'Halloran. 1987. Partition and the Limits of Irish Nationalism: An Ideology under Stress. Dublin: Gill & Macmillan, 1–2.
67. Under the terms of the Tourist Traffic Act of 1952, the Irish Tourist Board changed its name to An Bord Fáilte.
68. Anne Groutel. 2004. La coopération économique entre les deux Irlandes. Caen: Presses universitaires de Caen, 13–31.
69. Conor Cruise O'Brien to Michael Rynne, 10 September 1952, 415/267, NAI.
70. Stormont is the name of the castle that housed the Northern Ireland Parliament and Government.
71. Conor Cruise O'Brien to Michael Rynne, 10 September 1952.
72. Michael Rynne to William Fay, 13 September 1952, 415/267, NAI.
73. William Fay was Legal Adviser and Under-Secretary of the Irish Department of External Affairs.
74. William Fay to Michael Rynne, 15 September 1952, 415/267, NAI.
75. Walter Topping was Parliamentary Secretary to the Northern Ireland Minister for Finance and Chairman of the Unionist Party Parliamentary Group.
76. William Fay to Michael Rynne, 15 September 1952, 415/267, NAI.
77. Dictionary of Irish Biography. Frank Aiken. https://www.dib.ie/biography/aiken-francis-thomas-frank-a0070. Accessed 9 June 2025.
78. Department of Industry and Commerce, Memorandum for the Government, 11 October 1952, 415/267/1, NAI.
79. Michael Rynne to William Fay, 13 September 1952, 415/267, NAI.
80. Muiris Ó Muimhneachain to the Department of Industry and Commerce, 17 October 1952, S15297 A, NAI.
81. Michael Kennedy. 2000. Division and Consensus: The Politics of Cross-Border Relations in Ireland, 1925–1969. Dublin: Institute of Public Administration,147.
82. An Tóstal brochure, Ireland at home, S15297A, NAI.
83. Groutel, Economic cooperation, 41–44.
84. The Tánaiste is the Deputy Prime Minister of Ireland.
85. Address by Mr. Seán Lemass, T. D., Tánaiste and Minister for Industry and Commerce, to Commerce and Industry Association, New York, October 5th, 1953, 436/35, NAI.

86. On this topic, see: Organisations Are Inadequate, Says U.S. Survey Group. 1951. *The Irish Times*, 4 September; New I. T. B. Formed on Christenberry Lines. 1951 *The Irish Times*, 9 September.
87. Address by Mr. Seán Lemass, T. D., Tánaiste and Minister for Industry and Commerce, to Commerce and Industry Association, New York, October 5th, 1953.
88. Furlong, Irish Tourism, 173.
89. Ireland, parliamentary debates, Houses of the Oireachtas, Dáil Éireann (hereafter Dáil Éireann debates), 9 February 1955, 148, 1 (Seán Lemass).
90. Dictionary of Irish Biography. William Norton. https://www.dib.ie/biography/norton-william-joseph-bill-a6239. Accessed 9 June 2025.
91. Fine Gael, the Labour Party, and Clann na Talmhan were the three parties in the coalition government.
92. Dáil Éireann Debates, 9 February 1955, 148, 1 (Seán Lemass).
93. Dáil Éireann Debates, 6 March 1952, 129, 10 (William Norton).
94. John McQuillan (1920–1998) was an Irish parliamentarian (Clann na Poblachta), Roscommon constituency, who served from 1948 to 1969 (unlabelled from 1951 to 1961).
95. Dáil Éireann Debates, 9 February 1955,148,1 (John McQuillan).
96. John J Hearne to Conor Cruise O'Brien, 27 August 1952, 415/267, NAI.
97. John Leydon to the secretary of the Department of the Taoiseach, 29 April 1952, S15297 A, NAI.
98. Record of proceedings at An Tóstal conference held at the Consulate General of Ireland, New York, on Tuesday, 28th October 1952, 415/267, NAI.
99. Conor Cruise O'Brien to Joe Shields, 23 February 1953, 415/267, NAI.
100. Conor Cruise O'Brien to J. D. Brennan, 23 February 1953, 415/267, NAI; Conor Cruise O'Brien to Garth Healy, 23 February 1953; Conor Cruise O'Brien to Sean Murphy, 23 February 1953.
101. Dictionary of Irish Biography. Seán Nunan. https://www.dib.ie/biography/nunan-sean-a6270. Accessed 9 June 2025.
102. Handwritten note signed by Michael Rynne, dated 25 February 1953, found at the bottom of a note from Conor Cruise O'Brien to Michael Rynne also dated 25 February 1953, 415/267, NAI.
103. Tom Sheehy to Conor Cruise O'Brien, 2 March 1953, 415/267, NAI.
104. Dáil Éireann Debates, 9 February 1955,148,1.

CHAPTER 4

An Under-Exploited Diaspora Market in the 1950s

4.1 Political Belief in the Transatlantic Promise

Seán Lemass was inwardly convinced that neither agriculture nor industrial production for the domestic market could create sufficient jobs. He therefore considered it vital to boost exports in order for the economy to develop.[1] A belief that de Valera himself partly shared. In a message broadcast on American radio, he urged the diaspora to give preference to Irish products[2] whenever possible. Indeed, some politicians on the other side of the Atlantic believed that there was indeed a demand for such products from the Irish-American community. This was the case of Michael Disalle, Mayor of Toledo, Ohio, who visited Dublin in 1949:

> I think there are plenty of lines that this country could export [...] we have a population of about 300,000 in Toledo, a large proportion of whom are Irish or of Irish descent. The Irish in all parts of the United States could be very glad to get an opportunity of buying Irish goods and I believe a much closer trade relationship could be established.[3]

Although the ECA considered that tourism would provide Ireland with a quick financial return which would allow for the restoration of a healthy balance of payments,[4] exports of goods could in theory also contribute. To all appearances, the Irish diaspora in the United States could represent a huge potential market for products with an Irish image. Nostalgia and

A. Groutel, *The Two Irelands and the Diaspora*,
https://doi.org/10.1007/978-3-032-12355-8_4

sentimental attachment to Ireland would make it easier to get the Irish-American middle and upper classes to buy these goods. This was the message that Lemass conveyed to members of the Commerce and Industry Association in New York during his trip to the United States in October 1953. He spoke of the need to increase the country's dollar income, which would allow American imports to continue to flow to Ireland and its economy to function, while stressing that this difficulty was transitory. Ireland, he said, wanted to get to the root of the problem. The country's over-dependence on the United Kingdom, both in trade[5] and tourism, was making the Irish economy vulnerable. Recent problems with currency convertibility had unfortunately shown this. Ireland was a small country compared to the United States, he agreed, and increasing its transatlantic exports was a very difficult task. He insisted, however, that as part of the Marshall Plan, American experts had advised Irish industrialists on the requirements and characteristics of the American market. The diaspora market was an asset, he admitted, but it was necessary to provide an offer that met its requirements:

> We know that there are some 25 million American citizens of Irish origins, who retain a sentimental interest in the welfare of the Old Country, but, while sentimental considerations may occasionally produce a trade enquiry which might not otherwise be made, we understand that in this highly competitive market, sentiment is not a substitute for sound trading methods, nor do we intend to regard it as such.[6]

During this trip, he made another speech on the occasion of the opening of an Irish trade representation office in New York. The call for the contribution of the diaspora was renewed in an even more direct way:

> There are many men and women in important positions throughout the U.S. who were born in Ireland or have Irish origins or backgrounds; so are many more in ordinary walks of life. We hope that all will give us a helping hand in this effort at trade expansion by featuring Irish products in their homes or factories or by asking for them in the stores.[7]

Lemass did not like William Norton[8] who succeeded him as Minister for Industry and Commerce in June 1954. Yet both men were in agreement about the need to increase exports in order to overcome the growing balance of payments deficit in the mid-1950s. Increasing sales of Irish products to the Irish community in the United States could help.

Norton in turn tried to get this message across during his four-week stay in the United States in early 1956. He travelled over sixteen thousand kilometres and visited eighteen cities, including New York, Boston, Philadelphia, and San Francisco, where there was a large Irish-American community.

He appealed to the goodwill of the diaspora. If all twenty million Irish-Americans bought five dollars' worth of Irish goods on St Patrick's Day, he explained, it would give the industry a boost. He also sought to encourage them to spend their holidays in Ireland where "millions of salmon were lined up in the River Shannon waiting to be caught by the American fishermen".[9] The Irish press echoed this appeal to the Irish abroad, including those living in Britain:

> If all the Irish returning from Britain for holidays in 1956 could be persuaded to spend their loose money here as a regular patriotic move, then our boot and shoe factories, our textile factories, our whiskey distilleries would be advertising for workers, instead of letting them go.[10]

Increased exports would obviously have helped to boost the Irish economy. However, Norton must surely have been aware that this was wishful thinking. The characteristics of the industrial sector at the time meant that, with a few exceptions, it was simply not able or willing to meet the expectations of the diasporic market across the Atlantic.

4.2 Export Challenges: A Narrow Product Offer for Diaspora Markets

The Irish industrial sector consisted of many small family firms and only a few large companies, most of which had been founded before partition.[11] Some of them had built up a strong reputation in the brewing, distilling, and food processing sectors. In March 1936, an article in *The Irish Times* praised Ireland's long-standing exports to the world, particularly to the Commonwealth:

> Nigh on half a century ago you could buy Guinness's stout in a café in the shadow of the Taj Mahal[12]; purchase Jacob's biscuits in the bazaars of Hong-Kong; take a 'sundowner' of Irish whiskey at the headwaters of the Nile; or

> clothe yourself in Irish linen, Irish wool or Irish homespun in five continents. Every one of the Polar expeditions of the last fifty years was supplied with Cork butter; and during that time Irish beef, bacon, mutton and eggs have been rightly rated among the luxury products of the age. Irish goods are still held in high esteem throughout the world, for there are many products [...] that we make better than any other nation.[13]

Collateral victims of the protectionist policy implemented by Fianna Fáil[14] after 1932 and of the episode of the Economic War[15] between Ireland and the United Kingdom, these few large industrial companies found it much more difficult to export their products to England. In the same year, Guinness, an iconic company, even moved its headquarters to London and relocated some of its production to England in 1936 to avoid the retaliatory UK tariffs. Nevertheless, these large companies had the capacity to tap into the diasporic market that lay across the Atlantic and which was said to be lucrative.

In the aftermath of World War II, the Irish tweed and linen industries were booming.[16] The Irish label, although competing with the Scottish label, was recognised as a quality brand. The most important production of linen was north of the border,[17] but it was one of Ireland's main sources of exports. It was particularly popular in the United States, with the wealthy class of Irish origin, who appreciated being able to buy linen made from this material and manufactured in Ireland.[18]

In the food industry, Gateaux Ltd. was a great success story. Founded in 1949, the company quickly began exporting to Great Britain. By 1951, it had entered the Belgian, Swedish, and Dutch markets. By 1956, it was exporting to many countries around the world including Cyprus, Malta, Gibraltar, Sudan and other countries in East and West Africa, the British West Indies, and Mexico. Within seven years, its exports increased from two hundred to two thousand tonnes.[19] In 1953, after ensuring that its products met the stringent standards of the North American market, it set out to conquer it. The company, which had previously distributed its Gateaux of Ireland brand only in New York, intended to extend its reach to Boston, Chicago, and Los Angeles, cities with large populations of Irish origin. Of course, the latter contributed to the commercial success of Gateaux Ltd, but the company had realised that it needed to offer quality products at a good price to succeed in the United States.

However, it appears that companies advertising to the Irish diaspora were the exception rather than the rule. Indeed, most of the few large

Irish exporting companies preferred to get their message across to as wide a customer base as possible. W&R Jacob's, for example, at that time[20] one of the flagships of Irish industry,[21] exported worldwide. The company's advertising strategy never seems to have sought to exploit the emotional link between the diaspora and Ireland.[22]

Guinness has become an export model[23] and the brand is now closely associated with Irish identity. Indeed, for Irish expatriates, drinking Guinness abroad has become a way of both displaying their identity and maintaining an emotional connection with their country.[24] However, this is a relatively recent phenomenon. The first advertisements for the brand, which were launched in Britain in the late 1920s, used its health benefits as a selling point[25] and were not specifically aimed at the diasporic market.[26]

4.3 Successes and Failed Attempts to Organise Trade Between Ireland and the United States

It is clear that the vast majority of Irish businesses at that time were small. According to the Register of the Department of Industry and Commerce in 1948, three quarters of them employed fewer than twenty people and the remaining quarter employed an average of twenty-two.[27] Their lack of experience in international markets was an additional handicap for these companies, which consequently exported little. The key to export success was a joint effort, i.e. an initiative that would bring together several companies in the same sector of activity in order to limit the financial risks of such an undertaking.

In a parliamentary sitting, Patrick McGrath[28] reported the impressions that Mr Murphy, director of St Patrick's Woollen Mills, a tweed manufacturer, had given him on his return from a trade mission to the American continent:

> My visit to America was to increase our outlet for Irish-made tweeds and I found that there was a ready market there. With so many Irish people and people of Irish descent in America, there is quite a demand for goods bearing an Irish label. But I am only one individual, and one person cannot do a great deal on his own. If Ireland had a trade commissioner in the States, our exports could be increased considerably, for the prospects are very good.[29]

In 1935, Erskine Hamilton Childers,[30] then secretary of the National Agricultural and Industrial Development Association, contacted the

Department of External Affairs. After conducting a study of the tweed trade, he concluded that there was a need for increased advertising and marketing of tweed products in the United States. The companies in this sector were unwilling to collectively engage an agent who they felt could not fairly represent their individual commercial interests. But they were attracted by the idea of collectively creating an Irish Chamber of Commerce in New York. Childers therefore asked what the prerequisites were for the creation of such an organisation.[31] The Department of External Affairs was unenthusiastic and insisted that financial guarantees were essential to ensure the sustainability of such an institution which would have to employ full-time staff. In addition, the volume of Irish exports to the United States was minimal and it was unlikely that a sufficient number of companies would be able to participate in the project and make it viable.[32] As a result, the proposal was not pursued.

However, a few years later, the efforts of the Gaeltacht Services Division and its successor the Gaeltarra Éireann bore fruit. These government agencies, whose primary aim was to maintain employment in the remote areas of the West of Ireland, provided a framework for this largely cottage industry. After World War II, the Gaeltacht Services Division recruited sales agents in the United States, Canada, Britain, Germany, and France. Through these intermediaries, Irish tweed could be exported around the world.[33]

An Irish Chamber of Commerce was indeed established in New York City in 1939 on the initiative of four Irish-Americans. It was officially constituted on 28 August 1939. Although its creators had the best of intentions, for Leo T. McAuley, the Irish Consul General in the United States, the venture was amateurish:

> These gentlemen called upon me on the 15th inst. To inform me of the details of their scheme. We had a long and useful discussion in the course of which I gathered that, while their intentions were good, they had made no real effort to acquaint themselves with the practical problems involved in the successful establishment of a Chamber of Commerce, and they were not well acquainted with the causes responsible for the small volume of the present export trade from Ireland to the United States. Further, they had not yet approached the leading Irish American business men in this country and therefore were not in a position to say to what extent they could count on the support of such persons.[34]

The group did manage to compile a comprehensive list of missions that the Chamber of Commerce wanted to carry out, together with a letter of motivation, which they sent to McAuley in May 1940:

> Since there are upwards of twenty millions [sic] of Irish Americans in this country, there is unquestionably a tremendous potential market for Irish products and manufactures, if only this market were properly cultivated, and the Irish manufacturer competently represented. [...] There are literally thousands of Irish organizations, patriotic, historical, social and cultural throughout the United States, but not one which has interested itself in the material welfare of Ireland on a purely business basis. The fact that immigration to these shores is curtailed, makes it all the more necessary for Ireland to find new markets across the seas. The first and most logical of these markets is the United States where so many Irish born have made their permanent abode. The fact that 90 per cent of Ireland's exportable surplus goes to a nation, oftentimes at that nation's own prices, is truly a most unsound and unhealthy condition. If Ireland is to achieve that freedom which we all desire, she must strive to capture world markets for her products. In the life of a nation, as in the life of an individual, there can be no real political freedom unless it is based on economic freedom.[35]

Although they were not seeking financial support from the Irish state, they wanted to have its backing in order to be credible to the business community in both the United States and Ireland. Very cleverly linking the political dimension to the economic dimension to justify their approach was likely to be successful, as at that time the Irish authorities were still seeking to move away from the country's economic dependence on the United Kingdom. It should be noted that the group did not propose to take on trade relations with Northern Ireland, but was prepared to follow the advice of the Irish government in this regard.[36]

By the end of May 1940, the Chamber of Commerce had seventy-five members, according to Hugh Mullen, its director. McAuley remained sceptical, but in view of the group's efforts, he expressed a favourable opinion, albeit with some reservations, to the Department of External Affairs.[37] A year later, a telegram from the Irish Embassy in Washington to the Department of External Affairs about the Chamber of Commerce ended with the following assessment: "Substantial results improbable for a long time".[38] According to archival material, the war suspended the organisation's operations. In 1944, efforts to revive it failed for lack of adequate financial security and support from Irish-American businessmen.[39] Further attempts were made to establish an Irish Chamber of Commerce in the United States. In 1949, Michael C. Crotty, a native of Youghal, Ireland, and president of the Crotty Manufacturing Corporation (New York), was the bearer of a project to be implemented under the aegis of the Ancient Hibernian Order.[40] This initiative also fell through.[41]

From the early 1950s onwards, the Irish administration was even less inclined to support private sector initiatives to promote Irish exports to the US and to exploit the diasporic market there. The Foreign Trade Committee felt that the newly operational Córas Tráchtála Teoranta was the appropriate body to develop trade between Ireland and the dollar area and that responsibilities should not be spread too thinly.[42]

Norton, the Minister for Industry and Commerce and Tánaiste, revived the idea of promoting Irish exports to Irish-Americans on his return from the United States in February 1956. Although he had done much to encourage Irish-Americans to "buy Irish", he was aware that his message would have to be hammered home after his departure if it was to have any effect. He therefore expressed the hope that the many "Irish organisations"[43] in the United States would be brought together into one so that the goodwill of Irish-Americans could be harnessed to the benefit of the Irish economy.

Taoiseach John A. Costello[44] visited the United States a few weeks after Norton. He was very pleasantly surprised by the reception he received. Upon his return, he asked the Minister of Industry and Commerce to make recommendations for maintaining close contact with those groups and individuals in the United States who were sympathetic to Ireland.[45] Norton thus prepared a paper for the government's attention in which he expressed his desire to explore with his government colleagues how this might be achieved.[46]

In the absence of details of the project in question, some within the administration were wary: "It would appear that any form of organising Irish groups in the U.S. would have political overtones".[47] Great care had to be taken to avoid the suspicion that the Irish authorities were endorsing groups that openly displayed support for the IRA.[48]

The Ireland-America Council, created in October 1956, was entrusted with the mission "to develop and encourage the interest of American citizens, particularly those of Irish birth or descent, in the well-being and prosperity of Ireland".[49] But Norton had to contend with the reluctance of Irish government officials. So this group, despite its name, was based in Dublin and consisted solely of representatives of Irish companies or organisations.[50] A few meetings were held, but the council was dissolved in May 1957 when Fianna Fáil returned to power.

After leaving his post, Norton continued to hold the belief that it was necessary to work through Irish community organisations in the United States to penetrate the diasporic market there:

> There should be an enormous potential goodwill for Irish whiskey in America. There are 20,000,000 people of Irish birth or extraction there. We ought to have some special heart-call to them to help the motherland by buying Irish whiskey if they want to drink whiskey at all. [...] Some serious effort ought to be made to use these organisations as a nucleus for popularising Irish whiskey, not merely at their own functions but at all other functions they attend or over which they wield some influence. If we are merely to publish advertisements and then sit back to see the effect on the potential consumer, I am afraid we shall be disappointed.[51]

Lemass, Norton, and other politicians seemed to think that what was needed was to encourage Irish-Americans to do a good deed by buying Irish products and to organise the distribution network a little, using community organisations. When he spoke to representatives of the Irish-American community in New York, Lemass said without blinking:

> The hardest part of our export drive is, we believe, in getting it started. We will not ask those who support it to do so a second time if they find that the purchases of Irish products which they make are not sound and satisfactory in every way. It is in the conviction that, given the necessary impetus to get started, Irish products can advance in the American market on the basis of merit that we have launched our campaign.[52]

However, the dismaying findings of two studies by US consultants, delivered to the Irish government some time earlier, suggested that significantly increasing Irish exports to the United States would not be so easy.

4.4 A Critical Eye: American Perceptions of Ireland's Economy

An initial report on the potential of the Irish economy, known as the Stacy May Report,[53] which was the result of research by American consultants, was submitted to the Irish government in August 1952. It contained a list of products[54] that could be considered for export, but the authors made no secret of the fact that the road to success would be long and rocky for those who embarked on this path. Companies in the same sector would have to join forces to act in concert, a practice which they acknowledged was not used by Irish companies. The authorities were expected to provide active support to firms wishing to engage in such a venture. In addition, expert advice was strongly recommended to limit the risk of failure. And finally, Irish companies would have to agree to adapt the style and quality of their products to the markets to which they wished to export. Certain standards and contractual conditions would also have to be met.[55] To refine this initial analysis, the Córas Tráchtála Teoranta, the body responsible for developing trade between Ireland and the dollar zone, commissioned a team of American experts in marketing, business management, and production to assess whether certain Irish-made goods[56] could meet the expectations of American consumers. The aim was to select ten products that would make the country earn dollars as quickly as possible.

At the end of their review of 108 establishments, the consultancy team presented their findings[57] to the Córas Tráchtála Teoranta, which were particularly harsh on Irish entrepreneurs, a stark reminder of reality. It was true that some Irish products had gained international recognition, but they were the exception rather than the rule. In reality, the vast majority of Irish companies were simply not fit to compete in international markets. As a result, the experts were unable to propose a single product that met the criteria that had been established.[58] A list of products was proposed, but it was made clear that this was not a guarantee of their success in the US market, but simply that their potential was slightly higher than the products excluded from the list. No market research was recommended. This was because the conditions were not right for any of the products studied, as there was either no market or insufficient product quality and/or production volume. The experts recommended that manufacturers should adopt a more realistic attitude to the quality of their products compared to that of their foreign competitors. They also needed to work on improving their production methods and ensuring that quality was consistent before considering exporting.[59] In addition, hygiene in food processing plants, which left much to be desired, needed to be improved:

> Conditions of production in the plants visited are generally insanitary and do not come up to those of the U.S. and in a number of cases require attention even for the home market.[60]

This was of particular importance since, at the time, Irish exports of livestock and foodstuffs accounted for forty-four million out of a total of sixty-one million pounds.[61]

Irish government officials were outraged and questioned the relevance of the report's findings. Measuring the performance of Ireland's fledgling industrial sector against that of US companies was seen as simply absurd.[62] It is clear, however, that parts of Ireland's industrial sector could have benefited from US know-how under the Marshall Plan's technical assistance programme, which for political reasons was not available to the country.[63]

So, while there may have been a demand for certain Irish products from the diaspora market across the Atlantic at that time, the effort required by Irish companies to exploit it would have been considerable. At least, that was the opinion of the American consultants after a few weeks on the ground. Finally, the US consultants' report noted "psychological factors" which, according to its authors, played a large role in Ireland:

> They discovered no inclination among Irish producers to take any sort of risk. There is a real shortage of capital, but what there is remains buried. There is smugness, largely due to the prevalence of family-owned business which does not produce the drive necessary to make an impact upon the American market. Illusions exist amongst Irish manufacturers which interfere with the correct appraisal of the market, e. g. the illusion of superior quality of the Irish product, the illusion of appealing to Irish sentiment in the United States, the illusion of insufficient capacity in Irish plants, the illusion of United States without effort.[64]

This report recognised that there was a stated desire to encourage economic expansion in the country, but that in reality neither the authorities nor the business community nor the trade unions were doing anything to encourage this. The impetus and boldness needed for economic development was lacking. Furthermore, they noted that although the authorities in Ireland did not recognise the socialist model, the state did "stifle" individual initiative.[65] These internal contradictions were holding back Ireland's economic development.

The staff of the US Embassy in Dublin shared this uncompromising view of Irish society at the time.[66] In a report sent to Washington, Raymond J. Barrett, Second Secretary for Economic Affairs, painted an unflattering picture of the Irish population:

> Another consequence of the depressed and well-nigh hopeless economic conditions was the tendency to develop psychological compensations in other areas of human behavior for the impossibility of economic advancement. There was an attitude of devil-may-care irresponsibility – 'feckless-ness' it has been called - a lightheartedness toward obligations, an 'eat, drink and be merry' feeling, an indulgence in liquor and tobacco regardless of the consequences. [...] There is little need to point out how those characteristics have continued in present-day Ireland [...]. Their attitude of thought is often more emotional than logical or practical. There is a delight in earning a penny by devious means or without effort. The Embassy is steadily bombarded by letters from Irishmen hoping to gain a fat share of the supposed 'fortune' of a relative deceased in the United States. Few Irishmen are likely to lose sight of any possibility for a suit for libel or slander. Forms of chance abound in Ireland - Horse-racing, greyhound, footballs pools, raffles, etc. - and the world famous Sweepstakes[67] is Irish.[68]

For Barrett, emigration was the result of both desperation and this carelessness:

> An inability to improve one's lot in Ireland together with a lack of a feeling of binding obligations obviously bred a readiness to pack up and move, even thousands of miles, to a land where fortunes were reported to be available.[69]

In their defence, he conceded that once away from Ireland, "Irishmen, outside of this context, have done remarkably well".[70] Barrett also described the widespread inertia that gripped the entire state machinery. This was Barrett's personal view, with its element of subjectivity, but it is worth noting that his opinion and analysis were regarded as a reliable source and were taken seriously in Washington, which could be very damaging to Ireland's image:

> Particularly valuable is the provision of an analysis of basic psychological attitudes affecting both the political and economic policies of the

> Government, in addition to detailed economic data. The report demonstrates that Mr. Barrett has benefited from his long assignment in Ireland by acquiring thorough familiarity with both psychological and economic fundamentals of the Republic.[71]

But was this American perspective on Ireland and its economy an accurate reflection of reality? Historian Francis Stewart Leland Lyons argued that one of the main reasons for the sluggish growth of Ireland's industrial sector at the time was the lack of investment and the sector's limited capacity to compete in export markets. Compounding this were structural disadvantages: the country's scarcity of natural resources, the generally low standard of living, and the small size of the domestic market. As a result, Ireland was heavily reliant on exports. The agri-food industry formed the backbone of this export economy, but it too depended on an agricultural sector that had not undergone sufficient modernisation.[72] As a result, yields and productivity stagnated despite the financial resources allocated by the state.[73]

The Irish industrial sector also required private capital to modernise its manufacturing processes. However, as previously noted, such capital was scarce. In fact, Irish investors tended to direct their money abroad rather than into domestic industry. The Department of Industry and Commerce, which was actively seeking to promote industrial investment, suspected that many entrepreneurs were channelling funds into a narrow range of ventures that offered quick returns with minimal effort.[74]

4.5 Irish Entrepreneurs' Lack of Drive

The heyday of Irish whiskey[75] started in the eighteenth century and continued in the following century. In 1780, Irish distilleries were allowed to export their production to the British colonies. A century later, four hundred brands of Irish whiskey were marketed in the world. There were then 160 distilleries in Ireland. In 1805, John Jameson, who bought a distillery in Bow Street in Dublin in 1780, became the biggest whiskey producer in the world. John Powers & Son was another big name in the industry at that time.[76]

Yet, in the 1950s, the Irish whiskey industry was one of the sectors where a certain conservatism seemed to prevail. The Stacy May Report, which assessed the potential of whiskey, placed it among the few Irish products that could be successfully exported, provided that distillers adapted to the requirements of foreign markets.[77] Although the prohibition of alcohol consumption in the United States between 1919 and 1933, the consequences of the Irish War of Independence,[78] and the freeze on whiskey exports imposed by the Irish government during World War II were detrimental to the industry, this is not enough to explain its decline, which began in the nineteenth century and continued into the twentieth century. Indeed, when one of their compatriots, Aeneas Coffey,[79] presented his invention to Irish distillers, he was met with contempt: "[…] they poohpoohed the idea and would not accept it […]".[80]

In contrast, their Scottish competitors immediately saw the potential of this new process. When blended whisky was introduced, it quickly conquered the UK and international markets, making Scottish producers the world's leading whisky producers. While Scotland exported twenty eight million Irish pounds' worth of whisky in the first nine months of 1954, Irish exports amounted to only one hundred and fifty thousand pounds in the same period, a considerable loss of income for the Irish economy.[81] Of all industries, the Scottish whisky industry was, at that time, the one which brought in the most dollars to Britain.

Despite the growing success of blended whiskey with consumers, Irish producers, over the decades, refused to produce anything other than pot still whiskey, the only one, according to them, worthy of the name "whiskey". In fact, as early as 1874, they opposed the use of the name "whiskey" for blended whisky. In 1908, they lobbied the British government, which appointed a Royal Commission to decide the issue, but they were not successful.[82]

In the 1950s, some elected officials were highly critical of this attitude. One of them, John McQuillan, deplored the fact that Irish producers had exported only one gallon of whiskey to Australia in 1953.[83] There was indeed a potential market for the product in that country, since there was a large community of Irish origin whose size was increasing more rapidly than the Irish-American one.[84] McQuillan denounced the apathy of Irish producers:

> I believe that for the last 70 years our distillers have been prepared to jog along, that they have been satisfied with the home market. Their cry is and has been that their product is the best whiskey in the world. While they adopt this line and live in this cuckoo-land, the Scotch have swept the decks with their blended products. To-day, the Irish distillers strongly oppose the introduction of a blended product, just as they opposed it 70 years ago. […]

> Despite all the evidence available and the good, sound business reasons that existed, the Irish distillers stubbornly and pig-headedly refused to adapt themselves to changing world tastes and conditions with the consequent disastrous results we have to-day so far as the Irish product is concerned.[85]

But he still believed that there were opportunities and that the diaspora market was one of them:

> Surely, with our large Irish population in America, by giving the right commodity, producing the properly blended whiskey that will suit the American palate, we should be able to get a proper footing in that market.[86]

The Irish authorities were increasingly concerned that distillers were not making sufficient efforts to promote exports, particularly at a time when boosting dollar earnings was a national priority. However, as Norton pointed out, all government efforts since 1949 to encourage greater exports to the United States had failed. Distillers argued that there was no proven demand for their products abroad and that the financial risks were too high. As a result, they chose to continue focusing on pot still whiskey—the product that had traditionally ensured their success—and to remain oriented towards the domestic market. Yet this approach was equally precarious: of the twenty-seven distilleries operating in 1906, only five were still in existence by 1954.[87]

4.6 Cultural Obstacles: Materialism Versus Enterprise

Joseph J. Lee, a prominent historian and former Irish senator, has examined a range of economic, historical, and socio-psychological factors[88] that may explain the apparent lack of initiative within Irish society. Among his observations, he highlights the role of civil servants who, rather than acting as the crucial facilitators of decision-making and government implementation, had long served to slow down progress.[89] Tom Garvin concurs but adds that Ireland's economic underdevelopment was also largely the result of an ageing and stagnant political elite:

> Quite apart from the 1921 divisions, there was also a clear anti-modernist streak in Irish official and clerical thinking, generating a reluctance to engage seriously with the modern world. Most importantly, the notion of a static

> and unchanging order that was to be regarded as ideal was quietly accepted, gladly or fatalistically, by much of the population. In the minds of many, modernity was something to be shut out rather than welcomed and coped with. After all, if one really wanted modernity, one could go next door to Britain or over the Atlantic to America [...]. In turn, these mentalities encouraged a cultural pessimism, passivity or even hopelessness.[90]

As Barrett had noted,[91] Lee emphasises the centrality of land ownership to the Irish population.[92] For a people who had been colonised and suffered the Great Famine, land ownership was in itself a necessary guarantee of security on an island with a high population density and few employment opportunities:

> Loss of one's holding [...] normally brought with it not only the economic but the social ruin of the family. Economic loss involved psychic humiliation. [...] It was entirely rational in those circumstances for the individual to abhor risk taking when the price of failure was catastrophe.[93]

However, Lee explains that there was little incentive for those who worked the land, whether farmers or labourers, to excel at work, as effort was rarely rewarded and opportunities for upward mobility were almost non-existent. For Lee, what determined a farmer's place on the social ladder was the size of his farm, not productivity. Two major events in the nineteenth century improved the condition of farmers: the Great Famine, which gave surviving farmers the opportunity to exploit vacant land, and the reforms achieved through the political struggle of the National Land League.[94] But, as Lee points out, these advances were not the result of individual effort. Even the profits from the sale of agricultural produce depended more on British prices than on the farmer's own labour. Thus this culture of ownership, seen as a guarantee of security, would have taken precedence over the development of a "culture of achievement". For Lee, this mentality had rubbed off somewhat on other sectors of society. Industry was no exception:

> Family firms predominated. They were not incompatible with performance criteria. Some did achieve impressive records. But they were quite compatible with fairly comfortable stagnation [...]. The family firm had much the same ethos as the family farm.[95]

The protectionist policy implemented from the 1930s onwards did not, in his view, help to change these attitudes. He points out, however, that the Irish who had emigrated were one of the exceptions, as they were very dynamic, demonstrating that the predominance of a culture of ownership was a product of historical circumstances and not an innate trait of the Irish.

Garvin also emphasises the moral dominance of the Catholic Church over the leadership, and over the general mindset, in Ireland at that time. For this institution, he explains, commerce was synonymous with greed. Trade unions and professional organisations were also very important in Irish society. All of these actors had a great deal of influence on government decision-making and acted as brakes on change.[96]

By the 1950s, Ireland had achieved political independence, but the country was still extremely dependent on the United Kingdom as its main economic partner.[97] The opportunities offered by the diaspora market in the United States might have allowed some Irish agribusinesses and others to diversify and expand their operations abroad. However, although this market in the United States was presented as an El Dorado by some politicians, exploiting it remained in the realm of fantasy. Indeed, entrepreneurship and risk-taking were values that were not widely promoted in Ireland. Furthermore, a strong and sustained political will, which could have created a dynamic and encouraged Irish entrepreneurs to conquer the American market, seemed to be lacking at that time. According to Lee, Séan Lemass was determined to ensure that the culture of achievement replaced that of possession in Irish society.[98]

Notes

1. John Horgan. 1997. Seán Lemass: The Enigmatic Patriot, Dublin: Gill & Macmillan. 80.
2. Text of de Valera's Speech. 1932. *The New York Times*, 18 March.
3. A U.U. Mayor Seeks Irish Goods. 1949. *The Irish Times*, 1 October.
4. ECA, Subject Review of the 49–50 Program of the Irish Government, 14 January 1949, RG 469, entry 1247, memorandum no. 12, National Archives and Records Administration at College Park, MD, United States of America (hereafter NARA).
5. In 1949, 91% of Irish exports went to the UK. John O'Hagan, Patrick Murphy, Adrian Redmond. 2000. The Economy. In Central Statistics Office, ed. Adrian Redmond, That Was Then, This Is Now: Change in Ireland, 1949–1999. A Publication to Mark the 50th Anniversary of the Central Statistics Office: 91. Dublin: Stationery Office.

https://www.cso.ie/en/media/csoie/releasespublications/documents/otherreleases/thatwasthenthisisnow.pdf. Accessed 4 June 2025.

6. Address by Mr. Seán Lemass, T. D., Tánaiste and Minister for Industry and Commerce, to Commerce and Industry Association, New York, October 5th, 1953, 436/35, National Archives of Ireland (hereafter NAI).
7. Speech by Mr. Seán Lemass, T. D., Tánaiste and Minister for Industry and Commerce at opening of Trade Office, Ireland House, New York, October 5th, 1953, 436/35, NAI.
8. John Horgan, Seán Lemass,168.
9. William Norton quoted in: Mr. Norton Addresses New York Assembly. 1956. *The Irish Times*, 18 January.
10. George H. Burrows. 1956. With the Bundle on his Shoulder. *The Irish Times*, 7 January.
11. Following partition, the Free State was deprived of much of the industrial sector located in the north-east of the island, which remained under British control. Agriculture became, by necessity, the main engine of the new state's economy.
12. On Irish trade networks in India see: Barry Crosbie. 2012. Irish Imperial Networks: Migration, Social Communications and Exchange in the Nineteenth-Century India. Cambridge: Cambridge University Press, 24–62.
13. The Industrial Revival. 1936. *The Irish Times*, 9 March.
14. Denis O'Hearn. 2001. The Atlantic Economy: Britain, the US and Ireland, Manchester: Manchester University Press, 115.
15. As early as 1932, de Valera entered into conflict with London. He refused to pay land annuities to the British government. These annuities were paid to the Irish state by Irish farmers who had bought their land (Wyndham Act, 1903). Dublin then paid them back to the British government. London retaliated by imposing tariffs on Irish agricultural goods to recover the money. Dublin in turn imposed taxes on certain products from the United Kingdom. The "Economic War" episode ended with the signing of the Anglo-Irish Agreement of 1938. See: Christophe Gillissen. 2005. Une relation unique: les relations irlando-britanniques de 1921 à 2001. Caen: Presses universitaires de Caen, 129–208.
16. Irish Tweed, Gaeltarra Éireann. 1956. *The Irish Times*, 19 March.
17. W. H. Crawford. 1969. The Rise of the Linen Industry. In The Formation of the Irish Economy, ed. Louis M. Cullen: 23–35. Cork: Mercier Press.
18. Magee's of Donegal exported extensively to the United States and other destinations around the world. Magee's of Donegal. 1956. *The Irish Times*, 16 March. Greenmount & Boyne Linen Co. was another major company in this sector, also exporting extensively to Australia, Canada, and New

Zealand where there was a large Irish community. Linen: Greenmount and Boyne. 1956. *The Irish Times*, 19 March.

19. Gateaux Ltd. 1956. *The Irish Times*, 16 March.
20. The Jacob's brand still exists.
21. A Progressive Firm. 1929. The Irish Times, 12 September; The Biscuit Trade. 1932. *The Irish Times*, 21 January.
22. Some of the Jacob's advertising posters can be viewed at The Advertising Archives: http://www.advertisingarchives.co.uk/index.php?service=search&ac-etion=do_quick_search&language=en&q=jacob%27s+biscuit. Accessed 4 June 2025.
23. The brewery was founded in 1759 and shipped its first barrels to England in 1769. A century later, it was exporting to many countries around the world. In 2001, two billion bottles of the product were sold worldwide. Guinness Storehouse, https://www.guinness-storehouse.com/en/dis-cover. Accessed 4 June 2025.
24. Brenda Murphy. 2003. Pure Genius: Guinness Consumption and Irish Identity. New Hibernia Review, 7, 4: 53.
25. The famous slogan "Guinness is good for you" has remained attached to the brand's image. See also The Advertising Archives for posters advertising Guinness: http://www.advertisingarchives.co.uk/?a-service=search&action=do_quick_search&language=en&mode=&q=guinness&qw=&m d_1=&md_2=1930s&grid_layout=4. Accessed 4 June 2025.
26. Brenda Murphy, Pure Genius, 50–62.
27. John Horgan. Seán Lemass, 119.
28. Patrick McGrath was a Fianna Fáil elected member for Cork Borough.
29. Ireland, parliamentary debates, Houses of the Oireachtas, Dáil Éireann (hereafter Dáil Éireann debates) 1 June 1949, 115, 17.
30. Erskine Hamilton Childers was the fourth President of Ireland from 25 June 1973 to 17 November 1974. Dictionary of Irish Biography. Childers, Erskine Hamilton. https://www.dib.ie/biography/childers-erskine-hamilton-a1648. Accessed 10 June 2025.
31. Erskine Hamilton Childers to Leo T. McAuley, Consul General in New York, 30 August 1935, 315/262/1, NAI.
32. Secretary of the Department of External Affairs, to Erskine Hamilton Childers, 3 October 1935, 315/262/1, NAI.
33. Irish Tweed, Gaeltarra Éireann. 1956. *The Irish Times*, 19 March.
34. Leo T. McAuley to the Secretary of the Department of External Affairs, 18 September 1939, 315/262/1, NAI.
35. Hugh Mullen to Leo T McAuley, 25 May 1940, 315/262/1, NAI.
36. Leo T. McAuley to the Secretary of the Department of External Affairs, 31 May 1940, 315/262/1, NAI.

37. Leo T. McAuley to the Secretary of the Department of External Affairs, 2 January 1940, 315/262/1, NAI.
38. Telegram from Washington to the Department of External Affairs, 2 May 1940, 315/262/1, NAI.
39. Matthew Garth Healy, Irish Consulate General in New York, to Secretary of the Department of External Affairs, 15 February 1949, 315/262/1, NAI.
40. Michael C. Crotty to Donal Scully, Vice Consul, Irish Consulate General in New York, 25 February 1949, 315/262/1, NAI.
41. In 1952, Pádraig Pearse O'Sullivan, an Irishman living in New York, also proposed the establishment of an Irish Chamber of Commerce in the United States, but was not successful.
42. Foreign Trade Committee, Minutes of meeting held on 1st February 1952, 1590, Irish American Chamber of Commerce, 315/262/1, NAI.
43. This refers to ethnically-based community organisations. Mr. Norton Returns 'Satisfied with Results of Tour'. 1956. *The Irish Times*, 16 February.
44. Taoiseach is a Gaelic term commonly used to refer to the Irish Prime Minister. John A. Costello served twice as Taoiseach, from 18 February 1948 to 13 June 1951 and from 2 June 1954 to 20 March 1957. Dictionary of Irish Biography. John A. Costello. https://www.dib.ie/search?search_name=john+A+costello&search_fulltext=&field_contributor=&field_gender=All&field_religion=All&field_career=All&field_place_birth=All&field_place_death=All&field_date_of_birth_range%5Bmin%5D=&field_date_of_birth_range%5Bmax%5D=&field_date_of_death_range%5Bmin%5D=&field_date_of_death_range%5Bmax%5D=&field_floruit_range%5Bmin%5D=&field_floruit_range%5Bmax%5D=&sort_bef_combine=field_name_sort_ASC. Accessed 10 June 2025.
45. Memo for the Government, Report by the Taoiseach and recommendations following his visit to the United States of America, March 1956, P277/PTII, NAI.
46. Oifig an aire tionscail agus tráchtála [Department of Industry and Commerce], Memorandum for the Government, June 1956, 315/254, NAI.
47. Diarmuid Coffey to Michael McWhite, 30 August 1956, 315/254: exchange of remarks on William Norton's submission to the government dated June 1956, NAI.
48. Michael McWhite to Diarmuid Coffey, exchange of remarks on William Norton's submission to the government dated June 1956, 31 August 1956, 315/254, NAI.

49. Córas Tráchtála Teoranta, Establishment of America - Ireland Board of Trade (or Chamber of Commerce) in the United States, 27 October 1960, 315/262/1, NAI.
50. Bord Fáilte Éireann, Aer Lingus, Shannon Free Airport, and Córas Tráchtála Teoranta were part of this organisation.
51. Dáil Éireann Debates, 25 November 1958, 171, 7 (William Norton).
52. Speech by Mr. Seán Lemass, T. D., Tánaiste and Minister for Industry and Commerce at opening of Trade Office, Ireland House, New York, October 5th, 1953.
53. Stacy May led the team of American consultants who conducted the study.
54. This list included meat, stout, ale, confectionery, dairy products, whisky, flour cakes and confectionery, textiles of all kinds and clothing, leather goods including boots and shoes, glass, pottery, and cement products. IBEC Technical Services. 1952. Industrial Potential of Ireland: An Appraisal, New York: IBEC Technical Services Corporation, 88, S15389, NAI.
55. IBEC Technical Services, Industrial Potential of Ireland, 89.
56. This list included the products mentioned in the Stacy May Report and some others.
57. Department of Industry and Commerce, Report of American Experts engaged by Córas Tráchtála Teoranta, Memorandum for the Government, 7 October 1952, S14818 B/2, NAI.
58. Department of Industry and Commerce, Report of American Experts, 5.
59. Department of Industry and Commerce, Report of American Experts, 7.
60. Annex to summary, annex to the memorandum Report of American Experts engaged by Córas Tráchtála Teoranta, 2.
61. John O'Hagan, Patrick Murphy, Adrian Redmond, The Economy, 91.
62. Department of Industry and Commerce, Memorandum for the Government, Stacy May Report, 13 November 1953, S15389, NAI.
63. The Mutual Security Act of 1951 abolished the Economic Cooperation Administration and transferred its powers to the Mutual Security Agency (MSA), the agency that would henceforth manage the economic, technical, and military assistance that the United States would provide to its allies in Europe. Ireland did not want to give up its neutrality and had to do without the American technical assistance it should have received. See: Peter Murray. 2009. Facilitating the Future? US Aid, European Integration and Irish Industrial Viability, 1948–73. Dublin: University College Dublin Press, 19–45; Raymond J. Raymond. 1985. The Marshall Plan and Ireland, 1947–52. In The Irish in America: Emigration, Assimilation and Impact, ed. P. J. Drudy: 316–320. Cambridge: Cambridge University Press.

64. Ministry of Industry and Commerce, Report of American Experts engaged by Córas Tráchtála Teoranta, Memorandum for the Government, 7 October 1952, 1–2.
65. "[...] the heavy hand of Government controls has extended widely over all business operations in a manner that has tended to stifle private initiative". IBEC Technical Services, Industrial Potential of Ireland, 80.
66. Anne Groutel. 2016. American Janus-Faced Economic Diplomacy towards Ireland in the Mid-1950s. Irish Economic and Social History, 43, 1:16–19.
67. The Irish Hospitals' Sweepstakes was established in 1930 as a lottery to fund Free State hospitals.
68. Sociological and historical factors in Irish economic problems, Memorandum from the US Embassy in Dublin to the State Department in Washington, September 1957, RG 84, Classified General Records, 1956–1959, Foreign Service Dispatch, dispatch no. 107, NARA.
69. Sociological and historical factors.
70. Sociological and historical factors.
71. Foreign Service Economic Reporting Appraisal, 6 May 1958, RG 84, Department of State, General Records, 1953–1959, box 5, NARA.
72. Joseph J. Lee. 1989. Ireland, 1912–1985: Politics and Society. Cambridge - New York: Cambridge University Press, 530.
73. Francis Stewart Leland Lyons. 1985. Ireland since the Famine. London: Fontana Press, 624–628.
74. Denis O'Hearn, The Atlantic Economy, 119.
75. Irish producers chose to spell the word this way to differentiate their product from Scotch whisky.
76. See the history of Irish whiskey on the following page: https://en.wikipedia.org/wiki/Irish_whiskey. Accessed 4 June 2025.
77. Ibec Technical Services, Industrial Potential of Ireland, 88.
78. At the time of the Irish war of independence, London imposed trade sanctions on the sales of Irish whiskey in the British Empire. Many distilleries were forced to close their doors for good.
79. Blended whisky, lighter than traditional whisky, was produced using a column still. This new process, invented in 1830 by Aeneas Coffey, allowed the continuous distillation of grain alcohol to which a percentage of traditional whisky was then added. This invention revolutionised the industry by making it possible to produce whisky at a much lower cost than traditional malted barley-based pot still whisky.
80. Dail Éireann Debates, 3 November 1954, 147, 3 (John McQuillan).
81. Dail Éireann Debates, 3 November 1954, 147, 3 (John McQuillan).
82. Dail Éireann Debates, 3 November 1954, 147, 3 (John McQuillan).
83. Dail Éireann Debates, 3 November 1954, 147, 3 (John McQuillan)
84. "The Irish Abroad", *The Irish Times*, 21 May 1935.

85. Dail Éireann Debates, 3 November 1954, 147, 3 (John McQuillan)
86. Dail Éireann Debates, 3 November 1954, 147, 3 (John McQuillan)
87. Dail Éireann Debates, 3 November 1954, 147, 3 (William Norton).
88. See also: Bertram Hutchinson. 1970. On the Study of Non-Economic Factors in Irish Economic Development. Economic and Social Review, 1, 4: 509–529.
89. Lee, Ireland, 196–198, 275–277, 364.
90. Garvin, Preventing the Future.
91. Sociological and historical factors in Irish economic problems, Memorandum from the US Embassy in Dublin to the State Department in Washington, September 1957.
92. Lee, Ireland, 390–396.
93. Lee, Ireland, 391.
94. Pauline Collombier-Lakeman. 2014. Quels horizons politiques pour l'Irlande au XIXe siècle? Une étude de quelques caricatures du temps de Parnell. Revue LISA/LISA e-journal, 12, 4. https://doi.org/10.4000/lisa.6204
95. Lee, Ireland, 393.
96. Garvin, Preventing the Future, 3, 12.
97. The tourists Ireland received were mainly British and almost all of its exports went to the United Kingdom. Irene Furlong. 2009. Irish Tourism 1880–1980. Dublin – Portland: Irish Academic Press, 183; Ronnie Munck. 1993. The Irish Economy, London – Boulder: Pluto Press, 32.
98. Lee, Ireland, 390.

PART II

The Economic Policy Shift at the Turn of the 1960s and the Use of the Irish-American Business Elite

The late 1950s was a pivotal period for the two Irelands. Ireland's transformation in the late 1950s is often portrayed as a conscious move from protectionism to free trade, signalling the start of modernisation through economic growth and the rise of a more liberal, secular society. Historians such as Brian Girvin[1] and Terence Brown[2] interpret this period as a decisive cultural and ideological shift. While Lee sees the 1960s as a dramatic reversal of long-standing attitudes,[3] Daly offers a more measured interpretation. Her analysis stands out for its clarity, balance, and rigorous support through factual evidence and detailed data. She offers a persuasive counterpoint to more celebratory narratives, underlining the complex reality of an Irish modernisation process shaped as much by inertia and compromise as by ambition and transformation. Looking at the big picture, she argues that the extent of change has been overstated. She suggests that beneath the appearance of progress, deep-rooted values and lifestyles remained largely intact.[4] For Daly, the reforms were not the result of visionary leadership, but rather of limited political capacity and a desire to maintain influence by satisfying key groups such as farmers and the Catholic Church.[5] Economically, Daly emphasises that modernisation was less a strategic choice than a survival mechanism in response to global economic pressures.[6] Though Ireland embraced foreign investment and moved towards European integration, these steps were carefully managed to minimise disruption to the rural population. The 1965 Free Trade Agreement with Britain and the EEC application were not aimed at radically reshaping the economy but at maintaining social stability, even at the expense of domestic industries built under protectionist policies.[7]

While Daly's analysis invites us to look beyond surface-level narratives of progress and reconsider the true nature of Ireland's modernisation, it also opens the door to exploring less visible yet equally consequential dimensions of state policy during this period. In this second part, we will turn our attention to one such discreet initiative: the strategic efforts of both Irish and Northern Irish authorities to attract foreign investment by activating transatlantic ties with the business elite of the diaspora in North America in the 1950s to the 1970s.

The first instance of an Irish-American businessman investing in a major industrial project in Ireland dates back to 1917. While it would be several decades before other large-scale American investments followed, this case warrants inclusion in this introduction—not merely because Henry Ford is a well-known figure, but because his investment exemplifies, in many ways, the dual motivations that would later characterise other diaspora-driven initiatives: a desire to conduct business and, at the same time, to contribute to the well-being of Ireland, the land of his ancestors. Born in 1863 in Dearborn, Michigan, into a Protestant family, industrialist Henry Ford was struck by the poverty he encountered in Ireland, from which his father originated, during a business trip to Europe in 1912.[8] Ford historian Bob Kreipke said: "His family roots drew him to Ireland, he knew what he was able to do socially and economically in America and he figured he could apply the same formula to help the depressed area of Cork". The company founder hoped the Marina plant "would start Ireland along the road to prosperity".[9] At the time, Ford was the largest automobile manufacturer in the world, headquartered in Detroit.[10] The case of Ford has been extensively researched[11] and is particularly interesting. It illustrates, to a certain extent, John J. Teeling's findings[12] which show that investment decisions are not based solely on financial factors. But the Ford company's presence in Ireland was also shaped by complex interplays of economic calculation, political leverage, and international trade strategy. D.S. Jacobson has analysed the economic and political factors behind the businessman's decision to establish a manufacturing plant in Cork. While acknowledging that Ford's personal ties to Ireland undeniably came into play, he argues that the choice of this town was influenced less by Ireland's industrial capacity—then underdeveloped in automotive production—and more by strategic considerations including tariffs, political expectations, and wartime economic conditions.[13] Operating under the name Henry

Ford & Son Ltd., the company quickly established a plant in Cork—complete with an iron foundry—which became Ford's largest facility outside North America after Manchester.[14] From 1919 to 1972, Ford was the main employer in Cork.[15]

As the political landscape evolved with Irish independence, Ford's business in Cork was challenged by new tariffs.[16] The company lobbied intensely to preserve duty-free access to Britain but had mixed results. Although tractor production was halted in the early 1920s, Ford adapted the Cork plant for motor-car component manufacturing.[17]

Several Irish political leaders at the time were clearly interested in foreign investment, especially from the United States. In August 1919, De Valera, in a letter to Arthur Griffith,[18] stated that Ireland needed to gain the support of wealthy American businessmen who might be interested in developing the country's industrialisation, citing in particular the example of Ford who had already established a factory and could be open to other projects.[19] It is worth noting that in the autumn of 1919, during his stay in the United States, de Valera met Henry Ford in Detroit. But Ford, as a shrewd businessman, regarded de Valera's political convictions—strongly in favour of economic protectionism—with suspicion. As could be expected, the latter obtained nothing from Ford.[20] Griffith, for his part, met Edward Grace, Managing Director of Henry Ford and Son Ltd., in February 1922. As Jacobson points out,[21] this meeting was particularly important because Griffith, as President of the second Dáil Éireann (January to August 1922), had signed the treaty granting Ireland fiscal autonomy. Although Griffith—who had long been a proponent of protectionist policies—apparently assured Grace that trade in motor vehicles and parts would remain duty-free between Ireland and Great Britain, where Ford operated another factory, this commitment was not upheld following Griffith's death in August 1922. In fact, from 1932 onwards, Fianna Fáil's protectionist policy had an immediate impact on the company's operations, which ceased all exports. The plant then became an assembly facility for vehicles destined for the Irish domestic market.

As will be explained in what follows, the 1950s were marked by a gradual realisation that economic protectionism had reached its limits, and that only foreign investment could help modernise the Irish economy. In this second part, we will also focus on the means used by Irish political leaders to persuade the diaspora's business circles across the Atlantic to support their efforts. This political commitment not only helped to renew connections with expatriate communities, but also set in motion a new and far-reaching dynamic of economic development.

Notes

1. Brian Girvin. 1989. Between Two Worlds. Politics and Economy in Independent Ireland. Dublin: Gill & Macmillan, quoted in Mary E. Daly. 2016. Sixties Ireland. Reshaping the Economy, State and Society, 1957–1973. Cambridge: Cambridge University Press, 3.
2. Terence Brown. 1981. Ireland. A Social and Cultural History 1922–1979. London: Fontana, quoted in Daly, Sixties Ireland, 3.
3. Joseph Lee. 1989. Ireland. 1912–1985. Politics and Society. Cambridge: Cambridge University Press.
4. Daly, Sixties Ireland, 7.
5. Daly, Sixties Ireland, 10.
6. Daly, Sixties Ireland, 4.
7. Daly, Sixties Ireland, 6.
8. Frank Barry. 2023. Industry and Policy in Independent Ireland, 1922–1972. Oxford: Oxford University Press, 61.
9. Robert C. Kreipke quoted in Martin Brennan. 2017. Emigrant past drove Ford to set Ireland 'on road to prosperity'. *Irish Independent*, 1 January.
10. D. S. Jacobson. 1977. The Political Economy of Industrial Location: The Ford Motor Company at Cork 1912–26. *Irish Economic and Social History*, 4, 36–37.
11. See, for example, Robert C. Kreipke. 2013. *Faces of Henry Ford*. Evansville (Indiana): M.T. Publishing Company, Inc.; M. Wilkins and F. E. Hill. 1964. *American Business Abroad, Ford on Six Continents*, Detroit: Wayne State University Press.
12. John J. Teeling. 1975. The Evolution of Offshore Investment. DBA unpublished thesis. Harvard University. Quoted in Frank Barry. 2023. Industry and Policy in Independent Ireland, 1922–1972, 141. Oxford: Oxford University Press.
13. The Fordson tractor plant at Cork emerged during World War I when Britain faced food shortages, labour constraints, and the need to boost domestic agricultural production. Despite Ireland's small market and lack of industrial infrastructure, Cork was favoured due to its safer port (avoiding U-boat threats), lower wages, and incentives like cheap land and improved harbour facilities. Moreover, the British government's willingness to support the plant and the expectation of continued inclusion in the British customs union were key to Ford's decision. Jacobson highlights how the Ford company skillfully anticipated and influenced tariff policy, aiming to secure favourable trading conditions both during and after the

war. Ford's agents, including influential executives embedded in British government, played a critical role in promoting the Fordson over rival tractors.

14. Jacobson, Political Economy, 36.
15. Barry, Industry and Policy, 63.
16. Barry, Industry and Policy, 86.
17. Ford family members backed the plant despite considerable difficulties down the years. However, on 17 January 1984, it was announced that the assembly plant was to close with the loss of eight hundred jobs. Martin Brennan. 2017. Emigrant past drove Ford to set Ireland 'on road to prosperity'. *Irish Independent*, 1 January.
18. Dictionary of Irish Biography. Arthur Griffith. https://www.dib.ie/biography/griffith-arthur-joseph-a3644. Accessed 10 June 2025.
19. Dave Hannigan. 2008. The Rebel President's 1919 Campaign. Dublin: The O'Brien Press, 109.
20. Hannigan, The Rebel President, 109; Adams, Shadow of a Taxman, 173–174.
21. Jacobson, Political Economy, 51.

CHAPTER 5

Partition, Industrial Retreat, and Transatlantic Ambitions: Northern Ireland's Search for Economic Renewal (1920–1960)

5.1 The Economy of the North-East of the Island: A Short-Lived Prosperity

In the latter part of the nineteenth century, the economy of the north-east of the island of Ireland enjoyed a period of remarkable prosperity. Its main industry, linen weaving, was particularly successful, and production was now mechanised. By 1914 it was producing three quarters of the United Kingdom's output and exporting to markets where demand was growing, particularly the United States.[1] Ulster was the world's largest producer of linen cloth.[2] Shipbuilding, the most dynamic in the United Kingdom,[3] was the second largest sector of the local economy. Harland and Wolff, founded in 1850, and Workman Clark, established in 1879, two shipyards located in Belfast, were the largest companies in the city.[4] At that time, agriculture also constituted a significant portion of the economy in this region of the island.[5]

These sectors of the economy were particularly in demand during World War I.[6] The need for linen for uniforms, tents, sheets, etc. increased and the order books of the shipyards were full.[7] Butter, eggs, pork, and beef were also exported in large quantities. This period of economic expansion in the north-east culminated in 1920.

After the political partition of the island, Northern Ireland, which remained within the United Kingdom, was given a parliament and an autonomous government. Its institutions were allowed some room for

A. Groutel, *The Two Irelands and the Diaspora*,
https://doi.org/10.1007/978-3-032-12355-8_5

manoeuvre in the economic sphere.[8] At the time of partition, the economic situation in the north-east of the island, at its peak, gave the false impression that the new entity would not only be able to support itself, but would also contribute to the coffers of the British Treasury[9] with a surplus of income, the "imperial contribution", in the same way as other parts of the country. However, the three main industries of the Northern Irish economy began to slowly decline from the mid-1920s.[10]

Although the Northern Irish provincial authorities were not allowed to legislate on foreign trade or to conclude trade agreements with third countries, they did manage to obtain a favourable regime. Indeed, as early as 1923, Northern Irish representatives were invited to the Imperial Economic Conference in London, which was attended by many representatives of the Commonwealth countries. The stakes were high for Belfast, as there was an opportunity to establish direct contact with foreign governments,[11] which could prove useful in developing the province's exports around the world at a time when its traditional industries were stagnating.[12] In the months and years that followed, Stormont[13] maintained these relationships with its Commonwealth partners. For example, the province received an official visit in 1923 from William Massey, Prime Minister of New Zealand and a native of Ulster. It would seem that this special relationship allowed trade between the two countries to flourish.

Some economists[14] have attributed the continuing difficulties of the Northern Irish economy to the partition of the island. Ronnie Munck, for example, claims that its deleterious effects went beyond short-term economic consequences:

> This event [partition] damaged the economy and inhibited future development. It disrupted trade flows between North and South and weakened the already somewhat tenuous economic links between the two regions. More fundamentally, partition cemented political division in Ireland and prevented the formation of a sense of common purpose and determination to overcome the island's economic backwardness.[15]

John Bradley, while accepting that partition negated the creation of intra-island economic synergies, is more nuanced and questions Lars Mjøset's view that by depriving the south of Ireland of the island's industrial core, partition was a serious handicap to the economy of the new state. Indeed, Bradley doubts that the industries of the north-east of the island could have provided the dynamism and resources that the southern economy sorely needed since, as was also the case in Britain, they went into decline after World War I.[16] In fact, the highly political question of the true impact of partition has never been definitively settled.[17] Historian David S. Johnson,[18] for example, puts the impact of partition on both economies into perspective and shows that Ireland's protectionist policy in the early 1930s had a much more serious effect on economic relations between the two jurisdictions.

One thing is certain, however: the very small size of its domestic market was a handicap for the Northern Ireland economy, which remained dependent on its exports, the main destination of which was the geographically distant United Kingdom.[19] Furthermore, as an open economy is particularly vulnerable to external shocks, Northern Ireland was hit hard by the international economic crisis of the 1930s and by the protectionism many countries put in place to protect their industry. Unemployment soared to 28%. In 1932, seventy-two thousand people were officially unemployed.[20] The shipbuilding and linen industries, two pillars of the regional economy, were particularly hard hit.

Far from being a passing episode, the crisis lasted for a decade. Unemployment peaked at 29.5% of the labour force in July 1938.[21] By this time, the province was unable to pay the imperial contribution.[22] Living conditions for the working class deteriorated, as the unemployment benefit provided by the local authorities was not enough to guarantee the minimum subsistence for the many families living in substandard housing. Not surprisingly, infectious diseases were much more common than elsewhere in the United Kingdom, and in 1931 life expectancy was only fifty-seven years.[23] In addition, the base of the Northern Irish economy was very narrow. The Northern Ireland Government tried to diversify the region's industrial sector from the 1930s onwards, but without much success.[24] The province failed to attract new growth sectors such as the automotive and chemical industries, whose major names preferred to locate closer to the British capital.[25]

Like World War I, World War II was a boon for the shipyards and the linen industry,[26] whose activity was revived for a time. Moreover, the Labour government, which came to power in July 1945, promised the Stormont leadership that Northern Ireland would benefit from welfare state reforms[27] on the same basis as the rest of the United Kingdom. The economic upturn lasted for a few years after the end of World War II for the shipbuilding and Northern Irish linen industries, as the Korean War helped to fill the order books of both sectors.[28] However, after the end of the war, the linen sector, increasingly replaced by synthetic fibres, declined.

In the 1950s, Northern Irish agriculture became more modern and productive, but in the process employed less labour. Local authorities therefore had to cope not only with the downsizing of the linen industry, but also with the influx of a now unemployed rural population and the overall increase in its population.[29]

Stormont introduced new measures, such as the Re-equipment of Industry Act (NI) 1951 and the Capital Grants to Industry Act (NI) 1954, which provided grants to help existing industries modernise. The Industries Development Acts (1945–1953) were designed to encourage the establishment of British companies in Northern Ireland, with the aim of diversifying and expanding the province's industrial base. The industries that came to Northern Ireland created jobs at a rate of three thousand a year, while the existing companies did not create any.[30] It was clear that if it was to reduce unemployment, it had to try to attract companies from outside the province in growth sectors.

5.2 When Politics Gets in the Way of Business

The Unionist leadership, from the moment Northern Ireland was created as a political entity, ensured that it retained its grip on power at the expense of the Catholic minority. A deliberately skewed gerrymandering of electoral constituencies allowed it to retain the advantage. This was largely motivated by the fear of becoming a minority, a fear that may have been justified, since the Catholic birth rate was higher than that of the Protestants. The Special Powers Act,[31] an emergency law giving the Home Affairs Minister in Northern Ireland wide-ranging law enforcement powers, was passed in the aftermath of partition to restore order in the province. Apart from this very repressive legislative tool, the Stormont regime had at its disposal a police force, the Royal Ulster Constabulary, as well as the B Specials, a special police force made up of reservist volunteers. Even if there are differing views on the extent of the phenomenon,[32] it cannot be denied that the Catholic minority in Northern Ireland was politically and socially discriminated against, particularly in housing and employment,[33] for decades.

In 1950, Basil Brooke,[34] the Northern Ireland Prime Minister, visited the United States and Canada to promote trade and encourage businesses from these countries to come to Northern Ireland.[35] While he was warmly received in Canada, it was less the case in the United States. Indeed, President Truman refused to meet him. The Mayor of New York City, Bill O'Dwyer, did the same. It must be said that Brooke was known for his outrageous comments towards Catholics.[36]

In 1937, the nationalist MP Cahir Healy was one of those who argued that Stormont's discriminatory policy towards the Catholic minority had damaged the province's exports, particularly linen, to the United States:

> In the case of Ulster linen, when this Government came into office the industry was a flourishing one, because it had the best market in the world in the United States. The most consistent supporters of Irish linen were people of Irish birth and descent. You began preaching a sectarian policy [...] you described Irish linen as Ulster linen. You did not describe it as Northern Ireland linen. It is Northern Ireland when it suits you and Ulster when it suits you. In no case I can recall have you gone in for the national designation-Irish. From the moment that you limited the appeal in the United States there was a dramatic and tragic drop in the sales. It has never gained a margin of what was lost to this hour. I have no doubt if this Government advertised its linen as Irish linen, if it looked at the situation from the really national and not the provincial standpoint, it would still succeed in regaining a great deal of the market which it lost in the United States.[37]

Nevertheless, this rebranding was unlikely to have been the principal cause of the sector's decline, which was largely attributable to decreasing demand. Brooke, meanwhile, accused the nationalists of creating a climate of political instability that discouraged potential investors:

> If he and his friends continue to carry on agitation it creates a sense of uncertainty not only among industrialists in America but in England. They wonder whether it is worth while setting up industries here because in their view - not ours - Northern Ireland may possibly be absorbed into the Free State. Those are things which are very difficult to refute. If the hon. Member, who represents many workers in his area, would only appreciate that point he would realise that in doing what he does he is really harming his own people. I shall not ask him to desist, because that would apparently be a futile and probably a vain thing to do, but it is definitely harming this country by making all the more difficult the job we have of trying to induce industries to come here.[38]

There seemed to be an urgent need to improve the province's image abroad if these leaders were to attract investment. In 1955, Brooke undertook a two-month tour of Australia and New Zealand in an attempt to find opportunities for the linen industry and engineering products. He relied on the influence of three Australian government ministers of Ulster origin[39] to make the case for the province. But, for Ollerenshaw:

> The main problem of Northern Ireland was that whatever publicity machine the government put in place, it could never match those of Dublin or of Irish America.[40]

5.3 Some Businessmen of Good Will

By 1955, unemployment in Northern Ireland had become particularly worrying. It was therefore considered necessary, following consultation between Gwilym Lloyd George, the British Home Secretary, and Brooke, to set up a team whose primary task would be to find ways of overcoming this scourge and to advise the local government on economic development.[41]

The creation of the eight-member Northern Ireland Development Council (NIDC) was announced on 1 November 1955.[42] At his first press conference, Lord Chandos,[43] its chairman, was reassuring. It was true that Northern Ireland had twenty-six thousand unemployed while Britain had full employment. However, the province's unemployment rate had not been this low since 1951.[44] He therefore believed that the problem was not insurmountable provided that British and American companies could be persuaded to locate in Northern Ireland. The province, he argued, had many advantages. It had a willing and loyal workforce. Absenteeism was much lower than in the British workforce. British companies that had moved to Northern Ireland, such as Courtaulds, the Metal Box Company, and Lotus Shoes, were quite satisfied. In addition, the grants and low interest loans that the authorities offered to companies wishing to locate in Northern Ireland were also significant advantages.

At the first NIDC meeting, Chandos spoke of the need for an advertising campaign in North America and of the possibility of recruiting a group of people from Northern Ireland willing to participate in the NIDC's publicity effort in the United States and Canada.[45]

The Northern Ireland Trade Minister and Chandos decided on a small number of volunteers who were willing to help the NIDC.[46] Chandos met them during his trip to the United States at the end of May 1956. The United States Liaison Group was officially established on 1 June 1956. It consisted of seven people,[47] six of whom wished to remain anonymous. Only the name of A. E. Cooper would be released to the press. The group was given the task of considering and advising the NIDC on measures to attract American investment in Northern Ireland. Its members would also be responsible for disseminating information about the province and passing on the names of companies that might consider locating there.

When they met with Chandos, the group advised him against running a publicity campaign in the United States. Instead, they suggested that he contact the banks, as they were often aware of their clients' foreign investment plans. They could present the advantages of the province as part of their advisory work. Other targets of the Liaison Group were the large British consulting firms in the United States,[48] specialising in accountancy, large companies, and business schools.

While in the United States, Chandos met with representatives of the British Trade Promotion Centre and the British Chamber of Commerce and with the Scottish Council, whose mission was to encourage American investors to come to Scotland. Chandos had established friendly relations with the Scottish Council team who had undertaken to pass on the names of contacts that they were not interested in as there were now few opportunities in Scotland for overseas companies.[49] Chandos returned satisfied from his trip, an enthusiasm he shared with the Northern Irish Prime Minister:

> They practically worked me into the ground in the United States, but I was much gratified by the interest displayed by people in the matter. [...] Three enquiries in which, of course, I am most interested in at the moment are Dupont, Chemstrand and Reynolds Metal Company.[50]

In fact, a few weeks later, Dupont announced its decision to set up a production plant in (London)Derry[51] and thus create 1600 jobs. Chemstrand chose Coleraine in the northern part of the province.[52] Chandos also reported the positive impression he had received from the Liaison Group:

> We can count upon this committee for sound advice, and up-to-date knowledge of the American industrial scene, and general supervision of the work of developing our contacts with American industry.[53]

S. C. Leslie, another member of the NIDC, also visited the United States in September 1956. He attended the first meeting of the Liaison Group now known as the US Committee. His trip took him to New York, Washington, and Boston where he met with bankers, editors of major American newspapers, and businessmen. He also made contact with the American foreign trade authorities. While recognising that the latter had less influence on industry and business than the Board of Trade in the United Kingdom, he felt it was important to maintain close relations with the US Department of Commerce, which potential investors sometimes consulted for information. In addition, his various publications had some influence on the American business community. Leslie had heard of the visit to the United Kingdom of Eugene Kaplan, a senior official of the Department of Commerce, and was working to bring him to Northern Ireland.[54]

On his return from the United States, Leslie was convinced that the Scottish Council's approach should be used as a model for the NIDC. Alex Brackenridge, director of the Morton Sundour Company in the United States, who Leslie said was the driving force behind the Scottish Council's campaign, had been very supportive and given him valuable advice on attracting US investment:

> He summed up the secret of their success when he described the Scottish campaign in the United States as 'a heart affair'. They have certainly exploited the prestige of Scotland and the Scottish sentiment of many well-placed figures in the American business world. Northern Ireland has similar resources, perhaps to a greater extent than may be realised.[55]

Firstly, groups of thirty or forty businessmen of Northern Irish origin or well disposed towards the province were to be hand-picked. These would be invited to meetings chaired by a prominent banker or industrialist. Lord Chandos and a number of directors of American companies with operations in Northern Ireland would present its attractions. He had been told that this method was very effective:

> A gathering in New York on these lines arranged on behalf of the Scottish Council, at which the head of the American Burroughs Adding Machine Company described their Scottish operation, was mentioned to me by several different people in New York as a model of the way to influence the minds of American businessmen.[56]

This suggestion had also been made by Ferdinand K. Thun at the US Committee meeting and endorsed by the other members of the group. Indeed, industrial policy in Scotland was proving very popular with American investors.[57] According to an article in the *U.S. Journal of Commerce* on 3 September 1954, twenty-eight large American companies had opened factories in Scotland since the end of World War II, providing employment for ten thousand Scots.[58]

It was therefore envisaged that directors of American companies who had invested in Northern Ireland would be asked to promote the province in business circles across the Atlantic. Northern Irish businessmen with contacts in the United States would be given the same task.

Leslie thought it could be fruitful to make personal contact with potential investors. This method had also been tried and tested by the Scottish Council. Sir Francis E. Evans was approached to be the man for the job. A Belfast-born diplomat, he knew the United States well, having served in New York and Boston for some years.[59] On the verge of retirement, he agreed to meet potential investors on a trip to the United States where he was going for several weeks.

On his arrival in New York in October 1957, a reception was organised by the US Committee at the University Club. The British Consul General was also present. The Scottish Council's advice had been followed to the letter. There were about thirty people at the meeting, some representing companies, others banks and trade associations. Evans spoke to them about the attractions of Northern Ireland. In addition, two people representing Hughes Tool and Berkshire Knitting, American companies based in the province, spoke highly of it.

A few days before Evans' arrival, advertisements extolling the virtues of Northern Ireland appeared in *The New York Times*. According to W.E. Bell, the NIDC secretary who assisted Lord Evans on his trip,[60] enquiries were pouring in, so much so that he spent most of his time answering them, but he admitted that there was little to be gained in terms of investment:

> We have now had almost 300 requests for our literature, about half of these came from individuals, about 90 from manufacturing firms, and the remainder from bankers, investment consultants and public relations experts. We have paid particular attention to the requests from manufacturing firms but only a small number have come from firms well known in American business.[61]

In his report, Bell also praised the contribution of A. E. Cooper, a rare gem, whose help had proved invaluable:

> This report would be incomplete without a special word of thanks to Mr. Cooper, the convener of our U.S. Committee. His enthusiasm in the cause of Northern Ireland defies description. He has spent many hours in arranging our itinerary and in the distribution of our literature to American corporations. There has been a poor response to the direct mail campaigns which he has conducted but we are hoping for better results from the personal visits. Both Sir Francis and I have been particularly impressed by Mr. Cooper's close contact with American bankers and businessmen which seems to extend to every industrial center of any importance in the United States.[62]

After his stay in New York, Evans embarked on a tour of major American cities including Philadelphia, Pittsburgh, Wilmington, Houston, and Chicago, where there was a large community of Scots-Irish origin.[63]

Lord Evans' report to the NIDC on his return was similar to Bells'. The US Committee had been very helpful and was doing a good job of advising and connecting with potential investors. Through its high-level contacts in the business community, the US Committee was able to attract interest.[64] Evans believed that the experience could be replicated in other American cities:

> I would, however, welcome the strengthening of the Committee by the addition of members established in a number of regions outside the metropolitan area. These need not be Ulstermen, though it would naturally be preferable to harness the special sympathy men of Ulster origin might show. [...] The process of building up the Committee will be slow if this pattern is followed, but it would be progressively cumulative in effect. Others appropriate might be bank executives and persons in a position to acquaint us with firms in their areas likely to seek overseas expansion.[65]

In January 1958, Evans handed over to J. V. Morrison who became the permanent representative of the Northern Ireland Department of Trade and Commerce in the United States. Morrison took over much of the work previously done by the US Committee. The group remained at Morrison's disposal for the next two years before being officially disbanded in 1960.

5.4 Northern Ireland: A Province of the United Kingdom

At first, despite the assistance of the US Committee, only a very small number of American investors decided to invest in the province. For H. E. Jones of the Northern Ireland Department of Trade, the problem lay elsewhere:

> Since May 1956, when our American activities started, 22 American firms visited Northern Ireland to investigate the area as a plant location. That only two of these firms decided to establish in Northern Ireland is no reflection on the organisation for making contact - it shows, rather, that in the end it is economic factors which determine the issue.[66]

A. E. Cooper and some of the other members of the US Committee shared this view. They thought that the authorities should, as a matter of priority, rethink and improve the incentives offered to potential American investors. Otherwise, advertising Northern Ireland would be useless.[67] Two reports published in the late 1950s also urged the Northern Irish authorities to take more vigorous action to attract foreign investors. The conclusions of the first of these reports, *An Economic Survey of Northern Ireland*,[68] better known as the Isles and Cuthbert Report, were particularly pessimistic. They were summarised in a memorandum to the Department of Trade and Commerce in the following terms:

> The limited scope for profitable industry in Northern Ireland results in continuously heavier unemployment than in Great Britain. The existence of a higher rate over the last 30 years has not been a passing phase but a persistent condition. If in the United Kingdom the total demand for labour as a whole is great enough to match the labour force, it will generally not be great enough to yield full employment in Northern Ireland and so there will always be a need for special measures.[69]

For Isles and Cuthbert, the province's economy suffered from the combined effect of lack of natural resources, geographical remoteness, and insufficient investment. Because the industrial base was not sufficiently diversified, the skill mix of the workforce was limited. The report advocated attracting outside investment, particularly from large companies, in an attempt to reduce unemployment.

The report by the consultancy firm A. D. Little carried out for the NIDC assessed measures to attract US investors to Northern Ireland. Its findings were not much more encouraging than those of the Isles and Cuthbert report. Since the province had few assets, only a small number of industries would be interested, despite the incentives offered by the authorities. It was advised that a major publicity campaign should be conducted to publicise Northern Ireland in the United States and to emphasise the fact that it was part of the United Kingdom. At that time, Irish labour had a rather poor image with some of them. According to the report, few American industrialists distinguished between the two Irelands[70]:

> One view of several respondents who had little knowledge about Northern Ireland is that 'Irish labor is shiftless and irresponsible'; the inference is that there are no differences between labor in the North and in the Republic.[71]

Although this was not the majority view, according to the consultants, it had been expressed frequently enough which justified that "[…] the historical and ethnic differences between the two peoples should be stressed".[72]

It was also advised to act under the auspices of the British consular services. The Northern Irish authorities took these remarks very seriously and agreed with the report's recommendations. They accepted a joint invitation from the Board of Trade and the Foreign Office to share the office of the British Industrial Development Office (BIDO), a new body charged with attracting investors to the United Kingdom, which was established in February 1960. J. V. Morrison became the Deputy Director of BIDO. This change was very beneficial, as Belfast now had more financial resources and additional staff. Northern Ireland was presented as an integral part of the United Kingdom, which gave it a higher profile. In addition, Northern Irish representatives were allowed to run separate promotional campaigns if they felt it was necessary.[73] In Belfast, the new arrangement was welcomed and the opportunity to penetrate high-profile business circles in the United States through BIDO was welcomed.[74]

The most successful advertising campaigns and outreach took place in New York, California, Pennsylvania, Illinois, Ohio, Texas, and Canada.[75] Most of these states were part of the Manufacturing Belt where there was a large Scots-Irish community. The same was true in Texas and California[76] and in Canada. Although it took a few months for the Northern Irish authorities' efforts to attract American investment to bear fruit, the number of American companies that came to the province and the jobs they created increased dramatically from 1960 until 1968.[77] Indeed, the intensive canvassing efforts of the Northern Irish permanent representatives in the United States were complemented by ministerial missions, including that of Lord Glentoran, the Northern Irish Minister of Trade, who visited Texas, Illinois, and Pennsylvania for four weeks in the autumn of 1960.[78]

5.5 Terence O'Neill Looks to North America

For his part, Terence O'Neill,[79] as Minister of Finance (1956–1963) and later as Prime Minister of Northern Ireland (1963–1969), established contacts with community organisations in North America. He took an interest in the United States, but also in Canada, which had a booming economy and a large Northern Irish community. In his speeches, he was quick to mention the people who had left the province to become part of Canadian or American history. His attitude to emigration was not in any way disapproving or maudlin:

> I would never seek to discourage any individual from working out his personal destiny wherever it may lead him. These movements of people have enriched us all. In Northern Ireland our great linen industry received its critical impetus from the emigration of French Huguenots. Sometimes a transplanted flower blooms with renewed vigour in a different soil.[80]

Furthermore, he encouraged Northern Irish expatriates to integrate into the society where they had settled:

> Now of course I am extremely happy that many of these emigrants to Canada retain happy recollections of the land of their origin [...]. But at the same time I always make it clear that, in my view, the emigrant's first love and loyalty must unquestionably be to the nation with whose fortunes he has linked himself. I want the Ulster people in Canada to be first and foremost good Canadians. Indeed, the best service which they can perform to their kin-folk on the other side of the Atlantic is to show what responsible, productive and loyal citizens they can be. The position of a man coming to a new country is like that of the bridegroom who leaves the family home on marriage. He will, one hopes, never cease to love and respect his parents, but henceforth his primary responsibility must be to his partner. And so, if

an Ulsterman can make a good Canadian, I consider that is as good a way as any of showing his solid Ulster virtues.[81]

But these trips were not mere courtesy visits. After the accolades, O'Neill was pragmatic in making it clear to the Northern Irish diaspora that the province's economy needed foreign investment and welcomed it with open arms:

I also wanted to take the opportunity which such visit affords of obtaining the maximum publicity for our industrial promotion activities. In Canada comparatively little such promotion has been done, since the needs of a rapidly expanding domestic economy demand a very high proportion of local investment. I formed the impression however - and my estimate was confirmed by a number of prominent Canadians - that in the years which lie ahead Canadian business men may consider external investment, including the establishment of branch factories, to a considerably greater extent. In Press interviews, in personal contacts and through public speeches - including one to the influential Canadian Club in Ottawa - I stressed the inducements which Northern Ireland offer.[82]

The overseas visits of Stormont government dignitaries were also intended to neutralise the possible effects on public opinion across the Atlantic of the "border campaign",[83] i.e. the armed operations that the IRA had been conducting along the border between the two Irelands since 1956. Although the loss of life in this latent conflict, largely rural, was limited, it was likely to further tarnish the image of the Stormont regime abroad.

Indeed, the American press was concerned about the fate of political prisoners incarcerated without trial, both north and south of the border. Nationalist MP Cahir Healy was quick to point out the deleterious effects on the province's image abroad and on its economy:

The American Press has of late devoted a great deal of space to this particular question. [...] We have had for some time past representatives in America asking industrialists there to consider Northern Ireland as a venue to which to bring their plant. If we ignore American opinion [...] and even British opinion how can we expect them to pay much deference to the requests of our representatives and deputations that they should establish branches of their huge industries in this country?[84]

For O'Neill, people of Northern Irish descent abroad had to be the voice of the Unionist cause:

> A most valuable role is played, in many parts of the United States and Canada, by local Ulster, Ulster-Irish or Scots-Irish societies, which do a great deal to uphold the cause of Northern Ireland in those countries. I was glad therefore to be able to address the Ulster Associations of Toronto, the Ulster-Irish Society of New York and the Scotch-Irish Society of Pennsylvania.[85]

Despite the bad publicity, Francis E. Evans, Northern Ireland's representative in the United States, was not overly concerned about the economic consequences of the IRA's actions. On his return in 1957, he wrote in his report to the government:

> I am happy to report that in spite of frequent accounts in the American press of 'Irish Republican Army' activity, it seems unlikely to be a deterrent to American investment in Northern Ireland. A few questions were asked about the political situation, but there appeared to be no deep concern about the I.R.A. attacks.[86]

According to Andrew J. Wilson, at that time, the problems of Northern Ireland did not yet have a wide resonance abroad and even the Irish-American community was indifferent. In the 1950s, Irish-Americans, he argues, were mainly concerned with moving up the social ladder and their support for the nationalist cause was in steady decline.[87]

Indeed, the border campaign did not deter foreign investors, as between 1945 and 1968, two hundred and fifty new companies came to Northern Ireland. Most of these were British, but forty were American companies, including Monsanto, Goodyear, and DuPont.[88]

President John Fitzgerald Kennedy was more difficult to convince. Terence O'Neill was keen to maintain good relations with the American authorities. So he invited the US President to visit Northern Ireland during his official trip to Ireland in June 1963. O'Neill, unlike his predecessors, had advocated a more just policy towards the Catholic community in Northern Ireland. Despite this, Kennedy, aware that he could not displease his Irish-American electorate, declined the invitation. O'Neill visited the White House some time later, but was not received by the President, who subsequently declined a further invitation to visit Northern

Ireland. It cannot be ruled out, therefore, that O'Neill's decision to meet with Seán Lemass[89] in January 1965 was motivated, among other reasons, by a desire to project a favourable image abroad, and in the United States in particular. Both leaders, as we shall see, were seeking to attract American investors and this sign of appeasement could pay off in this regard, even if Northern Ireland in fact wanted to continue to go it alone in this sector.[90]

While Northern Ireland used a small group of diaspora businessmen to attract US investment in the mid-1950s, the experiment was short-lived. Its effects were not significant enough for similar groups to be established throughout the United States. It is not clear from the archival records whether, once they started working with BIDO, Northern Irish representatives in the United States sought to target businessmen from Northern Ireland and play on their feelings. One thing is certain, however: American investors did not flock until the image of Northern Ireland became associated with the United Kingdom. The end of the 1950s saw an even more radical shift in economic policy in Ireland, which was also affected by mass unemployment. It was also at this time that the Irish government's desire to harness the influence of the diaspora for the benefit of the country's economy began to take hold. There was less emphasis on persuading Irish-Americans to buy Irish-made goods. Instead, the interest of the Irish authorities in the Irish-American business elite grew.

Notes

1. Philip Ollerenshaw. 2013. Business and Finance, 1780–1945. In *Ulster since 1600: Politics, Economy, and Society*, Liam Kennedy and Philip Ollerenshaw, eds., 180–181. Oxford: Oxford University Press.
2. Ronnie Munck. 1993. *The Irish Economy*. London – Boulder: Pluto Press, 15.
3. Jonathan Bardon. 1992. *A History of Ulster*. Belfast: Blackstaff Press, 456.
4. *Bardon, A History of Ulster*, 182.
5. David S. Johnson. 1985. The Northern Ireland Economy, 1914–1939. In *An Economic History of Ulster, 1820–1945*, Liam Kennedy and Philip Ollerenshaw, eds. 184. Manchester: Manchester University Press,184.
6. Johnson, The Northern Ireland Economy, 184–187.
7. Bardon, *A History of Ulster*, 456–457.
8. Bardon, *A History of Ulster*, 514–515.
9. Sabine Wichert. 1991. *Northern Ireland since 1945*. London—New York: Longman, 23.
10. Bardon, *A History of Ulster*, 516–523.

11. Philip Ollerenshaw. 1996. Businessmen in Northern Ireland and the Imperial Connection, 1886–1939. In '*An Irish Empire?*' *Aspects of Ireland and the British Empire*, ed. Keith Jeffery: 180. Manchester—New York: Manchester University Press.
12. Ollerenshaw. Businessmen in Northern Ireland, 176–182.
13. In 1932, the Parliament of Northern Ireland moved to Parliament Buildings, at Stormont, on the eastern outskirts of the city. "Stormont" came to be a synecdoche referring both to the Parliament itself and to the Northern Ireland government.
14. See, for example, New Ireland Forum. 1983. *The Economic Consequences of the Division of Ireland since 1920*. Dublin: Stationery Office. For a diametrically opposed view, see: Bardon, *A History of Ulster*, 521.
15. Munck, *The Irish Economy*, x.
16. John Bradley. 1999. The History of Economic Development in Ireland, North and South. In *Ireland North and South: Perspectives from Social Science*, proceedings of the British Academy 98, Anthony F. Heath, Richard Breen, and Christopher T. Whelan, eds. 35–68. Oxford: Oxford University Press.
17. Johnson, The Northern Ireland Economy, 188–190; Wichert, *Northern Ireland*, 20.
18. David S. Johnson. 1981. Partition and Cross-Border Trade. In *From Plantation to Partition*, ed. Peter Roebuck: 229–246. Belfast: Blackstaff Press.
19. Valérie Peyronel. 2001. *Économie et conflit en Irlande du Nord*. Paris: Ellipses, 56–58.
20. To the number of unemployed people registered, we must add the thirty thousand not registered. Bardon, *A History of Ulster*, 526.
21. Bardon, *A History of Ulster*, 529.
22. Wichert, *Northern Ireland since 1945*, 23.
23. Bardon, *A History of Ulster*, 529–534.
24. The New Industrial Development Acts of 1932 and 1937 provided 0% loans and subsidies for industrialists wishing to establish themselves in the province.
25. Wichert, *Northern Ireland since 1945*, 22.
26. Munck, *The Irish Economy*, 47–55.
27. In 1945, Great Britain introduced the first family allowances, followed the next year by pension insurance, unemployment insurance, sick leave. and the National Health Service (a public health service guaranteeing free care for all), measures inspired by the Beveridge report.
28. Bardon, *A History of Ulster*, 612–615.
29. Bardon, *A History of Ulster*, 616–617.

30. Wichert, *Northern Ireland since 1945*, 60. See also: Richard T. Harrison. 1986. Industrial Development Policy and the Restructuring of the Northern Ireland Economy. *Environment and Planning C: Politics and Space*, 4, 1: 57. https://doi.org/10.1068/c040053.
31. Civil Authorities (Special Powers) Act (Northern Ireland) 1922.
32. See: Christopher Hewitt. 1983. Discrimination in Northern Ireland: A Rejoinder. *The British Journal of Sociology*, 34, 3: 446–451; https://doi.org/10.2307/590258. Denis O'Hearn. 1983. Catholic Grievances, Catholic Nationalism: A Comment. *The British Journal of Sociology*, 34, 3: 438–445. https://doi.org/10.2307/590257.
33. Martin Melaugh. 1995. Majority - Minority Differentials: Unemployment, Housing and Health. In *Facets of the Conflict in Northern Ireland*, ed. Seamus Dunn: 131–148. New York—Basingstoke: St Martin's Press.
34. Basil Brooke was Prime Minister of Northern Ireland from 1 May 1943 to 26 March 1963. Dictionary of Irish Biography. Basil Brooke. https://www.dib.ie/biography/brooke-basil-stanlake-a0985. Accessed 10 June 2025.
35. Philip Ollerenshaw. 2008. Northern Ireland and the British Empire-Commonwealth, 1923–61. *Irish Historical Studies*, 36, 142: 238–240.
36. Ollerenshaw, Northern Ireland, 238.
37. Northern Ireland, parliamentary debates, Stormont (hereafter Stormont debates), 1 June 1937, 19 (Cahir Healy).
38. Stormont parliamentary debates, 8 March 1950, 34 (Basil Brooke).
39. Ollerenshaw, Northern Ireland, 240.
40. Ollerenshaw, Northern Ireland, 238.
41. "Points from Prime Minister's speech at Reform Club on occasion of Home Secretary's visit, September 1955", PRONI, CAB/9F/188/8.
42. Government announcement, Northern Ireland Development Council, CAB/9F/188/8, Public Record Office of Northern Ireland (hereafter PRONI).
43. Oliver Lyttelton, 1er vicomte Chandos (Lord Chandos) was a World War I hero who later served in various British government departments before turning to a career in business. He was a member of the management team of the British Thomson Houston Company in Northern Ireland.
44. In 1951, the unemployment rate in Northern Ireland was 5.5%. Lord Chandos' statement to a press conference on Monday, 14th November 1955, at Crown House, Aldwich, London, CAB/9F/188/8, PRONI.
45. Minutes of the Northern Ireland Development Council, appendix A, statement by Chairman, 14 November 1955, CAB/9F/188/10, PRONI.
46. Report on publicity, 17 February 1956, CAB/9F/188/10, PRONI.
47. A. E. Cooper, representative of the Ulster Bank/Westminster Bank in the United States;

J. F. Cordner, Lybrand, Ross Bros. & Montgomery; J. V. C. Malcolmson, Texas Company; S. Milligan, Metropolitan Life Insurance Co; Edward W. Stitt, Bannister, Stitt, Holloway & Krauser; William A. Mayberry, Manufacturers' National Bank; Ferdinand K. Thun, Bershire Knitting Mills. Establishment of United States Liaison Group, undated document, CAB/9F/188/10, PRONI.

48. The paper cites Price Waterhouse as an example. Establishment of United States Liaison Group, CAB/9F/188/10.
49. Account of visit of chairman to United States, [June 1956], CAB/9F/188/10, PRONI.
50. Lord Chandos to Basil Brooke, 11 June 1956, CAB/9F/188/8, PRONI.
51. The official name of the city is Londonderry; however, nationalists and most Catholics in Northern Ireland use the name Derry, while Protestant Unionists refer to it as Londonderry, especially when they want to show their community affiliation. That said, the name Derry is used fairly commonly by both communities.
52. Report on publicity, seventh council meeting, 7 January 1957, CAB/9F/188/10, PRONI.
53. Lord Chandos, Report to the Prime Minister from the Northern Ireland Development Council, [November 1956], CAB/9F/188/8, PRONI.
54. S. C. Leslie, Report on America, 17 October 1956, CAB/9F/188/10, PRONI,
55. Leslie, Report on America.
56. Leslie, Report on America.
57. Pavlos Dimitratos, Ioanna Liouka, Duncan Ross, Stephen Young. 2009. The Multinational Enterprise and Subsidiary Evolution: Scotland since 1945. *Business History*, 51, 3: 402–407. https://doi.org/10.1080/00076790902844013.
58. Kevin Rush, Secretary of the Department of External Affairs, to the Secretary of the Department of Industry and Commerce, 12 November 1954, 315/254, National Archives of Ireland (hereafter NAI).
59. S. C. Leslie, United States Campaign: Outline Proposals, December 1956, CAB/9F/188/10, PRONI.
60. For its part, Bell visited Dallas, Milwaukee, Indianapolis, Cleveland and Columbus. Francis E. Evans, Tour of American industry, October–November 1957, Report to the Chairman from Sir Francis Evans, CAB/9F/188/14, PRONI.
61. W. E. Bell, American canvass: report from Mr. Bell, Washington, 11 October 1957, CAB/9F/188/10, PRONI.
62. W. E. Bell, American canvass.

63. Florida Irish Heritage Center. 4 January 2012. Where Are the Irish in America, https://floridairishheritagecenter.wordpress.com/2012/01/04/where-are-the-irish-in-america/. Accessed 4 June 2025.
64. Evans, Tour of American Industry,
65. Evans, Tour of American Industry.
66. H. E. Jones to A. J. Kelly (Offices of the Cabinet), Notes on Lord Chandos proposals, [Autumn 1959], CAB/9F/188/15, PRONI.
67. Promotion in America, note by the Council's sub-committee, undated document, CAB/9F/188/14, PRONI.
68. Keith Sydney Isles, Norman Cuthbert. 1957. *An Economic Survey of Northern Ireland*, Belfast: HMSO.
69. Department of Commerce, Northern Ireland Development Council, an economic survey of Northern Ireland, memorandum by the Ministry of Commerce, 17 October 1957, CAB/9F/188/10, PRONI.
70. It should be noted that the Irish authorities had unofficial access to the findings of this report. Document entitled Notes; the author is a vice-consul but the signature is illegible, 27 June 1961, 315/114/1, NAI. See also: Anne Groutel. 2016. American Janus-Faced Economic Diplomacy towards Ireland in the Mid-1950s. *Irish Economic and Social History*, 43, 1: 17–19. https://doi.org/10.1177/0332489316661066.
71. A program to attract American industry to Northern Ireland, report to Northern Ireland Development Council, Arthur Little Inc., October 15th 1959, 24, CAB/9F/188/17, PRONI.
72. A program to attract American industry to Northern Ireland.
73. Northern Ireland Development Council - 25th meeting - Tuesday, January 10th, 1961, CAB/9F/188/23, PRONI.
74. Northern Ireland Development Council, Note on the progress of the industrial promotion campaign in U.S.A. submitted to the 26th meeting of the council on April 17th, 1961, CAB/9F/188/23, PRONI.
75. The archive file contains the exact count of prospects by state. Report on American Activities - October 1961 to January 21, 1962, CAB/9F/188/23, PRONI.
76. Florida Irish Heritage Center, Where Are the Irish in America.
77. Harrison, Industrial Development Policy, 63. There was also a marked increase in investment from Britain, a trend that began as early as 1945. Harrison, Industrial Development Policy, 63.
78. NIDC, Note on the progress of the industrial promotion campaign in U.S.A. submitted to the 26th meeting of the council on April 17th, 1961, statistical footnote, CAB, 9F/188/23, PRONI.
79. Dictionary of Irish Biography. Terence O'Neill. https://www.dib.ie/biography/oneill-terence-marne-a6940. Accessed 10 June 2025.

80. Terence O'Neill, Ulster's Place in Britain Today, speech to the Empire Club of Canada,
Toronto, 19 October 1967. http://speeches.empireclub.org/60962/data?n=2. Accessed 4 June 2025.
81. O'Neill, Ulster's Place in Britain Today.
82. Stormont debates, 27 October 1959, 45.
83. The border campaign lasted from 12 December 1956 to 26 February 1962.
84. Stormont debates, 18 December 1962, 53.
85. Stormont debates, vol. XLV, 27 October 1959, 45.
86. Evans, Tour of American Industry.
87. Andrew J. Wilson. 1995. *Irish America and the Ulster Conflict, 1968–1995*. Washington: The Catholic University of America Press, 16.
88. Seán Cronin. 1987. *Washington's Irish Policy, 1916–1986: Independence, Partition, Neutrality*. Dublin: Anvil Books, 289.
89. Seán Lemass served as Taoiseach from 23 June 1959 to 10 November 1966.
90. John Horgan. 1997. *Seán Lemass: The Enigmatic Patriot*. Dublin: Gill & Macmillan, 272.

CHAPTER 6

The Republic of Ireland: From Protectionism to Economic Openness (1932–1960s)

In the early 1930s, Fianna Fáil saw economic protectionism as a way to develop an economy independent of Britain and to create enough jobs to stem emigration.[1] For a time, industrial production did increase significantly.[2] But this policy fell short of being a panacea. Firstly, industries, protected from external competition, were not competitive and had little incentive to be. Secondly, once they had reaped the rewards of the "easy phase"[3] of industrialisation by substitution, those who owned the capital in Ireland reinvested the profits in the British financial markets. Finally, although the country now produced many of the products it had previously imported, it still had to import the machinery needed for its industry.[4] John Horgan summed up the results of the policy of import substitution industrialisation in these words:

> Despite his [Lemass'] quite exceptional measures to encourage industrial growth, nascent Irish industry was precisely that: overwhelmingly small in scale and correspondingly vulnerable.[5]

The abandonment of economic protectionism in Ireland has long been presented as a sudden and radical shift following the publication of Thomas Kenneth Whitaker's[6] 1958 report *Economic Development*.[7] This report was undoubtedly the cornerstone of Lemass' economic policy in the years that followed. However, the move to a market economy was not a sudden

A. Groutel, *The Two Irelands and the Diaspora*,
https://doi.org/10.1007/978-3-032-12355-8_6

turnaround, but rather the result of a slow realisation[8] that protectionism had reached its limits.[9]

6.1 The Control of Manufactures Acts: An Embarrassing Sacred Cow

As part of its import substitution industrialisation project, Fianna Fáil, in addition to the various customs barriers it erected to protect the domestic industrial sector, also initiated the Control of Manufactures Acts of 1932 and 1934 which required 51% of the capital of companies to be in Irish ownership.[10] Daniel Morrissey, a member of Fine Gael, was very hostile to this legislation.[11] Once Minister for Industry and Commerce in the First Inter-Party Government (1948–1951), he did not hesitate to travel to New York in search of investors and people with technical knowledge,[12] even though the terms of the Act had not changed one iota. But in doing so he incurred the wrath of Vivian de Valera, Sean McEntee, and Michael Feehan, prominent members of Fianna Fáil, who publicly expressed their opposition to opening up the Irish economy to foreign capital, arguing that it would endanger it.[13]

This being said, there were informal contacts between American business circles and members of the Irish administration, as illustrated, for example, by the record of a meeting that took place on May 24, 1949, between decision-makers from the National City Bank of New York, William Gage Brady Jr., Charles Sheehan, Carl Hayden (from the Bank's London office), and C. Murray (Department of the Taoiseach), Sarsfield Hogan, and T.K. Whitaker from the Department of Finance. Con Cremin from the Department of External Affairs was present, as were the Governor of the Central Bank, the Deputy Governor of the Bank of Ireland, and the Chairman of the Revenue Commissioners.

During the conversation, the Irish-American businessmen voiced complaints about the tax regime in the United States. In their view, the high level of taxation was slowing the accumulation of venture capital. They also expressed concern about political instability and legislation in certain countries that hindered the arrival of foreign investment. Brady stated that American investors wanted to maintain control over the companies in which they invested. The message was therefore clear. If the newly established Industrial Development Authority[14] (IDA)—set up only days earlier—wanted to succeed in attracting American investment, the Control of

Manufactures Acts represented a major impediment. It is worth noting that on this occasion, Brady strongly criticised the nationalisation programme and the implementation of the social security system undertaken in the United Kingdom—a policy he described as "socialist".[15]

Yet it seems that, as early as the late 1930s, Lemass himself had begun to have doubts about the effectiveness of the Control of Manufactures Acts in the field of industrial policy.[16] Indeed, although he opposed the creation of the IDA on behalf of his party in 1949, it was not abolished when Fianna Fáil returned to power in 1951. Although officially no changes were made to the Control of Manufactures Acts, on his official trip to the United States in 1953, Lemass made it clear that American investors were welcome in Ireland provided that they could help to increase the productive capacity of Irish industry or introduce new techniques.[17] Lemass stressed the advantages of Ireland for investors. He argued that the country was geographically close to European markets. In addition, there was a double taxation treaty between Ireland and the United States[18] and the possibility of repatriating capital gains. The labour force in Ireland was plentiful, skilled, and adaptable to modern industrial methods. Finally, Lemass emphasised that the country enjoyed a particularly stable political situation:

> Investment in Ireland is as secure from violent political and social upheavals as in the U.S. We believe that it should be attractive to Americans seeking new outlets for their resources, and they may be assured that if they come to Ireland to participate in Irish industrial expansion they will be heartily welcomed.[19]

William Norton and Seán Lemass were well aware of the shortcomings of Irish industry, the shortage of capital, and the lack of dynamism of local entrepreneurs, and so they came to accept the idea, even though Lemass would not admit it in public, that foreign investors were needed to increase exports.

In late December 1954, Norton, then Minister for Industry and Commerce and Tánaiste, told William H. Taft, the US Ambassador to Ireland, of his determination to attract foreign companies. They would create the jobs and bring the technical know-how that the country needed.[20] Norton added that he took the matter very seriously. As did the Ambassador: "He [Norton] said that he felt as I did, that his predecessor, Mr. Lemass, had approached the problem too generally".[21]

But Taft was somewhat sceptical. Although there were ways of circumventing the law and obtaining exemptions, the Control of Manufactures Acts discouraged foreign investment. A report from the American Embassy in Dublin to the authorities in Washington left no room for doubt: "It is evident that the Act as presently constituted is a definite impediment to foreign investment in Ireland".[22] In a speech to the Association of Certified Accountants in Cork in January 1955, Taft called on the Irish authorities to face up to their responsibilities and repeal the Act: "You are not apt to get capital investment in your own country unless you make concessions to foreigners. By the 51% ownership investors abroad are discouraged".[23]

As a result, in the weeks leading up to Norton's trip to the United States in January 1956, Irish officials prepared a case to answer the questions that American businessmen were bound to ask.[24] A few weeks later, the subject was raised again at a meeting attended by members of the Department of Industry and Commerce, the Department of External Affairs, and the IDA. They felt that if the Minister committed himself to ensuring that all licences were granted for the production of goods for export,[25] this would be a sufficient guarantee.

Archival records show that Norton's initiative to attract foreign investors was unprecedented in its scope. The result was a close working relationship between US Department of Commerce officials and their Irish counterparts, who benefited from their advice and knowledge of US investor expectations in terms of incentives, particularly tax incentives.[26] However, the Irish Minister did not have the political courage to push for the repeal of the Control of Manufactures Acts, and it must be said that the results of these efforts were modest in terms of new foreign investment. However, it should be noted that some important measures were implemented during this period. For example, John A. Costello,[27] the Taoiseach, announced in October 1956 that an exceptional measure would be implemented to promote exports, despite reluctance within the Irish administration. As a result, the Finance Bill passed in 1956 provided for a 50% reduction in taxes on export profits.[28] Economist Frank Barry saw this as a measure designed primarily to attract foreign investors, but Costello did not mention it to avoid the wrath of Fianna Fáil.[29] Unexpectedly, after years in opposition, denouncing Norton's attempts to open up to foreign investment, this political party made a radical change in economic policy. The adoption of Whitaker's report by the Fianna Fáil government endorsed the move away from the protectionism that the party had advocated since its inception. The Control of Manufactures

Acts, the stumbling block to foreign investment, were finally repealed in 1958. Although there was a hiatus of over a year in the process of cooperation between the Irish and US ministries to encourage US investors to locate in Ireland, it resumed in early 1958.[30]

6.2 The Industrial Development Authority's Stranglehold on Foreign Direct Investment Promotion

Daly notes that throughout much of the 1960s, the IDA concentrated on drawing German and Dutch family-run companies to Ireland. The country's abundant labour supply was seen as a key advantage, particularly for West German firms facing significant labour shortages.[31]

However, attracting American investment in Ireland was also one of the main objectives of the Second Inter-Party Government.[32] In 1955, at a working meeting with Taft and Norton, John Leydon, Secretary of the Department of Industry and Commerce, pointed out that many of the leaders of major US companies were of Irish origin.[33] Playing on their attachment to Ireland could be an asset. Ware Adams, the Counsellor for Commercial Affairs at the US Embassy in Dublin, agreed and argued that, although financial considerations were paramount, the importance of this advantage should not be overlooked.

Indeed, in preparation for Norton's official trip to the United States in January 1956, Irish consuls in Boston, New York, Chicago, and San Francisco were asked to establish contacts with Irish-American industrialists who might be interested in the prospect of investing in Ireland.[34] The idea of bringing together a group of high-profile Irish-Americans from the business community was also floated by the US Department of Commerce. Brian Durnin of the Irish Embassy in Washington reported to Jack Molloy, an adviser to the Irish Department of External Affairs, the conversation he had had with an adviser from the US Department of Commerce:

> Mr. Dempsey suggested that one of the things we ought to do if at all possible would be to get a number of interested influential Irish-Americans who would be prepared voluntarily to cooperate with us in our efforts to attract American capital. He stated that this, in fact, is what is being done by the Scottish Council who have a number of American financers [sic], businessmen, etc. who are not paid officials, who meet once or twice a year to discuss ways and means of encouraging American investment in Scottish industries.

> The system works remarkably well according to Mr. Dempsey and imposes little or no burden on those cooperating. The individuals usually have the entrée to the right circles and should the question of investment arise they encourage the inquirers to consider investment in Scotland.[35]

In addition, the Irish Embassy in Washington reported that Mr Horrocopo, Director of the Investment Division of the American Bureau of Foreign Commerce, had spoken about Northern Ireland's efforts to attract US investors:

> Mr. Horrocopo alluded to the visit of Sir Francis and stated that 'Northern Ireland' had attracted a great deal of American investment in the past twelve months. He attributed this, not so much to the climate which had been developed by the Six Counties [sic] authorities, as to the readiness and willingness with which these authorities had accepted the advice and direction they had received from the American authorities. He emphasised the good work which had been done by the 'Northern Ireland' Development Council in New York and asked if anything had been done by the IDA in Dublin to encourage the establishment of a development council for investment in the Twenty-Six Counties.[36]

However, the IDA did not believe that an Irish Council in the United States would be useful because American businessmen were particularly keen to keep their foreign investment intentions confidential. The existence of such a group could undermine the discretion required by potential investors.[37] The idea was therefore discarded, at least temporarily.

6.3 A Growing Focus on the Status and Influence of the Irish Diaspora

At about the same time, the Irish Ambassador in London sent the Department of External Affairs a comprehensive report[38] on the social and economic position and influence of the Irish community in British business circles. Dublin had not commissioned the study from the Ambassador, who apparently did it of his own volition. The survey indicated that the number of Irish immigrants in Britain was around 900,000. However, it was impossible to give even an approximate figure for the number of people of Irish origin who were born in Britain.

The vast majority of the Irish who had migrated to the neighbouring island were employed in manual, low-skilled, or unskilled jobs. They fitted in relatively well with the local population. However, the higher up the social ladder they climbed, the more difficult it was for the Irish to gain acceptance, as they did not have access to the networks of alumni of prestigious British schools. As a result, the Irish in Britain sent their offspring to the "good" schools rather than "the cheaper schools for the Irish", so that they would not face this glass ceiling later on. The ambassador observed that while some Irish people were socially successful, they had not yet reached the pinnacle:

> It is clear [...] that the Irish do not in British domestic politics carry a weight in any way commensurate with their numbers. Nor, at a higher level, are they in a position to bring much influence to bear on the formulation of policy. At this level the influence of what has come to be known as 'the Establishment' is generally admitted to be of great importance [...]. This is a level to which the 'mere' Irish have as yet almost completely failed to penetrate.[39]

Moreover, there were few Irish high-flyers in the business world in Britain and they were thus not to be relied upon to influence the arrival of British investors in Ireland. In any case, the latter were not the first priority target, as reducing Ireland's economic dependence on Britain was always on the agenda.[40]

The Irish Department of External Affairs, however, found the idea of commissioning a report in the same vein in other countries with a significant ethnic Irish community very interesting. On 26 February 1958, Conor Cruise O'Brien sent instructions to Irish ambassadors to do so. Consulates were also to carry out the same exercise in order to have even more accurate information at the local level.[41]

Canada was one of the countries that could be of economic interest to Ireland. Indeed, as early as 1953, Lemass had invited Canadian entrepreneurs interested in investing in Europe to come to Ireland:

> The Canadian economy is expanding so rapidly that it is probable that all Canadian resources, financial and technical, are fully occupied in Canada but if in the future any Canadian business interests should consider that in Ireland, because of any special conditions prevailing there, or because of its geographical position in relation to European markets, there is scope for Canadian enterprise, they may feel certain they will be warmly welcomed in the expectation that closer commercial relations between the two countries will be mutually beneficial.[42]

A report[43] by T. J. Kiernan, the Irish ambassador in Ottawa, on the situation of the Irish in Canada reached the Secretary of the Department of External Affairs at the end of June 1958. It stated that 1.4 million Canadians had roots in Ireland. However, while the Irish-Canadian community represented 24.3% of the total population in 1871, by 1951 it had shrunk to a fraction.[44] Furthermore, the author of the report estimated that people of Protestant origin from Northern Ireland[45] made up about 70% of this group. This, it was pointed out, was in this respect different from the United States, Australia, or even Wales and England. However, it was expected that the gap would close. Indeed, since the early 1950s, the number of immigrants from the Republic of Ireland had surpassed[46] those from Northern Ireland.

Most of the emigrants from the island of Ireland were recruited in the construction sector or in industry where they worked in low-skilled jobs. However, a significant proportion of the new arrivals worked in clerical jobs and among the skilled were nurses, teachers, and engineers.

T. J. Kiernan also noted that, unlike the non-English-speaking ethnic minorities, the native Irish community had little interest in becoming involved in politics and consequently had little representation in institutions.[47]

As for the interest of Irish-Canadians in the homeland of their ancestors, it seems to have been very limited: "The Irish-origin Canadians are, in general, not interested in Ireland. They are poorly informed, and even the best informed are inclined to limit their interest to the Ireland of Yeats and the Irish Literary Renaissance".[48] According to Kiernan, even recent immigrants cared little about Ireland. The speed with which they were assimilated into the Canadian population and the absence of any contact with Ireland could, according to the ambassador, explain this. He concluded that there was little or no sense of an "Irish" identity within the Irish-Canadian community.

He also noted that Irish-Canadians did not seek to meet in associations or clubs. This, he said, was due to the lack of effort on the part of the Irish authorities to help the few existing associations to develop.

Kiernan had been ambassador to Australia before being transferred to Canada. In this report, he refers several times to Australia where the sense of identity of the Irish community was strong. Visits by Irish politicians such as John Redmonds, Joseph Devlin, and Michael Davitt, who had gone there to raise funds for the Irish cause, had helped to maintain these links. Kiernan lamented the lack of political will to cultivate a sense of identity in the Irish-Canadian community:

> The lesson to be learnt from this is that while no quick results should be expected from action taken to develop an understanding of Ireland in Canada, the long-term results of action can be profound and lasting. Unfortunately, such action calls for mental and physical energy; an alert continuation of policy. The lethargy which has characterized the Department's attitude to such activities in the past is paralleled by the indifference to Ireland which is the most noticeable feature of the Irish-born people who have come to settle in Canada.[49]

In another document,[50] the Ambassador made concrete proposals to address the weakening of ties between Ireland and the Irish abroad. He suggested that a visit by the President of Ireland could bring renewed attention to the country. It was also important to use television and radio to broadcast information and documentaries about Ireland. Materials should also be provided to schools that requested them. In order to take advantage, as much as possible, of even the small interest in the ancestral homeland, Kiernan suggested that the St Patrick's Day celebrations be used to promote tourism and trade between the two countries,[51] as the St Patrick's Day parades were jointly organised by Catholic and Protestant organisations in many cities across Canada.[52]

John M. Conway, the Irish Consul in New York, sent his report to the Department on 27 June 1958. He wrote his study in collaboration with a certain Eamonn Gallagher. Both shared a pessimistic view of Irish influence in the United States:

> We had many discussions on the contents, opinions and conclusions of the report and found that our varied experiences, over twenty-three years in my case and eight years in Gallagher's case, led us to the unhappy belief that our vaunted 'spiritual empire' is no longer an effective force in our behalf in these parts.[53]

In their comprehensive report, the authors dealt separately with the situation of Irish immigrants in the United States and that of Irish-Americans. While some Irish politicians liked to talk about all the goodwill that existed across the Atlantic towards Ireland, this report set the record straight.

Firstly, the number of Irish expatriates to the United States was decreasing and therefore the influence of this group alone was not to be relied upon. The report noted that although the proportion of skilled or highly skilled Irish arriving after World War II was higher than before, most immigrants were low-skilled or unskilled.

In this consular area, many Irish immigrants attended county clubs or societies. However, there were few white-collar workers among their members. As a result, they had little influence in the economic, political, and social sphere. In addition, they tended to support the IRA's border campaign, which the Irish authorities disapproved of.

In contrast, Irish-Americans[54] had risen up the social ladder over the generations and now occupied a very enviable place in American society. They were to be found in the upper echelons of finance, banking, industry, and the media. Some of them held high-profile positions in the political world. There were indeed many Irish-Americans in Congress and among the governors, which, on the face of it, boded well. But Conway and Gallagher were very cautious about the benefits that could be achieved:

> We are fortunate in having a number of individuals, in Congress and elsewhere, who will grant us more than a casual hearing. It would be a mistake to expect too much of them as they cannot be expected to feel under any obligation to submerge their American interests to ours.[55]

Both men were equally pessimistic about the chances of enlisting the help of the Irish-American business elite and exploiting it for Ireland's benefit:

> We have social contacts with Irish-Americans in the financial field. With one or two exceptions, however, we have generally found that their interest in Ireland is limited to a sentimental regard for their ancestry, which does not involve financial expenditure. They might, however, be attracted to us if social cachet were provided. [...] the number who have any interest in Ireland is extremely small and principally because our economic importance to them is so negligible.[56]

Indeed, the agency charged with attracting foreign investment to Ireland did not seem to have been very successful with Irish-American businessmen either:

> The Industrial Development Authority is also aware of the fact that Irish-born residents and Irish-Americans are not inclined to show any particular enthusiasm for Ireland merely because of their racial background. Irish-Americans undoubtedly represent tremendous economic power but such power is neither concentrated enough nor 'Irish' enough to risk very much for Ireland's benefit.[57]

Regarding market opportunities for Irish products, the outlook was equally unpromising. Although Irish immigrants were the main buyers of bacon and tea from Ireland, overall Córas Tráchtála Teoranta found the results of its efforts with the population of Irish descent disappointing. The agency had been assisted by Irish-American organisations such as the Ancient Order of Hibernians,[58] which had advertised Urney chocolates to its members in New York State, but only about thirty orders had resulted. The authors of the report concluded that Irish immigrants and Irish-Americans were, in general, not particularly interested in Irish products. This stark insight left little hope of using the influence of the diaspora for the benefit of the Irish economy. Its links with Ireland were weakening, a process that was becoming irreversible:

> Our influence in the United States is a function of the amount of interest Irish-Americans have in Ireland, rather than being 'Irish'. [...] It is remarkable the extent to which being 'Irish' does not involve any particular enthusiasm for, or even interest in, Ireland. [...] We, ourselves, have done little to avert the decline of Irish-American interest in us. There continues, of course, a natural race relationship. I feel, however, that our contact with Irish-Americans is so limited that we are in danger of losing any real connection with them.[59]

A fourth report focusing on the city of Philadelphia corroborated Conway and Gallagher's findings.[60] Edward Lee, the author of this paper commissioned by the Irish ambassador to the United States, made the following observation:

> There were two difficulties, the onetime settlements no longer exist and it is impossible to judge the extent to which the inevitable 'melting pot' has eradicated the 'Irish-ness' [sic] of the second and later generations. Friendliness for Ireland is universal but there is none of the identification which characterised the Irish community in Britain in which I was born. In speaking of our race we used the first person, the Irish-American refers to Ireland and the Irish as 'it' and 'them'.[61]

Not all Irish consulates in the United States responded to Conor Cruise O'Brien's appeal. Boston, San Francisco, and Chicago were dragging their feet and had not yet sent their study in 1961. The Department pressed them again. This extract from a letter to the Irish Ambassador to the United States clearly shows the link between the new economic policy in Ireland and Dublin's strong interest in the Irish-American community:

> As the present time, because of the efforts made to promote a better 'image' of Ireland in the United States and the various proposals which are being considered by this department with a view to furthering the aims of the programme for economic expansion,[62] the matter has assumed a new significance. In connection with these proposals, it is now essential that we have here a clearer picture of the political, economic and social standing of the Irish in the United States so we may be aware of their potentialities.[63]

If the Irish authorities were to take advantage of the social position held by some Irish-Americans, it was urgent, above all else, to revive their interest in Ireland. So it was decided to set up an organisation for this purpose. There was, however, much hesitation about the scope of the project. Should it be economic, as Whitaker had envisaged,[64] or more cultural, like the Scandinavian-American Foundation, as T. J. Kiernan had suggested?[65] Dublin decided to play on both fronts. On the one hand, the American Irish Foundation would promote relations between Ireland and the United States in the cultural, intellectual, literary, scientific, and educational fields by sponsoring exchanges of university professors, teachers, students, and artists and by awarding scholarships.[66] On the other hand, the Ireland-United States Council for Industry and Commerce Incorporated (IUSCICI) would be responsible for fostering economic relations between the two countries. Much publicity surrounded the plan to create the American Irish Foundation, announced during John Fitzgerald Kennedy's visit to Ireland in June 1963. However, the creation of IUSCICI in September 1962 was a low-key affair.

Notes

1. Ronnie Munck. 1993. The Irish Economy, London—Boulder, Pluto Press, 29–30.
2. From 1932 to 1939, production increased by 7.3% per year. Denis O'Hearn. 2001. The Atlantic Economy: Britain, the US and Ireland. Manchester: Manchester University Press, 118.

3. The initial phase in which industry protected from external competition produces basic goods for the domestic market. Ibid., 119.
4. O'Hearn, The Atlantic Economy, 118–119.
5. John Horgan. 1997. Seán Lemass: The Enigmatic Patriot, Dublin, Gill & Macmillan, 119.
6. Thomas Kenneth Whitaker (1916–2017) was a prominent figure in Ireland, known for his roles as an economist, politician, diplomat, and civil servant. He served as the Secretary of the Department of Finance from 1956 to 1969 and later as the Governor of the Central Bank of Ireland from 1969 to 1976. Additionally, he was a senator from 1977 to 1982, appointed by the Taoiseach. Whitaker is widely regarded as one of the most impactful civil servants in the history of the Irish State, with his economic policies playing a crucial role in shaping modern Ireland.
7. Thomas Kenneth Whitaker. 1958. Economic Development, Dublin, Stationery Office. Whitaker was Secretary of the Department of Finance.
8. Andy Bielenberg, Raymond Ryan. 2016. An Economic History of Ireland since Independence, London—New York, Routledge, 21–22.
9. See: Denis O'Hearn, The Atlantic Economy, 117–124.
10. Mary E. Daly. 1984. An Irish-Ireland for Business: The Control of Manufactures Acts, 1932 and 1934. Irish Historical Studies 24, 94, 246–272. doi:10.1017/S0021121400034672
11. Ireland, parliamentary debates, Houses of the Oireachtas, Dáil Éireann (hereafter Dáil Éireann debates), vol. 42, no. 10, 15 June 1932.
12. U.S.-Trained Technicians Needed for Irish Industry. 1949. The Irish Times, 4 January.
13. The future development and control of Irish industry, report prepared by John Patrick Walsh, 15 August 1949, RG 469, Europe Ireland Division, Deputy Director for Operations, Office of European Operations, subject files 1948–1953, box 2, despatch no 147, National Archives and Records Administration at College Park, MD, United States of America (hereafter NARA).
14. The Industrial Development Authority is the agency responsible for attracting foreign investment to Ireland. On the establishment of this agency, see: Frank Barry, Mícheál Ó Fathartaigh. 2015. The Industrial Authority, 1949–58: Establishment, Evolution and Expansion of Influence. Irish Historical Studies 39, 155: 460–478. doi:10.1017/ihs.2014.4
15. Anne Groutel. Autumn 2003. L'économie irlandaise et le spectre de la non-conquête. Sources, revue d'études anglophones, 15: 978.
16. Horgan, Seán Lemass, 91.
17. However, when he returned to the Opposition benches in 1954, Lemass did an about-face and continued to obstruct his successor when he, in turn, sought to attract foreign investment to Ireland. Horgan, Seán

Lemass, 167; Anne Groutel. 2016. American Janus-Faced Economic Diplomacy towards Ireland in the Mid-1950s. Irish Economic and Social History 43, 1: 13. https://doi.org/10.1177/0332489316661066

18. A double taxation agreement is a treaty between two countries for the avoidance of double taxation of persons and companies.
19. Address by Mr. Seán Lemass, T. D., Tánaiste and Minister for Industry and Commerce, to Commerce and Industry Association, New York, October 5th, 1953, 436/35, National Archives of Ireland (hereafter NAI).
20. Irish Government's Attitude towards Private American Industrial Investment in Ireland, Memorandum from the US Embassy in Dublin to the Department of State in Washington, 6 January 1955, RG 59, file 811.051 40A/1–655 HBS, 1954–1959, Foreign Service Dispatch, dispatch no. 220, NARA.
21. Irish Government's Attitude towards Private American Industrial Investment.
22. The future development and control of Irish industry, report prepared by John Patrick Walsh, 15 August 1949.
23. William H. Taft quoted in: Attracting American Investors to Irish Industry. 1955. The Irish Times, 19 January.
24. Memorandum, signed T. O'M. [T. O'Muireadhaigh], 1 June 1955, 305/57/97/1, NAI.
25. Report of meeting, signed J. Murray, 20 June 1955, 305/57/97/1, NAI.
26. Anne Groutel, American Janus-Faced Economic Diplomacy, 5–11.
27. Dictionary of Irish Biography. John A. Costello. https://www.dib.ie/biography/costello-john-aloysius-a2080. Accessed 10 June 2025.
28. Frank Barry. 2011. Foreign Investment and the Politics of Export Profits Tax Relief 1956. Irish Economic and Social History 38, 2011, pp. 60–64. http://www.jstor.org/stable/24338905
29. Barry, Foreign Investment, 67.
30. John J. Hearne, Irish Ambassador to Washington, to Cornelius Cremin, Secretary of the Department of External Affairs, 11 March 1958, 315/59/343/12, NAI.
31. Mary E. Daly. 2016. Sixties Ireland, Reshaping the Economy, State and Society, 1957–1973. Dublin: Cambridge University Press, 73.
32. Groutel, American Janus-Faced Economic Diplomacy. The Second Inter-Party Government (2 June 1954–20 March 1957) was a minority government of Fine Gael, the Labour Party and Clann na Talmhan.
33. Report of meeting, 23 January 1955, 315/59/343/1, NAI.
34. Memorandum, signed T. O'M. [T. O'Muireadhaigh], 1 June 1955; Report of meeting, signed J. Murray, 20 June 1955.
35. Brian Durnin to Jack Molloy, 5 August 1955, 315/254, NAI.

36. Brian Durnin to Secretary of the Department of External Affairs, 17 October 1957, 315/254, NAI.
37. Cornelius Cremin, Secretary of the Department of External Affairs, to John J. Hearne, Irish Ambassador to Washington, 17 May 1958, confidential letter, 315/59/343/12, NAI.
38. The Irish in Britain and some observations on Anglo-Irish Relations, report PR 7/58, marked confidential, from the Irish Ambassador in London to the Department of External Affairs, 29 January 1958, P115/I, UCD Archives, University College Dublin, Ireland (hereafter UCDA). This report is unsigned, but its author is most likely Cornelius Cremin who left his post as Irish Ambassador in London at the end of January 1958 to become Secretary of the Department of External Affairs.
39. The Irish in Britain and some observations on Anglo-Irish Relations.
40. In contrast, British tourists were welcome.
41. Conor Cruise O'Brien to Irish Ambassadors, 26 February 1958, P115/I, UCDA.
42. Foreign investment in Ireland, extracts from speeches by Mr Lemass, Ottawa Canadian Club, 25 September 1953, 2850B, NAI.
43. T. J. Kiernan, The Irish in Canada, report to the Secretary of the Department of External Affairs, 30 June 1958, 338/86/1, NAI.
44. The Irish community now represented only 10.3% of the Canadian population. Kiernan, The Irish in Canada.
45. These were members of the United Church of Canada (34.2%), Presbyterians (8.1%), Baptists (3.6%), Lutherans (0.6%), and members of various other churches (3.6%). Kiernan, The Irish in Canada.
46. The author estimated that 7500 people came to Canada from the Republic of Ireland in 1957 and 6800 from Northern Ireland. T. J. Kiernan, The Irish in Canada.
47. Montreal, however, was an exception. Although the Irish community represented only 6% of the city's population, it had significant political influence at the local level. Well-educated people of Irish descent held positions in the city's administration, the police, and the judiciary. T. J. Kiernan, The Irish in Montreal, report to the Secretary of the Department of External Affairs, 1 May 1959, 338/86/1, NAI.
48. Kiernan, The Irish in Canada.
49. Kiernan, The Irish in Canada.
50. T. J. Kiernan to Secretary of the Department of External Affairs, 13 November 1958, confidential letter, 338/86/1, NAI.
51. Kiernan, The Irish in Montreal.
52. Kiernan, The Irish in Canada.

53. John M. Conway, with Eamonn Gallagher, The Irish in the United States, New York consular area, report to Cornelius Cremin, Secretary of the Department of External Affairs, 27 June 1958, 338/86/1, NAI.
54. According to the authors of this report, approximately twenty-nine million Americans had Irish blood, about fifteen million were Catholic, nine million were Scots-Irish (i.e. Protestant) and five million were of a religion other than Catholic. Conway and Gallagher noted that the latter had few organisations to fall back on, so they tended to lose their Irish identity. Conway, Gallagher, The Irish in the United States, New York consular area.
55. Conway, Gallagher, The Irish in the United States, New York consular area.
56. Conway, Gallagher, The Irish in the United States, New York consular area.
57. Conway, Gallagher, The Irish in the United States, New York consular area.
58. The Ancient Order of Hibernians (1836–) is the oldest and largest Irish-Catholic organisation in the United States.
59. Conway, Gallagher, The Irish in the United States, New York consular area.
60. Edward Lee, The Irish in Philadelphia, report to T. J. Kiernan, 26 April 1961, P115/I, NAI.
61. Lee, The Irish in Philadelphia. This report was sent to Dublin.
62. The white paper First Programme for Economic Expansion (1958) followed Thomas Kenneth Whitaker's report Economic Development.
63. Seán S. Ronan, Assistant Secretary of the Department of External Affairs to T. J. Kiernan, Irish Ambassador to the United States, 26 April 1961, P115/I, NAI.
64. Proposed American Irish Foundation, [1962?], 338/76 I, NAI.
65. Letter to Miss Murphy [signature illegible], 13 August 1962, 338/76 I, NAI.
66. Dáil Éireann Debates, 16 July 1963, 204, 7.

CHAPTER 7

Formalising the Links With the Irish-American Business Elite in the 1960s

7.1 Forging Economic Ties: The Long Road to the Ireland–United States Council for Industry and Commerce

In January 1958, as Ireland embarked on the road to economic openness, Bernard B. Smith, legal advisor to Córas Tráchtála Teoranta in New York, drew the attention of Seán Lemass to the urgent need to enlist the support of influential Irish-Americans in political and economic spheres, who could advocate for Irish interests with the US authorities. The absence of such a lobby had seriously harmed the interests of Irish exporters during the public hearings, after which the quotas and tariffs on wool and worsted were altered by the US authorities. Smith proposed the creation of a small group of high-calibre American businessmen to act as a lobby for Irish trade interests. Its members would be given free rein to encourage investment and help promote tourism and imports of Irish products into the United States.[1]

The Ambassador, the Irish Consul General in the United States, and a representative of External Affairs welcomed the proposal. Vigilance was nevertheless required. Córas Tráchtála Teoranta and Seán MacEntee,[2] the Tánaiste, felt it was essential to keep Irish-American clubs and associations away from such a project, as their activities were often politically motivated. Smith assured that members would be carefully selected from business circles only.

A. Groutel, *The Two Irelands and the Diaspora*,
https://doi.org/10.1007/978-3-032-12355-8_7

Bord Fáilte[3] and Córas Tráchtála Teoranta were asked to draw up a list of eligible persons, knowing that the group would consist of no more than five or six people. The implementation of this project stalled for some years. In a memorandum dated January 1962, which records a meeting between Smith and John (Jack) Lynch,[4] the Irish Minister for Industry and Commerce, there was no longer any question of a board, as Smith had originally envisaged, but of a chamber of commerce that would be "[…] constituted by the right type of people which would serve the interests of Ireland and which would be indirectly under the control, and carry out the wishes, of the Irish Government".[5] Getting the "right type of people" was not an issue, according to Smith. "The main problem would be to select the people whose names were important enough to give the project weight and who would at the same time take an active interest and forward the objects of the chamber".[6]

Smith warned the Minister that action was urgently needed. The Irish economy was starting to flourish and there was nothing to stop anyone from setting up a chamber of commerce. It was therefore necessary to discourage any inclination in this direction in order to keep control of the situation. In addition, the prospect of the Kennedy Round, the sixth round of negotiations under the General Agreement on Tariffs and Trade (GATT), due to be launched in 1964, reinforced the urgency of creating a group to represent Irish interests.[7]

In the end, the establishment of a council was preferred to that of a chamber of commerce. The existence of the Ireland–United States Council for Industry and Commerce Incorporated (IUSCICI) was officially registered with the US government in New York on 17 September 1962.[8] However, its composition had not yet been finalised. Smith and Henry A. J. Ralph, vice-president of the Bank of America, were still trying to recruit leaders of major US companies from the twenty-two names selected by Córas Tráchtála.[9] Lynch and Ralph worked closely together in the months that followed. It was agreed that, in order not to overshadow the American Irish Foundation on a national level, the group's reach would initially be limited to New York.[10]

On 11 October 1963, the launch of IUSCICI was discussed at a luncheon attended by the Irish Minister for Industry and Commerce, several members of Córas Tráchtála, John L. Burke, President of B. Altman & Co. and John Maguire, President of John P. Maguire & Co, Inc. Maguire and Burke were very enthusiastic. The latter was of the opinion that the

IUSCICI would be very useful in promoting FDI in Ireland and giving "[...] a more truthful and realistic picture"[11] of the country.

The number of founding members eventually rose to eighteen.[12] While Irish descent was not a prerequisite, it is notable that the majority of members had Irish-sounding surnames. The organisation was officially inaugurated on 19 May 1964, at the St Regis Hotel in New York, in the presence of the Irish Minister for Industry and Commerce. John D. J. Moore, vice-president of W. R. Grace & Co. was the president of this council. Its members were hand-picked leaders of very large companies. Among them were the presidents of some of the most famous department stores in the United States such as B. Altman & Co.[13] and Lord & Taylor, founded in 1826, the oldest department store chain in the United States.

The IUSCICI was also composed of leading bankers,[14] industrialists,[15] and directors of publishing houses.[16] All of them expressed their willingness to help Ireland's economic development. Indeed, even before the official launch of IUSCICI, some of them,[17] such as John Galvin, director of the World Trade Center, had been working with the Irish authorities to promote the inflow of American investment into Ireland, a policy that had been approved at the highest level in the United States.[18]

7.2 Lemass in the United States: A Successful Charm Offensive

John Fitzgerald Kennedy visited Ireland in June 1963. This official visit by the first Catholic American President of Irish descent went straight to the heart of the Irish. This was followed by Lemass' visit to the United States at the end of October 1963. This political rapprochement served both Kennedy's electoral aims[19] and the ambitions of the Irish authorities who hoped to reap economic benefits. Kennedy had, according to Lemass, expressed the belief that the flow of American investment in Irish industry would increase as the country's economic situation improved.[20] Indeed, Kennedy's visit helped to raise American investor interest in Ireland.[21]

During his ten-day official visit to the United States, Lemass, for his part, made a point of highlighting the advantages his country offered to American investors in every speech he made. By this time, Ireland had overcome its ideological objections to the European Common Market.[22] Like the United Kingdom, it had already applied for membership in 1961. De Gaulle, however, vetoed the United Kingdom's entry because he felt it was too close to the United States. This decision conditioned the position of Ireland, whose economy was still closely linked to the British one.

But, according to the Treaty of Rome, on 1 January 1966, there was to be a third stage of the transitional period in which the voting arrangements in the Council of Ministers were to change.[23] In other words, unanimity would no longer be required to allow the entry of new members into the organisation.[24] Lemass tried hard to convince Irish-American captains of industry to participate in his government's efforts to attract investors, as Ireland's entry into the common market was now close, or so he thought.

At a dinner hosted by the Joint Irish Societies in Boston, he paid tribute to President Kennedy's visit to Ireland. For him, the enthusiasm it had generated was "the evidence of a re-awakening of deeply-seated feelings between Ireland and the Irish race abroad".[25] But it was now up to the Irish diaspora to maintain the memory of their roots: "This is not quite the same as tourism, which is really concerned with the passing of holidays. I am thinking of you re-establishing permanent connections with your own people in Ireland, studying history, knowing your culture and art etc."[26] The American Irish Foundation could help to maintain this connection, of course, but he added there were many other ways to achieve this:

> And as you are businessmen a connection with Ireland could be both pleasurable and profitable. [...] The mention of business-men brings to my mind that vast body of Americans of Irish ancestry who figure so largely in the business and industry of the new England states. For them I feel sure that the opportunities for successful development and expansion nowadays available in Ireland would complement, in a very satisfying way, a happy reunion with the land of their ancestors.[27]

Lemass was invited to a reception hosted by Peter Grace, president of W. R. Grace and Co., at the prestigious Links Club in New York. W. R. Grace was a multinational company with a wide range of activities, from banking to shipping, airlines, the chemical industry, and food processing. The company employed forty-five thousand people worldwide. Grace had inherited the company from his ancestor, William Russel Grace, who left Ireland for Peru during the Great Famine. He made his fortune in shipping in South America and then in the United States. He later became the first Catholic mayor of New York City.[28] W. R. Grace's vice-president, John D. J. Moore, was also of Irish origin.[29]

Grace planned to invite some forty people, most of whom had Irish-sounding names,[30] the ultimate in American business, as revealed in this excerpt from a letter from Moore to the Irish consul in New York who was actively involved in organising the event:

> We will probably invite the heads of the leading banks in New York, i.e. David Rockefeller,[31] George Moore,[32] Hap Flannigan[33] etc. and perhaps some investment bankers from top firms, such as Morgan Stanley, Merrill Lynch, etc. I suppose we will invite the heads of leading companies already established in Ireland, such as Standard Pressed Steel and others, but I suppose the most important category for the Irish Government's purposes would be the heads of prominent companies who are live prospects.[34]

Peter Grace clearly intended to give the Taoiseach the benefit of his address book and to open doors to circles that were difficult to access. A member of the very exclusive Links Club,[35] Grace had high-level connections in finance, industry, and politics. At this reception, he was apparently impressed by Lemass who spoke eloquently, without any notes, about the progress of the Irish economy and his awareness that only increased productivity could lead to a higher standard of living.[36] Some industrialists already established in Ireland corroborated Lemass' assertion when he spoke of the advantages offered to investors and the adaptability of the Irish workforce.[37]

The 1960s also witnessed the emergence of a small but influential group of dynamic Irish businessmen, some of whom played a pivotal role in forging stronger economic ties between Ireland and the United States. Brendan O'Regan, then serving as catering comptroller at Shannon Airport, was among those who participated in one of the ECA's familiarisation tours of the American hotel and leisure industry. During this trip, he met Conrad Hilton, a formative encounter that left a lasting impression.[38] From that moment on, O'Regan became an ardent admirer of the American model, deeply inspired by the energy, efficiency, and entrepreneurial spirit he encountered.[39] His time in the United States significantly shaped his thinking and provided him with a clear vision for transforming Irish tourism to appeal to American visitors. His biography provides a detailed account of his instrumental role in modernising the Irish tourism sector. Among his many achievements were the establishment of Shannon

College of Hotel Management, the first institution of its kind in Ireland, and the launch of the world's first duty-free airport store.[40] In 1957, Seán Lemass appointed O'Regan as chairman of Bord Fáilte Éireann, a position he would hold for sixteen years. In 1961, he successfully led the creation of Ireland's only regional development agency, the Shannon Free Airport Development Company, which went on to establish the Shannon Free Zone, the first of its kind globally.[41] By the early 1960s, Lemass and O'Regan had become closely aligned in their vision. They shared the conviction that strengthening ties with Irish America could bring a dual benefit: increasing tourism and attracting investment. O'Regan played a key role in drawing wealthy Irish-American businessmen to Ireland, some of whom went on to invest successfully in both the hospitality and industrial sectors, particularly in the west of the country. Notably, Bernard P. McDonough was persuaded to invest in Irish hotels, while Howard Thomas Hallowell, chairman of the Standard Pressed Steel Company in Pennsylvania, was one of the first to establish a factory in Shannon. Both men would go on to join the influential IUSCICI.[42]

7.3 Strategic Hospitality: The Power of Influence in Ireland's Investment Drive

The Irish authorities forged a close working relationship with IUSCICI and soon realised that it could be useful to stroke the egos of these important allies. As a result, the members of the group, along with their spouses, were invited to visit Ireland. Their acquaintances, looking for countries to invest in, were also welcome. To show what could be achieved in Ireland, a tour was organised of the production facilities of American companies located there.[43] The group stayed for three days at Dromoland Castle, a castle converted into a luxury hotel by one of their number, Bernard P. McDonough.

In return, IUSCICI members were expected to give evidence of their positive experience in Ireland. One of them, John A. Mulcahy,[44] having made his fortune in the United States, had invested in a factory in Cork and planned to go into mining in Kilkenny. He also intended to open a new factory in his home town of Dungarvan. When interviewed by *The Irish Times* while in Ireland, he said: "The Irish worker and the attitude of the Government towards foreign industrialists whereby they create a favourable climate is one of the best in the world".[45] Howard Thomas

Hallowell, chief executive of the Standard Pressed Steel Company, which owned a plant in Shannon employing four hundred and fifty people, agreed. He expressed his satisfaction with his investment and commended the Irish government for its unwavering support of foreign investors. In fact, he was on the verge of opening a new factory in Galway.[46]

Finally, the group was received with pomp and circumstance by Jack Lynch,[47] who had succeeded Lemass as Taoiseach, and, to complete the picture, by the President of Ireland himself, Éamon de Valera. John D. J. Moore's family were well acquainted with him. The latter, who was not accustomed to receiving groups of this size, agreed to make an exception.[48] John M. Conway, the Irish consul in New York, in his report on the Irish-American community, had stressed the importance of bringing a note of prestige to capture the attention of Irish-Americans.[49] Clearly, being received by the president was an honour designed to flatter potential investors. In addition, the opportunity to have direct contact with those at the top of the state was an asset for those businessmen who were well versed in the practice of influencing and pressuring state authorities.

For the Irish authorities, such visits had clear advantages. These visitors shared with them their impressions as businessmen and their suggestions. Some of them were delighted with their visit and decided very quickly to do business in Ireland. Tim Deegan, vice-president of Interpublic Inc., wrote directly to Jack Lynch expressing his gratitude and his intention to market Irish whiskey in the United States, just a few days after returning from his stay in the island.[50] Finally, these captains of industry, once they returned to the United States, acted as ambassadors for Ireland.[51] It was therefore decided to repeat the experience every two or three years.

IUSCICI members forged close links with successive Taoisigh of all political affiliations. In April 1973, Howard Thomas Hallowell, the group's president, contacted Liam Cosgrave,[52] the newly appointed Taoiseach leading a Fine Gael-Labour coalition. Until then, the IUSCICI had only dealt with Fianna Fáil governments, but Hallowell assured the Taoiseach that he could count on the group's support:

> At the assumption of your new responsibilities as Prime Minister of Ireland, I would like you to know that Ireland has an organization which is dedicated to furthering the efforts of industry and commerce in that good country of yours. The Ireland-United States Council for Commerce and Industry, of which I am president, is made up of a fine group of people in our country who have a mutual interest in the business activities of both our good coun-

> tries. The members of the Council are dedicated people of substantial stature who will go out of their way at any time and in any way to see that the industrial and economic objectives for which you are striving to achieve are met.[53]

John A. Mulcahy,[54] who had helped finance Richard Nixon's 1969 election campaign, told Dan Scully,[55] the director of Córas Tráchtála in the United States, that during a recent high-level visit to Washington he had spoken highly of the new Taoiseach and his government. He assured him that he would help the new Taoiseach as he had helped his predecessor.[56]

The IUSCICI soon managed to attract the interest of other American businessmen, many of whom were of Irish origin. Its third mission to Ireland in 1973 had sixty members, including wives.[57] By 1976, its membership had risen to two hundred and fifty, a dramatic increase, certainly due to Ireland's entry into the European Community in 1973. Indeed, there was a huge economic stake for American multinationals seeking to secure access to the European market. The IUSCICI now also had branches on the West Coast of the United States and in the Midwest.

In Dublin, the growing success of the IUSCICI was welcomed, as this publicity contributed to the economic development of the country. Needless to say, the group was particularly pampered when it came to Ireland. However, in 1975, the President of Ireland, Cearbhall Ó Dálaigh,[58] refused to meet with them, citing concerns that it appeared too commercial in nature. Moreover, he was not in the habit of receiving groups of this size.[59] This was unfortunate, since at the time of the group's visit most of the ministers had commitments related to the European presidency, which Ireland was holding for the first time since joining the organisation. Michael Killeen, the Director of the IDA, who worked closely with the IUSCICI, contacted D. O. Suilleabhain, the Secretary of the Department of the Taoiseach, to urge his cooperation in trying to change the President's mind. He recalled the importance of this group to Ireland:

> It is a voluntary association with a membership of distinguished Americans many of them of Irish descent, with an active interest in Ireland and Irish affairs. The Council helps in putting forward Ireland's viewpoint, in the United States, when occasion demands and has made a significant contribution to the country's economic development especially by encouraging industrial development here. The Council is representative of the majority

> of the U.S. industrial firms which have invested over £100 million in Ireland and have created almost 20 000 jobs. The visiting group also includes senior representatives of a number of firms which are potential investors under our programme. [...] If the group do not have an opportunity of meeting our new president on this occasion they will be deeply disappointed and their motivation could be adversely affected.[60]

On the same day the Irish ambassador in Washington sounded the alarm. He sent a telegram marked "very urgent" in which he reminded Dublin that given the economic situation in the country, it was essential that this group be received with honours and continue to work for the good of Ireland. As American businessmen liked to have their photographs taken with senior political figures, posing with the President outside Áras an Uachtaráin, his official residence, was one of the highlights of their stay. In addition, successive presidents had received the group during their visits who would not understand why it would not be the case this time.[61] In desperation, Michael Killeen wrote directly to the President, literally begging him to receive the group and agree to be photographed with them. Cearbhall Ó Dálaigh eventually agreed to his request.[62]

7.4 From Incentives to Investment: US Banks and Business in 1960s Ireland

The efforts of Lemass and the IUSCICI were soon rewarded. Ireland now offered a wide range of incentives to foreign investors, such as tax exemption on exports. In the mid-1960s, a number of US banks began to show an interest in Ireland. Perhaps it was whispered to them that there existed "a substantial amount of Irish capital lying under mattresses that could use a profitable home and that the United States [could] offer one".[63] In 1965, a year and a half after the Taoiseach's visit to the United States and when Ireland's entry into the European market was thought to be imminent, the First National City Bank of New York was the first American bank to set up in Ireland. Its chairman, George Stevens Moore, had been introduced to Lemass at the dinner hosted in New York by Peter Grace.

On the fifth anniversary of its opening in Ireland, its vice-president, Thomas Wilcox,[64] praised the institution's good results. "We've found Ireland a fertile field",[65] he said on that occasion. Some observers hoped that by pioneering in Ireland, it would set an example for others to follow.

In addition, the Chase Manhattan Bank and the Bank of America were said to be prepared to make a substantial loan to the Irish government.[66]

Indeed, Bank of America also established itself in Ireland in 1968.[67] Its vice-president, Henry A.J. Ralph, had been closely involved in the creation of the IUSCICI. In the same year, Chase Manhattan acquired a 50% stake in National City Bank, a subsidiary of the Bank of Ireland Group, one of the two major Irish banks. The new entity, which was named Chase and Bank of Ireland (International), was intended to serve foreign investors and help promote international trade.[68] It is worth noting that David Rockefeller, chairman of Chase Manhattan, who had also been introduced to Lemass at the Links Club dinner, was the guest of honour at the Irish Management Institute's annual conference in Killarney in late 1969.[69]

In the early 1960s, foreign investment in Ireland was mainly British and European. However, the American presence began to increase from the middle of that decade.[70] In 1970, Patrick Lalor, the Irish Minister for Industry and Commerce, stated that American companies had recently invested $67 million in Ireland and had opened eighty new factories employing eight thousand people.[71] This trend accelerated sharply with Ireland's entry into the European Community in 1973.

IUSCICI members were very active in bringing in investment from the United States. John A. Mulcahy, for example, is known to have played a major role in the establishment of a Pfizer factory in Ringaskiddy, near Cork, in 1969. He had made his fortune by selling his company to Pfizer in exchange for shares in the latter's capital. During the negotiations between the IDA and the American pharmaceutical giant, Mulcahy used his influence within the company to advocate the attractions in Ireland.[72] The arrival of this big name and the sustained efforts of the IDA helped the country to build a strong reputation among US investors of this sector. A letter from John J. Power,[73] Chairman of Pfizer, to George Colley, Irish Minister for Finance, shows that it was common for potential investors to gather information about Ireland from companies that were already located there:

> I have discussed the matter with a number of my associates here and have learned that in fact there is already a considerable amount of informal contact by Pfizer personnel with potential investors in Ireland. I have no doubt that other companies with investments have been similarly approached for advice and counsel with respect to their individual experiences.[74]

Indeed, other companies soon followed Pfizer's lead and the chemical/pharmaceutical industry became one of the two main sectors of the Irish economy.[75]

7.5 Reflections on a Decade of Foreign-Led Growth: Successes and Structural Challenges

IUSCICI members were heavily involved in Ireland's economic boom of the 1960s.[76] Michael Killeen estimated that they invested over £100 million in Ireland and created almost twenty thousand jobs. The influence of these Irish-American figures, although difficult to quantify, contributed to the influx of American investment into Ireland from the late 1950s onwards. Some of them, such as Peter Grace, brought Irish leaders into direct contact with the heads of the largest American companies in all economic sectors. Certainly, the tax incentives offered by Ireland were very competitive and investment was likely to be profitable. But IUSCICI members helped build confidence by paving the way for other US companies to follow once Ireland became a member of the common market.

Jack Lynch, the Taoiseach, at the 1970 IUSCICI annual dinner in the United States, paid tribute to the group's work for the Irish economy and the goodwill shown by its members:

> It is scarcely necessary for me to emphasise the importance of this organisation. The Council, as you know, is representative of some of the biggest investors in industrial development in this country and has been of considerable help in the industrial promotion drive. It has also been of great assistance in putting Irish interests before the United States administration. On my recent visit to the United States I took the opportunity of meeting some members of the Council to discuss our fears in relation to the new Trade Bill at present before Congress. I was quite impressed by their sympathetic approach and their readiness to take any action possible to ensure that our trade would not be adversely affected by any action taken under the legislation if eventually enacted.[77]

Indeed, IUSCICI members defended the interests of Irish exporters to the US authorities when they introduced quotas or taxes on imports of sugar, beef, dairy products, footwear, tweed, and crockery.[78] The Irish authorities could boast that they had set up a group of powerful Irish-American businessmen on whom Dublin could now rely. In 1963, Peter

Grace expressed his gratitude to the land of his ancestors in the following terms: "We would like to do a lot of things in Ireland. [...] We hope to help Ireland because Ireland certainly helped us when it sent my grandfather overseas".[79] Whether this was a genuine desire to contribute to Ireland's development or just a façade is difficult to ascertain. But it is clear that these Irish-American businessmen only became interested in Ireland when it became appealing for investment. If it gave them the feeling that they had done something useful for the ancestral homeland, all the better. The Irish authorities, for their part, benefited in terms of job creation, even if, as we shall see, these jobs were far from being permanent. Grace's support for Lemass was not purely altruistic. At the time, W.R. Grace, which had large investments in Latin America, viewed the growing political instability in that part of the world with suspicion and sought to limit the risks by relocating some of its investments to Europe.[80] At the beginning of the 1960s, this company and others were actively looking for business opportunities: "There are industrial holdings [...] such as W. R. Grace and Company and J. H. Whitney and Partners, who are constantly on the lookout for worthwhile Irish firms of sound potential but starved of capital".[81]

In 1963, W. R. Grace acquired a 50% stake in Urney Chocolates, one of Ireland's promising companies, which exported all over the world. In 1964, it also took over Hughes Brothers, another Irish company specialising in dairy products. In 1966, Hughes Brothers then acquired Lucan Dairies, a family ice cream business. Hughes Brothers Ltd. was then able to capture half of the Irish market share.[82]

The establishment of this American giant benefited the Irish economy, at least initially. By 1968, the company, which had also bought Leaf Ltd., a chewing gum manufacturer, employed a total of 1500 people in Ireland through its subsidiaries.[83] In the same year, Hughes Brothers opened a new automated factory in Rathfarnham (Dublin), one of the most modern in the world, an investment of one million Irish pounds. The entire manufacturing process was designed to maximise productivity. In addition, a profit-sharing scheme was introduced to increase motivation among the 250 employees.[84]

Within a year of W. R. Grace's entry into the company, Urney Chocolates saw a significant increase in exports to North America.[85] The company acquired Liam Devlin and Sons Ltd. and F. H. Steele, two Irish confectionery manufacturers. In 1969, the parent company decided to merge Urney Chocolates and Hughes Brothers, which became one of the largest food companies in Ireland.[86]

The arrival of W.R. Grace exemplifies the tangible benefits, such as job creation and modernisation, that could result from attracting major foreign industrial groups to Ireland. However, this example also shows the drawbacks of this strategy. These highly mobile companies can swiftly depart a country without hesitation when faced with challenging circumstances or when conditions appear more favourable elsewhere. In 1973, HB/Urney was sold to Unilever. In 1980, the group, renamed HB Chocolates, closed down.[87] As for Leaf Ltd.,[88] it was placed in receivership in 1978.[89]

At first sight, the work of IUSCICI had been very positive and was fully in line with the objectives set by the Irish authorities in 1958, i.e. to bring in foreign exporting companies to boost the Irish economy, stimulate growth, and create jobs. However, if one looks at the evolution of the Irish economy as a whole, it is clear that it followed a different course from that envisaged by Thomas Kenneth Whitaker in his 1958 report. The original plan was that indigenous businesses would become more competitive once faced with external competition and eventually become the driving force of the Irish economy. One of the tasks assigned to the IUSCICI was to assist in the development of Irish companies' exports to the United States. Foreign companies would then have only a secondary role.

There was indeed a brief economic boom that benefited some indigenous firms and sectors, such as the textile and footwear industries, through staff reductions, mergers, or increased exports to Britain. However, this boom was short-lived, largely because Britain had opened its market to EFTA[90] countries. At the same time, British firms increased their exports and expanded their share of the Irish market.[91] Many indigenous firms lagged behind. Rather than becoming more competitive, they suffered greatly from external competition. The subsidies they received from the state to mitigate this were ineffective.[92] The examples given above are only a small sampling; for a definitive, exhaustive account of the Irish industrial landscape, one should consult the book *Industry and Policy in Independent Ireland, 1922–1972*. In this fascinating and meticulously documented work on Irish enterprises, some founded even before independence, Barry guides the reader through the richness and diversity of native firms and traces their fortunes up to the eve of Ireland's entry into the European Common Market.

Yet, by the mid-1960s, foreign-owned companies were already driving industrial output and exports, but this apparent success came with structural weaknesses. Daly points out that the rapid growth of externally managed industries, often located in different areas and employing new workers, undermined the development of a cohesive industrial culture in Ireland. The absence of strong, domestically rooted industrial leadership meant that no influential group emerged to challenge the traditional dominance of farmers or the small native business class, which remained focused on property and distribution rather than innovation or manufacturing.[93]

In the late 1990s, Frank Barry, John Bradley, and Eoin O'Malley conducted a comparison between indigenous industrial companies and large foreign companies operating in Ireland. They concluded that the latter exported on average 89% of their output (95% for US companies) compared to 36% for Irish companies. The US companies were much larger,[94] five times more productive, and eight times more profitable.[95] Indeed, over the years, the dependence of the Irish economy on foreign companies kept on increasing.[96] These large companies, from all sectors of industry, were mainly looking for low-skilled, low-cost labour for factory assembly or packaging operations.[97] Decisions were made at the headquarters of the parent company. They sourced from abroad and had virtually no backward or forward linkages with indigenous industries.[98]

From the 1980s onwards, the IDA sought to address this problem by targeting the more technologically sophisticated electronics and pharmaceutical industries and selecting companies with the best long-term growth potential.[99] However, although these companies provided employment, this was not enough to offset the downsizing in indigenous firms in the 1980s and the increase in the working-age population.[100]

During the 1950s, the economies of both Irelands were relatively stagnant, unable to generate sufficient employment opportunities to address chronic unemployment. As demonstrated, foreign investment emerged as the solution to the investment deficit on both sides of the border.

South of the border, attracting foreign investors was an area in which the authorities had no experience. So they turned to the Irish-American captains of industry who, it was thought, would be willing to help. Lemass, following the tactic used by the Scottish Council, ostensibly sought to strike a chord with these figures at the mention of Ireland.

O'Neill, for his part, made a point of clearing up any confusion in the minds of his audience about the status of Northern Ireland when he spoke abroad.[101] He did attempt to mobilise businessmen from the province when he visited North America, but with less success than Lemass. Thus, in the early 1960s, Frank Hanna[102] suggested that the Northern Irish authorities should cooperate with Ireland and take advantage of the contacts and positive image that Ireland had with the Irish-American community. Moreover, he felt that such an initiative would have been very well received in London:

> [...] if one can place reliance on statements made from time to time by responsible members of the British Government one would say they would look with considerable favour on some degree of co-operation with the Government of the Republic of Ireland to see in what way joint efforts could be made with that Government towards improving the situation, towards the possible attraction of new industries from the Continent, towards the possibility of exploiting the predominantly strong Irish sentiment which is in America and which this Government by their peculiar and particular policy have simply jettisoned. Their name in America, as regards the Irish section, is simply mud.[103]

Frank Hanna was rebuffed by Terence O'Neill who refuted his claims:

> Is the hon. Member suggesting that the Southern Irish connection in America is having the effect of bringing American industry to Southern Ireland? If he is he is completely wrong. I discussed this with the Éire representatives in Washington and one of the things they are so worried about is the fact that they have been quite unable to attract American industry to Southern Ireland.[104]

In fact, as we have seen, Dublin was actively developing contacts with the Irish-American business elite at this time. On 14 January 1965, a historic meeting took place between O'Neill and Lemass. During their meeting, the two men discussed deepening economic cooperation between the two Irelands.[105] On this occasion, Lemass reached out to O'Neill and raised the possibility of working together to attract foreign investors. But from the outset, O'Neill pointed out the difficulties inherent in working together in this field:

> Mr Lemass said that there seemed to be cases where the Republic and Northern Ireland were 'bidding' against each other. He thought that there should be some degree of common effort, possibly involving pooling of

> information. It was pointed out to him, however, that one of the difficulties of such a course would be the fact that the Republic offers completely different and in some respects much larger inducements (eg tax concessions for exports).[106]

In reality, the Northern Irish authorities were hesitant to cooperate in this delicate area, fearing that it would weaken their ties with London and potentially bolster the concept of a unified island economy:

> The Republic Memorandum[107] goes on to speak of 'common objectives in regard to promotion of economic growth, attraction of foreign industries and capital, reduction of unemployment, regional development'. Since we have common objectives in these fields with Great Britain it is difficult to see how this could be achieved. We would not want to limit our ability to compete with the Republic in such fields as the attraction of foreign direct investment.[108]

In the late 1960s, the political situation in Northern Ireland deteriorated. What follows is not intended to be a summary of the complexities of the Northern Ireland conflict, but simply to provide some contextual background for the reader. The IRA's border campaign ended in 1962. The organisation went through a long period of inactivity. However, the early 1960s saw the emergence of an educated Catholic[109] middle class in Northern Ireland that was keen to increase its influence in the society in which it lived. In November 1959, a group of young Catholic graduates established National Unity. While advocating for reunification, the organisation acknowledged the legitimacy of Northern Ireland's status. Its members eschewed violence. The progressive ideas promoted by this movement spurred the Nationalist Party to engage within the established institutional framework of the province.[110] The Northern Ireland Labour Party and the Northern Ireland Committee of the Irish Congress of Trade Unions were also receptive to National Unity's arguments. In September 1966, they presented a joint document to the Northern Ireland Minister for Home Affairs in which they called, among other things, for the application of the "one man one vote" principle, the end of gerrymandering which favoured Unionists, as well as measures aiming to abolish discrimination in housing and employment.[111] A delegation was received at the Home Office in December, but their claims were dismissed by William Craig, the Northern Ireland Home Secretary. Symbolic gestures by

Northern Ireland's Prime Minister, Terence O'Neill, to the Catholic community had initially raised hopes that reform would follow. But nationalist leaders were now convinced that there was nothing to be expected.

The Black American struggle for civil equality was emulated in Northern Ireland. The Northern Ireland Civil Rights Association (NICRA), a peaceful, non-political, and non-sectarian movement founded in February 1967, campaigned on behalf of the province's Catholic minority. By organising non-violent demonstrations and occupations of premises, NICRA aimed to push the government to adopt a reform programme. In addition to universal suffrage in local elections on the basis of one man, one vote, and the abolition of gerrymandering, the organisation also called for the repeal of the Special Powers Act.[112]

On 24 August 1967, a march was organised from Coalisland to Dungannon (County Tyrone), attended by 2500 people. This was followed by another march led by loyalists. Craig, fearing that the situation might escalate, banned an NICRA demonstration planned for (London) Derry on 5 October 1968.[113] With the support of their followers, the leaders of the organisation defied the minister's authority. But the police stormed in and beat the demonstrators. These events marked the beginning of an escalation of violence that would last for decades. On 22 November 1968, O'Neill finally announced a series of reforms. However, they proved insufficient, failed to appease the nationalist camp, and provoked the anger of the loyalists. Disavowed by his cabinet and his party and under growing pressure from the civil equality movements, the Northern Ireland Prime Minister decided to call an early election at the end of February 1969, which he won by a narrow margin. On 23 April 1969, the government eventually announced its decision to adopt universal suffrage for local elections. However, O'Neill failed to win the support of the Unionists. Disillusioned, he resigned five days later. He was replaced by James Chichester-Clark.[114]

Despite the arrival of a new Prime Minister, July 1969 was a month of riots.[115] In August, (London)Derry was the scene of violent clashes, known as the Battle of Bogside, one of the city's districts.[116] The residents of this Catholic neighborhood entrusted the area to a local defence committee and transformed their block, known as "Free Derry", into a fortified stronghold to shield themselves from the B Specials.[117] Meanwhile, in Belfast, Protestant extremists conducted retaliatory raids into Catholic neighborhoods. With the specter of civil conflict looming, British army troops were deployed to restore order.[118]

The IRA, which previously aligned itself with proponents of civic equality, divided into two factions after the December 1969 convention. A number of its members, who disagreed with the official line, formed a parallel organisation, the Provisional Army Council. From June 1970 onwards, the situation changed in several respects. The Provisional IRA, in favour of a resumption of armed action, supported the vigilante groups that had sprung up in the province to protect Catholic neighbourhoods from loyalist attacks. In July 1970, the British army, in search of weapons, conducted a series of brutal raids in the Catholic neighbourhood of Falls Road.[119] Violent clashes broke out between the army and Catholics, who were incensed by the intrusions. These events marked the beginning of the Troubles.[120] Gradually, under the influence of the Provisional IRA, old themes of nationalism, such as reunification, were grafted onto civil rights demands. The protest movement then took a new turn. The Provisional IRA took up arms. The moderate members of the NICRA founded the Social Democratic and Labour Party (SDLP) on 21 August 1970[121] which was to become one of the main political parties in Northern Ireland.

In the following year, the Provisional IRA stepped up its bombing campaign. In September 1971, a loyalist paramilitary organisation, the Ulster Defense Association (UDA), was formed in response to the IRA's actions. Confronted by this chaotic situation that posed a serious threat to consume the province, Brian Faulkner,[122] using the Special Powers Act, reinstated internment, with the backing of Edward Heath's Conservative government. The situation only got worse. On 24 March 24 1972, just a few weeks after the notorious event known as Bloody Sunday, when British soldiers shot dead thirteen unarmed Catholic demonstrators in the town of (London)Derry, Heath announced the suspension of the Northern Ireland government for a year. London then took over the direct administration of the province (Direct Rule). This marked the onset of a long period during which potential investors were exceedingly rare:[123]

> During the last five years the department has promoted some 30,000 jobs in manufacturing of which only 5,000 originated outside Northern Ireland. In 1974, the percentage of inward investment jobs (14.7 %) was exactly half of what the percentage was in 1970 (30 %). There are few worthwhile enquiries from overseas investors and investors who can be persuaded to visit the Province rarely stay.[124]

Notes

1. Córas Tráchtála Teoranta, Establishment of America - Ireland Board of Trade (or Chamber of Commerce) in the United States, 27 October 1960, 315/262/1, National Archives of Ireland (hereafter NAI);
2. Dictionary of Irish Biography. Seán MacEntee. https://www.dib.ie/biography/macentee-sean-john-francis-a5202. Accessed 10 June 2025.
3. The organisation became known as Bord Fáilte Éireann in 1955 but was commonly referred to as Bord Fáilte.
4. Dictionary of Irish Biography. John (Jack) Lynch. https://www.dib.ie/biography/lynch-john-mary-jack-a4947 Accessed 10 June 2025.
5. Memorandum signed T. J. Cahill, 26 January 1962, S15245B/63, NAI.
6. Memorandum signed T. J. Cahill,
7. Córas Tráchtála Teoranta, Ireland/America Council, memorandum, 5 November 1963, S15245B/63, NAI.
8. This network still exists. Its annual activity report for 2017 can be found on its website: https://www.irelanduscouncil.com/2017/Council2017AnnualReport.aspx. Accessed 5 June 2025.
9. Department of Industry and Commerce [illegible signature] to Nicolas O'Nualláin, Secretary to the Taoiseach, 31 October 1962, S15245B/63, NAI.
10. John Lynch to Henry A. Ralph, 5 December 1962, S15245B/63, NAI; Henry A. Ralph to John Lynch, 11 January 1963, S15245B/63, NAI.
11. Córas Tráchtála Teoranta, Ireland/America Council, memorandum, 5 November 1963.
12. A full list of the founding members of this group appears on the front page of *The Irish Times* on 22 May 1964.
13. B. Altman was a popular chain of department stores founded by John L. Burke's father, Benjamin Burke, in 1906. The chain had two flagship shops, one on 5th Avenue and one on 34th Avenue in New York City.
14. Among them were: J. Brougham Wallace, vice-president of the Morgan Guaranty Trust Company; John A. Coleman, former president of the Wall Street Exchange; Frank J. Manheim, partner at Lehman Brothers; and Arthur Smyth, vice-president of the Marine Midland Bank.
15. Howard Thomas Hallowell, president of the Standard Pressed Steel Company of Pennsylvania; Bernard P. McDonough, president of the McDonough Corporation, a construction company in the late 1920s; John A. Mulcahy, president of the Quigley Company, a large company that manufactured thermal insulation.
16. The group included Richard Prentice Ettinger, owner of Prentice Hall Inc., and William Fine, publisher of *Harper's Bazaar*, the famous American fashion magazine, and other publications such as *Cosmopolitan*,

House Beautiful, and *Town and Country*. His articles and columns were published in thirty-seven magazines and hundreds of American, British, and Irish newspapers.

17. John Bowles to James J. O'Keefe, 24 September 1962, 2001/37/1154, NAI. According to Lemass, in October 1963, Galvin was organising a fact-finding mission to Ireland for a group of Irish-American businessmen interested in investing abroad. Address by Seán Lemass, Taoiseach at dinner by joint Irish Societies, Boston, 20 October 1963, S17400C, NAI.
18. It would appear that Ireland was given preferential treatment, as John Fitzgerald Kennedy, in an effort to solve the balance of payments problem, adopted certain measures to encourage US companies to invest in the United States rather than abroad and to tackle tax havens and tax evasion. Christian Deblock. September 2011. Les États-Unis et l'investissement direct étranger: une histoire à trois temps, Centre for Integration and Globalisation Studies, 13, https://ceim.uqam.ca/db/spip.php?article6969. Accessed 5 June 2025.
19. It was a way for the president to secure the votes of the Irish-American community while campaigning for re-election. Dermot A. Mullane. 1963. Hidden Assets in Lemass's Visit? Underlying Economic Aims", *The Irish Times*, 23 October.
20. U.S.-Irish Fishery Research Project: Lemass Outlines Joint Report. 1964. *The Irish Times*, 7 January.
21. Donoal O'Donovan. 1965. The Changing Face of Ireland Over There", *The Irish Times*, 3 May.
22. Marie-Claire Considère-Charon. 2002. Irlande, une singulière intégration européenne. Paris: Économica, 17–18.
23. Call to Boston Groups. 1963. *The Irish Press*, 21 October.
24. Unfortunately for Ireland, de Gaulle, unwilling to compromise on national sovereignty, opposed this change. France stopped participating in the main EU meetings ("empty chair policy") and demanded, in order to regain its place, a political agreement on the role of the Commission and majority voting, which implied an overall revision of the treaty system. On 30 January 1966, the Luxembourg Compromise provided a solution to the deadlock. According to the terms of this agreement, when very important interests of one or more countries are at stake, the members of the Council must try to reach solutions that can be adopted by all, while respecting their mutual interests. Thus de Gaulle was again able to veto the entry of the United Kingdom in November 1967.
25. Address by Seán Lemass, Taoiseach at dinner by joint Irish societies, Boston, 20 October 1963.
26. Address Seán Lemass, Boston.
27. Address Seán Lemass, Boston.

28. O'Donovan, The Changing Face of Ireland Over There; John MacCarthy. 1970. Now the Yanks Are Coming Back and Staying", *The Irish Times*, 23 May.
29. His ancestor, from Dingle in the west of Ireland, emigrated to the United States in the nineteenth century. Subsequently, the Moore family worked with Michael Davitt, John Devoy, and Éamon de Valera when they sought support for their cause across the Atlantic. Seán Cronin. 1971. The New Ambassador to Ireland. *The Irish Times*, 23 September.
30. Proposed list for Dinner for Prime Minister Lemass, 25 September 1963, P33/1/2, NAI.
31. David Rockefeller was, among other positions, chairman of the Chase Manhattan Bank.
32. George Stevens Moore was President of the First National City Bank.
33. Horace 'Hap' Flannigan was then President of the Chemical Bank of New York.
34. John D. J. Moore to John M. Conway, then Director of the IDA, 17 September 1963, P33/1/2, NAI.
35. The Most Powerful Club in the World? The Links. https://valuable-book.wordpress.com/2012/10/01/the-most-powerful-club-in-the-world-the-links. Accessed 5 June 2025.
36. Urney Chocolates in Partnership with American Company. 1963. *The Irish Times*, 16 November.
37. Dermot A. Mullane, Hidden Assets in Lemass's Visit?
38. Brian O'Connell, Cian O'Carroll. 2017. Brendan O'Regan, Irish Innovator, Visionary & Peacemaker. Newbridge: Irish Academy Press, 106.
39. Tom Callanan quoted in O'Connell, O'Carroll, Brendan O'Regan, 108.
40. O'Connell and O'Carroll, Brendan O'Regan.
41. The idea was first mentioned in a 1953 Department of Industry and Commerce minute. Frank Barry. 2023. Industry and Policy in Independent Ireland, 1922–1972. Oxford: Oxford University Press, 141. Two years later, the concept was also put forward in a document from the American administration which contained a list of recommendations to attract foreign investors addressed to the Irish government. Anne Groutel. 2016. American Janus-Faced Economic Diplomacy Towards Ireland in the Mid-1950s, Irish Economic and Social History 43, 1: 9. https://doi.org/10.1177/0332489316661066.
42. Anne Groutel. 2022. Ireland and the Marshall Plan: E.C.A.'s Manoeuvring to Promote Dollar Tourism. Irish Economic and Social History 49, 1:133. https://doi.org/10.1177/03324893221080610.
43. Report of meeting, 20 February 1967, 2008/148/106, NAI.
44. Refer to appendix for biography.

45. Strong U.S. Business Group Visit Ireland. 1967. The Irish Times, 28 April.
46. Strong U.S. Business Group.
47. Jack Lynch served as Taoiseach from 10 November 1966 to 14 March 1973 and again from 5 July 1977 to 11 December 1979.
48. [?] Jordans, Industrial Development Authority, to the Secretary of the Department of the Taoiseach, 18 April 1967, 2008/148/106, NAI.
49. John M. Conway, The Irish in the United States, New York consular area, report to Cornelius Cremin, Secretary of the Foreign Office, 27 June 1958, 338/86 (1), NAI.
50. Tim Deegan to John Lynch, 18 May 1967, 2008/148/106, NAI.
51. The Ireland / United States Council for Commerce and Industry, 24 March 1976, 2008/148/106, NAI.
52. Liam Cosgrave served as Taoiseach from 14 March 1973 to 5 July 1977.
53. Howard Thomas Hallowell to Liam Cosgrave, 17 April 1973, 2008/148/106, NAI.
54. Timothy J. Sullivan. 2009. New York State and the Rise of Modern Conservatism: Redrawing Party Lines. Albany: State University of New York Press, 130.
55. Dan Scully was the link between IUSCICI and the Irish authorities. The Ireland/United States Council for Commerce and Industry, 24 March 1976.
56. Kevin Rush, Irish Consul in New York, to Hugh J. McCann, Secretary of the Department of Foreign Affairs, 23 March 1975, 2008/148/106, NAI.
57. Joseph Hayes, Department of Foreign Affairs, to the private Secretary of the Taoiseach, 22 May 1973, 2008/148/106, NAI.
58. This was probably a pretext as it was common knowledge that Cearbhall Ó Dálaigh and the Taoiseach, Liam Cosgrave, were at odds with each other.
59. Ministry of the Taoiseach [illegible signature] [no addressee name], 23 May 1975, 2008/148/106, NAI.
60. Michael Killeen to D. O. Suilleabhain, 22 May 1975, 2008/148/106, NAI.
61. To HQ from Washington, 22 May 1975, 2008/148/106, NAI.
62. Michael Killeen to Cearbhall Ó Dálaigh, President of the Republic of Ireland, 23 May 1975, 2008/148/106, NAI.
63. Hugh O'Neill, Ireland's Appeal to Investors. 1965. *The Irish Times*, 10 February.
64. Thomas Wilcox was of Irish origin. His father was from County Cavan, Ireland, and his mother from County Fermanagh, Northern Ireland. Ireland Is a Fertile Field. 1970. *The Irish Times*, 22 September.
65. Ireland Is a Fertile Field.
66. O'Donovan, The Changing Face of Ireland Over There.

67. Bank of America Dublin Branch Officially Opened. 1968. *The Irish Times*, 21 September.
68. Chase Manhattan Bank to Take Half Share in National City. 1968. *The Irish Times*, 28 February.
69. Largest Ever IMI Conference Opens at Killarney. 1969. *The Irish Times*, 25 April.
70. Denis O'Hearn. 2001. The Atlantic Economy: Britain, the US and Ireland. Manchester: Manchester University Press, 143.
71. Irish Attractions for U.S. Are Firm. 1970. *The Irish Times*, 23 December.
72. Ray Mac Sharry, Padraic White. 2000. The Making of the Celtic Tiger. Cork: Mercier Press, 189–190.
73. Power is a name of Irish origin.
74. John J. Power to George Colley, 7 August 1972, 2003/20/105, NAI.
75. Mac Sharry, White, The Making of the Celtic Tiger, 189–190; Andrew Whittaker. 1972. Series of Major U.S. Pharmaceutical Firms May Establish Here. *The Irish Times*, 8 December; U.S. Company to Set Up £5 m. Factory in Ireland. 1972. *The Irish Times*, 8 December; IDA Takes Comfort from Health Care Success Story. 1993. *The Irish Times*, 5 March.
76. Between the late 1950s and 1973, manufactured exports grew at an annual rate of 23% and output increased two and a half times. Ronnie Munck. 1993. The Irish Economy. London—Boulder: Pluto Press, 33–34.
77. Jack Lynch to Paddy [Patrick] Lalor, 30 September 1970, 2008/148/106, NAI.
78. The Ireland/United States Council for Commerce and Industry, 24 March 1976.
79. Urney Chocolates in Partnership with American Company.
80. O'Donovan, The Changing Face of Ireland Over There.
81. O'Donovan, The Changing Face of Ireland Over There. See also: Hugh O'Neill, Ireland's Appeal to Investors.
82. Hughes Taking over Lucan Dairies. 1966. *The Irish Times*, 28 June.
83. Company's Irish Holdings. 1968. *The Irish Times*, 16 July.
84. £1 million Plant Geared for Optimum Investment Return. 1968. *The Irish Times*, 16 July.
85. Urney's Win Record Export Order. 1966. *The Irish Times*, 22 November.
86. Grace Forms New Division. 1969. *The Irish Times*, 12 June.
87. HB Chocolates Closure to Cost 300 Their Jobs. 1980. *The Irish Times*, 26 April.
88. However, the company was taken over by Huhtamaki, a Finnish group, then by CSM, a Dutch group, and finally, in 2001, by ZED Gum, an Irish company, which closed the Kilcock factory and relocated production to China. Zed Candy. 2009. *The Irish Times*, 15 June.

89. Bill Murdoch. 1978. Losses Force Leaf Ltd. into Receivership. *The Irish Times*, 26 July.
90. The European Free Trade Association (EFTA) was established on May 3, 1960, as an alternative trade bloc for European states that were unable or unwilling to join the then European Economic Community (EEC), the main predecessor of the EU. The Stockholm Convention (1960) established EFTA and was signed by seven countries known as the "Outer Seven": Austria, Denmark, Norway, Portugal, Sweden, Switzerland, and the United Kingdom.
91. Daly, Sixties Ireland, 65–66.
92. Kieran A. Kennedy, Thomas Giblin, Deirdre McHugh. 1988. The Economic Development of Ireland in the Twentieth Century. London: Routledge, 1988, 72, 241; O'Hearn, The Atlantic Economy, 146–147.
93. Daly, Sixties Ireland, 31, 380.
94. They were larger both in terms of numbers and production.
95. Frank Barry, John Bradley, Eoin O'Malley. 1999. Indigenous and Foreign Industry: Characteristics and Performance. In Understanding Ireland's Economic Growth, ed. Frank Barry: 51. London: Palgrave Macmillan.
96. See: National Economic and Social Council. "A Review of Industrial Policy: A Report Prepared by the Telesis Consultancy Group", Dublin, Stationery Office, 1982; O'Hearn, The Atlantic Economy, 145–148.
97. Proinnsias Breathnach. 1998. Exploring the "Celtic Tiger" Phenomenon: Causes and Consequences of Ireland's Economic Miracle. European Urban and Regional Studies 5, 4: 308. https://doi.org/10.1177/096977649800500402.
98. Cormac Ó Gráda, A Rocky Road, 116.
99. The IDA also sought to attract internationally traded services, particularly in financial services, IT and back office operations. Breathnach, Exploring the 'Celtic Tiger' Phenomenon, 309.
100. Joseph Durkan. 1992. Industrial Policy from the 1930s to Culliton, Policy Paper PP92/4, Dublin, University College Dublin, School of Economics, Centre for Economic Research, 6–8; Peadar Kirby. 2002. The Celtic Tiger in Distress: Growth and Inequality in Ireland. Basingstoke: Palgrave, 19–20.
101. Terence O'Neill, 19 October 1967, Ulster's Place In Britain Today, speech to the Empire Club of Canada, Toronto, https://speeches.empireclub.org/60962/data. Accessed 5 June 2025.
102. Frank Hanna was an independent Labour MP for the Belfast Central constituency.
103. Northern Ireland, parliamentary debates, Stormont (hereafter Stormont debates), 30 October 1962, 52.
104. Stormont parliamentary debates, 30 October 1962, 52.

105. The authorities of the two Irelands cooperated on a few occasions in the economic field in the 1950s. Anne Groutel. 2004. La coopération économique entre les deux Irlandes. Caen: Presses universitaires de Caen; Michael Kennedy. 2000. Division and Consensus: The Politics of Cross-Border Relations in Ireland, 1925–1969. Dublin: Institute of Public Administration.
106. Meeting with the Prime Minister of the Irish Republic, 14 January 1965, CAB/9/U/1, Public Record Office of Northern Ireland (hereafter PRONI).
107. This is a document, which the Irish authorities sent to Belfast, containing a number of proposals for economic cooperation.
108. Untitled and undated document, CAB/9/U/1, PRONI.
109. The Butler Education Act, a British legislation passed in 1944, made education compulsory until the age of 15, and the Education (Stormont) Act of 1947 provided easier access to education. The Catholic community in Northern Ireland was one of the beneficiaries. Paul Brennan. 1991. The Conflict in Northern Ireland. Paris: Longman, 38.
110. Michael Farrel. 1980. Northern Ireland: The Orange State. London: Pluto Press, 238–239.
111. Farrel. Northern Ireland, 243.
112. This emergency law, passed in 1922, was made permanent in 1933. It gave the executive particularly extensive powers of repression. The auxiliary police, the B Specials, knowing that they were protected, indulged in numerous abuses. NICRA called for its disbandment. Brennan, The Conflict, 34, 39.
113. Jonathan Bardon. 1992. A History of Ulster. Belfast: Blackstaff Press, 654–655.
114. James Chichester-Clark was Prime Minister of Northern Ireland from 1 May 1969 to 23 March 1971.
115. Bardon, A History of Ulster, 665–666.
116. Located at the foot of the city walls, it was, at the time, one of the most disadvantaged areas of the city where Catholics lived. In the 1990s, the area was almost completely rebuilt. Only a section of wall bearing the inscription "You are now entering free Derry" bears witness to the Battle of the Bogside.
117. Barry White. 1983. From Conflict to Violence: The Re-emergence of the IRA and the Loyalist Response. In Northern Ireland: The Background to the Conflict, ed. John Darby: 184. Belfast: Appletree Press.
118. Bardon, A History of Ulster, 670.
119. White, From Conflict to Violence, 185.

120. A term used in Northern Ireland to refer to the climate of violence that prevailed in the province between that time and the paramilitary ceasefires in 1994.
121. Paul Bew, Gordon Gillespie. 1993. Northern Ireland: A Chronology of the Troubles, 1968–1993. Dublin: Gill & Macmillan, 30.
122. Brian Faulkner was First Minister of Northern Ireland from 23 March 1971 to 30 March 1972. He succeeded James Chichester-Clark who had resigned shortly before. Dictionary of Irish Biography. Brian Faulkner. https://www.dib.ie/biography/faulkner-arthur-brian-deane-a3021. Accessed 11 June 2025.
123. Richard T. Harrison. 1986. Industrial Development Policy and the Restructuring of the Northern Ireland Economy. Environment and Planning C: Politics and Space 4, 1: 57–58. https://doi.org/10.1068/c040053
124. J. T. Quan, Review of industrial strategy in Northern Ireland, 29 August 1975, COM/63/1/746, PRONI.

PART III

The Growing Economic and Political Influence of Irish-American Businessmen Over the Two Irelands (1990s–2010s)

In this third part we will see that, at the request of the Irish authorities, the Irish-American business elite again played an important role when Ireland was hit by the economic crisis on two occasions. In addition, some of these individuals also attempted to help break the political and economic deadlock in Northern Ireland in the 1990s. Was this driven by financial interest, or was it motivated by a desire to aid the economy of their ancestral land purely out of altruism? While it is not easy to decipher the motivations of these diaspora figures, we will see that each side had something to gain.

The now very open Irish economy was hit hard by the oil shocks of 1973 and 1979.[1] As a result, in the 1980s, the combined effect of slowing global growth, soaring inflation,[2] and a sharp increase in foreign debt caused by escalating oil prices plunged the Irish economy into a crisis that lasted until the end of that decade.[3] At that time, despite the presence of large foreign companies on its soil, Ireland was still one of the poor relations of the European Community. By 1985, unemployment had reached 17% of the Irish population[4] with emigration resurging as a consequence after a brief period of respite.[5]

The 1970s were even worse for Northern Ireland. At that time, it produced a third of the United Kingdom's synthetic fibre output,[6] a very oil-intensive industry. When the first oil shock hit, Northern Ireland-based companies in this sector saw the price of their raw material soar and faced rising transport and electricity costs.[7] Consequently, many companies were forced to lay off workers. Industrial jobs were lost at a rate of 3% per year between 1973 and 1979.[8] Meanwhile, industrial production fell by 5% per year.[9] In addition, the violence of the conflict, reported by the international media, deterred potential investors. The economist John Simpson has estimated that between thirty thousand and thirty-five thousand jobs were lost as a direct result of the conflict.[10] Indeed, during the 1980s, the trend continued. Northern Ireland was then the most disadvantaged province in the United Kingdom.[11] Unemployment, at an average of 20%, was twice as high as in the rest of the country. The Industrial Development Board[12] was still unable to attract new investment, despite offering very attractive incentives.[13] However, the number of large US companies operating in the province remained stable[14] during the decade, primarily attributable to grants provided by the International Fund for Ireland.[15]

Yet, the process of deindustrialisation continued inexorably. Between 1979 and 1981, 110 industrial companies closed.[16] A further deterioration in international economic conditions was compounded by the effects of Margaret Thatcher's monetary policy.[17] Forty thousand industrial jobs were lost between 1979 and 1989 in Northern Ireland.[18]

However, it would appear it was relatively unaffected by the cuts to the British public services during the Thatcher years.[19] Indeed, the increase in the number of civil servants offset the losses in the industrial sector[20] but this only increased the province's economic dependence on London.

The opening of the European single market in 1992 caused some concern in the business community both in Northern Ireland and south of the border. This new step towards economic integration, which presaged increased competition, was to be critical, as had been the entry of the United Kingdom and Ireland into the Common Market in 1973. The early 1990s were therefore marked by the desire of Irish and Northern Irish business organisations to strengthen their links in order to create synergies between the two economies. The aim was to promote an "integrated island economy" better able to cope with the influx of foreign companies.[21] Dublin expressed its willingness to work with the Northern Irish authorities. As a result, a study on the possibilities of North-South cooperation was commissioned by the Taoiseach Albert Reynolds.[22] The foreword he wrote might have suggested that a new era was beginning:

> I hope that the removal of trade barriers this year will be followed, in the years ahead, by an even greater recognition of our common European destiny and by the erosion of less tangible barriers which have for too long prevented both parts of the island from realizing their full economic potential and from developing a much stronger single island economy. [...] The

> challenge which confronts us in both parts of Ireland, from the Single Market and European Union, is to ensure that we maximize the benefits which are being made available to us. I believe that this challenge can best be met on an island-wide basis, with the development of a coherent economic strategy which can build on our considerable strengths.[23]

Although a number of projects to renovate North-South infrastructure were implemented and some agencies worked more closely together, particularly in the field of tourism, the common economic strategy remained a dead letter.[24]

In reality, Reynolds had his eyes on the United States. The single market was opening up new opportunities for American companies. The Taoiseach was convinced that Ireland should seize this opportunity to become "… an economically-strategic trading bridgehead between Europe, America and third countries".[25] But, faced with increasingly fierce competition to attract foreign investors, Ireland had to stand out.[26] Albert Reynolds adopted a pragmatic attitude: "If we are as good as the next it sometimes takes extra push, influence and muscle to try to get industries to locate here".[27]

Moreover, there was a danger that the Clinton administration, which came to power in 1993, would limit the tax advantages granted to companies that relocated their production abroad. Ireland, home to four hundred US multinationals,[28] could be directly affected. It was therefore vital to mobilise all available forces in the United States against the proposed changes.

During the 1980s, collaboration between the Irish authorities and Irish-American businessmen continued, albeit in a more subdued fashion, leading Niall O'Dowd to say that all this goodwill was not being used.[29] Patrick J. Daly, Director of the IDA, was taken aback by O'Dowd's comments: "Indeed, it is through the strong support of Irish-Americans at senior management level in the United States that many of the 350 US companies who are already here set up their Irish operations".[30] Still, Reynolds decided it was time to rekindle this relationship. Over the next two decades, the fortunes of the two Irelands were to take unexpected turns. Ireland, one of the poorest countries in the European Community, saw its growth rate soar and became one of its most prosperous members. But just as the "Celtic Tiger" seemed invincible, Ireland was hit by a financial crisis that brought it to its knees. Northern Ireland, meanwhile, embarked on a lengthy peace process. In the subsequent part, we will examine the involvement of certain individuals from what is referred to in

Ireland as "the diaspora" in each of these significant events, and how they utilised these opportunities to bolster their influence in both Irelands.

Notes

1. Ronnie Munck. 1993. The Irish Economy. London—Boulder: Pluto Press, 37–38.
2. In 1981, Ireland's inflation rate was 20.5%. Ray Mac Sharry, Padraic White. 2000. The Making of the Celtic Tiger. Cork: Mercier Press, 37.
3. Public debt reached 140% of GDP in 1988. Michael Burda, Charles Wyplosz. 2003. Macroéconomie: une perspective européenne. 3rd edn. Paris—Brussels: De Boeck University, 316. Moreover, Ireland's annual growth rate of gross national product of 4.8% in the period 1960–1973 fell to 2.2% in the period 1973–1979 before collapsing to 0.2% between 1979 and 1986. Munck, The Irish Economy, 38.
4. Mac Sharry, White, The Making of the Celtic Tiger, 38.
5. Munck, The Irish Economy, 83–84.
6. Jonathan Bardon. 1992. A History of Ulster. Belfast: Blackstaff Press, 719.
7. Bardon, A History of Ulster, 718.
8. Bardon, A History of Ulster, 720.
9. Bardon, A History of Ulster.
10. Bardon, A History of Ulster.
11. Richard T. Harrison. 1986. Industrial Development Policy and the Restructuring of the Northern Ireland Economy. Environment and Planning C: Politics and Space 4,1: 54. https://doi.org/10.1068/c040053
12. The Industrial Development Board, established in 1982, was charged with attracting large foreign investment projects.
13. Sabine Wichert. 1991. Northern Ireland since 1945. London—New York: Longman,180–182.
14. Harrison, Industrial Development Policy, 57–58.
15. Francis M. Carroll. 2005. The American Presence in Ulster: A Diplomatic History, 1796–1996. Washington: The Catholic University of America Press, 193. The International Fund for Ireland is an independent international organisation established in 1986 by the Irish and British governments under the Anglo-Irish Agreement (1985). Its aim is to promote social and economic progress and to encourage reconciliation between the Unionist and Nationalist communities. The United States, Canada, Australia, and New Zealand also contribute financially to the fund.
16. Bardon, A History of Ulster, 782.
17. Following Arthur Laffer's supply-side economics, the Chicago Monetarist School and the Austrian School (championed by Friedrich Hayek), Margaret Thatcher implemented these and other theories by making deep

cuts in public spending and direct taxes. She fought the inflation that was plaguing the United Kingdom in the late 1970s with high interest rates. Finally, she removed subsidies to unprofitable industries, such as the mines, and encouraged FDI.

18. Bardon, A History of Ulster, 734.
19. Valérie Peyronel. 2001. Économie et conflit en Irlande du Nord. Paris: Ellipses, 55–56.
20. Munck, The Irish Economy, 62–63.
21. Anne Groutel. 2004. La cooperation économique entre les deux Irlandes. Caen: Presses universitaires de Caen, 96–110.
22. Albert Reynolds served as Taoiseach from February 1992 to December 1994. Dictionary of Irish Biography. Albert Reynolds. https://www.dib.ie/index.php/biography/reynolds-albert-a10167. Accessed 11 June 2025.
23. Albert Reynolds. 1992. Foreword. In Ireland in Europe: A Shared Challenge. Economic Cooperation on the Island of Ireland in an Integrated Europe. Dublin: Stationery Office, 7–8.
24. Groutel, Economic cooperation,106–110.
25. Albert Reynolds quoted in: Denis Coghlan. 1992. US-Irish Trade Body Planned. *The Irish Times*, 15 September.
26. In the early 1990s, fifty-eight countries were added to the forty-eight that had already implemented a programme to attract FDI. Nathan M. Jensen. 2006. Nation-States and the Multinational Corporation: A Political Economy of Foreign Direct Investment. Princeton: Princeton University Press, 35.
27. Ireland, parliamentary debates, Houses of the Oireachtas, Dáil Éireann, 13 October 1992, 423, 4.
28. Conor O'Clery. 1997. Daring Diplomacy, Clinton's Secret Search for Peace in Ireland. Boulder: Roberts Rinehart Publishers, 213.
29. Niall O'Dowd. 1990. The Missing Irish-American Connection. *The Irish Times*, 14 September; Niall O'Dowd. 1990. Harnessing a Heritage for the Homeland. *The Irish Times*, 21 September. Niall O'Dowd is an Irish-born writer and journalist living in the United States. He founded *Irish-America Magazine* and the New York-based *Irish Voice* newspaper. He was the first to publish Business 100, portraits of the 100 most important Irish-American businessmen. Refer to appendix for biography.
30. Patrick J. Daly. 1990. Selling Ireland. *The Irish Times*, 29 September.

CHAPTER 8

Irish-American Businessmen and the Rise of the "Celtic Tiger" (1992–2002)

The Ireland-America Economic Advisory Board (IAEAB) was established in September 1992 at the initiative of Albert Reynolds. This group provided the "extra push" that the Taoiseach sought to attract foreign investment. Like the IUSCICI in the 1960s, the IAEAB was made up of captains of industry and other influential Irish-American figures who said they were willing to work for the good of Ireland, officially on a voluntary basis.[1] Initially consisting of about twenty members, this number grew over the years to forty-two in 2008. They came from a wide range of backgrounds including finance, insurance, information and communication technology, pharmaceuticals, and tourism.

The task assigned to the IAEAB had much in common with that of the IUSCICI. Like the latter, the members of the new group were tasked with presenting a favourable image of Ireland to potential investors or within their respective companies. They were also to examine ways in which the economic relationship between Ireland and the United States could be diversified and move towards "a more balanced pattern of economic relations than that which concentrates on attracting US multinational companies with the lure of low taxation and high profits".[2]

The Social and Economic Policy Division (Unit 2) within the Department of the Taoiseach set the agenda for the group's meetings in consultation with the Irish Ambassador to the United States, who usually acted as a liaison between the group members and the Irish authorities.

A. Groutel, *The Two Irelands and the Diaspora*,
https://doi.org/10.1007/978-3-032-12355-8_8

This division was also responsible for conveying the IAEAB's recommendations to the various government departments and agencies.[3]

Journalist Niall O'Dowd was particularly enthusiastic. He believed that the IAEAB's experience in development and distribution could help promote Irish exports across the Atlantic. He also believed that large Irish companies and concerns in which the state had a stake could open their boardrooms to these businessmen and benefit from their experience.[4]

8.1 Irish-American Businessmen Acting as Facilitators

When he set up the group, Reynolds was well aware of the benefits of working with this elite group, which held financial power and economic intelligence.[5] During the 1970s and 1980s, the upward mobility of Irish-Americans as a whole had continued.[6] There was now a critical mass of businessmen among them:

> [...] directors on other boards throughout the United States and would also have knowledge of developments that can take place. They can be of immense help to the IDA or SFADCo[7] by putting their weight behind them to get investment to come to Ireland.[8]

According to Stephen D. Cohen, multinationals consider a multitude of factors before deciding to locate in a country, but:

> No single formula exists because specific strengths and weaknesses of a country or region might receive high priority by one team of corporate evaluators and be ignored by another [...]. Calculating trade-offs between positive and negative country characteristics is an art, not a science.[9]

That said, in general, multinationals give priority to countries whose authorities provide guarantees of stability in economic policy and work to maintain a favourable climate for economic activity.[10] In the 1990s, Ireland had both of these advantages. The Irish government's consistent policy of fiscal discipline, across the political divide, had led to a consolidation of public finances. This policy had been implemented in a climate of social peace, the result of agreements between trade unions and employers (social partnership).[11] Furthermore, Ireland was part of the European single market and, as a member of the European Union, it benefited from the organisation's development funds which contributed, among other things, to the modernisation of the country's infrastructure.[12]

But Ireland had other trump cards. The country had a young, abundant, English-speaking and now more skilled workforce. Indeed, free secondary schooling from 1967 onwards and a policy of facilitating access to education, including higher education, had raised the general level of educational attainment of the Irish population.[13] Ireland also offered a range of advantages for investors, including a particularly favourable corporate tax rate.

Yet, these assets had to be promoted. One of the IAEAB's tasks was to bring them to the attention of potential investors in the United States. The IDA, which had developed strong negotiating skills,[14] could take over once a potential investor was identified.

The ensuing period of economic expansion,[15] of an unprecedented magnitude since the creation of the state, has been much talked about.[16] The massive presence of multinationals, mainly American, is cited as one of the major reasons for the Irish economic "miracle".

The Irish-American business elite was clearly instrumental in bringing them to Ireland. The IDA has never publicly mentioned the companies that decided to establish in the country after contact with the IAEAB. However, Bertie Ahern[17] made no secret of the fact that the members of this group had allowed many high-level contacts to be built up across the Atlantic in the previous decade.[18]

Niall O'Dowd welcomed, for example, the contribution of Donald Keough,[19] former Chairman and CEO of Coca-Cola and a founding member of the IAEAB. The latter accompanied a large number of potential investors on fact-finding trips to Ireland, including some of the world's richest men such as Warren Buffett, a friend of Keough's, and Bill Gates.[20] These initiatives were successful, with both Berkshire Hathaway (Buffett) and Microsoft (Gates) subsequently investing in Ireland. These Irish-American contacts also proved to be very useful in the financial sector when the Irish authorities decided, in the late 1980s, to create the International Financial Services Centre (IFSC), a business hub specialising in financial services. Indeed, the IAEAB included among its members high-ranking individuals who could help the IDA[21] establish contacts in this sector, which it was not very familiar with at the time. In 1995, the IAEAB formed a subcommittee whose members were specifically tasked with providing advice and promoting the centre among their business connections.[22] In 2003, Ahern publicly thanked Daniel P. Tully,[23] a member of the IAEAB, for having played a key role[24] in attracting Merrill Lynch, of which Tully was then the CEO.[25]

8.2 A Role of *Eminence Grise*

The IAEAB was also to provide advice and new ideas on economic policy. One of the first pieces of advice given to the Irish authorities was to rebrand the country to revitalise inbound tourism, which had been stagnant for a decade.[26] Several members of the IAEAB were tasked with devising a strategy, recognising the sector's capacity to stimulate growth and generate numerous employment opportunities.[27]

Studies were also carried out, one by external consultants,[28] the other by Bord Fáilte, as a result of which a partnership between the state and the tourism industry was implemented in 1994. Subsequently, a £3 million advertising campaign was launched in the United States.[29] The image of Ireland was reworked, with leprechauns[30] and other symbols of Irish folklore, previously prevalent in such campaigns, being pushed into the background.[31] In addition, the IAEAB insisted that the new image be carried by all Irish government agencies operating in the United States in order to convey a consistent message.[32]

Furthermore, as Ireland's economic situation had improved significantly, the Irish government was aware that EU structural funds would diminish starting from 1999.[33] However, the process of upgrading the country's infrastructure was not complete and promised to put a strain on the state budget. The amount of work needed to upgrade the water distribution system, sewage disposal, and drainage, for example, was estimated at IR£ 1.5 billion in 1998.[34] The IAEAB therefore urged the Irish authorities to promote public–private partnerships (PPPs),[35] a practice common in the United States. It drafted comprehensive guidelines outlining the steps the Irish government should take to secure the required private funding.[36] The government's plan to create public–private partnerships was indeed included in the National Development Plan 2000–2006 and the next one.[37]

The IAEAB also supported the government's efforts to liberalise the Irish economy, particularly in the area of telecommunications. In the late 1990s, the Irish authorities recognised the urgency of taking action in this area to maintain the country's attractiveness to foreign investors. Indeed, in 1998, Microsoft preferred London to Dublin to establish its European Mirror website, because "For large-scale global digital communications,"

Ireland was "a marginal and uncompetitive location".[38] An advisory committee was therefore set up to study the issue. This group, chaired by Brian Thompson,[39] one of the members of the IAEAB, was composed of influential players in the US telecommunications sector. They made a number of recommendations[40] including the privatisation of Telecom Éireann, the state-owned company that held the monopoly of the fixed-line and mobile networks in Ireland. The committee also advocated the creation of a body that could give a trust mark to Irish companies in e-commerce. Furthermore, it was considered imperative to decrease tariffs and align them with those in the United States for both domestic and international communications. It was also essential to guarantee nationwide availability of broadband Internet. Finally, the report suggested the creation of a network of business angels.

8.3 Enlightened Philanthropy

In the field of higher education, the role of Irish-American billionaire Charles "Chuck" Feeney[41] was crucial.[42] Feeney's interest in the sector began in the late 1980s, even before he became a member of the IAEAB. His meeting with Ed Walsh,[43] then in charge of the development of the Limerick National Institute for Higher Education,[44] was decisive. Walsh's ambition was to transform the institute into a university that would offer technical courses of study along the lines of the technical universities in the United States.[45] Feeney was attracted by Walsh's personality and his proposal. He thus introduced the Irishman to several academics from Cornell University and leading figures in the world of business in the United States. Inspired by his encounter with the billionaire, Walsh accepted the latter's suggestion to set up an endowment for the institution, which was granted university status in 1989.[46] Although very common in the United States, this method of funding universities had never been used in Ireland before. The University of Limerick was therefore a pioneer in this field, a decision it never came to regret. Feeney was the first president of the foundation. Lewis L. Glucksman, another billionaire, succeeded him a few years later. He was not of Irish descent, but he was familiar with Ireland, where he spent his leave as a submariner during World War II. He later married Loretta Brennan,[47] an Irish-American.[48] Glucksman gave very generously to the foundation, but Feeney's financial involvement was unparalleled. Walsh obtained funds from the Irish authorities for the project as well. The combined monies made the

University of Limerick one of the best endowed institutions of higher education in Ireland.[49] It was also the first to train people to meet the exact needs of the economy, which probably contributed significantly to the establishment in Ireland of multinational companies such as Analog Devices and later Dell, Microsoft, and IBM.[50]

In the following years, Feeney through The Atlantic Philanthropies, his foundation, extended his contribution to the whole of Irish higher education. In 1999, the Programme for Research in Third Level Institutions (PRTLI) was launched by the Irish government. According to Ferdinand von Prondzynski, former President of Dublin City University, the project was the brainchild of Feeney, who persuaded the Irish authorities to implement it.[51] Von Prondzynski notes that prior to the creation of this programme, due to a lack of funding, none of the Irish universities were recognised in the field of research at the international level. The PRTLI was a partnership between the Irish state, the universities, and The Atlantic Philanthropies, which provided 30% of the funding for the first three phases of the project.

Some fifteen higher education institutions benefited from the funds available under this programme. They were used to build the necessary infrastructure for research and researchers (state-of-the-art laboratories, classrooms, libraries, on-campus accommodation, etc.) in the "hard" sciences and in the humanities and social sciences.[52] But, for von Prondzynski, the most important thing was that Ireland's image was now associated with research and innovation:

> Most of the key investments that the IDA has attracted to Ireland over the past few years would not have come at all but for the research culture that we have created. And because we can no longer credibly look for new investment in low-skills manufacturing or call centres, this is our future.[53]

Between 1987 and 2014, Atlantic Philanthropies provided Ireland with 1.2 billion euros, of which 553 million euros went to higher education.[54]

This, combined with supplementary funding from the state, amounted to 1.3 billion euros for the sector. Feeney unquestionably played a significant role in the transformation of higher education and research in Ireland[55] and, by extension, the rise of the Celtic Tiger in the 1990s.[56]

8.4 A Controversial Neoliberal Influence

The IAEAB played a significant role in encouraging the Irish authorities to adopt an "American-style" approach, marked by a more liberal economic outlook. With the benefit of hindsight, one might question the consequences of these recommendations and, more broadly, the board's direct or indirect involvement in what Peadar Kirby described as the authorities' "Irish-style" neoliberal agenda.[57] Some intellectuals voiced strong opposition to this newly established emphasis on purely economic priorities. Kathleen Lynch,[58] among others, criticized the growing marketisation of higher education, which had become increasingly focused on meeting the needs of the economy—often at the expense of the public interest.[59] It is clear that, although research in the humanities and social sciences was allocated a share of the budget under the Irish Research Programme for Higher Education Institutions, it remained the poor relation. In the first three phases, these disciplines received only 15% of the total budget. This disparity reflects the commercial logic underpinning resource allocation in the sector—an approach reinforced by a study which found that these areas had a commercial impact of "0%."[60]

The tourism sector, by contrast, experienced clear benefits. Between 1994 and 1997, the number of foreign visitors increased annually by 11%. From 1987 to 1997, the industry created 58,000 jobs, accounting for nearly 9% of all employment opportunities in Ireland.[61] However, the transformation of Ireland's image provoked discontent among some observers. Jim MacLaughlin, a researcher at University College Cork, lamented that Ireland's image had been reduced to "a mere commodity to promote tourism", resulting in the commercialization of Irish history and culture and the erosion of their intrinsic value.[62]

Other aspects of government policy, endorsed by the IAEAB, were also met with mixed reactions. Despite expectations that the public–private partnership (PPP) model would prove more efficient in terms of cost and time than exclusive public sector procurement, Eoin Reeves' analysis of PPPs within Ireland's National Roads Programme suggests otherwise.[63] Kieran Allen likewise criticised the privatisation of public services, arguing that it "does not systematically guarantee lower prices, better service or greater efficiency".[64] The case of Telecom Éireann, as we shall see, stands as a textbook example of these issues.

8.5 Growing Dependence on Foreign Investment

From a broader perspective, the IAEAB supported a strategy that allowed the Irish economy to climb the global value chain. At the same time, however, it contributed to growing dependence on foreign direct investment (FDI)—despite then-Taoiseach Albert Reynolds' initial hope that economic ties with the United States would not rely solely on the arrival of multinational corporations seeking tax advantages. In the early 1980s, Ireland was compelled to abandon export tax incentives deemed incompatible with European Community regulations. The government instead adopted a very low corporate tax rate (12.5%), which attracted—and continues to attract—numerous foreign investors.

Some commentators repeatedly warned that overly generous corporate tax breaks would ultimately harm Ireland's international image.[65] Over the decades, the dangers of over-reliance on FDI have also been highlighted by several Irish academics.[66] In 2010, Peadar Kirby observed that despite these long-standing warnings, the Irish authorities—driven by the goal of transitioning to a knowledge-based economy at all costs—remained largely indifferent:

> [...] there seems little willingness thoroughly to investigate the shortcomings of public policy and to design a policy more likely to succeed and more in keeping with the nature of the Irish economy. Small and medium-sized enterprises are poorly supported by state policy which still seems captivated by the needs of multinationals despite decades of warnings that such a policy focus is unwise for the long-term.[67]

Journalist Niall O'Dowd had expressed hope that IAEAB members would support the development of indigenous businesses by sharing their expertise in exports and international markets. In fact, the IAEAB did recommend that financial institutions extend greater support to small businesses[68] and encouraged the creation of start-up incubators, particularly in software development and electronic commerce.[69] However, this component of its original mission does not appear to have been a strategic priority. As the Enterprise Strategy Group noted, between 1990 and 2002, growth in the sales and exports of indigenous firms was "negligible".[70]

The IFSC, by contrast, has been a clear success since the 1990s. Today, the centre is home to over 500 companies and, as of 2022, employed 38,000 people. It contributes 7.4% to Ireland's gross national product and generates €2.1 billion in tax revenue annually for the state.[71] Nevertheless, the companies based there maintain limited commercial ties with indigenous firms.[72] However, Fintan O'Toole, one of Ireland's leading journalists, argued that the IFSC's success owed much to a deliberate policy of regulatory leniency: "Its very success has also encouraged a reluctance to ask too many questions [...] the notion of lax regulation is part of our competitive advantage".[73]

Lastly, the relationship between major IFSC-based corporations and Irish authorities appears to have grown uncomfortably close.[74] A series of scandals, compounded by the economic crisis that began in 2007, had deeply damaging consequences for both the international reputation of the IFSC and Ireland as a whole.[75]

Notes

1. The members of the group were not paid but their expenses (transport, board, and lodging) were covered by the Irish Department of Foreign Affairs. The amount could vary from year to year. In 2006 they amounted to €21,765 but only €4443 the following year. Ireland, parliamentary debates, Houses of the Oireachtas, Dáil Éireann (hereafter Dáil Éireann debates), 13 February 2008, 647,1.
2. Albert Reynolds quoted in: Denis Coghlan. 1992. US-Irish Trade Body Planned. *The Irish Times*, 15 September.
3. Government of Ireland, Department of the Taoiseach, "Strategy Statement of Department of Taoiseach 1998–2001", May 1998, 36.
4. Niall O'Dowd. 1993. US's Second Largest Ethnic Group Rocks into Minority. *The Irish Times*, 13 March.
5. "[This group] have a lot of financial muscle and intelligence operations within their own companies." Albert Reynolds, Dáil Éireann Debates, 13 October 1992, 423, 4.
6. Mercator. 1983. Irish America our Most Under-Utilised Asset. *The Irish Times*, 17 October.
7. SFADCo, or Shannon Development, was established by the Irish Government in 1959 to promote Shannon Airport and the surrounding area. Until 2014, SFADCo was responsible for promoting tourism in the region and attracting inward investment. The agency managed the Shannon Free Zone and the National Technology Park where the University of Limerick is located.
8. Dáil Éireann Debates, 13 October 1992, 423, 4 (Albert Reynolds).
9. Stephen D. Cohen. 2007. Multinational Corporations and Foreign Direct Investment. Oxford: Oxford University Press, 155.

10. Nathan M. Jensen. 2006. Nation-States and the Multinational Corporation: A Political Economy of Foreign Direct Investment. Princeton: Princeton University Press, 2.
11. Ray Mac Sharry, Padraic White. 2000. The Making of the Celtic Tiger. Cork: Mercier Press, 121–145, 367.
12. Mac Sharry, White, The Making of the Celtic Tiger, 180–182, 372–373.
13. Mac Sharry, White, The Making of the Celtic Tiger, 364–366.
14. "The IDA is now considered one of the best agencies in the world for promoting FDI". Denis O'Hearn. 2001. The Atlantic Economy: Britain, the US and Ireland. Manchester: Manchester University Press, 171.
15. This period runs from the early 1990s to 2001/02. After a temporary slowdown due to the bursting of the dot-com bubble, the growth rate of the Irish economy picked up again until the financial crisis hit in 2007–2008.
16. See: Mac Sharry, White, The Making of the Celtic Tiger; Peadar Kirby. 2002. The Celtic Tiger in Distress: Growth and Inequality in Ireland. Basingstoke: Palgrave; Paul Sweeney. 1999. The Celtic Tiger: Ireland's Continuing Economic Miracle. Dublin: Oak Tree Press; Frank Barry (ed.). 1999. Understanding Ireland's Economic Growth. London: Palgrave Macmillan; Alan Gray (ed.). 1997. International Perspectives on the Irish Economy, Dublin, Indecon.
17. Bertie Ahern was Taoiseach from June 1997 to May 2008.
18. Dáil Éireann Debates, 19 November 2002, 557, 4 (Bertie Ahern).
19. Donald Keough died in 2015. He was also the chairman of Allen & Company Incorporated, a major US investment bank, and a member of the board of directors of numerous companies including McDonald's, *The Washington Post*, and H. J. Heinz. Refer to appendix for biography.
20. Niall O'Dowd. 2010. The Corporate Chieftain. Irish America, 1 January.
21. Donald P. Brennan (Morgan Stanley & Co.), William J. Flynn (Mutual of America), Denis P. Kelleher (Wall Street Access), Edmund F. Kelly (Liberty Mutual Group), Mary B. Maguire (The Chase Manhattan Bank), Thomas J. Moran (Mutual of America), Arthur F. Ryan (The Prudential Insurance Company of America), Daniel P. Tully (Merrill Lynch & Co., Inc.).
22. Dáil Éireann Debates, 4 April 1995, 451, 5.
23. Bertie Ahern. Speech on Acceptance of an Honorary Degree of Laws at Fairfield University, Connecticut, USA, 25 September 2003. Refer to appendix for Dan Tully's biography.
24. On the role of the diaspora in promoting the IFSC, see: Fiona Reddan. 2008. Ireland's IFSC: A Story of Global Success. Cork: Mercier Press, 232, 234.
25. Merrill Lynch moved to the IFSC in 1995.

26. Michael Clancy. 2011. Re-presenting Ireland: Tourism, Branding and National Identity in Ireland. Journal of International Relations and Development 14, 3: 296. https://doi.org/10.1057/jird.2010.4
27. Dáil Éireann Debates, 22 March 1994, 440, 4; Dáil Éireann Debates, 16 February 1994, 438, 8.
28. AD Little Consultants conducted an independent study of Bord Fáilte's activities. Dáil Éireann Debates, 5 October 1995, 456, 5.
29. Dáil Éireann Debates, 10 May 1995, 452, 6.
30. A leprechaun is an imaginary creature from Irish folklore.
31. Michael Clancy, Re-presenting Ireland, 297–298.
32. Dáil Éireann Debates, 17 November 1998, 496, 6.
33. EU aid was to be cut from one billion to one hundred and fifty million Irish pounds. Marc Hennessy, Kyran Fitzgerald. 1998. Anger as EU Cuts Set to Take a Heavy Toll. The Irish News, 19 March.
34. Dáil Éireann Debates, 24 June 1998, 493,1.
35. Dáil Éireann Debates, 17 November 1998, 496, 6.
36. Ahern Plan to Seek Private Investment. 1998. *Irish Examiner*, 20 March.
37. Government of Ireland, Department of the Taoiseach, "National Development Plan 2000–2006", Pn. 7780, Dublin, Stationery Office, 2003. https://www.drugsandalcohol.ie/5076/1/NDP_complete_text%5B1%5D.pdf. Accessed 5 June 2025. See also: Government of Ireland, Department of the Taoiseach, "Framework for Action on Infrastructural Development Including Public Private Partnership", Dublin, February 2000. https://www.yumpu.com/en/document/read/30483625/framework-for-action- on-department-of-taoiseach. Accessed 5 June 2025; Government of Ireland, Department of the Taoiseach, "National Development Plan 2007–2013. Transforming Ireland, a Better Quality of Life for All", Pn. A7/0004, Dublin, Stationery Office, 2007. http://www.socialinclusion.ie/documents/NationalDevelopmentPlan2007-2013_000.pdf. Accessed 5 June 2025.
38. Robert Herbold, Chief Operating Officer at Microsoft, quoted in: Harvey Thompson. 3 May 1999. Irish Government Sells Off State Telecom Company. World Socialist Web Site, International Committee of the Fourth International. http://www.wsws.org/articles/1999/may1999/tele-m03.shtml. Accessed 5 June 2025.
39. Brian Thompson was previously President and CEO of LCI and Global Telesystems Group, Inc.
40. See: Siobhan Creaton. 1998. Minister Sets Target Date for Telecoms Market Liberalisation, *The Irish Times*, 10 June; Karlin Lillington. 1998. Ireland Takes its First Stride on the Road to Digital Economy. The Irish Times, 19 November; Karlin Lillington. 1998. Telecom Eireann to Cut

Internet Cost by 33%. The Irish Times, 19 November; Principal Elements of Report. 1998. *The Irish Times*, 19 November.

41. Refer to appendix for biography.
42. For more details on Chuck Feeney's influence on the Irish economy and the country's political life, see: Anne Groutel. 2024. Irish Diaspora Business Elite philanthropy: Boon or Bane? *Revue Lisa/Lisa e-journal* 22, 57, Ondine Aza, Anne Groutel, Caixia Tan (eds.), special issue on: Diasporas, States and Economic Development in the English-speaking World: Opportunities and Threats. https://doi.org/10.4000/lisa.15866
43. After studying engineering at Cork University, Ed Walsh moved to the United States for ten years. He worked there while continuing his studies at Iowa State University where he obtained a Master's degree in nuclear physics and a PhD in electronics. He eventually decided to return to Ireland where he was offered the opportunity to develop the Limerick National Institute for Higher Education. Louise Holden. 2009. Limerick Leader Is True Original. *The Irish Times*, 10 February.
44. Higher education institution that provided technical education.
45. Holden, Limerick Leader Is True Original.
46. Conor O'Clery. 2007. How the West Lured a Billionaire. *The Irish Times*, 27 August.
47. Refer to appendix for biography.
48. Lara Marlowe. 2010. A Gift that Keeps on Giving. *The Irish Times*, 25 September.
49. O'Clery, How the West Lured a Billionaire.
50. Holden, Limerick Leader Is True Original.
51. Ferdinand von Prondzynski. 29 May 2010. PRTLI Wars. A University Blog. Diary of Life and Strategy Inside and Outside the University. https://universitydiary.wordpress.com/2010/05/. Accessed 5 June 2025.
52. Gerry O'Sullivan. 2005. Le Programme irlandais pour la recherché dans les établissements de troisième degré (PRTLI). PEB Échanges, revue du Programme pour la construction et l'équipement de l'éducation, Programme 3: 1316. https://doi.org/10.1787/566838767166
53. Ferdinand von Prondzynski. 2009. Ireland's Future Depends on Continued Investment in Research. *The Irish Times*, 10 November.
54. Ned Costello. 2017. Building on the Legacy of Chuck Feeney's Philanthropy. *The Irish Times*, 6 January.
55. Higher Education Authority, "Transformations: How Research is Changing Ireland", Dublin, 2008, vi.
56. Interview with Chuck Feeney on CBS news, 25 February 2008.
57. Peadar Kirby. 2010. Celtic Tiger in Collapse: Explaining the Weaknesses of the Irish Model. 2nd edn. Basingstoke: Palgrave Macmillan, 146–164.

58. Kathleen Lynch is a University Professor at University College Dublin.
59. Kathleen Lynch. 2006. Neo-Liberalism and Marketisation: The Implications for Higher Education. European Educational Research Journal 5, 1, 1–17. https://doi.org/10.2304/eerj.2006.5.1.1
60. PA Consulting Group, "Ten Years On: Confirming Impacts from Research Investment. A Case Study Focusing on the Direct Commercial and Economic Impacts From Exchequer Investment into Centres and Initiatives", August 2011, 36, https://hea.ie/assets/uploads/2017/06/Ten-Years-On-Confirming-Impacts-From-Research-Investment.pdf. Accessed 5 June 2025.
61. In 1987, the sector employed 119,000 people in Ireland. Dáil Éireann Debates, 1 December 1998, 497, 5.
62. Jim MacLaughlin. 1997. Ireland in the Global Economy: An End to a Distinct Nation? In Under the Belly of the Tiger: Class, Race, Identity and Culture in Global Ireland, Ethel Crowley and Jim MacLaughlin, eds. 1–19. Dublin: Irish Reporter Publications; Anne Groutel. 2013. L'art et la culture au service de l'économie irlandaise: perspectives, stratégies et controverses. Special issue: Les nations celtiques et le monde contemporain, ed. Frédéric Armao, Revue Babel 27, 8:153–165. https://fredericarmao.wordpress.com/wp-content/uploads/2017/05/les-nations-celtiques-et-le-monde-contemporain.pdf. Accessed 5 June 2025.
63. Eoin Reeves. An Economic Analysis of Public Private Partnerships: The Case of the Ireland's National Roads Programme, paper presented at the conference "Highways: Cost and Regulation in Europe", Università degli studi di Bergamo, Italy, 27 November 2004. Eoin Reeves is a Senior Lecturer in Economics at the University of Limerick.
64. Kieran Allen. 2007. The Corporate Takeover of Ireland. Dublin: Irish Academic Press, 45–50.
65. Siobhan Creaton. 1998. Abuse Mars Financial Credibility. *The Irish Times*, 13 February.

    American Rumblings of Discontent over Irish Benefits Cause Concern. 2005. *The Irish Times*, 28 November.
66. See for example: O'Hearn, The Celtic Tiger: The Role of Multinationals, in Under the Belly of the Tiger, 21–34.
67. Peadar Kirby, Celtic tiger in Collapse, 156.
68. Dáil Éireann Debates, 17 November 1998, 496, 6.
69. See: Eoin O'Malley. April 1998. The Revival of Irish Indigenous Industry 1987–1997. Quarterly Economic Commentary: 3556; Eoin O'Malley. Winter 2004. Competitive Performance in Irish Industry. Quarterly Economic Commentary: 66–86.
70. Eoin O'Driscoll. 2004. Ahead of the Curve: Ireland's Place in the Global Economy. Dublin: Enterprise Strategy Group, 8.

71. See the IFSC website: https://www.ifsc.ie/ifsc-facts-history
72. Marc C. White. 2005. Assessing the Role of the International Financial Services Centre in Irish Regional Development. European Planning Studies 13, 3, 2005: 391–392, 401. https://doi.org/10.1080/09654310500089365
73. Fintan O'Toole. 2009. Liechtenstein on the Liffey. *The Guardian*, 27 February.
74. Mark Malone. January 2013. IFSC Clearing House: What the Irish Times Doesn't Say and Why It Matters. Irish Left Review 1, 1, 77–92. https://soundmigration.wordpress.com/2012/10/26/ifsc-clearing-house-what-the-irish-times-doesnt-say-and-why-it-matters/. Accessed 5 June 2025.
75. Caroline Madden. 2009. IFSC Plummets in International Competitiveness Ranking. *The Irish Times*, 17 November.

CHAPTER 9

From Philanthropy to Pressure: The Double-Edged Influence of the Irish-American Economic Network (1990s–2000s)

9.1 Investing in the Homeland: The Dual Motives of Irish-American Powerful Businessmen

Donald P. Brennan is one of the IAEAB members who invested in Ireland. In 1990, while a director of Morgan Stanley Bank, he acquired a stake in Waterford Wedgwood, a famous Irish manufacturer of luxury crystal and china, of which he was once chairman.

Another example is Kevin Melia. Born in Ashford, Co. Wicklow, Ireland, he emigrated to the United States where he founded Manufacturers Services Ltd. (MSL)[1] in 1994. The following year the company moved to Athlone (Co. Westmeath, Ireland). In 2000, MSL invested twenty million dollars in Ireland and set up its European headquarters in Galway, in the west of the country.[2] The company, whose turnover was one billion dollars, employed five thousand people, of which one thousand were in Ireland (Athlone, Galway, and Dublin). In addition, Melia acquired a stake in Iona Technologies, one of Ireland's flagship companies. He served as the chairman of the company on two occasions: first in 2007, the year the company went public on NASDAQ, and then again in 2008, when it was acquired by Progress Software. Chris Horn's tribute to Melia, co-founder of Iona Technologies, following the news of his death in 2014 is interesting in that it highlights a different facet of the role that some members of the diaspora play in the Irish economy:

A. Groutel, *The Two Irelands and the Diaspora*,
https://doi.org/10.1007/978-3-032-12355-8_9

> He was my personal coach and mentor as chairman [...]. He guided me a lot as a first-time CEO and was a great help to me personally when growing Iona. I benefitted hugely from his wisdom and great experience.[3]

This mentoring role was all the more important because in the 1990s the majority of Irish entrepreneurs had no experience of business development. Melia held a wide variety of positions in a number of Irish companies. He served as a director of Eircom in the early 2000s. Additionally, he acted as the non-executive chairman of Horizon Technology Group Plc., an Internet services company, and held a non-executive directorship at DCC, a publicly traded Irish conglomerate, where his contributions are fondly recalled. Michael Buckley, the chairman of DCC, said that the group benefited from Melia's "considerable corporate and entrepreneurial expertise".[4] He was also a director of Merrion Capital Group, an Irish company specialising in brokerage and corporate finance. Melia was among the IAEAB members who made tangible and diverse contributions to the advancement of the Irish economy. He found his investment worthwhile, as apart from the profits generated by his company MSL in Ireland, he also realised substantial capital gains from selling shares in Iona and Horizon.[5] This came on top of the salaries and bonuses allocated to senior company executives.[6]

Whether driven by the attraction of profit or by an altruistic desire to contribute to the country, deciphering the motivations behind why certain members of the IAEAB invested in Ireland proves challenging. Conor O'Clery has written a book about Chuck Feeney, who for many years avoided publicity about his philanthropic activities. He describes the billionaire's attachment to Ireland:

> Like most Irish Americans, Feeney had a sentimental attraction to the land of his ancestors [...]. He carried in his wallet a 'Thornsticks'[7] card, stating he was an Irish American, passionately proud of Irish culture and customs but without publicity, fanfare, or personal reward.[8]

O'Clery recounts the occasion when Feeney brought his wife and children to Ireland for the first time. They stayed at the Dromoland Castle Hotel in County Clare:

> They remember tears trickling down his face as he listened to a harpist play melancholy Irish melodies [...]. The more he reconnected with Ireland, the

more Feeney became convinced that Irish Americans like himself should be doing more to help.[9]

During the 1980s, the economy of the Republic of Ireland was stagnant. However, Feeney remained resolute in his determination to invest in Ireland. Consequently, he tasked Padraig Berry, someone well acquainted with the country, to conduct some reconnaissance. In addition, Feeney travelled to Ireland in person to look for business opportunities.[10] At one point he considered buying director John Huston's Georgian mansion near Craughwell in the west of Ireland as a base for his family. However, being a savvy businessman, he opted against it due to the excessive cost. Instead, he bought the Kilternan Golf Course and Country Club, nestled in the foothills of the Dublin Mountains, home to Ireland's only synthetic ski slope, and Heritage House, one of Dublin's finest Georgian buildings.

During the same decade, Chuck Feeney, Anthony "Tony" O'Reilly,[11] and Dan Rooney[12] —two other prominent members of the IAEAB—made strategic investments in Ireland. The three men were part of a consortium that purchased Ashford Castle[13] in 1985 for $7 million. Ashford Castle, a thirteenth-century medieval estate converted into a luxury hotel, had previously been acquired in 1970 by Irish-American businessman John A. Mulcahy. The property was later sold in 2007, at the peak of the property boom, to developer Gerry Barrett for €50 million.[14] Around the same time, Feeney divested all his Irish properties, including the Castletroy Park Hotel, which was sold for €25 million.[15]

Other Irish-American tycoons have used their corporate influence to encourage their companies to expand into Ireland. For example, Bertie Ahern told the Dáil on two occasions that Donald Keough had lobbied within his company for Ballina Beverages[16] (Co. Mayo), a subsidiary of Coca-Cola, to set up in Ireland:

> To be bluntly honest, it is not there because it is profitable but because the top two people involved are Irish and wanted to do something for Ireland. In many other instances Irish people intervened.[17]

Whatever Bertie Ahern said, it was not just a good deed, as the company was far from loss-making. Indeed, at that time, US companies in Ireland producing soft drinks were making profit margins of up to 70%.[18] Although costs rose in the 2000s, investing in Ireland remained highly profitable for multinationals.[19]

Therefore, although IAEAB members who invested in Ireland were demonstrating their dedication to the country, their motivations were not solely altruistic. Some cynics might even say that while they made a point of ostensibly donating to The Ireland Funds, a charity set up by Tony O'Reilly and Dan Rooney, many of them were recouping some of their donations through the profits, dividends, or capital gains from their investments in Ireland.

9.2 When Profit Collides with National Interest

Until 1995, the telephone operator Telecom Éireann was a public company. In 1995, the Irish government initiated the privatisation of the company, leading to its transformation into Eircom. By 1999, Eircom was publicly listed on the Dublin, London, and New York stock exchanges. Numerous small investors were urged to buy shares in the company, but those who did so ultimately regretted it deeply as it was followed by a significant decline in share prices when the Internet bubble burst in 2001.[20]

In 2001, Eircom sold its mobile phone subsidiary Eircell to Vodafone before being taken over by the Valentia[21] consortium headed by O'Reilly, who became Eircom's chairman. The company's decisions drew swift criticism. Indeed, Eircom, which oversaw 80% of the nation's fixed telephone lines, raised rental prices by 27% over two years, laid off 1800 employees, and divested assets yielding 285 million euros.[22] Now thriving with profitability, the company distributed generous dividends to its shareholders, including O'Reilly who reportedly pocketed 55 million euros in the first two years.[23] But it is worth noting that this strategy was pursued at the expense of implementing a long-term policy. The company was singled out by the Organisation for Economic Co-operation and Development (OECD) for failing to invest in broadband Internet, a service that would have made the Irish economy much more attractive to foreign investors.[24]

It is surprising that O'Reilly didn't prioritise this strategic matter for Ireland, especially considering his investment of €400 million in an attempt to salvage jobs at Waterford Wedgwood,[25] and guaranteed its debts, which amounted to 300 million euros. Ultimately, these efforts were futile, as the company was placed into receivership in 2008.[26]

9.3 Silent Partners: The Secrecy and Power of the IAEAB

For François Denord, the notion of a network:

> [...] often has a positive connotation when used in relation to an organisational form [...]. In the field of management, the network thus refers to flexible and decentralised organisational forms, which are thought to be more efficient than traditional hierarchical structures.[27]

The IAEAB's statute was indeed flexible, but somewhat unclear. When asked about this by Labour MP Proinsias De Rossa, Albert Reynolds confirmed that the members of the group were not elected. Rather, in his words, it was:

> [...] an arrangement by which prominent Irish business people who have made it to the top in Irish-American business would come together to try to pool their resources and impart knowledge to our various agencies on how to improve business for Ireland, be it by buying and selling, investment, tourism, infrastructure and so on.[28]

Reynolds described this group as:

> An extremely powerful, influential and knowledgeable force which could help the United States' economy to grow abroad and help reduce the Irish economy grow faster so that we can reduce the unacceptably high level of unemployment.[29]

Ahern also paid glowing tribute to the IAEAB that he described as "[...] enormously important [...]",[30] "[...] immensely helpful [...]",[31] or "[...] extremely useful [...]".[32] Yet both the Department of the Taoiseach[33] and John Bruton[34] sought to downplay the role of the IAEAB in our interviews. This despite the fact that the former Taoiseach had previously publicly expressed "[...] his thanks to each and every one of them for this very practical expression of their goodwill towards Ireland".[35]

If Denord concedes that networks have benefits, he also points out that they are "frequently associated with secrecy, clandestine activities and struggles for influence when it comes to the economic, media, political or administrative worlds".[36] Thus, it is worth noting that while successive Irish Prime Ministers have from time to time provided parliamentarians with an overview of the IAEAB's recommendations, the agendas and minutes of these meetings have never been published. Furthermore, even if Reynolds, in his autobiography, mentions a few names,[37] the full list of members was never made public.[38] The reason given for the secrecy surrounding the identity of the group was that they were not acting on behalf of their company, but in their personal capacity.[39]

9.4 Behind the Curtain: Power, Politics, and Influence in Irish-American Business Relations

The close relationship between these Irish-American tycoons and the Irish authorities raises a number of questions. Documents and testimony released at the time of the Moriarty Inquiry shed light on the pressure that certain members of the IAEAB exerted on the Irish government during the award of the second mobile phone licence. The Moriarty Tribunal was set up in 1997 to investigate suspicions of corruption against Irish politicians. As part of this inquiry, the Tribunal was tasked with determining whether Michael Lowry, then Minister for Telecommunications, exerted undue influence in advocating for the second telecommunications licence to be awarded to Esat.

It was rumoured that when Reynolds was Taoiseach, he had "promised" to award the licence to Motorola.[40] In return, the multinational company was said to have committed itself to further investment in Ireland and to creating jobs. In 1996, Esat Digifone, a company owned by Denis O'Brien, a wealthy Irish businessman, was preferred to Persona Group (a consortium in which Motorola had a 26.6% stake) and Irish Cellular Telephone Ltd., another consortium headed by O'Reilly. John F. Mitchell,[41] vice-president of Motorola and member of the IAEAB, wrote to the then Taoiseach, John Bruton, expressing his dismay at the government's decision:

> We were surprised that the decision was not reviewed by the government since our people were informed it would have government review and approval, with a final decision and announcement in the middle of November.[42]

He pointed out in passing that "[...] to an increasing extent Ireland has been chosen over other locations that were favoured in the past".[43] He explicitly stated that the decision went against Motorola's interests.

Mitchell subsequently penned a second letter to Bruton a few weeks later, informing him of his intention to attend the upcoming IAEAB meeting. In addition, he emphasised that his Irish staff were consistently updating him on the licensing process's developments.[44]

Tony Boyle, who headed Persona, and Michael McGinley, who was also a member of Persona, gave evidence to the Moriarty Inquiry. They confirmed that the news of the award of the licence to another group was very badly received at Motorola's headquarters.[45] The retaliation swiftly followed. The multinational company, which employed 1500 people in Ireland and was planning to expand its operations, left the country.[46] In addition, Motorola also took the Irish state to court to get to the bottom of the irregularities in the award of the licence. O'Reilly, another member of the IAEAB whose consortium was also among the unsuccessful bidders, did not excuse the government either. At the time, he wielded considerable influence in the Irish business community, particularly through Independent News and Media (INM), Ireland's largest media group. Called to testify on 31 March 2004,

Bruton said that in a private meeting O'Reilly had expressed his "Unhappiness"[47] about the way the licensing process had been led. It was certainly a disappointment to O'Reilly's partners too. Indeed, Jean Kennedy, then US Ambassador to Ireland, told Seán Donlon, a senior government adviser, that American businessmen she knew were convinced that they would win the bid because they had O'Reilly as a partner.[48] During this interview with Bruton, O'Reilly is reported to have said that he felt the value of his potential contribution had been underestimated.[49] The latter also expressed his grievances about what he considered to be inadequate subsidies from the Irish state to a Heinz factory.[50] At the time, O'Reilly was the managing director of the multinational.

On 6 March 1997, the day of the general election, the front page editorial of the *Irish Independent* urged voters not to return the Rainbow Coalition to power. Bruton felt that the latter,[51] which he led, had been "punished" for not giving in to O'Reilly's demands.

In any case, Fianna Fáil won the election. It is clear that the new leadership did not challenge O'Reilly's control of the media in Ireland; rather it was quite the reverse. Indeed, despite O'Reilly's growing influence in the communications sector, Mary Harney, Tánaiste in the Fianna Fáil government from 1997 to 2006, took the decision not to refer the Valentia takeover of Eircom to the competition authority. This allowed O'Reilly and members of his family, who already owned a stake in Chorus and controlled Independent News and Media,[52] to become majority shareholders in the country's largest telecoms group.[53] Moreover, documents released under the Freedom of Information Act reveal that, in the midst of the Eircom takeover battle, Charley McCreevy, then Minister of Finance, agreed to hastily introduce an amendment to the Finance Act 2002. This change is alleged to have indirectly benefited Valentia.[54] In his 2009 book, writer and journalist Matt Cooper revealed the links between O'Reilly and Ahern, which proved it to be a mutually beneficial relationship.[55]

9.5 Strategic Silence: US Influence and Ireland's Cautious Diplomacy

But the links between some very influential Irish-American businessmen and Irish leaders may have had even deeper implications. In 2002, Joe Higgins challenged Ahern while answering a question on the IAEAB in the lower house of the Irish Parliament. The socialist TD criticised the Ahern government for being too timid to condemn US foreign policy for fear of offending "powerful US multinationals".[56] Ahern dismissed these allegations with a wave of the hand: "I would not get too excited or hung up about us being too much into the pockets of the United States". Yet the end of his reply indicates that the Irish authorities had adopted a cautious stance: "[…]We should not go out of our way to have a go at the US at every possible opportunity".[57]

A few weeks before the summit between EU representatives and the United States in June 2004, during the Irish presidency of the organisation, Ahern firmly discouraged potential troublemakers:

> He [Joe Higgins, TD] should not talk about mass protests and antagonism when people come to this country for a summit during our Presidency of the EU. This country's close relationship with the United States has been built up over 150 years. We derive significant benefits from it for our people who work in the United States and in this country. It does no good to anybody in this House to be ranting an old antagonistic doctrine of senseless proportions.[58]

It is true that the Irish authorities, aware of the possible repercussions for the country's economy, kept a low profile during the Iraq War and even went so far as to make Shannon airport available to American troops en route to the combat zones, ignoring the country's neutrality and the massive opposition of Irish public opinion.[59]

The latter and the media were difficult to contain, which at times irritated the IAEAB and led two of its members to express their annoyance at what they saw as an anti-American campaign. For example, Thomas J. Moran, Managing Director of Mutual of America, expressed dismay at the criticism of US foreign policy from the Irish public.[60]

But the starkest warning came after Vincent Browne and John O'Shea of the non-governmental organisation Goal criticised the Irish government's decision to send €1 million in aid to Hurricane Katrina victims. Denis P. Kelleher,[61] Managing Director of Wall Street Access, spoke bluntly:

> This animosity towards America has done a lot of damage - immeasurable damage between Ireland and Irish-America. [...] we are sick of it [...]. Yes I do believe this has the potential, longer term, to be harmful to American business relocation to Ireland. Of course other factors, such as being competitive, will also play a role. But if goodwill is damaged, then the path of least resistance will choose more friendly environments. Others on this side of the world feel exactly as I do. I have spoken to them. [...] We have all been heartened that Ireland is on the up economically and I have been honoured to be asked by the Taoiseach to sit on the AIEAB, but it should be remembered that these things are highly cyclical and this America bashing will be remembered into the future.[62]

It is not unreasonable to suggest that the continued support of the IAEAB may have been contingent upon Ireland's accommodating posture towards the United States and its alignment with American foreign policy. In any case, the Irish authorities refrained from taking any action that might have strained this relationship. Nevertheless, Kelleher's warnings should be interpreted with caution. It is unlikely that critical public discourse in Ireland would have significantly deterred foreign direct investment. Indeed, despite France's outspoken opposition to the Iraq War, US investment in the country rose markedly between 2002 and 2003.[63]

When the Irish economy was lagging in the 1980s, IAEAB members helped the Irish authorities to attract foreign investment by facilitating access to key figures in the US business community. Most of its members, having successfully invested in Ireland themselves, were living proof that Ireland was a profitable destination and that its authorities were determined to attract FDI. In doing so, the group provided Ireland with a vital competitive advantage. The IAEAB also conveyed the message that the Irish authorities were receptive to informal requests from foreign companies and could be accommodating if necessary. Ahern acknowledged that the group had helped to ensure "[...] deeper involvement on the part of corporate America in Irish affairs".[64] These words are sobering given the pressure some companies put on the Irish authorities to defend their interests. Multinationals generally see it as an advantage to have direct links with policymakers.[65] However, the question arises as to how far they should be allowed to influence the affairs of the country. The IAEAB has always supported pro-business government policy to the extent that it also served the interests of certain members of the group. But what has happened to Ireland's long-term economic interests? The answer to this question, as we have seen, is far from unanimous.

Notes

1. Manufacturers Services Ltd. was an international company based in Concord, Mass. It offered comprehensive electronics manufacturing and supply chain management services. In 2004, the company merged with Celestica, a Canadian company. https://www.celestica.com/about-us/history-and-milestones. Accessed 5 June 2025.
2. Jamie Smyth. 2000. Melia Firm to Set up HQ in Republic. *The Irish Times*, 6 December; Lorna Siggins. 2000. MSL to Create 700 Jobs for Athlone, Galway. *The Irish Times*, 3 March.
3. Ciarán Hancock. 2014. Death of Former Chairman of Iona Technology", *The Irish Times*, 19 June.
4. Hancock. Death of Former Chairman.
5. Iona Shares Sold. 1998. *The Irish Times*, 16 May; Iona Share Transactions. 1998. The Irish Times, 20 May; Sale of Iona Shares. 1998. *The Irish Times*, 28 July; Naji Takes Chairman Role at Horizon. 2001. *The Irish Times*, 27 February; Graeme Davies. 2001. Melia Fades from Horizon, Citywire, 30 April. http://citywire.co.uk/money/melia-fades-from-horizon/a222811. Accessed 5 June 2025.
6. Jamie Smyth. 2005. New Iona Boss to Earn Base Salary of €259,000. *The Irish Times*, 1 June; Four Eircom Directors Share €3.39 m. 2005. *The Irish Times*, 24 June.
7. The Thornsticks is an organisation founded in 1982 by Tom Dunn, an American politician of Irish origin. The aim of this organisation is to maintain a sense of identity in the Irish-American community and to help families in need.

8. Conor O'Clery. 2007. The Billionaire Who Wasn't: How Chuck Feeney Secretly Made and Gave Away a Fortune. New York: Public Affairs, 134.
9. O'Clery. The Billionaire.
10. O'Clery. The Billionaire, 135.
11. Anthony O'Reilly is Irish by birth. After playing professional rugby, he pursued a business career in the United States where he became president of the H. J. Heinz Company. He also invested heavily in Ireland. Refer to appendix for biography.
12. Daniel Milton "Dan" Rooney was the president of the American football team the Pittsburgh Steelers. Dan Rooney was the United States Ambassador to Ireland from 2009 to 2012. He passed away in April 2017. Refer to appendix for biography.
13. Ashford Castle is located on the border of counties Galway and Mayo in the West of Ireland.
14. Ciaran Hancock. 2007. Barrett Now King of Ashford Castle", *The Irish Times*, 28 September.
15. Jack Fagan. 2004. Limerick Hotel Sold for €25 m. *The Irish Times*, 23 June.
16. Ballina Beverages produces the syrup concentrate which is then sold to the various bottlers that own a Coca-Cola franchise around the world.
17. Houses of the Oireachtas, Dáil Éireann (hereafter Dáil Éireann debates), 10 November 2004, 592, 2. See also: Dáil Éireann Debates, 19 November 2002, 557, 4.
18. Denis O'Hearn. 1997. The Celtic Tiger: The Role of Multinationals. In Under the Belly of the Tiger: Class, Race, Identity and Culture in Global Ireland, Ethel Crowley and Jim MacLaughlin, eds. 27. Dublin: Irish Reporter Publications.
19. Kieran Allen. 2007. The Corporate Takeover of Ireland. Dublin: Irish Academic Press, 77–106.
20. Firm May Change Hands for Fifth Time in Six Years. 2006. *The Irish Times*, 15 April.
21. Valentia was supported by the famous financier George Soros and the US bank Goldman Sachs. Firm May Change Hands.
22. Buoyant Tone as Revamped Eircom Embarks on Second Float. 2004. *Irish Independent*, 1 March; The Insider: Barefaced Cheek of Eircom Chiefs. 2004. *The Sunday Business Post*, 18 January.
23. John McManus. 2004. O'Reilly to Earn More than €36 m in Eircom Float", *The Irish Times*, 27 February.
24. Eamon Quinn. 2004. Revealed: Eircom's Share Millionaires. *The Sunday Business Post*, 22 February.
25. This group was created in 1987 following the merger of Waterford Crystal and Wedgwood (porcelain), two high-end brands whose origins date back to the eighteenth century.

26. Barry J. White. 2014. Tony O'Reilly: How the Billionaire's Fortune Unravelled. The Daily Business Post, 26 June.
27. François Denord. Réseaux, Théorie des. Encyclopædia Universalis. https://www.universalis.fr/encyclopedie/theorie-des-reseaux/. Accessed 5 June 2025.
28. Dáil Éireann Debates, 13 October 1992, 423, 4.
29. Dáil Éireann Debates, 13 October 1992.
30. Dáil Éireann Debates, 10 November 2004, 592, 2.
31. Dáil Éireann Debates, 12 October 2005, 607, 3.
32. Dáil Éireann Debates, 28 February 2001, 531, 4.
33. Interviews conducted on 22 April 2009 with Paul McGarry and George J. Shaw of the Department of the Taoiseach.
34. Interview with John Bruton on 8 October 2003. John Bruton succeeded Albert Reynolds as Taoiseach on 15 December 1994. He held this position until 26 June 1997.
35. Dáil Éireann Debates, 4 April 1995, 451, 5.
36. Denord, Réseaux, Théorie.
37. Albert Reynolds. 2009. Albert Reynolds: My Autobiography. London: Transworld Ireland, 257–258.
38. Members of the Irish Parliament could, however, access it on request.
39. Dáil Éireann Debates, 21 November 2001, 544, 4.
40. The Moriarty Commission did not bring any charges against Reynolds. Moriarty Hears of Letter to Reynolds. RTÉ news, 29 January 2003.
41. Refer to appendix for biography.
42. John F. Mitchell, Letter to An Taoiseach John Bruton dated 6 November 1995. Letter accessed online on 11 June 2012 but no longer available. The website moriartytribunal.com on which this letter was published was opened by Denis O'Brien, who was highly critical of Justice Moriarty's methods. Internal documents from the Irish Department of Telecommunications and correspondence such as this letter, which were not included in the official report published by the Commission of Inquiry, were made available to the public on the Internet.
43. John F. Mitchell, Letter to An Taoiseach John Bruton, 6 November 1995.
44. John F. Mitchell, Letter to An Taoiseach John Bruton, 19 February 1996, letter accessed on 11 June 2012 at moriartytribunal.com but no longer available.
45. Sam Smyth, Elaine Byrne. 2012. Motorola Warned of Job Cuts over Licence, *Irish Independent*, 1 April.
46. Smyth, Byrne, Motorola Warned; State Lost Motorola Investment, Bruton Was Told in Letter. 2004. *The Irish Times*, 26 March.

47. John Bruton quoted in: Ex Taoiseach Details 1996 Meeting with O'Reilly. 2004. *The Irish Times*, 24 March. See also: Matt Cooper. 2009. Who Really Runs Ireland? The Story of the Elite Who Led Ireland from Bust to Boom ... and Back Again. Dublin: Penguin Ireland, 17–22.
48. O'Reilly Was 'Unhappy' at Not Getting Licence. 2004. *The Irish Times*, 29 March.
49. Ex Taoiseach Details 1996 Meeting with O'Reilly.
50. O'Reilly Was "Unhappy" at Not Getting Licence.
51. The Rainbow Coalition was in power from 1994 to 1997.
52. Chorus was the second largest cable operator in Ireland and Independent News and Media the most powerful media group.
53. John McManus. 2001. Regulatory Problems Await O'Reilly Bid", *The Irish Times*, 24 April.
54. Oliver Emmet. 2004. Minister Faces Queries on Tax Changes Prior to Eircom Sale", *The Irish Times*, 16 February; see also: Dáil Éireann Debates, 18 February 2004, 580, 2.
55. Cooper, Who Really Runs Ireland?, 3–12.
56. "There is also a great danger of this government being compromised in taking an independent position on US foreign policy for fear of offending many of these powerful multinationals". Dáil Éireann Debates, 19 November 2002, 557, 4.
57. Dáil Éireann Debates, 19 November 2002.
58. Dáil Éireann Debates, 18 February 2004, 580, 2.
59. Paul Brennan. 2004. L'Irlande et la guerre d'Irak. Études irlandaises. Special issue In Memoriam Paul Brennan:165–168. https://doi.org/10.3406/irlan.2004.1682.
60. Conor O'Clery. 2002. Businessman Philanthropist Plays Key Role as Irish US Ally. *The Irish Times*, 12 April.
61. Refer to appendix for biography.
62. Jerome Reilly. 2005. Enough of that Anti-American Rant. *The Irish Times*, 20 September.
63. France, Assemblée nationale, Commission des Affaires étrangères, "Rapport d'information sur les relations entre l'Europe et les États-Unis", 11 October 2005, 41.
    https://www.assemblee-nationale.fr/12/pdf/rap-info/i2567.pdf. Accessed 5 June 2025.
64. Dáil Éireann Debates, 12 October 2005, 607, 3.
65. Nathan M. Jensen. 2006. Nation-States and the Multinational Corporation: A Political Economy of Foreign Direct Investment. Princeton: Princeton University Press, 2006, 78–79.

CHAPTER 10

The Northern Ireland Conflict: Irish-American Business Leaders Working for Peace (Mid-1970s–2010s)

According to Irish diplomats stationed in North America during the 1960s, the Irish-American community's sense of ethnic identity had gradually diminished over successive generations. However, the outbreak of violence in Northern Ireland in the late 1960s served to rekindle this connection. Disturbed by media coverage and graphic images of the conflict, some members of the community responded by making financial contributions to the Irish Northern Aid Committee (NORAID),[1] an organisation suspected of raising funds in the United States to finance the IRA's armed struggle in Northern Ireland.[2] It is interesting to note that the Ulster Defence Association (UDA) and the Ulster Volunteer Force (UVF), Protestant Loyalist paramilitary organisations, also sought to raise funds abroad, particularly in Canada, where many Ulster Protestants emigrated in the nineteenth century. According to Steve Bruce, Ontario was to Ulster Protestants what Boston was to Irish Catholics. Orangeism was popular there. Bruce recounts how, in 1972, a group of Canadian businessmen shipped arms to the UVF.[3] But he agrees that these loyalist organisations were not able to gain the same political and financial support abroad as the IRA.[4]

However, many prominent Irish-Americans were opposed to the use of violence. Concerned about the growing success of NORAID, they preferred to join the Ireland Fund, the organisation founded in 1976 by Tony O'Reilly and Dan Rooney. The Fund was a non-political charity, and from

A. Groutel, *The Two Irelands and the Diaspora*,
https://doi.org/10.1007/978-3-032-12355-8_10

its inception it declared its intention to distance itself from NORAID and to work for peace through peaceful means. O'Reilly appealed to the feelings of the Irish diaspora in the United States:

> The Irish-American people have an enormous debt to Ireland, and there are millions of both traditions, orange and green, who have never given anything to Ireland. [...] we are trying to alert them to their debt.[5]

From the outset, the organisation was a great success. In 1987, it merged with the American Irish Foundation and became the American Ireland Fund. Over the years, it expanded its work to all parts of the world where there is a community of Irish origin and became known as The Ireland Funds.[6] Beyond its charitable work, the American Ireland Fund established a setting in which members of the diaspora elite, including the Northern Irish diaspora, could meet on a regular basis[7] and a circle in which one had to be seen. Working for peace in Northern Ireland became socially rewarding as it reflected positively on the individual image of Fund members.

In addition, the MacBride Principles[8] were introduced in 1984 as a set of corporate codes of conduct for US companies operating in Northern Ireland. They were named after Seán MacBride, Irish human rights advocate, Nobel Peace Prize laureate, and former foreign minister of Ireland, to reflect his lifelong commitment to justice and equality. The campaign was launched by Irish-American activists, particularly Fr. Sean McManus, president of the Irish National Caucus, along with labour unions and civil rights advocates in the United States. Fr. McManus was instrumental in crafting and promoting the principles through his lobbying efforts on Capitol Hill and among American public institutions. They were supported by figures in the US Congress (notably Congressman Ben Gilman and later Senator Tom Harkin) and by human rights groups, aiming to use economic influence to push for fair employment practices in Northern Ireland during the Troubles. The goal of the MacBride Principles was to combat systemic religious discrimination—especially against Catholics—in hiring, promotion, and workplace conditions in Northern Ireland. The principles encouraged corporate accountability, linking American investment to human rights standards. The MacBride Principles became a powerful tool of economic and moral pressure, widely adopted by US states, cities, universities, and pension funds, many of which passed legislation requiring investment only in companies that adhered to them. This amplified US influence in encouraging equal opportunity reforms in Northern Ireland and set a precedent for ethical investment linked to human rights.

However, by the end of the 1980s, neither the IRA's armed action nor attempts at a political resolution had resolved the Northern Ireland issue. The conflict was bogged down. Thus, in the early 1990s, some diaspora leaders in the United States decided to get involved in the Northern Ireland peace process.

10.1 Soft Power Diplomacy: Irish-America's Role in Conflict Resolution

In a book on the influence of the Clinton administration[9] on the Northern Ireland peace process, Conor O'Clery recounts how Bill Clinton, during his (first) election campaign, pledged to put the Northern Ireland issue on his foreign policy agenda if elected.[10] Journalist Niall O'Dowd was invited by Chris Hyland, who was responsible for building support among ethnic minorities, to join Bill Clinton's campaign.[11] O'Dowd was one of those who set up a support group for the Democratic candidate, Irish-Americans for Clinton. Bruce Morrison,[12] a former congressman, and Raymond Flynn, the mayor of Boston, were also among its founding members.[13] After their candidate's victory, they formed Americans for a New Irish Agenda, a group that made proposals for a settlement of the Northern Irish question.[14] One of these was to send an American envoy to Northern Ireland. However, this was put aside at the urging of Albert Reynolds. The Taoiseach, engaged in confidential negotiations with London to resolve the conflict, was apprehensive that external intervention might complicate matters further.[15]

The leaders of the Americans for a New Irish Agenda remained resolute and proceeded to arrange a fact-finding mission to both North and South Ireland. Despite numerous challenges, Morrison and O'Dowd, joined by millionaire Chuck Feeney and Bill Flynn,[16] another affluent Irish-American businessman, embarked on the journey in early September 1993.[17] They met with the protagonists of the Northern Irish conflict, including representatives of paramilitary organisations. Throughout the following year, they acted as intermediaries between the US authorities and the various parties involved in the conflict. O'Clery reports that, in mid-August 1994, O'Dowd handed a Sinn Féin member a document in which the

Irish-American mediators pledged to support a number of demands if the Republican movement renounced the use of arms.[18] They hoped to ensure that Sinn Féin president, Gerry Adams, and members of the party would be able to travel freely to the United States and be treated by the White House on the same basis as other Northern Ireland political leaders. There was also an expectation that Sinn Féin would be allowed to open an office in Washington. Discussions further included the possibility of transferring IRA members imprisoned in the United States to Ireland, and of ending surveillance activities by the Federal Bureau of Investigation (FBI). The Irish-American group claimed that they could persuade Washington not only to endorse the peace process but also to guarantee support for any eventual agreement. Finally, the mediators pledged to develop ways of attracting investment to Northern Ireland. Feeney's presence in the group added credence to this objective.[19]

The IRA declared a ceasefire on 31 August 1994. On 13 October 1994, the Combined Loyalist Military Command followed suit. Although a final settlement of the conflict was not yet in sight, it was a momentous occasion. The Good Friday Agreement of 1998 was another turning point in the peace process. Under its terms, Northern Ireland was allowed to have an autonomous parliament and an executive, provided that the latter is multiparty. In addition, the Northern Ireland authorities were given a certain amount of freedom in economic development and other fields.

In the years following the ceasefires, Feeney personally paid for much of the cost of the office that Sinn Féin opened in Washington.[20] Bill Clinton, for his part, made the economic side of the Northern Ireland question a priority. He was convinced that peace and prosperity went hand in hand. In other words, external financial assistance had to be an integral part of the peace process. It was therefore decided that the White House would organise a conference to link Northern Irish businesses with American companies with a view to attracting American investment to Northern Ireland. The province's political leaders were invited to attend the event which took place in May 1995. It would appear, however, that despite the efforts of the US authorities, the immediate results, in economic terms, were modest.[21] They persevered, however. A similar conference was held in Pittsburgh in 1996 and trade missions between the United States and Northern Ireland were organised in the following years.[22] Eventually, these initiatives paid off, with an additional forty US companies coming to the province over a four-year period, bringing the total to 165 by 2000.[23]

The impetus from the US authorities and the peace process encouraged some prominent figures in the Irish diaspora to promote tripartite economic and scientific cooperation between the United States, Ireland, and Northern Ireland. In September 2002, Susan Ann Davis, founder and president of her eponymous company[24] and an active member of the Republican Party,[25] organised a summit in Washington as part of the US-Ireland Business Summit, a non-profit organisation.[26] Several members of the US administration, including Don Evans, Secretary of Commerce, and Tommy Thompson, Secretary of Health and Human Services, attended. Mary Harney, the Tánaiste, and Reg Empey, the Northern Irish Minister for Enterprise, Trade, and Investment, were also present. So were Pat Cox, the President of the European Parliament, Martin Naughton, the Director of Intertrade Ireland,[27] as well as academics and the directors of several multinational companies based in Ireland, such as Wyeth, Galen, EMC, and Liberty Mutual.[28]

Reg Empey emphasised the importance of fostering entrepreneurship in Northern Ireland and highlighted what Northern Irish businessmen could learn from the United States in this regard.[29] The plan to create a transatlantic science partnership between the United States, Ireland, and Northern Ireland was announced at the event. The US-Ireland Research and Development Partnership, formally inaugurated in 2006, promotes cooperation between the three countries in the fields of biotechnology, nanotechnology, and information and communications sciences.[30]

Presidents George W. Bush and Barack Obama also showed an interest in Northern Ireland. Their administrations thus continued the work of the Clinton administration.[31] For example, in September 2009, the Secretary of State,[32] Hillary Clinton, appointed Declan Kelly as US Special Envoy for Economic Affairs in Northern Ireland. He served for two years with some success, reportedly creating 1500 jobs.[33] He was succeeded in 2014 by former Senator Gary Hart.

While the initiatives of the American authorities were certainly very beneficial for Northern Ireland, it should be noted that, in parallel, a group of businessmen ready to contribute to the economic development of the city of Belfast, the Friends of Belfast, was created at the initiative of the Belfast City Council (BCC).

10.2 Investing in the Future: A Diaspora-Driven Economic Role

High-profile Irish-Americans, less directly involved in the political side of the peace process, also began to take an interest in Northern Ireland. John Cullinane[34] was one of them. Having amassed wealth in the US software industry, he sold his company, Cullinet,[35] in 1989. It was then that he began to actively engage in Ireland's software industry and invested in the homeland of his ancestors, expressing a sense of indebtedness to it.[36] Upon Barry Murphy's invitation, a prominent figure in the Irish software industry, Cullinane convened with some forty Irish software entrepreneurs. Subsequently, he resolved to provide seed capital to the most promising companies:

> It was inevitable some of them would become software entrepreneurs, I was seeing the first wave, so I decided to help them in a variety of ways because entrepreneurship was something new in Ireland.[37]

Among others, he helped Iona, one of the most dynamic companies in the sector, to establish itself in the United States.[38] Cullinane's investments south of the border attracted the attention of leading figures on Northern Ireland's political and economic scene. The first contact with BCC representatives was in October 1994, when they were seeking to develop economic relations between their city and Boston. The latter had already established links with the Republic of Ireland through Boston Ireland Ventures, an organisation chaired by Frank Costello,[39] a close associate of Cullinane.[40] One of their early successes was to convince the US, UK, and Irish authorities of the value of setting up a fund under the International Fund for Ireland (IFI)[41] which would provide seed money for Northern Irish and Irish high-tech companies in the border counties to develop partnerships with US businesses. According to Willie McCarter, these resources were instrumental in the development of the sector on both sides of the border:

> He came before the International Fund for Ireland when I was chairman to urge funding through IFI for two vital programmes, RADIUS and RADIAN, that had successfully engineered partnerships and would be a good fit for similar partnerships between Northern Ireland hi-tech companies, border counties of the Republic and US and Canadian companies. In

> typical John Cullinane fashion, this was a pioneering step which not only led to many hi-tech partnerships but also helped the whole hi-tech scene in Ireland, north and south, to develop to the point where it is today.[42]

In the years that followed, Cullinane became increasingly involved in promoting the Northern Irish economy in the United States and worked closely with the BCC's Development Committee. In October 1997, the Council appointed him as Special Economic Adviser for the promotion of Belfast in the United States, a role which he fulfilled pro bono.

10.3 "Friends" in High Places: Irish-American Support for Post-Conflict Development

In its five-year economic development plan (1995–2000), the BCC emphasised the need to stimulate economic activity and attract foreign investment to the city. The decision was made to develop economic links with North America. Reg Empey, serving as the mayor of the city at the time, along with Alasdair McDonnell,[43] who was a city councillor then, embarked on fact-finding trips to Washington, Boston, and Pittsburgh in October 1994. White House conferences in Washington and Pittsburgh cemented the links between Belfast and the two cities. In 1996, the BCC established contacts with the Canadian province of Nova Scotia, which led to the signing of a memorandum of understanding committing the two partners to establish an economic alliance. In November 1997, a comparable protocol was signed with Boston. The subsequent year, the city of Portland (ME) followed suit. These various partnerships became the pillars of the Atlantic Rim Initiative.[44] At the same time, the BCC set up Investment Belfast Ltd., an agency to attract investors and promote business relationships between companies based in Belfast and in the partner cities (Boston, Halifax, and Portland).

In February 1998, Cullinane, together with Costello, established the Friends of Belfast group in Boston.[45] The goal was to promote the economic development of Northern Ireland by showcasing it to North American business circles and serving as a facilitator. Priority was given to the development of a network in North America, while not ruling out opportunities within the European Union. By September 1999, the network had expanded to include 180 members from academia, industry, and government. Cullinane assumed the responsibility of chief recruiter. However, it soon became evident that there was a necessity to strategise and formalise the group's activities, lest the momentum be lost. It was therefore decided that one member in each city would be appointed to lead and motivate the groups and that specific objectives would be set.[46]

In 2000, the Council reported that the network had helped bring Liberty Mutual Insurance Company and Segue Software, two companies that created forty and two hundred jobs respectively, to Northern Ireland.[47] In addition, Joe Corcoran, an American developer and member of the network, was also planning to invest in the Titanic Quarter, a new area of Belfast to be built on the site of the Harland and Wolff shipyards where the famous liner of the same name was built.[48]

As the model proved successful in Boston, it was decided to expand the network. Interestingly, among the newly appointed Friends tasked with aiding the network's leader at the local level were numerous individuals with Irish-sounding names.[49] The BCC minutes never explicitly refer to the Friends of Belfast group as comprising members of the diaspora, yet in practice this appears to have been the case.

By 2000, there were six representatives of the Friends group in the Pittsburgh area, a city known for its strengths in banking, life sciences, health, fibre optics, and high technology.[50] Dan Gallagher, a leading lawyer, was charged with taking over the group, as Cullinane had done in Boston. In New York, there were seven Friends of Belfast. It was thought important at the BCC to establish contacts there, particularly in finance, but also in the high-tech sector that was developing in Manhattan. John Connorton, a Wall Street lawyer, John Sharkey, a well-known telecommunications industry figure, and people from Belfast were given the reins of the local network.

In 2000, Belfast was to receive a visit from the Northern California World Affairs Council, a delegation of twenty-five senior people from various sectors. During this visit, it appeared crucial to enlist additional Friends to add to the group, which at the time only comprised two members in California.[51]

Ted McConnell, who had connections with numerous immigrants from Northern Ireland, was tasked with expanding the network in Toronto. Denver was also identified as another city where cultivating contacts would be beneficial, given the presence of many well-established companies in the biotech, electronics, and software sectors. There was also potential in the creative industries and cultural tourism. Jim Lyons, President Clinton's special adviser on Northern Ireland from 1993 to

2001, was a frequent visitor to Belfast[52] and seemed to be the right person to facilitate the group in the US city.

A preliminary evaluation of the network's situation was conducted in 2002. The recruitment of new members willing to actively promote economic ties between Belfast and North America was progressing smoothly. Within a few months, membership had surged from 170 to 347.[53] The Friends of Belfast now included senior people in the financial world, in sectors ranging from e-commerce to the energy industry, and in the legal profession.[54] Harry Grill, for example, was employed at one of Boston's leading law firms. Among the firm's clients were large life sciences and healthcare companies that were looking to expand into Europe. Members of the BCC's economic development sub-committee felt that Grill could be very useful in helping to organise fact-finding missions for companies in these sectors.

John Kirkwood, another Friend, was setting up a $10 million investment fund to help Belfast companies exploit the opportunities in Pennsylvania.[55] In addition, Rick Dimino, director of the Big Dig project in Boston,[56] offered to put the BCC in touch with some of his acquaintances to set up a World Trade Centre in Belfast.[57] This came to fruition some years later.

The December 2002 review of the network's activities reveals that it facilitated the organisation of seventy US trade missions to Belfast between 1998 and 2002. Additionally, it played a role in coordinating several trade missions to Boston and Pittsburgh, resulting in Northern Irish companies signing contracts worth $5 million.[58] The Economic Development Sub-Committee believed that the network's efforts required improved coordination and a sharper focus. Consequently, a strategy was devised to formalise this approach. One of its goals was to examine successful public policies in the United States regarding urban regeneration, economic development, and cultural tourism, with the aim of learning from them and applying insights gained to the activities of the BCC. The network could also work to promote Belfast's cultural and tourism potential internationally, aiming to portray the city positively to potential investors. The influence and expertise of the Friends could benefit Northern Irish businesses and Invest Northern Ireland, the agency responsible for attracting foreign investors to the province. It was decided that the network's efforts should focus on no more than one or two sectors in each US city. Distinct strategies were crafted for Boston, Denver, New York, and Pittsburgh to capitalise on the unique potential offered by each city. For instance,

New York boasted the most promising prospects in finance and creative industries, Pittsburgh in cultural tourism, Denver in environmental industries. Quantifiable targets and evaluation criteria were to be agreed later with the Friends' groups that would be responsible for implementing the strategies.[59]

However, despite providing each network member with a roadmap, an internal evaluation in 2004 unveiled that they expressed dissatisfaction regarding the irregular communication with the BCC:

> [...] weaknesses mentioned were [...] a lack of detailed briefings to the head chairs, infrequent city visits with a lack of follow-up, with the result that the Council was at risk of being perceived as yet another Northern Ireland organisation visiting a US city with few tangible outcomes as a result.[60]

The year 2004 was therefore marked by a commitment to enhancing communication between the BCC and group leaders, as well as expanding the promotion of Belfast in the realms of culture, arts, and tourism. Emphasis was also to be placed on creating business links that could benefit companies located in the provincial capital.

In 2005, two trade fairs dedicated to the promotion of Northern Ireland's creative industries took place, one in New York and the other in Boston. A dozen Northern Irish companies with good export potential were selected to attend. Robert M. Johnson, Chairman of the Executive Council of New York City and a member of the Friends of Belfast, collaborated closely with the BCC in coordinating these events. Notably, Johnson had significant connections in software, digital media, film, and television companies. Additionally, he was acquainted with venture capitalists in the media sector. As a direct outcome of the trade fairs, two Northern Irish companies successfully persuaded two venture capitalists to invest a combined total of one million dollars.[61] It was also an opportunity for these companies to establish many contacts across the Atlantic. In January 2006, the BCC's Economic Development Committee developed an action plan for the coming year in which the Friends of Belfast network was to be closely involved. The person overseeing economic initiatives at the BCC emphasised the necessity of regularly organising such events to sustain the momentum and visibility of Belfast. However, there was no mention of the Friends of Belfast in the BCC minutes in the subsequent years. The network faced challenges due to the Council's change in economic development goals. Indeed, the BCC was worried it may become ineligible for certain EU grants, which were previously utilised to attract Foreign Direct Investment (FDI), among other purposes. This uncertainty prompted a reassessment of priorities.[62] In the 2010s, there were several attempts to reactivate this network,[63] but without any follow-up.

However, it would appear that many of the contacts established between Friends of Belfast members and the business community in Northern Ireland have been maintained.[64] One example is the visit of Boston Mayor Marty Walsh to Belfast in 2014. On this occasion, he was received by the directors of Liberty IT, a subsidiary of the insurance company Liberty Mutual Insurance,[65] which has been based in Belfast since 1997. During his visit, Walsh emphasised the cooperation between his city and Belfast:

> 'Belfast was a natural choice for the first Sister City agreement of my Administration,' said Mayor Walsh. 'Historically, these agreements have been exclusively about cultural exchange and the promotion of tourism, but we want to use this program to work toward a broader base of economic partnerships: a strategic alliance in the global economy that will bring growth and good jobs to both cities. We build that partnership with the support of businesses like Liberty Mutual and others who are investing in their workforce in both Boston and Belfast'.[66]

Liberty Mutual Insurance, Boston, and the two Irelands had a close relationship. James McGlennon, the company's Executive Vice President and Chief Information Officer, was present to express gratitude to Walsh, who had been recently honoured as Irish-American of the Year by the online magazine Irish America[67]*:*

> We are honored to host Mayor Walsh during his travels home to Ireland and thank him for his contributions to economic development including his support of our Boston Home Office expansion while he was a member of the Massachusetts legislature. Speaking from my own experience as a native of Ireland now living in the Boston area, I have no doubt that the Mayor will enjoy his time here.[68]

Liberty Mutual's links with Ireland go back several decades, to the time when Edmund F. Kelly[69] was Chairman and CEO of the company.[70] Liberty Mutual IT set up in Belfast when he was head of the parent company. The Irishman knew the city well, having studied there before emigrating to the United States. He was a member of the IAEAB and was also close to the Irish government.

In addition, links between Belfast and New York have been maintained through Máirtín Ó Muilleoir's initiative, the New York - New Belfast Conference, which has been held annually since 2009. Ó Muilleoir was a Sinn Féin councillor in the City of Belfast before becoming Mayor in 2013–2014. He was also Northern Ireland's Minister for Finance (2016–2017). The event has become a major event attended by many prominent figures in the Irish diaspora including John Connorton of the Friends of Belfast.[71]

Initially, the combined effect of the opening up of the single market and globalisation resulted in a significant gap between the Northern Ireland economy and the Irish economy, which, as we have seen, experienced an unprecedented boom.[72] In fact, Northern Ireland continued to be hindered by the structural weaknesses within its economy. However, from 1997 until the global economic crisis of 2007–2008, it also enjoyed a significant upturn.[73] Although not as spectacular as Ireland's boom, between 1996 and 2007 the province's growth rate of around 3% was the highest of the UK regions, with an average of 2.8%.[74] Between 1998 and 2008, 100,000 jobs were created. Moreover, in 2008 its unemployment rate, at around 4.2%, was lower than the rest of the United Kingdom (5.2%). The ceasefires in 1994 undoubtedly played a significant role in these positive outcomes, as they paved the way for a peace process from which substantial economic benefits, known as the "peace dividend", emerged.

10.4 Irish-American Businessmen Invest in Northern Ireland

The participation of the main Northern Irish political parties in the provincial government and the impetus given by the US administration certainly provided confidence to US investors. Between 2003 and 2008, some of them invested around $1 billion in Northern Ireland in the technology, financial services, and pharmaceutical sectors.[75]

Influential businessmen, predominantly of Irish-American origin, played a significant role in attracting these investments to Northern Ireland.[76] The participation of politicians from the Social Democratic and Labour Party (SDLP)[77] and Sinn Féin in the Northern Ireland Executive undoubtedly bolstered the connections between these individuals and the region. For instance, the establishment of Seagate, in[78] the city of (London)

Derry, is a prime illustration. Silicon Valley Global magazine recounts how "[...] a quiet drink he shared in a Los Angeles bar with Seagate executive Brendan Hegarty changed the fortune of his native Derry in a way that would match any of Hume's[79] laudable political efforts".[80]

Additional multinational corporations set up research and development facilities in Northern Ireland. This included Microsoft in 2000 and the Japanese electronics conglomerate Fujitsu in 2007. In 2011, Hewlett Packard inaugurated a global centre of excellence for software research, later joined by Intel.[81]

Citigroup, ranked twelfth in the world by Forbes Global 2000,[82] was one of the groups that moved to Northern Ireland in the early 2000s. The company opened a technology centre of excellence and a finance academy in Northern Ireland. Bill Mills, an Irish-American and active member of the American Ireland Fund,[83] who was the company's chief executive at the time, emphasised the strategic importance of these investments in Belfast.[84] It is worth noting the presence of other Irish-born personalities in Citigroup's management team, such as Jim O'Donnell and Daniel Keegan, both of whom were members of the board of directors of the American Ireland Fund at the end of the 2010s.[85]

In addition to the 375 jobs created, Citigroup's presence in Northern Ireland has attracted other companies. For example, Polaris, an Indian financial software company, came to Northern Ireland because Citigroup, one of its largest customers, was located there. Once it was established, the company decided that it was a good place to set up a financial and technology centre.

In the early 2010s, another significant investor in Belfast was the New York Stock Exchange Euronext (NYSE), led by Duncan Niederauer, an Irish-American who also served as a board member of the American Ireland Fund[86] and was close to Enda Kenny,[87] the then Taoiseach. In 2011, the New York Stock Exchange (NYSE) hosted its inaugural Ireland Day on Wall Street, with the Taoiseach's participation. This event has since become an annual tradition. Additionally, in the same year, Niederauer presided over the annual dinner of the American Ireland Fund, which was attended by Enda Kenny.

When the establishment of the NYSE in Belfast was announced in 2009, Niederauer openly acknowledged that in 2007, he had been visited on Wall Street[88] by Ian Paisley[89] and Martin McGuinness.[90] They had urged him to invest in Northern Ireland. Perhaps he was moved by the significance of this visit—two former adversaries joining forces to promote job creation and economic prosperity in the region.

In 2012, the Mercantile Chicago Exchange (MCE) followed the lead of the NYSE. In the following years, this group opened a financial innovation lab at the University of Ulster at Jordanstown, Belfast.[91] The MCE was headed by Terence A. Duffy, another Irish-American who was then an adviser to the regional (Chicago) branch of the American Ireland Fund.

Also worth mentioning is William McKiernan, head of Cybersource, a large Silicon Valley company specialising in online payments. The company set up a research and development unit in Belfast in 2008. McKiernan, an Irish-American, is also a member of the board of the American Ireland Fund.[92] Although he no longer has family in Ireland, he claimed that "[…] his executives jumped at the chance to work in Belfast. […] Now the Irish-American wants to help the land of his forebears".[93] The Northern Ireland economy thus entered a period of transition in the 2010s. In the first half of 2017, the information and communication technology sector was the fastest growing sector of the regional economy (+4%).[94] It is gradually specialising in new areas such as financial technology (fintech), a fast-growing sector that alone employs three and a half thousand people in the province. In 2015, Paddy Cosgrave, the founder of Web Summit, organised MoneyConf in Belfast. This event, which brings together professionals from the financial services sector, has helped to promote the city's desire to make a name for itself in this field.[95]

In the manufacturing sector, too, Northern Ireland has seen new investment, including Coca-Cola HBC.[96] The company invested £93.5 million in a factory at Knockmore Hill, near Lisburn, Co Antrim. The plant, the group's largest on the island of Ireland, opened in 2008 and employs four hundred and fifty people.[97] The move was the result of two years of negotiations with Coca-Cola HBC, whose managing director at the time was Irial Finan,[98] an Irish immigrant to the United States. Finan, who is also a member of the board of directors of the American Ireland Fund,[99] makes no secret of its attachment to Ireland:

> Finan tries to stay as close as possible to what's happening in Ireland, but admits he doesn't 'get home enough', particularly not to his native Roscommon, although he does closely follow his county's GAA performance and is happy with last weekend's win over New York. He can't be accused of losing his Roscommon accent either, although all those years in the Coca-Cola 'system' may have allowed a few 'vacations' and 'sidewalks'

to creep in. Not forgetting his roots, Finan likes to promote Ireland where he can. Emphasising that his opinions are personal, not corporate views, he says he still thinks Ireland 'has an awful lot going for it'.[100]

10.5 "Hollywood Comes to Belfast" to Film

In the past decade, the province has also benefited from the assistance of diaspora business networks in the Hollywood film industry. From 2004 onwards, as mentioned earlier, the BCC made the development of the creative industries a priority.[101] In this context, it worked with John Connorton, Michael Flannery, and Bob Johnston of the New York Executive Council and the Friends of Belfast network. Contacts were established with the American television channels PBS and Discovery Channel. But in 2007, Twentieth Century Fox became the first major US film company to embark on a Tom Hanks-produced feature film, *City of Shadows*, at the Titanic Quarter Studios in Belfast. In 2009, HBO followed suit and came along to film the pilot of the *Game of Thrones* series in Northern Ireland. The worldwide success of the cult series has had a very positive impact on the Northern Irish economy and has helped the province establish its reputation in the film industry. In 2016, the local authority estimated that the series brought in 148 million pounds.[102] In addition to the film industry, the series has also boosted the tourism sector and the image of Northern Ireland. This was made possible by the Northern Ireland Tourist Board and HBO working together to use digital and social media to attract fans of the series to twenty filming locations, in natural settings, around the province. In 2013, the *Game of Thrones* exhibition at the Titanic Belfast Museum attracted 18,000 visitors in ten days and raised $4.5 million.[103]

Jay Roewe, vice-president of the HBO production company, said that when his teams went on a fact-finding mission to Northern Ireland, they found what looked like "a sleeping giant", but quickly realised the "creative potential" that Belfast holds. He admits that his company was very lucky to be able to "wake"[104] this giant. He speaks highly of the province, cherishing fond memories of it, and aims for Belfast to be perceived globally as "a great place to do business".[105]

It is worth noting that Roewe is an Irish-American whose name appeared in the 2012 list of the fifty most influential Irish-American figures in the US entertainment industry published by the Irish Technology Leadership Group (ITLG)[106] business network.[107] He gave a talk on technology and entertainment at an ITLG event at Sony Pictures Studios in California in September 2011. Some three hundred people attended the event, which brought together senior executives from Warner Bros, Twentieth Century Fox, Walt Disney Studios, Sony Pictures, Paramount Studios, NBC Universal, Dreamworks, Google, Intel, Motorola, etc.[108] The Irish diaspora, which is particularly well represented in the film industry across the Atlantic, responded to the ITLG call. Indeed, a few weeks later, in November 2011, this business network organised a visit to Belfast by a group of senior executives from Silicon Valley and the Hollywood film industry as part of its "Hollywood Comes to Belfast" initiative. A number of meetings were organised in which private investors took part. These few examples give an idea of the role that a number of businessmen, mostly of Irish origin, played in attracting this American investment to Northern Ireland whose reputation as a "safe" place to do business needed to be strengthened. Máirtín Ó Muilleoir paid tribute to them in the following terms:

> I'm long familiar with the famous Irish American tome by Thomas Cahill, 'How Ireland Saved Civilization'. But as I come to the end of a one-year adventure as mayor of Belfast, I am more convinced than ever that we need a scribe to write a new volume on 'How Irish America Saved Ireland'. [...] Whether it is tourist visitor numbers, which are off the charts thanks to rocketing numbers from North America, or new job creation projects which are being spearheaded by American companies, the fact remains that the U.S. is Belfast's greatest ally [...].
>
> The message from Belfast is that there is a real thirst for more relationships of mutual benefit with Irish America. Far from having seen the best days of transatlantic partnership, it's my conviction that the greatest days of Irish American co-operation with those who wish to build the peace in the North of Ireland are still ahead of us.[109]

10.6 The Importance of Developing Entrepreneurship in Northern Ireland

In the aftermath of the global financial crisis of 2007–2008, the Cameron government imposed drastic budget cuts and reforms on the UK civil service as part of a broader austerity agenda. However, these planned reforms were met with resistance in Belfast.[110] Northern Ireland's economy continues to rely heavily on an oversized public sector,[111] which represents a significant financial burden for the UK Treasury. As a result, the region's structural economic weaknesses have persisted, despite a notable increase in US investment during the 2010s. Nonetheless, Northern Irish political leaders have long recognised the imperative of developing the private sector and fostering entrepreneurship as essential steps towards strengthening the region's economic foundations and preparing for an eventual reduction in financial support from London.[112]

But decades of political conflict stifled the entrepreneurial spirit that had once helped make Belfast one of the most dynamic cities in the British Isles. Indeed, for at least a generation, parents, aware of the economic impact of the conflict on private sector employment, steered their offspring towards careers in the civil service or the professions.[113] It seems that the arrival of foreign multinationals has helped to restore hope as many of them now employ qualified personnel from the province in their research and development units. After gaining experience in these companies, it seems that some of them are starting to become entrepreneurs and create innovative companies in the new technology sector.[114] The Northern Ireland Science Park (NISP), renamed Catalyst Inc., was established in 1999 and is one of the signs of economic renewal in Belfast City. The park, located in the Titanic Quarter, is the largest in Northern Ireland.[115] In 2017, it was home to 160 technology and biotechnology companies employing a total of 2300 people. With this growing success, plans were made to open new premises in (London)Derry to meet the demand. Joan Stuart, Development Director, planned to create 5000 new jobs as part of the cluster's ten-year development plan. It was expected to grow to 100,000 square metres. One hundred million pounds was to be invested in the cluster with the aim of making Northern Ireland one of the world's leading entrepreneurial knowledge economies in the next fifteen years.[116] The NI KEI (Northern Ireland Knowledge Economy Index)[117] reveals that in 2018 the growth rate of Northern Ireland's knowledge economy sector was the second highest of the United Kingdom's regional economies.[118] According to two 2018 reports published jointly by Catalyst Inc., Bank of Ireland, and the University of Ulster, the most recent data revealed that 40,250 people,[119] 91,000 if indirect and induced employment is counted,[120] were employed in this industry in Northern Ireland. In 2016, the sector was worth £3.8 billion and accounted for 10% of the regional economy.[121]

Novosco,[122] PathXL,[123] and 8over8[124] were among the many Northern Irish start-ups with a bright future at the start of the 2010s, but Sisaf was probably the most iconic of them. Founded in 2008, this highly innovative biotech start-up was the first company in the sector to receive a $900,000 investment from Silicon Valley.[125] However, it is less acknowledged than south of the border, Irish-American businesspeople have therefore contributed to the development of entrepreneurship in Northern Ireland. Thanks to the ITLG, the company has been able to benefit from this financial windfall, which has enabled it to expand its research team. In 2017, its headquarters and research department were still located at Catalyst Inc. in Belfast, but the company also had a presence in Silicon Valley, where it was housed at the Irish Innovation Center in San Jose (California). Today the company's headquarters are located in Guildford (United Kingdom).

In 2013, Sisaf again received 500,000 pounds of funding from a consortium of investors of which Silicon Valley Global Ventures (SVG Ventures), the ITLG's angel fund, is a member.[126] This network closely monitored the advancement of its investment, with its director, John Hartnett, subsequently being appointed vice president of the company. Indeed, Sisaf expanded meteorically. By September 2016, it had managed to raise $4.9 million from investors to fund its development plans, mainly from Asia.[127]

Therefore, it appears that investments in research and development facilities in Northern Ireland by major US companies have contributed to creating a positive feedback loop. However, it required a combination of factors to stimulate their arrival. The active support of the US administration undoubtedly played a decisive role. Additionally, the wholehearted commitment of Northern Ireland's governing parties was essential. Working together, Peter Robinson[128] and Martin McGuinness effectively highlighted the province's advantages during significant meetings with US investors coordinated by Washington. By the early 2010s, Northern Ireland stood a good chance of rivalling the Republic of Ireland. One observer noted how Robinson and McGuinness adeptly leveraged Ireland's economic challenges to their advantage:

> I was able to see Peter Robinson and Martin McGuinness up close and in action. To say that they were 'on message' would be an understatement. Northern Ireland was at peace, it had outstanding infrastructure and a great education system, and it was attracting high-tech investment. United around economic development, Robinson and McGuinness subtly made an ironic but essential point in their presentations. Northern Ireland was likely to be

> a better investment than the Republic, given the economic catastrophe there. Its smaller size, top-class universities, non-eurozone status, government willingness to work with companies, and overall infrastructure made the North a great investment. Though the corporate tax would remain high, and the recession had caused significant cuts in services, Northern Ireland was open for business.[129]

As the eurozone debt crisis[130] raged, the province's leaders emphasised the strength of the UK banking system, which was not part of it. All of these factors worked in Northern Ireland's favour, and this was not lost on the large US companies.[131] Furthermore, in the ensuing period, Northern Ireland-based businesses and regional authorities banded together to obtain permission from London to set a corporate tax rate on a par with that of the Republic of Ireland.[132] After years of fruitless negotiations, Belfast obtained this right, which was to take effect from 2018,[133] but which, due to the suspension of the Northern Ireland Executive in January 2017, could not be implemented. The Northern Ireland Executive has since committed to setting the rate of corporation tax at 12.5% to apply to certain trading income. While legislation has been passed, the final devolution is subject to agreement between the UK Government and the Northern Ireland Executive. Such a measure would be welcome. Theresa Villiers, then Secretary of State for Northern Ireland, noted in early 2015 that the prospect had attracted the interest of certain members of the US Congress and several American companies. She also highlighted the fact that many of the latter already had a "strong affinity with the island of Ireland due to ancestral ties".[134] She went on to recall some of the advantages of the province:

> 'It has high quality infrastructure, a highly skilled workforce, its quality of life - and low rates of company taxes could provide another powerful incentive for US companies to come and invest,' she said. 'And there are also matters relating to heritage. So you will have perhaps an interest in investment in Northern Ireland partly reflecting people's own heritage in relation to the island of Ireland'.[135]

This brings us back to the question of the motivations of diaspora business leaders investing in Northern Ireland since the early 2000s. Most of them have received an award from the American Ireland Fund as a token of recognition from the diaspora community in the United States.

However, there is no doubt that their investments in Northern Ireland were not driven solely by altruism or a sense of duty. In October 2010, Declan Kelly, while attending a major meeting in Washington to promote economic development in Northern Ireland, said:

> American companies are looking at the pure business case. They are not looking at investing in Northern Ireland as a favor - it is if the business case adds up, and Northern Ireland is a very positive region.[136]

In addition to the benefits already mentioned, Invest Northern Ireland offers incentives to foreign investors. It is known, for example, that the agency contributed £7.6 million to the establishment of Citigroup in Belfast.[137]

However, when conditions are no longer favourable, the attachment to Ireland no longer comes into play. Seagate Technology, a company that John Hume brought in, did not hesitate to close one of its Northern Ireland factories and move the unit to Malaysia where labour is cheaper.[138] It is also possible that some investors chose Northern Ireland in the late 2000s when Ireland's economic future looked uncertain because of the financial crisis.

Notes

1. For a detailed analysis of NORAID's role, see: Jack Holland. 1987. *The American Connection: U.S. Guns, Money, and Influence in Northern Ireland*. New York: Viking.
2. Andrew J. Wilson has written a book on the Irish-American contribution to the conflict in Northern Ireland. Andrew J. Wilson. 1995. *Irish America and the Ulster Conflict, 1968–1995*. Washington: The Catholic University of America Press.
3. Steve Bruce. 1992. *The Red Hand. Protestant Paramilitaries in Northern Ireland*. Oxford: Oxford University Press, 168–169.
4. Bruce. *The Red Hand*, 171.
5. Tony O'Reilly quoted in: Details Announced of Ireland Fund Awards. 1980. *The Irish Times*, 21 August.
6. Kingsley Aikins, Anita Sands, Nicola White. 2009. *The Global Irish Making a Difference Together: A Comparative Review of International Diaspora Strategies*. Dublin: The Ireland Funds, 92–93.
7. American Fund Raisers Present £40,000 for Peace and Charity. 1976. *The Irish Times*, 25 August.

8. The Nine MacBride Principles include: Increase representation of under-represented religious groups in the workforce, Prohibit provocative religious or political emblems in the workplace, Ensure security for minority employees at work and while commuting, Publicly advertise all job openings, Eliminate discriminatory job reservations, apprenticeships, or training schemes, Develop training programmes to promote advancement of minority workers, Appoint a senior management official to oversee affirmative action efforts, Establish grievance procedures to handle complaints and resolve disputes, Monitor progress and report on implementation of fair employment goals.
9. See also: Joseph E. Thompson. 2001. *American Policy and Northern Ireland: A Saga of Peace Building*. Westport: Praeger, 162–241.
10. Conor O'Clery. 1997. *Daring Diplomacy, Clinton's Secret Search for Peace in Ireland*. Boulder: Roberts Rinehart Publishers, 15–16.
11. O'Clery. *Daring Diplomacy*, 25.
12. Morrison chaired the House Immigration Subcommittee from 1989 to 1991. He was responsible for the Immigration Act of 1990, which provided for the creation of forty thousand visas per year for three years for countries that had been adversely affected by the Immigration Act of 1965. A total of sixteen thousand (40%) of these visas were allocated to applicants from the Republic of Ireland and Northern Ireland.
13. O'Clery, *Daring Diplomacy*, 26–27.
14. O'Clery, *Daring Diplomacy*, 35.
15. O'Clery, *Daring Diplomacy*, 46–47. Sometime later, on 15 December 1993, the British Prime Minister, John Major, and Albert Reynolds, made a joint statement, the Downing Street Declaration. This document recognised the right to self-determination of Northern Ireland. In other words, London would not oppose the unification of Ireland if that was the will of the majority of the people of the province.
16. Refer to appendix for biography.
17. O'Clery, *Daring Diplomacy*, 62–64.
18. O'Clery, *Daring Diplomacy*, 144.
19. O'Clery, *Daring Diplomacy*, 145.
20. In 1996, he donated $244,000 to cover staff salaries and office rent. Joe Carroll. 1996. American Says Donation to SF Personal, *The Irish Times*, 12 December.
21. Andrew J. Wilson. 2003. 'Doing the Business': Aspects of the Clinton Administration's Economic Support for the Northern Ireland Peace Process, 1994–2000. *The Journal of Conflict Studies* 23, 1, 2003: 155–176. https://journals.lib.unb.ca/index.php/JCS/article/view/355
22. Wilson, 'Doing the Business'; Thompson, *American Policy and Northern Ireland*, 179–180.

23. Valérie Peyronel. 2017. US Investment in Northern Ireland: Strategies, Incentives and Perspectives. In *Revisiting the UK and Ireland's Transatlantic Economic Relationship with the United States in the Twenty-First Century: Beyond Sentimental Rhetoric*, Anne Groutel, Marie-Christine Pauwels, and Valérie Peyronel, eds. 78. London: Palgrave Macmillan.
24. Susan Davis International is a world-renowned communications and public relations consultancy based in Washington DC.
25. Susan Ann Davis was then president of the National Assembly of Irish-American Republicans. United States of America, *Congressional Record*, 10 October 2002 to 8 November 2002, vol. 148, Pt. 15, p. 20557.
26. Irish-US Summit Reveals New Trade Partnerships. 2002. *The Irish Times*, 5 September.
27. IntertradeIreland is one of the North-South bodies established under the Good Friday Agreement. Its mission is to promote trade between the two Irelands.
28. Liberty Mutual Insurance is an insurance company, founded in 1912, with its headquarters in Boston. It is present in thirty countries. The company is ranked seventy- sixth in the Fortune 100 list of the largest American companies.
29. Vincent Boland. 2014. Northern Ireland Seeks to Revive its Private Sector. *The Financial Times*, 29 May.
30. Science Foundation Ireland, US-Ireland R&D Partnership Programme. https://www.sfi.ie/funding/funding-calls/us-ireland-rd-partnership. Accessed 5 June 2025.
31. Valérie Peyronel, US Investment in Northern Ireland, 82–85.
32. In the United States, the Secretary of State is the equivalent of the Minister of Foreign Affairs.
33. U.S. North Envoy Declan Kelly Resigns. 2011. *The Irish Echo*, 18 May, https://www.irishecho.com/2011/5/u-s-north-envoy-declan-kelly-resigns. Accessed 5 June 2025.
34. John Cullinane's parents, originally from Dunmore East (Co. Wexford, Ireland), emigrated to the United States in 1929. Refer to appendix for biography.
35. Cullinet was the first software company to be listed on the New York Stock Exchange in 1982. Boston Honorees, John Cullinane. 2006–2007. *Irish America Magazine*, January–December.
36. Wilson, Doing the Business; Bill O'Donnell. 2015. Cullinane's Success as a Software Pioneer. *Boston Irish Reporter*, 2 March.
37. Wilson, Doing the Business.
38. Boston Honorees, John Cullinane, *Irish America Magazine*.

39. Born in the United States, Frank Costello was educated in Ireland. After a career overseas, he returned to Northern Ireland and has lived in Belfast for the past fifteen years. He is a historian, author of several books, and a lecturer at Queen's University (Belfast). He is also a venture capitalist and runs Costello Associates, a company that invests in community development. In the late 1990s, he was the North American economic advisor to the BCC.
40. Wilson, Doing the Business.
41. The International Fund for Ireland is an independent international organisation established in 1986 by the British and Irish governments to promote economic and social progress and dialogue and reconciliation between unionists and nationalists on the island of Ireland.
42. Willie McCarter quoted in: Bill O'Donnell. 2015. Book Details Cullinane's Success as a Software Pioneer. *Boston Irish Reporter*, 2 March 2015, https://www.bostonirish.com/around-town/book-details-cullinane%E2%80%99s-success-software-pioneer. Accessed 5 June 2025.
43. Alasdair McDonnell was leader of the SDLP from 2011 to 2015.
44. Belfast City Council, Minutes of the Economic Development Sub-Committee meeting, 8 September 1999.
45. At the first meeting of the group, seventy people expressed their willingness to work for the benefit of the economy and the people of Belfast City. Following the meeting, the members were divided into eight sub-groups, each of which was given a task in a different economic sector. Each of them was tasked with attracting investment or business opportunities in one of the following sectors: software, education, finance, telecommunications, property, environment, or health. A sub-group was also tasked with promoting the image of Belfast. Belfast City Council, Internal Report of the Economic Development Sub-Committee, 3 June 1998.
46. These objectives do not appear in the publicly available parts of the BCC minutes.
47. Belfast City Council, Minutes of the Economic Development Sub-Committee Meeting of 2 August 2000.
48. The area is home to the Science Park, film studios, Belfast Metropolitan College, and residential buildings.
49. One set of minutes mentions Michael Flannery, Jack Deacy, Tim Sullivan, Dan Gallagher, etc. Belfast City Council, Minutes of the Economic Development Sub-Committee meeting of 8 May 2002.
50. Belfast City Council, Minutes of the Economic Development Sub-Committee meeting of 2 August 2000.
51. Wilford Welch, a prominent lawyer, led the group on this visit. He joined the Belfast circle of Friends shortly afterwards.

52. Heather Draper. 2014. Denver Litigator Jim Lyons Chronicles Northern Ireland Peace Work in New Book. *Denver Business Journal*, 19 November. http://www.bizjournals.com/denver/blog/finance_etc/2014/11/denver-litigator-jim-lyons-chronicles-northern.html. Accessed 5 June 2025.
53. Belfast City Council, minutes of the Economic Development Sub-Committee meetings, 7 February 2001; Belfast City Council, minutes of the Economic Development Sub-Committee meetings, 7 August 2002.
54. The minutes of the Belfast City Council meetings held on 5 December 2001 and 8 May 2002 mention the names of some of Belfast's US "friends".
55. Belfast City Council, Minutes of the Economic Development Sub-Committee meeting, 5 December 2001.
56. The Big Dig was the largest urban infrastructure construction project in North America.
57. Belfast City Council, Minutes of the Economic Development Sub-Committee meeting, 8 May 2002.
58. Belfast City Council, Minutes of the Economic Development Sub-Committee meeting, 4 December 2002.
59. The BCC minutes of 6 August 2003 reveal what the expected results were. Not all were quantified. Belfast City Council, Minutes of the Economic Development Sub-Committee meeting of 6 August 2003.
60. Belfast City Council, Minutes of the Economic Development Sub-Committee Meeting, 2 June 2004.
61. Belfast City Council, Minutes of the Economic Development Sub-Committee meeting, 11 January 2006.
62. Belfast City Council, Minutes of the Economic Development Sub-Committee meeting, 2 June 2004; Belfast City Council, Minutes of the Economic Development Sub-Committee meeting, 8 September 2004.
63. Belfast City Council, minutes of the Development Committee meetings, 21 May 2013.
64. Belfast City Council, Minutes of the Development Committee meeting, 14 April 2010.
65. Belfast City Council, Minutes of the Development Committee meeting, 14 April 2010.
66. Boston Mayor Celebrates Belfast Connection with Liberty IT, 25 September 2014, http://liberty-new.open.wp-dev.web.tibus.net/boston-may or-celebrates-belfastconnection-with-liberty-it. Accessed 5 March 2020. Note: this link is no longer active.
67. Boston Mayor Marty Walsh: Irish American of the Year. 2014. *Irish America*, 27 June
68. Boston Mayor Marty Walsh.

69. Refer to appendix for biography.
70. Edmund F. Kelly was chairman and CEO of Liberty Mutual Insurance from 1992 to 2011. Taryn Luna. 2013. Edmund "Ted" Kelly's Salary Generated Controversy. *The Boston Globe*, April 10.
71. Steve Lenox. 2015. Face to Face Still the Best Connection. *The Irish Echo*, 1–7 July.
72. Michael D'Arcy. 2007. "NDP Bolsters an All-Island Economy". *The Irish Times*, 26 January.
73. For a summary of the province's economic performance, see: UK Parliament, Northern Ireland Affairs Committee, Memorandum submitted by the Northern Ireland Chamber of Commerce and Industry, 16 May 2000.
74. Jonathan Saul. 2008. Northern Ireland Looks to Make Peace Dividend Pay. 6 May. http://www.reuters.com/article/us-irish-economy/northern-ireland-looks-to-make-peace-dividend-pay-idUSL0283780420080506. Accessed 5 June 2025.
75. Saul, Northern Ireland.
76. Saul, Northern Ireland.
77. The SDLP is a political party in Northern Ireland that advocates a rather moderate nationalism.
78. Seagate is a world-renowned provider of digital storage solutions.
79. John Hume (1937–2020) was one of the founding members of the SDLP. He was awarded the Nobel Peace Prize in 1998, a prize shared with David Trimble (1944–2022), then leader of the Ulster Unionist Party. Both helped to shape the Good Friday Agreement (1998).
80. Celebrating Seagate. Fall 2014 *Silicon Valley Global*, 27, https://issuu.com/argyll1/docs/svgmi6_web/27. Accessed 8 May 2020. Note: this link is no longer active.
81. Intel Marks 1st Anniversary in Belfast, 2 May 2014, online: https://newsroom.intel.ie/news-releases/intel-marks-1st-anniversary-in-belfast. Accessed 6 August 2020. Note: This link is no longer active.
82. World's Largest Public Companies in 2017. 2017. *Forbes*, 3 May. https://www.forbes.com/pictures/5924acd8a7ea434078d451ab/2017-global-2000-top-25. Accessed 5 June 2025.
83. The Ireland Funds. 2016. New York Dinner Committee Reception 2016″, 12 September. https://irelandfunds.org/event/new-york-dinner-committee-reception-2016. Accessed 5 June 2025.
84. Invest Northern Ireland. Annual Report and Accounts 2004–05, 43. https://www.investni.com/sites/default/files/documents/static/library/invest-ni/documents/annual-report-investni-2004-2005.pdf. Accessed 5 June 2025.

85. Jim O'Donnell was honoured at the 2017 American Ireland Fund Gala Dinner, chaired by Daniel Keegan. The Ireland Funds. 2017. New York Annual Dinner Gala 2017. 4 May. https://irelandfunds.org/event/new-york-annual-dinner-gala-2017. Accessed 5 June 2025.
86. The Ireland Funds, Board of Directors, online: https://irelandfunds.org/about-us/theireland-funds-america/board-of-directors. Accessed 5 June 2025.
87. Enda Kenny served as Taoiseach from 9 March 2011 to 14 June 2017.
88. Henry McDonald. 2009. NYSE to Create up to 400 Jobs with New Belfast Office. *The Guardian*, 19 October.
89. Dictionary of Irish Biography. Ian Paisley. https://www.dib.ie/biography/paisley-ian-a10164. Accessed 12 June 2025.
90. Dictionary of Irish Biography. Martin McGuinness. https://www.dib.ie/biography/mcguinness-james-martin-pacelli-a10375. Accessed 12 June 2025.
91. Chicago Mercantile Exchange Opening Ulster University 'Trading Floor' to Help Train Students. 2015. *Belfast Telegraph*, 26 August.
92. The Ireland Funds, Board of Directors.
93. Mark Paul. 2011. Visionary Presses the Right Buttons. *The Sunday Times* (Irl.), 9 October.
94. Connor Lambe. 2017. Northern Ireland Economy to Keep Growing - But a Slowdown Is Still Expected. *The Irish Times*, 20 June.
95. Vincent Boland. 2015. Belfast Takes a Shine to Financial Technology. *The Financial Times*, 15 June.
96. Coca-Cola HBC Ireland and Northern Ireland. Plants and Processes. https://ie.coca-colahellenic.com/en/local-impact/plants-and-processes. Accessed 5 June 2025.
97. Coca-Cola HBC Ireland and Northern Ireland, Plants and Processes.
98. Irial Finan was an executive vice president of Coca-Cola and president of Coca-Cola Bottling Investments from 2004 until the end of 2017. He retired in March 2018, The Coca-Cola Company. https://www.coca-colacompany.com/press-releases/irial-finan-to-retire-from-coca-cola. Accessed 5 June 2025. Refer to appendix for biography.
99. The Ireland Funds, Board of Directors.
100. Una McCaffrey. 2011. The Real Thing, *The Irish Times*, 6 May.
101. Northern Ireland Assembly, Belfast, Parliamentary Committee on Culture, Arts and Leisure, Hansard Official Report: Inquiry into Maximising the Potential of the Creative Industries: Belfast City Council, 9 February 2012.
102. *Game of Thrones* is one of HBO's biggest hits. The series was broadcast in 173 countries and thus entered the record books in 2016. Game of Thrones entre dans le livre des records. 2015. *L'Express*, 3 September.

https://www.lexpress.fr/culture/tele/game-of-thrones-entre-dans-le-livre-des-records_1712204.html. Accessed 5 June 2025.

103. Noel Martin Murray. 2016. GoT Belfast? How a Television Epic about a War-Torn Land Was Employed to Rebrand Northern Ireland. In *Global Place Branding Campaigns Across Cities, Regions and Nations*, Ahmet Bayraktar and Can Usley, eds. 11. Hershey: IGI Global.
104. *"When we finally came and scouted and looked around, we felt that there was a lot of creative potential. But you need an infrastructure, you need people to make good production with, but what we found was a little bit of a 'sleeping giant'. I think we have been very fortunate to kind of wake that sleeping giant and discover a great creative community here, that* [sic] *has really come to work with us at a world class level*". BBC. 2013. *Game of Thrones* 'Attracts Success' to Northern Ireland. BBC News, 11 October, https://www.bbc.com/news/uk-northern-ireland-24493594. Accessed 5 June 2025.
105. John Kennedy. 2012. Northern Lights Shine on the Crossroads of Hollywood, Wall Street and Silicon Valley. Siliconrepublic.com September 18. https://www.siliconrepublic.com/life/northern-lights-shine-on-the-crossroads-of-hollywood-wall-street-and-silicon-valley. Accessed 5 June 2025.
106. The activities of this network will be discussed in detail in part four of this book.
107. John Kennedy. 2012. ITLG Announces Hollywood 50 at Sony Pictures Studios - Irish-American Execs Take Centre Stage, 22 September. https://www.siliconrepublic.com/life/itlg-announces-hollywood-50-at-sony-pictures-studios-irish-american-execs-take-centre-stage. Accessed 5 June 2025.
108. John Kennedy. 2011. Silicon Valley's Irish Conquer the Heart of Hollywood, 14 September. https://www.siliconrepublic.com/play/silicon-valleys-irish-conquer-the-heart-of-hollywood. Accessed 5 June 2025.
109. Máirtín Ó Muilleoir. 2014. American Investment Is Key to Stable Future. *The Irish Echo*, 28 May–3 June.
110. Vincent Boland. 2014. Irish Two-Speed Economy Puts Integration under Pressure. *The Financial Times*, 20 October; Vincent Boland. 2015. Northern Ireland Shows No Sign of Bowing to Austerity Push. *The Financial Times*, 5 May.
111. The public sector accounted for 65% of Northern Ireland's GDP in the early 2000s. In Place of Strife. 2004. *The Economist*, 14 October. By the early 2010s this had risen to 70%. Vincent Boland. 2014. Northern Ireland Seeks to Revive its Private Sector. *The Financial Times*, 29 May. In the last quarter of 2015, 25% of the workforce was employed in the

public sector, a much higher percentage than other UK provinces. Matthew Ward. 2016. UK parliament. The Northern Ireland Economy. House of Commons Library, debate pack no. CBP-2016-0104, 10 May.

112. As Violence Recedes, Ulster Must Wean Its Economy Off State Subsidies. 2011. *The Economist*, 30 June.
113. Vincent Boland, Northern Ireland Seeks to Revive its Private Sector.
114. John Mulgrew, 2015. Start-ups Driving Northern Ireland Tech Successes, Says Microsoft Man, *Belfast Telegraph*, 24 September.
115. United Kingdom Science Park Association, Catalyst Inc., https://wearecatalyst.org. Accessed 5 June 2025.
116. John Mulgrew. 2016.Northern Ireland Science Park Rebranded Catalyst Inc. as 10-Year Plan Seeks to Be the Catalyst for Economic Boost, *Belfast Telegraph*, 20 June.
117. The index was developed by NISP CONNECT (a centre that houses many of Northern Ireland's high-tech companies) and is modelled on the San Diego CONNECT's Innovation Report. This index is used by the Northern Ireland Department of the Economy. See: Northern Ireland Executive, Department of the economy, "*Innovation Strategy for Northern Ireland 2014–2025*", September 2014. https://www.economy-ni.gov.uk/sites/default/files/publications/deti/Innovation-Strategy-2014-2025_2_0.pdf. Accessed 5 June 2025.
118. Catalyst Inc., Bank of Ireland, University of Ulster, *The 2018 Northern Ireland Knowledge Economy Report. Overview, Performance, Challenges*, 8. https://wearecatalyst.org/wp-content/uploads/2019/08/Knowledge-Economy-Report2018.pdf. Accessed 5 June 2025.
119. Catalyst Inc., Bank of Ireland, University of Ulster, *The 2018 Northern Ireland Knowledge Economy Report*, 9.
120. University of Ulster, Bank of Ireland, Catalyst Inc., *The Knowledge Economy in NI. The Whole Story 2018*", January 2018, 29. https://pure.ulster.ac.uk/en/publications/the-knowledge-economy-in-ni-the-whole-story-2018. Accessed 5 June 2025.
121. University of Ulster, Bank of Ireland, Catalyst Inc., *The Knowledge Economy,* 28.
122. In October 2019, Novosco was acquired by German group Cancom in a £70 million deal.
123. PathXL was founded in 2004 as a Queen's University Belfast spin-out company and was purchased by Philips in 2016. In 2020, Cirdan announced that it had acquired the Belfast-based Philips Digital and Computational Pathology business (formerly known as PathXL).
124. 8over8 was sold to AVEVA Group plc for £27 million in 2015.

125. Northern Ireland Biotech Company Secures US$900 K, 4 April 2011. https://www.siliconrepublic.com/start-ups/northern-ireland-biotech-company-secures-us900k. Accessed 5 June 2025.
126. Co-Fund NI and Innovation Ulster, two investment funds, are also involved.
127. Bhargavi Rathi. SiSaf Gets S$4.9 M in Series A for Its Tech that Improves the Way Drugs Are Administered to Patients, 20 September 2016. https://thetechportal.com/2016/09/20/sisaf-series-a/?amp. Accessed 5 June 2025.
128. Peter Robinson served as First Minister of Northern Ireland from 2008 until 2016 and Leader of the Democratic Unionist Party (DUP) from 2008 until 2015.
129. Seán Kay. 2011. *Celtic Revival? The Rise, Fall, and Renewal of Global Ireland*. Lanham: Rowman & Littlefield, 161.
130. This term refers to a series of events that took place in the early 2010s. In the summer of 2011, a stock market storm arose partly as a result of the Greek public debt crisis. Ireland's public debt crisis, caused by the state bailout of its national banks, also contributed to the eurozone crisis.
131. Seán Kay, *Celtic Revival*, 164.
132. Vincent Boland. 2014. Tax Devolution Unites Northern Ireland. *The Financial Times*, 2 December.
133. Northern Ireland Executive, "*A Fresh Start. The Stormont Agreement and Implementation Plan. An Agreement to Consolidate the Peace, Secure Stability, Enable Progress and Offer Hope*", 17 November 2015, 21, https://www.executiveoffice-ni.gov.uk/publications/fresh-start-stormont-agreement-and-implementation-plan. Accessed 5 June 2025.
134. Theresa Villiers quoted in: David Young.2025. Cutting Northern Ireland's Corporate Tax 'Powerful Incentive' to United States. *Belfast Telegraph*, 5 February.
135. Theresa Villiers quoted in: David Young.
136. Declan Kelly quoted in: Seán Kay, *Celtic Revival?*165.
137. Invest Northern Ireland. Annual Report and Accounts 2004–05, 43. https://www.investni.com/sites/default/files/documents/static/library/invest-ni/documents/annual-report-investni-2004-2005.pdf. Accessed 5 June 2025.
138. Jonathan Saul, Northern Ireland Looks to Make Peace Dividend Pay.

CHAPTER 11

From Collapse to Recovery: Ireland's Financial Crisis and the Strategic Turn to the Diaspora (2007–2015)

During the so-called Celtic Tiger period, a significant improvement in the standard of living of the Irish population,[1] a high rate of immigration, and historically low interest rates fuelled a sudden rise in consumption and demand for housing. Irish banks began to borrow heavily from foreign banks (mainly German and French) to meet the growing demand from individuals and property developers.

11.1 Structural Vulnerabilities and the Celtic Tiger Model: When the Unthinkable Happens

From 2003 onwards, the construction and property sectors became the main engines of Irish economic growth.[2] As early as 2004, *The Economist* expressed concern that house prices in Ireland were soaring as a result of the combined effect of strong demand for housing and the European Central Bank's imposition of lower interest rates on an already fast-growing Irish economy. Irish banks such as Bank of Ireland and Allied Irish Bank, major lenders, would be very exposed if the housing bubble burst: "Clearly there are big risks ahead, with a property crash perhaps the most threatening".[3]

In 2006, some Irish journalists and economists sounded the alarm. They denounced the excessive dependence of the Irish economy on the construction sector, which employed 13% of the workforce and accounted

A. Groutel, *The Two Irelands and the Diaspora*,
https://doi.org/10.1007/978-3-032-12355-8_11

for 23% of GDP,[4] and on the property sector. They also highlighted the worrying parallel between the situation in the United States[5] and Ireland. Economist Morgan Kelly feared a rapid collapse of the housing market of between 40% and 50%[6] and emphasised the extremely perilous position in which Irish banks found themselves. When demand for new homes actually began to wane in 2006, many developers who had not anticipated this trend found themselves unable to sell off their stock.[7] They were forced to cut prices to meet their bank liabilities. This was all it took to convince potential buyers to postpone their purchases, as the market trend was now downwards. The situation became critical in the aftermath of the stock market shock of 29 September 2008, which followed the announcement that the US Congress had rejected the Paulson plan, a seven hundred billion-dollar rescue plan to deal with the financial crisis in the United States. On 6 October 2008, the stock markets recorded the biggest week-on-week decline in their history. This led to a freeze in the financial markets.

As early as October 2007, *The Economist*, questioning the possible impact of falling house prices and record levels of household debt in Ireland, published an article entitled "Ailing Celtic Tiger?"[8] In February 2009, the same weekly magazine ran the headline "Rykjavik-on-Liffey",[9] leaving no room for doubt this time. It has to be said that Morgan Kelly's forecast, then accused of being a doomsayer,[10] turned out to be correct. Ireland was the first European country to enter recession in September 2008.[11] The Irish economy, after more than a decade of high praise, suddenly fell off its pedestal. By the end of the 2000s, Ireland was even experiencing a return to emigration, a phenomenon thought to belong to the past. Between 2011 and 2015, the number of people leaving Ireland fluctuated between 80,000 and 89,000 per year.[12]

It is true that the financial crisis,[13] which began in the sub-prime mortgage market in the United States before spreading to all financial markets and the real economy worldwide, had repercussions in Ireland.[14] However, much of Irish public opinion, as well as many business journalists, public intellectuals, and some economists, agreed that the causes of the crisis were mainly endogenous and attributed responsibility for the debacle to the Fianna Fáil administration.[15]

The successive government measures taken in response to the banking crisis had far-reaching consequences in both economic and political terms. The freezing of the financial markets in September 2008 left Irish banks without short-term funding. Thinking that this was a temporary liquidity crisis, the Irish government hastily decided that the state would guarantee the debts and deposits of the six major Irish banks for a period of two years to the tune of 440 billion euros. By taking this decision, the government initiated a downward spiral: successive recapitalisations, nationalisations of certain banks, and finally the creation, at the end of 2009, of the National Asset Management Agency (NAMA),[16] which was given the task of buying up the banks' toxic loans. Predictably, the Irish government's decision to bail them out put a strain on public finances. By 2010, the public deficit had risen to 32% and the debt to 95% of GDP.[17] In November of that year, Dublin was thus forced to turn to the European Union and the International Monetary Fund (IMF). The two organisations provided Ireland with an eighty-five billion euro rescue package at an interest rate of 5.8%, a rate considered far too high by the Irish population.[18] Indeed, Fine Gael, the centre-right party, which together with the Labour Party formed the coalition that succeeded Fianna Fáil in power, made the renegotiation of the terms of the rescue package one of their main electoral promises during the 2011 general election campaign.[19]

Furthermore, the EU/IMF bailout gave these organisations a say in Irish public finances. This was very unpopular with the Irish people who considered it as an infringement of national sovereignty. The following excerpts are taken from a long article by Fintan O'Toole, a well-known Irish intellectual and columnist, which appeared in *The Irish Times* at the time of the visit of the IMF and EU representatives to Dublin in November 2010. The author expresses and explains both the feelings of the Irish population at the time and the particular historical resonance of what was, no less, a direct supervision of the Irish public finances by international organisations:

> The sense of having returned to the status of a subject people, obedient now to the whims of money men rather than of a monarch, is palpable. It may be a gross oversimplification of our plight, but it is not without a basis in plain truth. This sense of national humiliation accounts for the addition of another feeling to the stew of unhappy emotions that is simmering away in the Irish psyche. Fear, rage, despair, distrust and helplessness have all been in the pot for the past two years. The new ingredient added this week is shame. [...] Ireland is being placed under adult supervision. And that cuts right through to the most tender nerve of a former colony. What colonial overlords tell their subject peoples is: 'You're not fit to govern yourself'. That taunt is deeply embedded in our historical consciousness. Much of modern Irish history has been shaped by the attempt to disprove it. The Proclamation of

> Easter 1916 declares 'the right of the people of Ireland to the ownership of Ireland, and to the unfettered control of Irish destinies [...]'. The struggle to assert this idea of popular sovereignty goes back at least to the United Irishmen[20] of the late 18th century. Their revolutionary idea of the 'sovereignty of the people' is the cornerstone of modern Irish nationalism.[21]

Furthermore, the increase in household taxes and the cuts in social spending to facilitate the repayment of the loan to Ireland led to public anger at the government and to some extent at the European Union. Indeed, the Irish felt it was unfair that they should have to suffer the consequences:

> The terms of the European element of the bail-out arouse particular ire. There is something of a consensus in Ireland that the country rescued Europe (specifically, German and French investors that had lent heavily to Irish banks) last November, rather than the other way around. There have been heated exchanges between Irish and EU politicians over how to apportion the blame for Ireland's crash. Some compare Ireland's bank guarantee unfavourably with Iceland's decision, after similar meltdown in October 2008, to let the banks go to the wall, creditors be damned.[22]

In addition to its incompetence in managing the crisis, the Irish government was also blamed for having failed to put in place a system to effectively supervise the banks and to curb corruption and nepotism. Fianna Fáil itself came under fire for having close ties with property and construction magnates who provided funds for the party coffers.[23] The economic crisis was thus coupled with a deep political crisis arising from the Irish people's loss of confidence in the country's institutions. There was an overwhelming desire for a fresh start,[24] which necessarily involved the removal of Fianna Faíl leaders.

11.2 A Friend in Need Is a Friend Indeed: Diaspora Investment and Financial Stabilisation

The Irish authorities by rushing to the rescue of the country's banks put the public finances at risk. However, the providential intervention of a few businessmen from the diaspora helped Ireland to limit the damage.

Indeed, in 2011, when Bank of Ireland was on the brink of nationalisation, a consortium of American and Canadian investors acquired 34.9% of its capital. By reducing the state's share from 36% to 15.1%, this transaction helped to contain the risk of bankruptcy that threatened it. It also helped to restore some of the lost investor confidence in the Irish economy.[25] Financial magnate Wilbur Ross,[26] an Irish-American, was the driving force behind the consortium.[27] Needless to say, Ross' initiative, as a specialist in buying out failing companies, was timely. As a member of the board of directors, he became involved in the bank's affairs and gave it valuable advice.[28] The billionaire was awarded the American Irish Historical Society's Gold Medal in November 2014 for his role in the rescue of the financial institution. But while Ross' intervention was a boon to the Irish government, the Irish-American billionaire also benefited. In 2014, he sold his shares in Bank of Ireland, which had tripled in value since 2011. Indeed, he bought them for $400 million and received $1.2 billion.[29] In addition, in May 2012, the Irish government announced its decision to sell its 25% stake in Aer Lingus, the Irish airline privatised in 2006. James Hogan,[30] the then CEO of Etihad,[31] said during a visit to Dublin that he was willing to consider the offer. In fact, his company had been discreetly buying shares in Aer Lingus for several months through Bank of America and Merrill Lynch. The deal was not made public as it represented less than 3% of the company's total shares.[32] Aer Lingus had valuable landing slots at Heathrow, an advantage for Etihad, which purchased 2.98% of the former's shares from the Irish state. In the years that followed, Etihad continued to increase its stake in the Irish airline, reaching 4.9% of the total in 2014. This acquisition provided some relief to the Irish state finances. At the same time, Etihad struck a good deal. When it sold its stake in Aer Lingus to the IAG Group[33] in 2015, the Irish airline's shares had doubled in value.[34]

In a different economic sector, John C. Malone bought up properties and offices that were in the hands of NAMA as a result of the 2008 financial crisis. Malone, an Irish-American with an estimated fortune of $7.5 billion, has been successful in the cable TV and communications sector. UPC, the cable TV provider in Ireland, is one of the subsidiaries of his company Liberty Global. Malone says he fell in love with the land of his ancestors during a business trip to Ireland. Having heard about the good business opportunities in the property sector after the crisis, he decided not only to buy a "pied-à-terre" on the island—Humewood Castle in Co. Wicklow—but also to invest in properties, luxury hotels, and horse farms. Between 2012 and 2015,[35] Malone invested two hundred million euros in Ireland, helping to boost state coffers.[36] Interestingly, he also purchased

Castlemartin, the estate of Tony O'Reilly, who was compelled to sell his property due to financial misfortune.[37]

11.3 State–Diaspora Relations in Times of Crisis

In the late 2000s, the financial crisis in Ireland prompted the Irish authorities to seek to reinvigorate their relationship with the diaspora, particularly its entrepreneurial elite, who could help pull the country out of its downturn. While some of these figures extended a helping hand to the Irish authorities amid the country's financial difficulties, others lamented the ingratitude of the Irish population and the prevailing anti-American sentiment. The latter were less eager to help. They made this clear to the Taoiseach in September 2005 during one of his official visits to New York. Dermot Ahern, the Irish Foreign Minister, reported their misgivings:

> I think the difficulty is that Irish-America in particular has is their growing feeling that Ireland, with its new wealth and confidence, is beginning to turn a little sour on the US. We want their peace money, their inward investment and jobs and special treatment in terms of visas for our young people. But at the same time we want to keep them locked away in the back room like an old demented uncle who is out of step and very embarrassing to our new friends.[38]

Dublin therefore had to find the right words to encourage diaspora figures to respond to its call. The invaluable contribution of the Irish diaspora to Ireland was recognised in a document published by the Department of Foreign Affairs in 2009[39]:

> The significant part played by Irish America in advancing the Northern Ireland peace process is recognised as a particular example of the enormous impact which a highly motivated and committed diaspora can have. The current economic downturn represents a timely stimulus to look again at our overseas communities, particularly in the US, and to see how this valuable resource can be elevated to a new and even more dynamic level. [...] The Minister for Foreign Affairs is looking at a number of initiatives involving our global Irish community aimed at helping to address the current economic situation. The Irish American business leadership is, of course, central to any such initiatives and it can be anticipated that they will wish to play their part in working closely with us in support of the economy.[40]

The message is cleverly formulated. It is not a cry for help from a country at the bottom of the abyss. On the contrary, "the economic downturn", a euphemism for the crisis Ireland was then experiencing, was presented as an opportunity to strengthen ties with Irish-American captains of industry, who were expected to cooperate willingly.

Beyond recognising the importance of the diaspora, this document is significant because it illustrates that Ireland, while keen on cultivating its relationship with prominent Irish-American business leaders, had also recognised the necessity of engaging with emerging powers and establishing a global diaspora business network.

11.4 The "Global Tribe": An Unrivalled "Sales Force"

As Ireland's economic situation continued to deteriorate, David McWilliams, a returning expatriate, economist, and journalist, published a book entitled *The Generation Game*,[41] a eulogy of the diaspora. In this book, which was a great success in Ireland, McWilliams argued that the diaspora is a unique resource that new technologies now make it possible to leverage. The following excerpt, from an article published by the author on his website, depicts, with a hint of cold pragmatism, what Ireland could achieve from a closer relationship with the diaspora, a relationship driven by interest:

> The diaspora want to be part of our story and we, the homeland of the tribe, seem to turn our backs on them. With so many prominent Irish people in positions of power around the world, this is quite an oversight. [...] They are our networks, our sales force, the people who maintain our brand - and they can be of great service to us, if we let them. Because they want to be part of our story, we can fill a gap that they feel in terms of their heritage. [...] Think about the power of the diaspora in a world where communication is immediate. [...] We should be promoting much freer travel between Ireland and America for people of Irish heritage; we could see our potential workforce increase from four million to 70 million. These people would not have to move here - although some undoubtedly would - but by telling them that Ireland is open to them and vice versa, you create the network necessary to compete. If we just consider the Irish in America, the commercial power of the diaspora is irrefutable.[42]

He pointed out that out of the thirty-four million Irish-Americans recorded in 2005, eleven million had a tertiary degree; 40% were senior executives or professionals; 72% were homeowners; and the average household income of Irish-Americans was 53,000 dollars. Similarly, McWilliams noted that the 3.8 million Irish-Canadians, the 1.9 million Irish-Australians, and the half a million Irish-Argentines had an equally interesting profile.[43] This clearly contrasts with Mary Robinson's comforting 1995 call to the Irish people to cherish the diaspora.

It must also be admitted that McWilliams' speech sometimes has nationalistic overtones when he talks about his vision of a greater Ireland:

> It is time to see the island of Ireland in the 21st century as the cradle of a global nation. […] All we have to do is imagine a New Hibernia. […] Anything that makes the tribe stronger makes the homeland stronger. In time the relationship becomes symbiotic. […] Globalisation could be the golden era of the Irish.[44]

But while McWilliams believed that members of the diaspora could eventually return to Ireland if they so wished, the country had to select who it accepted into its territory:

> The gardener will be cautious about introducing new plants which might overshadow some of the existing varieties. […] Ireland - given that we are a magnet for immigrants […] could find its culture diluted quite easily.[45]

11.5 The Global Irish Economic Forum: "An Irish Davos"[46]

McWilliams proposed consulting with the global diaspora elite on strategies to help Ireland overcome the crisis. He presented his proposal to Irish leadership, who agreed to adopt it. In September 2009, distinguished members of the Irish diaspora were invited with honours to Farmleigh House[47] to a summit meeting, the Global Irish Economic Forum (GIEF). One hundred and eighty leading figures from the worlds of business, the arts, and communications attended. They deliberated for three days on ways to get Ireland back on track and on the best way to unite the Irish diaspora. Donald Keough and Denis P. Kelleher, two members of the AIEAB, had already made their contribution, as they were part of the group of Irish-American businessmen who had invested $5 million a few months earlier in Irishcentral.com, a website dedicated to fostering links between the Irish diaspora and Ireland.[48]

The agenda of the event was made public. In addition, the advice and suggestions of the working groups were published[49] as was the list of participants. Although most of the working sessions were held behind closed doors and participants had to adhere to the Chatham House Rule,[50] this represented a significant departure from the practices of the Irish authorities in the 1990s, who were very discreet about their contacts with influential IAEAB figures.

It is likely that the Irish government's primary objective was to mobilise the Irish-American business community to leverage their influence in restoring Ireland's reputation abroad and attracting foreign investment, as they had done in the past. However, the content of their message at the forum was somewhat different from what the Irish authorities might have expected. While the participants supported the government's efforts to transform the Irish economy into a knowledge-based economy, they strongly emphasised that in order to do so, the country needed to develop its own strengths in certain sectors.[51] Consequently, it was considered essential to rebrand the country so that it would stand out with unique characteristics. This would help indigenous companies to compete internationally and to find new markets.

For example, it was necessary to capitalise on Ireland's "green" image.[52] This would help to revive the Irish agri-food sector, which was experiencing major difficulties at that time. In 2009, it represented 38.8% of indigenous industry sales and 46% of exports by local companies. In that year, the industry recorded a 15% drop in export sales, due to the unfavourable exchange rate of the euro against the pound sterling.[53] Forum participants believed in the growth potential of the sector, particularly in Asia and the Middle East.[54] A focus on product traceability and environmentally friendly agriculture could make a difference in international markets. It was proposed that an international network of key players from the diaspora could help promote the image of Ireland as a place of bountiful nature and healthy food. However, beyond this postcard image, Ireland needed to innovate in order to increase productivity and profit margins in the industry. It was also suggested that biopharmaceutical research into the pharmacological properties of foods and their impact on health should be developed. Ireland could become a centre of excellence in the development of nutritional products, alongside promoting "green" technologies as another viable idea.

Ireland's cultural heritage and protected nature image were also to be exploited as a priority to promote ecotourism. It was also felt that there was a need to publicise the vibrancy of the arts and culture sector as this would have a positive impact on the wider economy and help to restore the country's reputation which had been damaged since the onset of the crisis.[55] Indeed, a study by DKM Consultants showed that in 2008 the value added by the sector was €11.8 billion, representing 7.6% of Irish Gross National Product, and it accounted for 8.7% of employment.[56] Consequently, during the forum, Dermot Desmond, a well-known Irish businessman, proposed the creation of a world-class performing arts university. This new centre would not only be a centre of excellence in arts education, but would also aim to bring together the arts and technological innovation. In general, the participants in this forum wanted to encourage the Irish authorities to adopt a broader vision of research and development, a vision that had previously been confined to new communication technologies and life sciences.[57]

John McColgan, the creator of Riverdance, also proposed the creation of another website for the Irish diaspora to communicate and stay updated on current affairs in Ireland.[58] Furthermore, in the area of tourism, a project to encourage the diaspora to come and holiday in Ireland was considered. Finally, the establishment of a global diaspora network was also discussed. As will be seen, some of these initiatives have been implemented and have made a valuable contribution to the Irish economy.

11.6 Institutionalising Engagement: The Global Irish Network

The Global Irish Network (GIN) was officially launched by the Irish Minister for Foreign Affairs, Micheál Martin, in February 2010. This network, whose aim was to maintain links between the individuals who participated in GIEF, was placed under the aegis of the Irish Abroad Unit in the Department of Foreign Affairs. In general, new technologies have undoubtedly helped to strengthen ties and promote the engagement of diasporas in the affairs of their countries of origin.[59] Indeed, the creation of the GIN truly marked a turning point in the relationships between the Irish authorities and businesspeople of Irish descent. First and foremost, the network facilitated the establishment of very useful contacts in forty countries, including emerging markets. This is fully in line with the Irish foreign policy whose main objective is to establish links with markets where Irish companies can export[60] or invest.

The mission of this network has some similarities to the IAEAB's in the 1990s. At the onset, network members were expected to help improve Ireland's image abroad, as the country's reputation had suffered badly during the crisis. Nowadays, they should also, as far as possible, help the IDA and Irish companies to establish contacts with decision-makers in large foreign companies. Helping companies in the agri-food industry, the largest indigenous industry, is one of the network's main objectives. Furthermore, GIN members are also committed to acting as a conduit when the Irish authorities wish to organise a trade mission to the country where they reside.[61]

However, the GIN differs from the IAEAB in several respects. Firstly, while the latter was surrounded by a certain level of opacity, the existence and names of the GIN members are known to all. Moreover, the GIN functions as a network and does not aim to provide strategic advice to the government. However, this possibility was available to its members during the GIEF, which was organised every two years until recently. After each of these events, a summary report was published on the network's website, hosted by the Irish Department of Foreign Affairs. While the IAEAB was a small group of Irish-American magnates, the GIN draws its strength from its numbers and its presence on almost every continent. It undeniably represents a significant asset for a country that does not benefit from trade relations inherited from a colonial past.

11.7 The Gathering: Rallying "the Tribe"

At the 2011 GIEF, it was announced that a series of cultural events would be held throughout Ireland during 2013, encouraging people to invite family and friends from abroad to celebrate the occasion. This idea was not new, as it was very similar to the An Tóstal of the early 1950s.[62]

Tourist numbers had been falling for several years,[63] so the country needed to find ways to boost tourism activity. The diaspora was seen as an easier market to exploit in the short term than, for example, the Chinese market, where Ireland is not well known and where much remains to be done in terms of advertising.

In the months leading up to the start of the festivities, there were doubts about the fate of the initiative. In fact, Scotland organised a comparable event that resulted in financial losses.[64] Some journalists were ironic about what some called "the government's latest scheme",[65] a project whose intentions seemed vague. Others wondered whether or not the Irish would decide to invite friends and family to come to Ireland. Would the diaspora answer the call?[66] Moreover, actor Gabriel Byrne's statements in the media disrupted the entire operation. Despite his appointment as an ambassador for Irish culture by Dublin a few months earlier, he unexpectedly criticised the Gathering, describing the initiative as "a scam" during a radio interview with well-known journalist Matt Cooper:

> And when you talk to older people, Irish-American people here, and they say 'we are sick to death of this, because the only time the diaspora, or the Irish-Americans, are ever mentioned is as tourists, and how can we get these people here to boost our tourism, and how can we get people back here so that we can shake them down for a few quid'.[67]

He remembered the attitude of some Irish people towards Irish-Americans in search of their origins:

> We used to ridicule the busloads of 'Yanks' who came to Ireland to investigate their ancestral links. We happily took their money with one hand while we used the other to hide our derision at their endeavours to discover their Irish roots.[68]

Fiach Mac Conghail—senator and director at the renowned Abbey Theatre—and Mannix Flynn, writer, actor, and Dublin City Councillor, expressed their agreement with Byrne.[69] However, the President of the Republic of Ireland, Michael D. Higgins, a friend of the actor, sought to qualify Byrne's comments, pointing out that the latter's main concern was to ensure that the project had content.[70] Byrne was reportedly supported by most of those who wrote to Irish newspapers and by commentators on social networks.[71] Furthermore, some journalists praised his honesty:

> Byrne did us all a favour. He punctured the bubble of hogwash surrounding the Gathering and articulated an unease and confusion that many people have about the project [...]. Byrne also did everyone a favour by sweeping aside the façade that this is about something other than money. To express otherwise is disingenuous. Sentiment is only used to grease the till.[72]

Michael O'Leary, chairman of the Irish airline Ryanair, also denounced the initiative which he called "the Grabbing".[73] While he said he thought it was a good idea, he strongly disapproved of the fare increases planned by Dublin Airport, the railways, and bus companies. Indeed, at the end of 2012, Ryanair announced that it was not planning to increase the number of flights for the Gathering.[74]

The year 2013 did not begin with the best of auspices for this project, for which the Irish authorities had high expectations. However, the Gathering was considered a success in several respects. Firstly, although fewer tourists came specifically to the festival than expected,[75] it brought in an additional 170 million euros, a sum that exceeded projections.[76] North American tourists were the most numerous.[77]

Furthermore, according to a study by an independent consultancy,[78] local communities participated actively, since they held at least 5000 events, 70% of which were organised specifically for the festival.[79] The report highlights the important role of volunteers who contributed greatly to the success of the event.[80]

It should be noted, however, that Fáilte Ireland's report on the Gathering advised against organising such a festival more than once every five years, as sustaining that level of national and international mobilisation on an annual basis would be difficult to achieve. Moreover, the Tailteann Games and An Tóstal have demonstrated the difficulty in achieving long-term success for such events, which eventually lose momentum. On the other hand, it was recommended to maintain the contacts established with the diaspora networks and to integrate them into the country's tourism strategy.[81]

Tourism figures for Ireland in 2014 were good, despite initial fears that visitor numbers would fall in the year following the Gathering. In fact, they increased by 6% and tourism revenues by 9% compared to 2013. North American visitors, in particular, reached a record high of 1.1 million, 10% more than the previous year.[82]

However, there were also other factors that explained these good figures. Firstly, Ireland was better served by airlines than before. Secondly, growth had resumed in the United States, the United Kingdom, and Germany, which are among Ireland's main markets for tourism. Thirdly, the government lowered VAT on the hotel industry and abolished the tax on airline tickets.[83] The combined effect of all these factors is likely to have added to the positive spin-offs of the Gathering in terms of image.

The Irish authorities, it appears, achieved their objective. They succeeded in generating much-needed revenue for the state coffers by leveraging the substantial potential of the Irish diaspora. The report prepared by the organisers states that the Gathering helped enhance Ireland's image as a tourist destination,[84] but it does not elaborate. Fitzpatrick & Associates was commissioned to produce a final report on the economic impact of the event, which was due in April 2014. This was indeed the case, as it is mentioned in another report, but to date it has not been made available to the public.[85]

11.8 Farmleigh: Criticism and Limitations of Diaspora Mobilisation Policies

GIEF was not unanimously supported and some were quick to criticise the government's initiative.[86] First, some observers questioned the usefulness of organising an event that cost the Irish taxpayer 300,000 euros at a time when the country was in the midst of a financial crisis. They saw it as an attempt by a government which was out of breath and out of ideas to maintain appearances and pretend it was seeking a way out of the deadlock. Michael O'Leary, known for his outspokenness, refused to participate on the grounds that the event was "just a talking shop for yakkitiyaks flying home to attend the All-Ireland final".[87] He defended his stance in the following terms:

> I wouldn't participate in a three-day photo shoot, listening to the great and the good of the Irish diaspora, a lot of whom, like Bob Geldof, don't employ anybody in Ireland, don't pay taxes in Ireland. I'd happily go along for four hours on a Tuesday in Government Buildings, with no press, no photo-calls, and come up with a list of decisions, and then let's implement them.[88]

There were also negative comments about the elitist nature of the forum, with participants seemingly so far removed from the day-to-day lives of the Irish people.[89] There was also some criticism of the absence of social scientists who could have challenged participants to rethink Ireland's economic and societal model, a model that some felt was based on unbridled consumerism and ever-increasing growth, and which was seen to be responsible for Ireland's woes.[90]

The forum may have suffered from the poor image of the Fianna Fáil government, whose reputation had been tarnished by its disastrous handling of the crisis. In hindsight, those who had criticised the Gathering before the event remained just as unconvinced of its usefulness afterwards. Brendan Hughes[91] was one of them: "There were some big ideas, but to be honest I don't think anyone would suggest there was a silver bullet and I'd be very worried if anyone were to suggest that any of these were the answer to our problems".[92] O'Leary, standing firm on his positions, remained severe:

> It didn't work because the government has no will to take tough decisions. They prefer photo ops with the great and the good, instead of sitting down with real business people, agreeing a small list of decisions and then implementing them. The course of Bertie which was 'all dither and no action' prevails.[93]

This view was shared by other observers[94] of Irish political and economic life, such as the economist Constantin Gurdgiev[95] who, in the aftermath of the publication of the first progress report on the projects proposed by the forum, offered a scathing critique of the Fianna Fáil administration. He concluded:

> What Farmleigh report does well, then? It shows a deep degree of incompetence and insecurity amongst the political and bureaucratic masters of Ireland Inc.[96] It's [sic] comprehensive lack of new ideas, lack of departure from the status quo are frustrating, especially since we know many of those of who were at Farmleigh last September really do have good ideas. It is simply that DofFA [Department of Foreign Affairs] and this Government had no desire to hear them speak their minds. Which brings me to the revelation that was not made before (to my knowledge) about Farmleigh. In months of preparation for Farmleigh, DofFA took over the lists of invitees, prepared by the idea originators and mercilessly cut out all potential invitees they did not approve of.
>
> From that list gone were a number of public figures very active in policy debate in this country and internationally [...]. How do I know this? The original owners of the Farmleigh idea actually told me this a week before Farmleigh took place![97]

It seems that the "filtering" by the Department of Foreign Affairs was not rigorous enough, as some of those invited expressed their criticisms of the country's economic policy in an extremely direct,[98] even crude, manner.[99]

After falling very low, the Irish economy made a spectacular, almost miraculous recovery. Between 2014 and 2017, it had the highest growth rate in the European Union (26.3% in 2015 and 5.2% in 2016). Ireland adhered strictly to the austerity policies dictated by Brussels, but it is uncertain whether this alone accounts for the economic recovery. One thing is clear, however: US multinationals did not abandon Ireland during its crisis. Indeed, the financial crisis had the effect of driving down wages and property prices, making it more competitive. Although US investment in Ireland fell by 13% in 2009, by the following year the trend had been reversed and US investment in Ireland had risen by more than 10%. The export sector dominated by US multinationals is probably the only indicator that remained positive during the financial crisis.[100]

However, it is essential to clarify what makes Ireland particularly appealing to foreign multinationals and to explain the factors behind the potentially misleading figures of Irish growth. This will provide a clearer perspective on the country's economic health during that period. Apart from a particularly attractive corporate tax rate, Ireland is known for loopholes in its tax system. The "double Irish",[101] for example, was a method used by multinationals such as Apple, masters of tax optimisation, to have their profits booked in tax havens *via* Ireland. This allowed them to largely avoid paying tax. However, in view of the loss of revenue, both the American and the European authorities, which had previously tolerated these practices, have become much more vigilant since the 2008 crisis. The European Union even ordered Ireland to recover €13 billion from Apple, the amount of unpaid tax to the Irish state.[102] Consequently, in 2014, Ireland announced its intention to remove the ability of companies to use the "double Irish" by changing the residency rules. All companies in Ireland must now be tax resident in the country. That said, there are other avenues available to multinationals such as tax inversion mergers.[103] Foreign companies, by merging with indigenous companies, can become domiciled in Ireland and benefit from the Irish corporate tax rate.

Yet, all these practices, which are in the eyes of some "morally reprehensible but perfectly legal",[104] have had a number of drawbacks for Ireland. Firstly, they have given the country the image of a tax haven, which is not good for its reputation. Secondly, for years, they had the effect of artificially inflating economic indicators, particularly GDP, which did not reflect the state of the real economy. For instance, Ireland's 26.3% growth rate in 2015 is believed to have been due to several multinationals exploiting the tax inversion merger mechanism during that year.[105] For Romaric Godin, the impressive Irish growth rate does not mean that it was fictitious since household consumption increased by 4.4% and all sectors grew by more than 5% in 2016, but it was certainly not as high as the GDP would suggest.[106] Consequently, the Central Statistics Office, Ireland's statistical agency, announced in 2017 that it would be abandoning GDP as a statistical tool for measuring the health and size of the Irish economy and switching to adjusted gross national income (GNI). Since the latter does not take into account the effects of the re-domiciliation of these multinationals or the transfer and depreciation of their financial assets, it is considered a more reliable benchmark.

To conclude, some Irish-American tycoons played a direct role in rescuing the Irish state's finances by purchasing government shares in various companies. While the post-financial crisis growth of the Irish economy cannot be solely attributed to them, it is plausible that they leveraged their influence to attract investment to Ireland during its challenging period. However, this involvement has also resulted in increased influence and obligations in return.

Notes

1. Europe: qui sont les riches, qui sont les pauvres?. 2013. Le Point, 12 December. http://www.lepoint.fr/economie/europe-qui-sont-les-riches-qui-sont-les-pauvres-12-122013-1768553_28.php. Accessed 6 June 2025.
2. Cathal O'Connell. 2007. The State and Housing in Ireland: Ideology, Policy and Practice. New York: Nova Science Publishers, 138.
3. Why Worry? 2004. The Economist, 16 October.
4. John Walsh. 2006. Not a Stone Will Stand upon a Stone. *The Guardian*, 9 May.
5. Alan Ahearn. 2006. Ireland Exposed by Reliance on Faltering US Economy. *The Post*, 31 December.
6. Morgan Kelly. 2006. How the Housing Corner Stone of Our Economy Could Go into Rapid Freefall. *The Irish Times*, 18 January; Morgan Kelly. 2007. Banking on Very Shaky Foundations. *The Irish Times*, 7 September.
7. Morgan Kelly. 2008. Property Market Approaching Critical Point. *The Irish Times*, 18 January.
8. Ailing Celtic Tiger? 2007. *The Economist*, 12 October.
9. This title refers to the bankruptcy of the Icelandic state at the end of 2008. The Liffey is the river that flows through Dublin. Reykjavik-on-Liffey. 2009. *The Economist*, 5 February.

10. Louise Holden. 2010. The Doom Merchant Whose Warnings Don't Seem So Far-Fetched Anymore. *The Irish Times*, 13 April.
11. Irish GDP contracted by 0.3% in the first quarter of 2008 and by 0.5% in the second quarter. France 24. 2008. Ireland officially enters recession, 25 September. https://www.france24.com/en/20080925-ireland-enters-recession-economy. Accessed 6 June 2025; see also the Central Statistics Office website (Ireland) for more detailed information: https://www.cso.ie/en/releasesandpublications/ep/p-mip/mip2014/economy/ef. Accessed 6 June 2025. As in the United States, in Ireland the economy is considered to be entering a recession when GDP contracts for two consecutive quarters.
12. Central Statistics Office (Dublin). Table 1: Components of the Annual Population Change, 1987–2015. https://www.cso.ie/en/releasesandpublications/er/pme/populationandmigrationestimatesapril2015/. Accessed 6 June 2025.
13. For a clear and detailed summary of the causes and consequences of the subprime crisis, see: Jean-Charles Bricongne, Vincent Lapègue, Olivier Monso. March 2009. La crise des "subprimes": de la crise financière à la crise économique. In La récession se prolonge. Note de conjoncture de l'Institut National de la Statistique et des Études Économiques. https://www.insee.fr/fr/statistiques/1407821. Accessed 6 June 2025. See also: Valérie Peyronel, Catherine Coron, Régine Hollander (eds). 2010. La crise financière et les économies du monde anglophone. Paris: Presses Sorbonne Nouvelle, 2010.
14. See: Marie-Claire Considère-Charon. 2011. Regards sur la crise irlandaise. Politique étrangère 2: 429–440; Anne Groutel. 2011. L'Irlande: un avenir très incertain. Grande Europe 32: 3–9.
15. Anne Groutel. 2015. Une nouvelle gouvernance: une condition nécessaire à la reprise économique en Irlande? Revue LISA / LISA e-journal 13, 2. Martine Azuelos (ed.). Special issue: Anglo-Saxon Capitalism and the Anglophone World(s). https://doi.org/10.4000/lisa.8396
16. NAMA functions as a bad bank. These structures buy high-risk assets from public or private financial institutions above their market value. The aim is to avoid systemic bank failures by socialising losses. In other words, the state or a local authority takes over the initial costs incurred by the failing institutions.
17. Anne De Guigné. 2010. L'Irlande, un pays malade de ses banques. Le Figaro, 22 November; Charles Forelle, David Enrich. 2010. Ireland's Fate Tied to Doomed Banks. *The Wall Street Journal*, 10 November.

18. John Spain. 2010. The Irish Are the Patsys of Europe. 1 December. https://www.irishcentral.com/opinion/others/the-irish-are-the-patsys-of-europe-111104154-238056261. Accessed 6 June 2025.
19. Statement of Purpose. 2011. *The Irish Times*, 7 March.
20. The Society of the United Irishmen was originally an Irish liberal political organisation created to achieve parliamentary reform in Ireland. Inspired by the American and French Revolutions, it evolved into a revolutionary republican organisation.
21. Fintan O'Toole. 2010. Fear, Rage, Despair and Distrust Have Been in the Pot for Two Years. The New Ingredient Is Shame. *The Irish Times*, 20 November.
22. After the Race. 2011. *The Economist*, 17 February.
23. Shane Ross. 2010. The Bankers: How the Banks Brought Ireland to Its Knees, Dublin: Penguin Books.
24. David McWilliams. 2008. Crisis Is an Opportunity Too Valuable to Squander. Irish Independent, 23 July; Kieran Mulvey. 2010. The Crisis Is an Opportunity to Reshape Nation's Destiny. *Irish Independent*, 27 April; Fintan O'Toole. 2010. Enough Is Enough: How to Build a New Republic. London: Faber and Faber.
25. Wilbur Ross Jr. 2015. Tales from the Vault. Irish America, December/ January. http://irishamerica.com/2014/12/tales-from-the-vault/ Accessed 6 June 2025.
26. Wilbur Ross Jr. served as Secretary of Commerce in the Trump administration. He took office on 27 February 2017 and served in that position throughout President Donald Trump's term.
27. Lisa O'Carroll. 2011. Wilbur Ross and Fairfax Rescue Bank of Ireland. *The Guardian*, 28 July.
28. Laura Noonan, Freya Berry. 2014. U.S. Billionaire Wilbur Ross to Sell Landmark Bank of Ireland Investment. 9 June. http://www.reuters.com/article/us-bank-of-ireland-ross-idUSKBN0EK1PH20140609. Accessed 6 June 2025.
29. Patrick Counihan. 2014. Billionaire Wilbur Ross Sells Off His Interest in Bank of Ireland, Triples Investment, 10 June. https://www.irishcentral.com/news/american-billionaire-wilbur-ross-sells-off-his-interest-in-bank-of-ireland-and-triples-investment. Accessed 6 June 2025.
30. James Hogan, an Australian of Irish origin, participated in the Global Irish Economic Forum in 2009 and 2011.
31. Etihad is the national airline of the United Arab Emirates.
32. David Black. 2012. Etihad Takes 3 Per Cent Stake in Aer Lingus. *The National* (Abu Dhabi), 2 May.

33. IAG (International Airlines Group) comprises British Airways, Iberia, and Vueling.
34. John Mulligan. 2015. Etihad Flying High as Shares Double in Aer Lingus. Belfast Telegraph, 16 January; John Mulligan. 2015. Etihad to Sell 5pc Aer Lingus Stake to IAG for €66 m. *Belfast Telegraph*, 9 June.
35. Simon Carswell. 2015. John Malone: The US Billionaire Buying Up Ireland. *The Irish Times*, 21 February.
36. Malone was not alone in buying up NAMA-owned properties; other vulture funds have done the same. Attracta Mooney. 2017. 'Aggressive' Vulture Funds Swoop In on Irish Property. *The Financial Times*, 20 February.
37. Barry J. White. 2014. Tony O'Reilly: How the Billionaire's Fortune Unravelled. The Daily Business Post, 24 June.
38. Jerome Reilly. 2005. US Economic Big-Wig Warns: 'We're Sick of Your America-Bashing'. Irish Independent, 25 September.
39. Government of Ireland, Department of Foreign Affairs, Irish Embassy in Washington. "Ireland and America: Challenges and Opportunities in a New Context", March 2009, http://studylib.net/doc/7647330/ireland-and-the-usa-a-strategic-review-ofopportunities-. Accessed 6 June 2025.
40. Government of Ireland, Ireland and America, 13.
41. David McWilliams. 2007. The Generation Game. Dublin: Gill & Macmillan.
42. David McWilliams. 2009. Diaspora Can Foster Future Success. 30 August. https://www.skyscrapercity.com/threads/economy-discussion-thread.844202/?u=141167&sortby=newest. Accessed 6 June 2025.
43. McWilliams, Diaspora Can Foster Future Success.
44. David McWilliams. 2007. The Jack Charlton Theory of Economics, 10 September. http://www.davidmcwilliams.ie/the-jack-charlton-theory-of-economic. Note: This link is no longer active.
45. McWilliams, The Jack Charlton Theory.
46. David McWilliams coined the expression "An Irish Davos".
47. The Irish State purchased Farmleigh House and its estate from the Guinness family in 1999. Farmleigh House is the home of Heads of State on official visits to Ireland.
48. Michelle Devane. 2008. Site for Irish Diaspora. *The Sunday Business Post*, 9 November.
49. Government of Ireland, Department of Foreign Affairs, "Global Irish Economic Forum Report", Dublin, 2009.
50. The Chatham House Rule allows participants in a meeting to disclose information about what was said at the meeting. However, they undertake not to reveal the names or affiliations of the speakers.

51. Noreen Bowden. 2009. High Profile Members of the Diaspora Asked for Advice, 21 September. http://www.emigrant.ie/index.php?option=com_content&task=view&id=74,069&Itemid=369. Note: this link is no longer active.
52. Government of Ireland, Global Irish Economic Forum Report, 27.
53. Government of Ireland, Global Irish Economic Forum Report, Annex IV, 31; Forfás, 2010, Annual Business Survey of Economic Impact 2009, November, 9–10. http://edepositireland.ie/bitstream/handle/2262/70638/forfas101123-ABSEI_2009%20-%20Results.pdf?sequence=1&isAllowed=y. Accessed 6 June 2025.
54. Government of Ireland, Global Irish Economic Forum Report, 32.
55. Anne Groutel. 2013. L'art et la culture au service de l'économie irlandaise: perspectives, stratégies et controverses. In special issue: Les nations celtiques et le monde contemporain, ed. Frédéric Armao: 153–165. Revue Babel, 27,8.
56. Cullen Hails Success of Irish Arts at Global Economic Forum. 2009. Hotpress.com. 19 September. www.hotpress.com/archive/5829319.html. Accessed 6 June 2025.
57. Government of Ireland, Global Irish Economic Forum Report, 27.
58. Riverdance is a traditional dance show consisting of Irish tap dancing, singing, ballet, and music. The show has toured the world and has helped to raise the profile of Irish culture.
59. See: Jennifer M. Brinkerhoff. 2009. Digital Diasporas: Identity and Transnational Engagement. Cambridge: Cambridge University Press.
60. Anne Groutel. 2017. Irish Exporting Companies: Looking East, Looking South but Still Going West. In Revisiting the UK and Ireland's Transatlantic Economic Relationship with the United States in the twenty-first Century: Beyond Sentimental Rhetoric, Anne Groutel, Marie-Christine Pauwels, and Valérie Peyronel, eds. London: Palgrave Macmillan, 210–214.
61. Government of Ireland, Department of Foreign Affairs, Global Irish Network.
    https://www.dfa.ie/global-irish/business-and-education/global-irish-network. Note: This webpage has been removed.
62. Eithne Shortall. 2012. The Gathering Storm; Tourism Venture or Cynical Bid for Emigrants' Cash? *The Sunday Times* (Irl.), 11 November.
63. Ireland experienced a 25% decline in visitor numbers between 2007 and 2010. Government of Ireland, Department of Foreign Affairs, "The Report of Second Global Irish Economic Forum, Dublin Castle, 7–8 October 2011", Dublin, 22 November 2011, Annex 2, Appendix 3: 14.

64. Dan Griffin. 2012. We're Not Alone in Hosting a Global Homecoming. *The Irish Times*, 10 November; Seán McCárthaigh. Organisers Defend Gathering Tourism Targets. *The Irish Times*, 27 August.
65. Michael Clifford. 2012. Gathering Storm: Byrne Brings Home Truth. *Irish Examiner*, 10 November.
66. Donald Clarke. 2012. Tourism Initiative a Debate Gathering Momentum. *The Irish Times*, 10 November; Eithne Shortall, The Gathering Storm; Campaign Postcards Gathering Only Dust. 2012. *Irish Independent*, 15 November; Criticising the Gathering. 2012. *The Irish Times*, 10 November.
67. Michael Clifford, Gathering Storm: Byrne Brings Home Truth.
68. Gabriel Byrne quoted in: Maybe I'm Naive, Gabriel, but I Think Diaspora Still Has a Bit of a Grá for Us. 2012. Irish Independent, 7 November.
69. Joanne Hunt. 2012. Abbey Director Criticises 'Lip Service' to Culture", *The Irish Times*, 8 November.
70. Lost in Translation? The President Steps in to Explain Gabriel's 'Sham'. 2012. *Irish Daily Mail*, 24 November.
71. Eithne Shortall, The Gathering Storm.
72. Shane Hegarty. 2012. The Gathering Special Quality: Leo's Smugness. *The Irish Times*, 10 November.
73. Gathering Naysayers Urged to Cut the Criticism. 2012. *Irish Examiner*, 5 December.
74. Campaign Postcards Gathering Only Dust.
75. The Irish authorities had expected an additional three hundred and fifty thousand tourists; the number achieved was between two hundred and fifty thousand and two hundred and seventy-five thousand. Fáilte Ireland, "The Gathering - Final Report", December 2013, 3.
76. The target set by the Irish authorities was 168 million. The budget allocated by the State was a modest 13 million euros. Fáilte Ireland, The Gathering.
77. The final report mentions that these North American tourists generally stay longer in Ireland and spend more than other tourists. Fáilte Ireland, The Gathering, 51.
78. Ziene Mottiar, Bernadette M. Quinn, Theresa Ryan. 2014. A Study of the Social and Community Impacts of the Gathering in Counties Kerry and Westmeath. Dublin: Dublin Institute of Technology, School of Hospitality Management and Tourism, 1 March. https://doi.org/10.21427/D70R2J
79. Fáilte Ireland, The Gathering - Final Report, 19.
80. Ziene Mottiar et al., A Study of the Social and Community Impacts, 33.

81. Fáilte Ireland, The Gathering - Final Report, 52. This is included in the strategy formulated by the Irish Department of Transport, Tourism and Sport, but the details are not specified. Government of Ireland, Department of Transport, Tourism and Sport, "People, Place and Policy - Growing Tourism to 2025" Dublin, March 2015, 56.
   https://assets.gov.ie/19625/0740208ab1524fa3962da51e46bd43af.pdf. Accessed 6 June 2025.
82. Fáilte Ireland, "Annual Report", Dublin, 2014, 5.
   https://www.failteIreland.ie/FailteIreland/media/WebsiteStructure/Documents/4_Corporate_Documents/Annual_Reports/Failte-Ireland-Annual-Report-2014.pdf?ext=.pdf. Accessed 6 June 2025.
83. Fáilte Ireland, Annual Report.
84. Fáilte Ireland, The Gathering - Final Report, 45.
85. Fáilte Ireland, Fitzpatrick Associates. The Gathering Ireland 2013 - Economic Impact Study - Final Report", 2014, cited in: "Tourism Marketing Fund. Value for Money and Policy Review. Appendix 2: Literature Review", Department of Transport, Tourism and Sport, June 2019, 11. https://assets.gov.ie/static/documents/tourism-market-fund-value-for-money-and-policy-review.pdf. Accessed 6 June 2025.
86. For humorous and wry articles on this subject, see: Lise Hand. 2009. Superheroes of the Irish Diaspora Know How to Talk, Now Let's See Action. *Irish Independent*, 21 September;
   Diarmuid MacShane. 2009. Diaspora, Schmiaspora! How about the Chickens Who Came Home to Roost. http://www.macshane.ie/2009/09/diaspora-schmiaspora-time-to-forget-about-the-wild-geese/. accessed 30 May 2017. Note: this link is no longer active. See also two letters from readers of *The Irish Times*. 2009. Farmleigh Forum. 23 September.
87. Michael O'Leary quoted in: Conor McMorrow. 2010. The Hot Éire Balloon. *The Sunday Tribune*, 7 February.
88. Michael O'Leary quoted in: Ciarán Hancock. 2009. Will Farmleigh Make a Difference. *The Irish Times*, 26 September.
89. Mark Little. 2010. A Few Closing Thought, 20 September. Mark Little's blog at rte.ie. http://www.rte.ie. Accessed 5 February 2010. Note: this link is no longer active.
90. Colm O'Doherty. 2009. The Fetishists of Farmleigh. 22 September. https://www.tasc.ie/blog/2009/09/22/fetishists-of-farmleigh/. Accessed 6 June 2025.
91. Brendan Hughes, was the author of the blog Brendanhughes.ie.
92. Brendan Hughes. 2009. Big Ideas from Global Irish Economic Forum. 20 September https://brendanhughes.ie/?s=big+ideas+from+p-global+irish+forum. Note: this link is no longer active.

93. Michael O'Leary quoted in: Conor McMorrow, The Hot Éire Balloon.
94. See for example: Diarmuid McShane. 2010. Status Report of the Global Irish Economic Forum", 16 March. Accessed online on 24 May 2017 but no longer available.
95. Constantin Gurdgiev is the former editor-in-chief of Business and Finance Magazine. He has a PhD in macroeconomics and finance. He has taught at Johns Hopkins University, University College Dublin and is a visiting lecturer at Trinity College Dublin.
96. This expression, which is now part of everyday language, appeared in the media a few years ago. Competitiveness and innovation have become the watchwords of this businesslike Ireland.
97. Constantin Gurdgiev. 2010. Why Farmleigh Report Falls Flat", 13 March. http://trueeconomics.blogspot.fr/2010/03/economics-13032010-why-farmleighreport.html. Note: This webpage has been removed.
98. Denis O'Brien, the telecoms magnate, lamented that Eircom was on its fifth takeover and advised nationalisation of the company because the necessary investment to modernise the network had not been made. Elaine Byrne. 2011. So Who's Afraid of Denis O'Brien? Enda Kenny Is. Irish Independent, 16 October.
99. See Bob Geldof's comments on hotels and Ireland's tourism product. Ciarán Hancock, Will Farmleigh Make a Difference.
100. Vanessa Boullet, The Irish-US Economic Relations: End of an Era or a Promising Future? in Revisiting the UK, 62–64.
101. The Irish tax system allowed multinationals "to establish a subsidiary in Ireland whose tax residence is in another country. The main function of the subsidiary may be to charge other Irish and non-Irish subsidiaries of the same multinational for intellectual property rights relating to patents and the use of the multinational's brand. This reduces the profits of these subsidiaries that are taxable in these countries and the so-called double Irish mechanism allows most of the multinational's profits to be transferred to the subsidiary whose tax residence is most often in the Cayman Islands or the Bahamas and thus to evade most of the corporate tax". Jean-Christophe Defraigne, Patricia Nouveau. 2017. Introduction à l'économie européenne. 2nd edn. Louvain-la-Neuve: De Boeck Supérieur, 481.
102. Upsetting the Apple Cart. 2016. *The Economist*, 8 September.
103. Transfer pricing is another process used extensively in Ireland and elsewhere by the parent companies of multinationals who "dump the components they export to their subsidiaries in Ireland for assembly. This allows the Irish subsidiaries of these multinationals to make higher profits that are less taxed than in the US or other EU countries". Jean-Christophe Defraigne, Patricia Nouveau, Introduction à l'économie européenne, 479.

104. Christopher Dembik. 2016. +26.3% for Gaelic GDP: the real explanation for Little Ireland's over-performance. 13 July. http://www.atlantico.fr/decryptage/263-forgaelic-gdp-veritable-explanation-over-performance-little-irland-christopher-dembik-2762566.html#FpsPtJ1zQdp6hRYW.99. Note: This webpage has been removed.
105. Dembik. +26.3% for Gaelic GDP.
106. Romaric Godin. 2016. Ireland: 26.3% growth artificially inflated", *La Tribune*, 12 July.

PART IV

Ireland and the Diaspora Entrepreneurial Elite: Partnership or Interference?

In the aftermath of Ireland's accession to the European Economic Community, a limited number of large Irish firms managed not only to endure the transition but to expand their operations. One notable example is Smurfit Kappa, a packaging company originally founded in the 1930s. After consolidating its position in the domestic market through mergers, the company pursued an ambitious strategy of international expansion from the 1970s onward, first acquiring firms in Britain and subsequently extending its reach to the United States, continental Europe, and Latin America. Today, it employs approximately 45,000 people across thirty-five countries.[1]

CRH represents another case of successful adaptation. Formed in 1970 through the merger of two leading Irish public companies—Cement Limited (established in 1936) and Roadstone Limited (established in 1949)—CRH has become a major global player in the production of cement and construction materials. It now employs 77,000 individuals worldwide.[2] Kerry Group, a company operating in the agri-food sector and established in 1972, has similarly evolved into a multinational enterprise.[3] More recent examples of successful Irish firms include Ryanair and Paddy Power.[4]

As Barry notes,[5] a number of legacy firms dating from the pre-independence era, such as Guinness and Jacob's, managed to remain competitive for a time. However, they were ultimately acquired by larger multinational groups. It was arguably through these acquisitions that the development and long-term viability of their iconic brands were secured.

A similar trajectory can be observed in the case of Irish Distillers, which is particularly illustrative. As previously explained, Irish whiskey had suffered a prolonged decline since the early twentieth century, leading to the closure of numerous distilleries. By the 1960s, the industry was in a state of crisis, and radical intervention was necessary. In 1966, the three remaining distilleries in the Republic—John Power & Son, John Jameson & Son, and the Cork Distilleries Company—merged to form Irish Distillers Limited, pooling their resources in an effort to revitalise the sector. A pivotal moment came in 1988, when the company was acquired by the French conglomerate Pernod Ricard, providing access to global distribution networks. Somewhat ironically, the renewed international enthusiasm for Irish whiskey in recent decades has led to the re-emergence of Single Pot Still—a historically distinctive and authentically Irish style of whiskey—as a prominent product on global markets. Jameson, in particular, has enjoyed remarkable success in the United States, helping to reignite international interest in the Irish whiskey category more broadly.

John Fitzgerald and Patrick Honohan argue that the achievements of these firms effectively disprove the long-standing assumption that Ireland lacked entrepreneurial capability or was structurally incapable of attaining industrial productivity.[6] However, they also cite the examples of Irish Shipping, Waterford Glass, and GPA as reminders that consolidation, scale, and international expansion have not invariably guaranteed long-term success. Furthermore, they point out that Ireland's most successful indigenous firms have largely emerged outside the sectors of information technology and pharmaceuticals, which remain primarily dominated by foreign direct investment. This distinction is crucial, as it underscores the fact that, for a considerable period, linkages and spill-overs from foreign multinationals into the domestic economy were limited in scope and impact.[7]

This dependency on foreign investment and its inherent vulnerabilities were becoming increasingly apparent. In 2004, *The Economist* expressed concern that rising inflation was eroding Ireland's competitiveness, which was so dependent on FDI.[8] To cushion the effects of rising costs[9] and to avoid the risk of foreign multinationals leaving the country, Ireland needed to focus on attracting research and development activity to move the economy up the value chain towards a knowledge-based economy. During an official visit to the United States in 2002, Mary Harney, the then Tánaiste, emphasised what had become the new priority of the Irish authorities: "Ten years ago, we would have said jobs, jobs, jobs. […]

Ireland now needs to become drivers of technology [...]. Instead of simply playing the tune, we've got to become the composers".[10]

This shift in discourse seemed to reflect a broader policy reorientation. Indeed, in the 2000s, reports from Irish bodies such as Forfás[11] or think tanks such as the Small Business Forum[12] and the Enterprise Strategy Group[13] emphasised the critical need to develop entrepreneurship, believing that local businesses have a key role to play in the transition of the Irish economy to a "smart" economy. However, since the late 1950s, the Irish authorities had prioritised the inflow of foreign investment rather than an industrial policy focused on developing entrepreneurship in Ireland.

In light of this historical context, this final section will first shed light on the reasons why entrepreneurship was long considered a less respected career path in Ireland. We will then examine how and why, in recent decades, the image of the entrepreneur has changed, and how the development of entrepreneurship has become a national priority. The Irish-American diaspora elites have played a key role by providing concrete support to Irish technological start-ups, while also benefiting themselves. However, as we will see, this is only one aspect of the growing influence and decision-making role these elites aspire to have in Ireland, both in the economic and political sphere.

Notes

1. John Fitzgerald, Patrick Honohan. 2023. Europe and the Transformation of the Irish Economy, coll. Elements in Economics of European Integration. Cambridge: Cambridge University Press, 16.
2. John Fitzgerald, Patrick Honohan, Europe.
3. John Fitzgerald, Patrick Honohan, Europe, 19.
4. Paddy Power is an Irish gambling company founded in 1988. Its product offering includes sports betting, online casino, online poker, and online bingo.
5. Frank Barry. 2023. Industry and Policy in Independent Ireland, 1922–1972. Oxford: Oxford University Press, 169–197.
6. John Fitzgerald, Patrick Honohan, Europe, 16.
7. John Fitzgerald, Patrick Honohan, Europe, 15.
8. Why Worry? 2004. *The Economist*, 14 October 2004.
9. See: Anne Groutel. 2007. Irish Economy and Globalisation. In Le Tigre celtique en question, ed. Catherine Maignant: 91–104. Caen, Presses universitaires de Caen.

10. Mary Harney quoted in: US-Ireland Business Summit—Washington. 2002. The Irish Emigrant, 8 September. The Irish Emigrant was an e-weekly published from 1987 to 2012.
11. Forfás, "Towards Developing an Enterprise Strategy", Dublin, Forfás, September 2007; Forfás, "Making It Happen. Growing Enterprise for Ireland", Dublin, Forfás, September 2010. http://edepositireland.ie/bitstream/handle/2262/70642/Forfas100924Making_It_Hap-ppen-Growing_Enterprise_for_Ireland.pdf?sequence=1&isAllowed=y. Accessed 6 June 2025. Forfás (1994–2014) was an independent body with a government mandate to advise on industrial development, economic policy, and innovation.
12. Small Business Forum. 2006. The Report of the Small Business Forum: Small Business Is Big Business, Dublin, May.
13. Eoin O'Driscoll. 2004. Ahead of the Curve: Ireland's Place in the Global Economy, Dublin, Enterprise Strategy Group.

CHAPTER 12

Ireland and Entrepreneurship: From Cultural Barriers to Diaspora-Driven Innovation

12.1 A Society Long Suspicious of Entrepreneurs

A first study, dating from 1973, and a second, conducted ten years later, tend to show that Irish society was not perceived by entrepreneurs themselves as a society that encouraged entrepreneurship. One of the findings of the first of these studies, published by the Economic and Social Research Institute (ESRI), a leading Irish economic research institute, is quite revealing:

> One of the most disturbing features of these interviews [with Irish entrepreneurs] was how often informants came back to the thesis that what families, schools, the Church, the social system, and the business system itself failed to produce in Ireland is people with the basic virtues of honesty, integrity, and hard and purposeful work.[1]

The second study, also conducted among Irish entrepreneurs, indicated that they felt that the education system placed too much emphasis on "security" and the importance of having a stable job. A career in business was not seen as such.[2] In addition, the entrepreneurs surveyed said they suffered from the public image of their profession:

> In the public's mind, the recurring popular picture of business people in Ireland is based on the stereotype of the 'gombeen man',[3] a tradition deeply rooted in Irish culture.[4]

A. Groutel, *The Two Irelands and the Diaspora*,
https://doi.org/10.1007/978-3-032-12355-8_12

However, the authors of this study noted the beginning of a change in attitude towards entrepreneurship in the early 1980s. Yet, in the early 2010s, some observers of Irish economic life were still very pessimistic. In his book, *Ireland's Malaise: The Troubled Personality of the Irish Economy*, Michael Casey[5] praises entrepreneurship, but at the same time expresses scepticism about the ability of Irish society to instill entrepreneurship spirit in its population: "The evidence [...] suggests that the Irish gene pool does not produce entrepreneurs in great numbers and that our culture does not nurture them".[6] He offers a scathing critique of his fellow countrymen, deploring their casualness, a cultural trait that, in his view, is enduring: "For many farmers of the time, leisure was preferable to work. [...] It is possible that some version of this attitude survives among Irish entrepreneurs of today".[7] According to Casey, this preference for ease may have driven some to resort to illegality:

> Then, just as social and cultural norms were becoming somewhat more welcoming to the emergence of an entrepreneurial class, at least in the cities, it transpired that the prevailing model of enterprise was one of cunning and stroke-play.
>
> The emphasis was on making money for little or no effort, usually on the basis of cronyism and inside information. Risk-taking was for the race, not for business. [...] The entrepreneurs who emerged in the period (the Haughey era)[8] were not good role models for the next generation. Their legacy contributed to the property bubble and the economic collapse of 2008.[9]

Casey noted that at no time since the 1950s had Ireland been able to generate growth through internal means[10] and went so far as to question whether the various EU funds Ireland had received and FDI had helped perpetuate the Irish penchant for ease and inhibit their entrepreneurial spirit[11]:

> Family-run firms are still the norm and these tend not to grow beyond the point where the family might lose control. The owners are reluctant to hire professional managers, or go public, and they rarely want the hassle of exporting. These firms reach a certain size and then remain in that 'comfort zone'.[12]

This view is reminiscent of Joseph J. Lee's view of his fellow countrymen.[13] In the same vein, Casey summarised his thinking as follows: "In general, it appears that we are still rather more interested in possessing than in performing".[14]

However, it should be noted that Irish attitudes towards entrepreneurship have changed significantly since the 1980s. Indeed, the 2017 Global Entrepreneurship Monitor report revealed that distrust has been replaced by admiration for successful businesspeople. However, only 53% of those surveyed thought it was a good career choice.[15]

12.2 Entrepreneurship Policy in Ireland: The Persistent Policy Void

Casey also criticised the Irish authorities for taking the easy way out. When a multinational company left, they gave in to local pressure and immediately sought to bring in another to replace it, without considering alternatives:

> There is never the slightest suggestion that local entrepreneurship might come to the rescue, perhaps because it is recognized that this is inadequate or non-existent. The idea of self-help seems to be absent in many parts of the country.[16]

Indeed, the example of the Collison brothers, two gifted inventors,[17] illustrates perfectly the low regard in which young entrepreneurs in the new technology sector were held in the 2000s. The two young men approached Enterprise Ireland for seed money to fund their project. The agency, which was responsible for helping small Irish businesses, had at that time a reputation for being unresponsive, conservative, and administratively cumbersome.[18] Perplexed by the complexity of the process, the brothers decided to try their luck in California. They have since become millionaires. In 2008, Richard Delevan, in an article about the Collisons' success, noted that:

> Because the success of Patrick Collison is a symbol of Ireland's colossal failure to develop an indigenous technology industry to match the story we told ourselves. It is an indictment of our hypocrisy. His narrative has a simple message: if you are a creative entrepreneur of talent and drive, Ireland is not the place for you.[19]

Dan Breznitz,[20] an economist with expertise in innovation policy, pointed to the lack of a coordinated government strategy to promote Irish technology companies.[21] Indeed, Forfás published a paper in 2007 that was intended to serve as a blueprint for the development of a policy to promote entrepreneurship.[22] The benefits to growth, competitiveness, and innovation, as well as to regional development and social cohesion, were cited as the rationale for the approach. Making Ireland one of the most entrepreneurial nations in the world was the ambitious goal set by the authors of this study.[23] However, the long-awaited policy targeted at entrepreneurship development was not developed by the Fianna Fáil administration. Instead, a few months later, it released a more comprehensive plan to stimulate innovation and boost the Irish economy.[24] While the importance of developing entrepreneurship was recognised, the role assigned to Irish companies was only peripheral. It was not intended that they should be the next engine of growth, but rather that they should be involved in creating an ecosystem that would attract multinationals and foreign entrepreneurs.[25]

12.3 The Wake-Up Call From the Irish-American Business Community

In this context, Craig Barrett's[26] words at the first GIEF in 2009 caused a stir. The former chairman of the multinational Intel and a prominent member of the diaspora was forthright when he stated that of the fourteen reasons that had convinced Intel to come to Ireland twenty years earlier, only one remained: the extremely low corporate tax rate.[27] Barrett argued that Ireland needed to reinvent its business model and spend at least 3–4% of its GDP on research and development. Furthermore, the quality of the education system was poor. Creativity had to be encouraged and more graduates had to be trained, especially in mathematics and science. In addition, Barrett, who was very pessimistic about the future of the US economy at the time, argued vigorously that Ireland was too dependent on foreign multinationals: "We are watching the decline and fall of the United States as an economic power - not hypothetically - but as we speak".[28] Robert Shapiro, an advisor to Barack Obama and[29] former Under Secretary of Commerce for Economic Affairs, had also warned Ireland some time earlier:

> Ireland must wean itself from dependence on FDI. A low corporate taxation rate is not the most important factor moving forward, it goes beyond that. The next stage is not FDI but a series of policies that actively promote spill-overs from FDI corporations to Irish indigenous firms. The best way forward is for young Irish people to become entrepreneurs and force existing business to compete and become the best in the world. If you look at the Chinese model, FDI is a transitional strategy, not an end game strategy, that creates a lasting impact. The key to Ireland's next stage is to make the entire economy a modern economy and not one that depends on the success of foreign companies.[30]

On 29 September 2009, a few days after Craig Barrett's dramatic statement, Mary Coughlan, Tánaiste and Minister for Enterprise, announced that she would implement a strategy to promote a true entrepreneurial culture in Ireland.[31] However, this strategy was not formulated by the Fianna Fáil administration, whose long period in power ended in 2011. In that year, the discontented Irish people inflicted a stinging electoral defeat on the incumbent government. It was succeeded by a coalition of Fine Gael and the Labour Party.

12.4 The Fine Gael Administration and the Diaspora: A Shared Commitment to Promoting Entrepreneurship in the 2010s

Enda Kenny became Taoiseach in March 2011 in the midst of the economic crisis and at a time when the Irish people had lost faith in their country's institutions. Fine Gael was elected largely on the promise that the new government would improve the governance of the country. A number of reforms were indeed implemented to break with past practices,[32] but it is worth noting that the new administration did not question the formalisation of links with the Irish-American business elite, but rather the opposite.

Eamon Gilmore, the Tánaiste, acknowledged before the lower house of the Irish Parliament that the Global Irish Economic Forum (GIEF) and The Global Irish Network (GIN) had been constructive initiatives: "The deputy knows I criticised the previous Government on many issues but this is not one of them. This was a very good initiative which was very successful".[33] The Government thus decided to renew GIEF every two years but Eamon Gilmore indicated that the forthcoming GIEF agenda would be more specific and focused on concrete actions.[34]

This was in response to criticism that most of the initiatives envisaged in the first GIEF had not been implemented. The world-class university of the performing arts, one of the grand ideas that had sprung from Dermot Desmond's mind, for example, never came to fruition.

Until 2011, only a secretariat, liaising with the ambassadors, coordinated the network's activities. At the second GIEF, the Tánaiste announced that a steering committee, the Global Irish Network Advisory Group, consisting of nineteen members of the diaspora elite representing several continents, chaired by the Taoiseach and the Tánaiste, would be responsible for monitoring the implementation of some of the measures suggested during GIEF and assisting the secretariat in coordinating GIN activities.[35] The Irish authorities wanted to show that they were committed to taking GIEF's recommendations to the next level; otherwise there was a risk that diaspora leaders would be unwilling to assist in the future.

Recognising the importance of developing Ireland's relations with the rest of the world in this era of globalisation, particularly with emerging economies where there are significant economic opportunities for key sectors of the Irish economy, such as agri-food and construction, the new leadership placed greater emphasis than its predecessors on the development of entrepreneurship and the promotion of exports by indigenous businesses.[36]

China, of course, but also Saudi Arabia, Qatar, the United Arab Emirates, and South Korea were among the markets that some Irish companies had begun to exploit.[37] As a result, the number of trade missions to these countries, led by ministers or senior Irish government officials, increased. In order to intensify and diversify Ireland's foreign relations, foreign trade was placed under the aegis of the Department of Foreign Affairs and Trade. Diplomatic Staff became much more actively involved in the promotion of economic activities than it was in the past. The assistance of GIN members is invaluable and is regularly sought when the DFA wishes to organise a mission abroad.

In addition, the Entrepreneurship Forum, a think tank chaired by Seán O'Sullivan, was commissioned by the Fine Gael administration to prepare a report on how to promote entrepreneurship in Ireland. An engineer by training, O'Sullivan is a serial entrepreneur who has invested in some twenty technology companies. Among other ventures, he is the founder of MapInfo Corporation, a NASDAQ-listed company and pioneer in geographic information systems, and of SOS Ventures, a venture capital firm. Born in the United States to Irish parents, O'Sullivan lived in County Cork at the time, where he founded Avego, a technology company.[38]

The Entrepreneurship Forum report[39] marked a clear departure from previous publications on the subject, and O'Sullivan's distinctly American influence is hard to miss. While it echoed familiar recommendations[40]—such as the importance of business mentoring, networking, and embedding entrepreneurship across all levels of education—its real shift lay in tone and focus. The report placed strong emphasis on individual responsibility, urging Irish people to embrace entrepreneurship regardless of age, gender, or educational background. Citizens, it argued, needed to become more self-reliant and temper their expectations of the state, which should concentrate on fostering an environment supportive of entrepreneurial activity.

Unlike previous reports, the Entrepreneurship Forum's report was followed by action. Nine months after its publication, the Irish government published its strategy[41] devoted exclusively to the promotion of entrepreneurship, a first in Ireland. The importance of the latter is clearly expressed, as well as the ambition of the Irish leaders to make Ireland one of the most dynamic countries in the world in this field. While the measures included in this strategy were not revolutionary, it is worth noting that, in the same vein as the Entrepreneurship Forum report, the Irish authorities made it clear that they intended to leave entrepreneurs in the driving seat and limit their action to areas that are directly under the responsibility of the State, i.e. the promotion of entrepreneurship in the education system, tax policy, or the simplification of administrative procedures and company law.

12.5 The Irish Technology Leadership Group: A Bridge Between Ireland and Silicon Valley

Craig Barrett, the outspoken former CEO of Intel, is the chairman of the Irish Technology Leadership Group (ITLG),[42] but John Hartnett[43] is the leader of this highly influential network and a founding member. Originally from Limerick, Hartnett has served, among other roles, as Managing Director of G24 Innovations and Vice President at Palm, Inc.[44] Barry O'Sullivan, Vice President and General Manager of Cisco's Collaboration Technology Group, is one of the founding members of this network and is also part of the ITLG leadership team.

Promoting links between Ireland and Silicon Valley in the fields of innovation, investment, education, and entrepreneurship is the primary mission of this network whose objectives are perfectly in line with those of the Irish authorities. Indeed, how to transform Ireland into the Silicon Valley of Europe was one of the themes proposed during GIEF 2009.

This network was originally set up in 2007 in the United States. Its members are Irish expatriates and Irish-Americans from the Silicon Valley business community who hold senior positions in the sectors of new technologies and finance (Wall Street), and in the seventh art (Hollywood). In a few years, its membership has grown from six hundred to six thousand[45] to twenty thousand.[46] These include senior business leaders, prominent figures on Sand Hill Road in Menlo Park, California, famous for its concentration of venture capitalists, and senior government officials in Washington and Dublin.[47]

The Irish government has supported the ITLG by serving as a facilitator for the network, which has been particularly active from its inception.[48] Among its various initiatives, the ITLG organised the visit of Silicon Valley entrepreneurs to an annual event where Irish entrepreneurs seek transatlantic partnerships. This event, titled *"Silicon Valley Comes to Ireland"*, has been hosted in different Irish cities on several occasions.

The Irish Innovation Centre was established in San Jose (California) at Hartnett's initiative. This centre, which served as a "base camp" for companies from the island of Ireland seeking to explore opportunities in Silicon Valley, also hosted Californian start-ups.[49] Around 100 entrepreneurs could meet, network, share, and learn from each other.[17] Furthermore, having an address in the capital of Silicon Valley is an important asset for a small company trying to conquer the American market.

The ITLG is also working to address some of the key objectives identified during GIEFs, such as securing finance, which is one of the key challenges facing Irish businesses in their development phase. Indeed, in the early 2010s, Irish investors were investing heavily in property, which was the most popular sector at the time, to the detriment of investment in start-ups. In 2010, only $300 million was invested in venture capital for start-ups. By comparison, Israeli companies received $1.5 billion. Indeed, in the same year, while Israel boasted 140 science and technology companies listed on NASDAQ, Ireland had only three.[50]

As a result, John Hartnett, Brendan Richardson, and Richard A. Moran founded Irish Technology Capital, a $100 million venture capital fund that invested in selected Irish and Northern Irish innovative technology companies, or start-ups. Hartnett ran this fund as well as SVG Ventures, a similar investment fund based in San Jose, which invests in the same type of companies.[51]

In 2010, SVG Ventures also opened the Silicon Valley Global Accelerator, a business incubator that housed over forty companies and organisations in downtown San Jose.[52] In October 2013, SVG reported that since 2011, fifteen Irish companies[53] had received funding through SVG, which announced its intention to launch a new $25 million fund, again with the aim of helping Irish start-ups to grow.

SVG Ventures also entered into an agreement with Eircom to invest in a ten-million-dollar fund, the Lab353 Accelerator. Ten Irish start-ups, specialising in mobile telephony, cloud computing, or the Internet of things, were be able to benefit from it to develop in Europe and the United States.[54]

The ITLG also worked in collaboration with Silicon Valley Bank, which had a significant role in the development of innovative Irish start-ups with high growth potential. Claire Lee, who began her career at IBM in Ireland, was the Director of the Start-up Unit at Silicon Valley Bank. She was also an advisor to the US State Department and on the advisory board of ITLG. This bank, which specialised in lending to technology companies, announced in 2012 that it would lend €97 million to Irish start-ups.[55] It also worked closely with the Ireland Strategic Investment Fund, a sovereign wealth fund managed by the National Treasury Management Agency (NTMA).[56] The latter's mission is to invest in commercial enterprises and thereby support economic activity and employment in Ireland.

At the 2009 GIEF, the Taoiseach asked those invited to identify promising economic sectors.[57] As noted earlier, the diaspora entrepreneurial elite recommended developing an economic model that was less dependent on FDI and suggested that indigenous businesses should take over in areas where the country already had some expertise. However, it was stressed that there was a need to increase productivity and specialise in niches. While agri-food was seen as a declining sector, those attending GIEF tried to convince the Irish authorities otherwise.

The ITLG has worked in the spirit of these recommendations. In 2012, for example, it announced that it was collaborating with several Irish and American universities and the Steinbeck Innovation Cluster on an initiative to promote agricultural technology and the concept of smart farms in the Salinas agricultural region, the rural part of California south of Silicon Valley. Education, incubation, investment, and business engagement were the four key words of the Steinbeck Innovation Cluster, which aimed to create hundreds of jobs in the Salinas region. Indeed, Hartnett says that precision agriculture, viticulture, and aquaculture are areas of opportunity. The use of technology in agriculture will be essential in the future to cope with the world's growing population.[58] In 2014, SVG Partners announced the launch of THRIVE, an incubator in Salinas for agricultural technology companies. The partnership between SVG Partners and Forbes is designed to provide funding, advice, and contacts with leading companies in the region for up to fifteen entrepreneurs with innovative projects.[59] In March 2016, the ITLG announced that two Irish companies, selected from among 200 from thirty-five countries, had joined the incubator.[60]

12.6 The Rapid Emergence of Irish Start-Ups in the 2010s

In light of what was said at the beginning of this section, the sudden increase in the number of Irish start-ups, fifty of which had moved to Silicon Valley, by 2014,[61] could come as a surprise. Yet, as a journalist noted at the time: "In the last three to four years there has been a blossoming level of respect towards Irish companies in Silicon Valley. Ireland is on the move".[62] For John Ryan,[63] we were witnessing the beginnings of a change in attitude among young Irish people who were less hesitant to become entrepreneurs: "Irish graduates are as fired up as any Americans you meet. It's not the way it was 20 years ago, where people who came to the US took a more lax approach to things".[64] The massive presence of American technology companies (Google, Apple, Facebook, etc.) in Ireland had clearly sparked off vocations.[65] Silicon Valley, with its promise of sources of funding and a dynamic market, had many attractions. Where previously few would take the risk, the presence of the ITLG, whose members act as guarantors, encouraged them to do so.[66] Quite judiciously, the possibility of developing a business mentoring system was indeed raised at the 2009 GIEF. This was intended to allow Irish entrepreneurs to benefit from the experience of experienced businesspeople from the diaspora. This suggestion has been implemented. For example, the companies that SVG takes under its wing benefit from advice and introductions from businessmen who know the field well, a contribution that is just as valuable as financial assistance. Hartnett believes that this mentoring is crucial to instilling in Irish entrepreneurs the "right" attitude for success:

> The focus is ongoing big early, but people are not overly concerned about risk. They are hyper-aware of making the right decisions, but ultimately if the idea has a chance it is about making it as big as possible early on. […] The first thing to do is hook up immediately with people like the ITLG; you can make a lot of mistakes very easily out here but we are well connected and we'll show you where to go and what to do, which will save a lot of time, money and energy. […] Entrepreneurs from Ireland tend to waffle a bit. […] They may have great technology but they need to pitch in a refined way. The first challenge is to get your story right; the other is to turn up for meetings early.[67]

Finally, the Web Summit phenomenon, by projecting the image of Ireland as a home for innovative companies to the world, has most likely contributed to the atmosphere in which innovative companies can be set up in Ireland. The Web Summit, created by Paddy Cosgrave, is a trade fair for seed and early stage start-ups. The first edition of this event, which brings together investors, companies, and the media, took place in 2010. Since then, its success, driven by Cosgrave's entrepreneurial energy and aggressive marketing, has continued.[68] In 2014, John Collison said:

> Ireland is a good place to start a company, with some advantages over the US. […] When we started out in 2010, it would have been much harder for us here because our business depended on dealing with banks and none of them would talk to us here. Also, some of the people we needed to hire were in Silicon Valley. But I can't see why a company like ours couldn't set up from Ireland now.[69]

In addition to the reassuring message they conveyed, the Collison brothers could now serve as role models in the eyes of potential Irish entrepreneurs.[70] It is notable that the percentage share of new entrepreneurs rose from 9.3% in 2014 to 12.4% in 2019, indicating that there was momentum in the new technology sector at the end of the 2010s. Although it is difficult to determine its exact reach, the "Think big" message promoted by ITLG members has been positive, and the group's practical initiatives on the ground have served as a clear incentive.

12.7 Profits and Pitfalls: Investment in Irish Start-Ups

Investing in these start-ups can be very profitable. In recent years, these companies have increasingly been seen as a safe bet. As pioneers, ITLG members have personally invested in Irish start-ups. Thus, the technology companies that the group deals with managed to raise a sum of fifty million euros between 2007 and 2013, ten million of which was contributed by ITLG members.[71] Working closely with these companies through the network and advising them has increased their chances of becoming profitable. Nevertheless, investing in start-ups can be risky. Mcor Technologies was one such company with a promising future. It specialised in 3D colour printers and had a unique process. In the first ten months of 2013, it announced a 600% increase in sales. This enabled it to benefit from an additional $2 million from the Irish Technology Capital Fund.[72] John Hartnett, as well as being one of the venture capitalists, was also a member of the board of directors of this young company. Yet, Mcor entered into receivership in 2019.

It seems that ITLG members inspired others, as the 2010s witnessed a proliferation of investment funds eager to back Irish start-ups. Some of them have prospered while others have closed down. Atlantic Bridge, for example, injected €100 million to help Irish seed-stage companies expand in Silicon Valley. Brian Long, its founder and director, himself invested in some of these start-ups. In 2016, the fund announced returns on investment of three times for GolNav, four times for Maginatics, and up to five times for Mataio. Atlantic Bridge has indeed enjoyed lasting success.[73] In contrast, SmartInvest, another investment fund, which was to invest seventy million dollars (fifty-six million euros) in thirty start-ups[74] ready to develop in the United States, seems to have closed down.

As for Frontline Ventures, it succeeded in convincing An Post, the Allied Irish Bank, and Enterprise Ireland, among others, to contribute to a forty million investment fund.[75] Silicon Valley Bank also appeared to be keen to continue to exploit this opportunity. Indeed, in May 2016, it announced that a further €96 million would be made available to innovative Irish start-ups.

Venture capital is complemented by other types of funding such as government grants, crowdfunding, etc.[76] Although Silicon Valley Bank went bankrupt in March 2023, securing funding to create and develop a start-up internationally is now less of a challenge, thanks to the groundwork laid by prominent Irish-American venture capitalists and the momentum generated.

Thus, high-profile diaspora businesspeople have been helping to promote entrepreneurship, particularly in the technology sector, on the island of Ireland for several years. On the surface, this trend might suggest the emergence of a domestic engine of economic growth—one that could help reduce Ireland's heavy dependence on multinationals. However, a closer look reveals that this is not yet the case. While the past decade has seen the creation of a multitude of indigenous technology start-ups, many of their owners are selling their companies to larger foreign firms. In fact, like Apple or Google,[77] many multinationals now prefer to acquire such companies with ready-to-use technologies rather than invest directly in research themselves. In the past, this has allowed some start-ups, such as Iona, Parthus, or Elan, to develop but unfortunately not on Irish soil. One thing is certain: between 2000 and 2015, over three hundred shareholders and executives of two hundred Irish start-ups became millionaires through the sale of their companies, and the trend is accelerating[78] at the risk of turning Ireland not into an entrepreneurial society with a balanced mix of small, medium, and large enterprises but into a nursery of innovative start-ups for foreign multinationals to harvest.

12.8 Turning Connection Into Capital: Diaspora-Driven Ventures

The Irish diaspora received significant attention from the late 2000s, prompting businessmen within the diaspora to recognise potential business opportunities. As a result, a number of businesses related to the diaspora have emerged since then.

After the first GIEF, John McColgan, co-producer of the Riverdance show, announced his intention to create a web portal—a kind of social network—for the diaspora to find all kinds of information about Ireland and to maintain the link with the island. WorldIrish.com was subsequently introduced as a fairly innovative platform that aimed to aggregate information from Twitter, Facebook, and other websites. Dermot Desmond, Denis O'Brien, and Terry Clune, well-known entrepreneurs, were also involved in the project.[79] The venture appeared promising, with McColgan stating that €1.5 million out of €3 million had already been invested in the project by the time of its launch in October 2011. However, he was looking to raise a further seven to ten million euros to develop the site.[80] He projected a profit of twenty million euros per year in the following five years[81] and anticipated the site would recruit one hundred thousand members in its first year.[82] In addition to creating a large connected diasporic community, WorldIrish.com would serve as a showcase for Ireland, potentially attracting foreign investors.

From the outset, there was some scepticism about the project's viability.[83] Moreover, a similar site had already been launched in March 2009 by Niall O'Dowd. Indeed, IrishCentral.com, the Irish version of the *Huffington Post*, already offered a wide range of information about Ireland, videos, blogs, and online discussion forums. By 2011, the site, which was updated in real time, had 71,000 subscribers and seven hundred thousand visitors per month. Its advertisers included Coca-Cola, Jameson, Guinness, Aer Lingus, and Continental Airlines.[84] Dennis Fitzgerald and Dennis P. Kelleher, two prominent Wall Street personalities of Irish origin, were among the backers of the site.[85]

Although a study showed that forty-nine million people from the diaspora were connected,[86] the challenger, WorldIrish.com, only managed to attract fifty thousand subscribers, far short of the targets set by the management. Predictably, the two sites announced their intention to merge in early September 2013. The new entity was named IrishCentral.com. However, quite unexpectedly, in May 2016, Niall O'Dowd sold the site to a group of Irish-born venture capitalists who had already invested in technology start-ups. Liam Lynch, who headed the group, said he wanted to double the number of visitors to the platform.[87]

Other diaspora tycoons embarked on diaspora-related business initiatives in the 2010s. Neville Isdell,[88] former chief executive of Coca-Cola, personally invested €12 million in Epic Ireland, a first-of-its-kind fully digital museum dedicated to 321 Irish diaspora celebrities. The museum, which opened in Dublin in 2016, hoped to match the success of the Titanic museum in Belfast, which aimed to attract 400,000 visitors but doubled that number in its first year of existence.[89]

An other example is ConnectIreland (CI) founded in 2012 by Terry Clune in partnership with the IDA. The principle consisted in recruiting as many members of the diaspora as possible who would then act as "connectors" helping to attract foreign investors to Ireland. They were expected to identify overseas expansion opportunities for companies and promote Ireland as an ideal business location. If the connector succeeded in generating interest in the country, they would pass the contact to CI, which, in collaboration with the IDA, would then take charge of the matter and see it through to completion. Clune, who invested €5 million in the project in 2013, committed to covering all costs associated with running the business. In return, the Irish state was expected to offer a "reward" of €1500 (up to a maximum of €150,000 per person) to the intermediary, along with a commission ranging from €1000 to €2500 per permanent job created. This arrangement was anticipated to benefit the Irish Treasury, as it would reduce state expenditures on unemployment benefits and increase tax revenue.[90]

In 2013, Clune projected the creation of five thousand jobs and a gross return of ten million euros.[91] A document published by the Irish government in March 2015 stated that there were forty thousand connectors. It indicated that they had brought thirty-six new investment projects to Ireland and contributed to creating one thousand jobs.[92] In June 2016, the CI website listed the number of connectors as 72,300 and announced that sixty-eight companies had set up in Ireland thanks to CI between 2012 and 2016.

It is worth pointing out that the website did not show the number of jobs actually created, but referred to a number of "jobs in the process of being created" and "potential jobs". The study carried out by the consultancy DKM, commissioned by CI, was not much more precise. It gave an estimate of between six thousand four hundred and seven thousand three hundred jobs for the period 2014–2020.[93] By May 2019, the CI website showed a number of connectors of 89,652. These supposedly allowed investments from ninety-four foreign companies. However, it is clear that the number of jobs created, 2822, was minimal.[94]

The Irish authorities had clearly taken a new step by harnessing the diaspora as a collective asset for the Irish economy in an organised and systematic manner. While appealing to the sentiments of diaspora members, this initiative transformed their connection with Ireland into a commercial relationship and cemented the notion of mutual material benefit. The words of Joanna Murphy, then Chief Executive of ConnectIreland in an interview with *The Irish Times* in 2015 were unequivocal:

> We're in daily contact with many of our brightest and our best, so they can help us to generate leads, generate jobs in their home counties so emigrants can return home to rear a family surrounded by their grandparents, so their children can attend the schools they did. [...] All we require from our connectors is a name and some information. [...] And every successful connector

receives cash reward of up to €1,500 per sustainable job created. It really is as simple as that.[95]

CI did not disclose the profile and motivations of these connectors, but it is interesting, and indeed reassuring, to note that those who provided such information to CI generally donated the money to charity.[96]

Notes

1. Michael Patrick Fogarty. 1973. Irish Entrepreneurs Speak for Themselves. Dublin: Economic and Social Research Institute, 96–97.
2. Industrial Development Authority, Joyce O'Connor, Mary Lyons, "Enterprise - The Irish Approach", Dublin, 1983, 13.
3. The term "gombeen man", or pawnbroker, refers to traders and merchants who, during the Great Famine, sold food or goods at exorbitant interest rates.
4. O'Connor, Lyons, Enterprise - The Irish Approach, 5.
5. Michael Casey was Chief Economist at the Central Bank of Ireland. He worked with Thomas Kenneth Whitaker and served as Secretary General in the Irish Department of Finance.

   He was also a member of the Executive Board of the IMF in Washington for three years.
6. Michael Casey. 2010. Ireland's Malaise: The Troubled Personality of the Irish Economy. Dublin: The Liffey Press, 67.
7. Casey, Ireland's Malaise, 77.
8. Charles Haughey (Fianna Fáil) was Taoiseach from December 1979 to 30 June 1981, from 9 March 1982 to 14 December 1982 and from 10 March 1987 to 11 February 1992. He was convicted of receiving money from businessmen, embezzlement, and tax evasion.
9. Casey, Ireland's Malaise, 79.
10. Casey, Ireland's Malaise, 62–63.
11. Casey, Ireland's Malaise, 71.
12. Casey, Ireland's Malaise.
13. Joseph J. Lee. 1989. Ireland, 1912–1985: Politics and Society. Cambridge—New York: Cambridge University Press, 528.
14. Casey, Ireland's Malaise, 71.
15. Enterprise Ireland - Department of Business, Enterprise and Innovation, Paula Fitzsimons, Colm O'Gorman, Global Enterpreneurship Monitor. The 2017 Survey of Entrepreneurship in Ireland, Dublin, June 2018.
16. Casey, Ireland's Malaise, 72–73.

17. For a biography of the Collison brothers see: Derek Andersen. [2012]. The Collison Brothers and Story behind the Founding of Stripe. https://www.startupgrind.com/blog/the-collison-brothers-and-story-behind-the-founding-of-stripe/. Accessed 6 June 2025.
18. Patrick Freyne. 2009. A Lean, Keen Enterprise Machine. Business & Finance, 21 May.
19. Richard Delevan. 2008. Emigrant Irish Entrepreneurs. Business & Finance, 11 April.
20. Dan Breznitz is a world-renowned academic and author of a book comparing the policies and strategies of Israel, Taiwan, and Ireland. Dan Breznitz. 2007. Innovation and the State: Political Choice and Strategies for Growth in Israel, Taiwan, and Ireland. New Haven: Yale University Press.
21. Nicole Matthews. 2009. Leading the Way to Success. Business & Finance, 26 March.
22. Forfás, "Towards Developing an Enterprise Strategy", Dublin, Forfás, September 2007.
23. Forfás, Towards Developing an Enterprise Strategy, 5.
24. Government of Ireland, Department of the Taoiseach, "Building Ireland's Smart Economy: A Framework for Sustainable Economic Renewal", Dublin, Stationery Office, 2008.
25. "The Smart Economy has, at its core, an exemplary research, innovation and commercialisation ecosystem. The objective is to make Ireland an innovation and commercialisation hub in Europe - a country that combines the features of an attractive home for innovative R&D-intensive multinationals while also being a highly-attractive incubation environment for the best entrepreneurs in Europe and beyond". Government of Ireland, Building Ireland's Smart Economy, 8.
26. Refer to appendix for biography.
27. The corporate tax rate in Ireland was 12.5% for all companies. However, this rule has recently changed. See Government of Ireland, Department of Finance, press release, 31 December 2023.
28. Craig Barrett quoted in: Michael Hennigan. 2009. Home Truths on Irish Exports as Ireland Faces a Changed Global Economy in the Decade Ahead, 4 May. http://www.finfacts.ie/irishfinancenews/article_1016593.shtml. Note: This webpage has been removed.
29. It should be noted that the Obama administration aimed to encourage investment to stay in the United States rather than go abroad.
30. Finfacts Team. 2008. Obama Advisor Says "Ireland Must Wean Itself from Dependence on FDI", 5 November. http://www.finfacts.ie/irishfinancenews/article_1015171.shtml. This webpage has been removed. Robert

Shapiro was in Ireland in November 2008 to participate in a seminar on FDI in Ireland organised by the University College Dublin Business School.
31. Tánaiste Urges Unions to Negotiate. 2009. *The Irish Times*, 29 September.
32. Anne Groutel. 2015. Une nouvelle gouvernance: une condition nécessaire à la reprise économique en Irlande? In Revue LISA / LISA e-journal 13, 2. Martine Azuelos (ed.). special issue: Anglo-Saxon Capitalism and the Anglophone World(s). https://doi.org/10.4000/lisa.8396
33. Ireland, parliamentary debates, Houses of the Oireachtas, Dáil Éireann (hereafter Dáil Éireann debates) 2 June 2011, 734.
34. Dáil Éireann debates) 2 June 2011.
35. Carl O'Brien. 2011. Initiatives to Bring Funds and Tourists Unveiled at Global Forum. *The Irish Times*, 8 October.
36. See: Anne Groutel. 2013. Diaspora irlandaise et entrepreneuriat de croissance: vers un développement transnational des PME irlandaises. In Les sociétés entrepreneuriales et les mondes anglophones, ed. Jacques-Henri Coste: 161–179. Paris: Presses Sorbonne Nouvelle.
37. Anne Groutel. 2017. Irish Exporting Companies: Looking East, Looking South but Still Going West. In Revisiting the UK and Ireland's Transatlantic Economic Relationship with the United States in the Twenty-First Century: Beyond Sentimental Rhetoric, Anne Groutel, Marie-Christine Pauwels, and Valérie Peyronel, eds. 205–226. London, Palgrave Macmillan. doi.org/10.1057/978-1-137-58550-9_10
38. John Kennedy. 2011. Tech Entrepreneur Is RTÉ's Newest 'Dragon', 28 November. https://www.siliconrepublic.com/start-ups/tech-entrepreneur-is-rtes-newest-dragon. Accessed 6 June 2025.
39. Government of Ireland, Department of Jobs, Enterprise and Innovation, "Strengthening the Startup Community. Report of the Enterpreneurship Forum", Dublin, January 2014.
40. Anne Groutel. 2015. Les entreprises irlandaises: nouveau moteur de la croissance économique nationale au lendemain de la crise? In Irish Studies, 40, 2, Martine Pelletier and Valérie Peyronel, eds. 31–44, special issue: The crisis? What crisis? https://doi.org/10.4000/etudesirlandaises.4731
41. Government of Ireland, Department of Jobs, Enterprise and Innovation, "National Policy Statement on Entrepreneurship in Ireland", Dublin, September 2014, 8, 20–23.
42. The ITLG assists technology companies in Ireland and Northern Ireland and tries to attract investors to the province.
43. Refer to appendix for biography.
44. G24 Innovations is a manufacturer of dye-sensitized photovoltaic cells. Palm, Inc. (NASDAQ listed) was an American company in the handheld computer industry, PDA.

    It was acquired in 2010 by Hewlett-Packard.

45. John Kennedy. 2013. Irish Tech Start-Ups Need to Embrace the Fast, Competitive Culture of Silicon Valley. 9 July. https://www.siliconrepublic.com/start-ups/irish-tech-start-ups-need-to-embrace-the-fast-competitive-culture-of-silicon-valley. Accessed 6 June 2025.
46. See ITLG website. https://itlg.org/. Accessed 24 June 2025.
47. Tom McEnery. 2014. Beyond Guinness: Irish Software Companies Pour into Silicon Valley, 14 March. http://www.mercurynews.com/opinion/ci_25344699/beyondguinness-irish-software-companies-pour-into-silicon. Accessed 6 June 2025.
48. The Irish government has provided financial support to the ITLG in the amount of $250,000. Government of Ireland, Department of Foreign Affairs, "The Global Irish Economic Forum, One Year On. A Report on the Follow Up to the Global Irish Economic Forum at Farmleigh", Dublin, October 2010, 5.
49. The centre was officially opened by Taoiseach Brian Cowen. He served as Taoiseach from 7 May 2008 to 9 March 2011.
50. John Kennedy. 2011. The Silicon Valley Way, 13 October. https://www.siliconrepublic.com/business/the-silicon-valley-way. Accessed 6 June 2025.
51. John Kennedy. 2009. Irish Technology Leaders' ITC Group to Raise US$100 Million Venture Capital Fund, 22 October. https://www.siliconrepublic.com/start-ups/irish-technology-leaders-itc-group-to-raise-us100-million-venture-capital-fund. Accessed 6 June 2025.
52. John Kennedy, SVG Partners Kicks Off Second Venture-Capital Fund.
53. Mcor Technologies (a pioneering company specialising in 3D photocopying) and Flint Mobile (a company specialising in mobile phone payments) are among the companies that received funding through this channel. Flint Mobile received a further $6 million from SVG in October 2014. Kennedy, SVG Partners.
54. Irish Startups Can Ride the Wave of a "Real Tech Boom", 2014. Thejournal.ie, 9 October http://www.thejournal.ie/ireland-tech-boom-1714291-Oct2014. Accessed 6 June 2025.
55. Colm Kelpie. 2016. Silicon Valley Bank Set to Double Irish Lending Pot. *Irish Independent*, 12 May.
56. The NTMA is an agency that manages, among other things, the assets and liabilities of the Irish Government and the debt of the State.
57. Government of Ireland, Department of Foreign Affairs, "Global Irish Economic Forum Report", speech by Taoiseach, Mr. Brian Cowen, T. D., at the Global Irish Economic Forum in Farmleigh House on Friday, Dublin, 18 September 2009, 50.
58. John Kennedy. 2012. ITLG and CoderDojo Pioneer Farms of the Future in Rural California, 12 December. https://www.siliconrepublic.com/sci-

ence/itlg-and-coderdojo-pioneer-farms-of-the-future-in-rural-california. Accessed 6 June 2025; John Kennedy. 2014. SVG Partners Joins Forces with Forbes to Launch Ag-Tech Accelerator, July 9. https://www.siliconrepublic.com/start-ups/svg-partners-joins-forces-with-forbes-to-launch-ag-tech-accelerator. Accessed 6 June 2025.
59. Kennedy, SVG Partners Joins Forces.
60. John Kennedy. 2016. Two Irish Start-Ups to Join THRIVE Agritech Accelerator in California, 25 March. https://www.siliconrepublic.com/start-ups/agritech-salinas-food-accelerator-thrive-forbes-svg-partners. Accessed 6 June 2025.
61. Barbara McCarthy. 2014. The Successful Irish Entrepreneurs Who Have Moved to Silicon Valley and Are Taking On the Tech World. *Irish Independent*, 31 August.
62. Naoimh Reilly. 2014. New Irish Tech Companies Are Taking on Silicon Valley Irish Independent, 20 July.
63. John Ryan is a retired inventor and businessman. He made his fortune in Silicon Valley with his company Macrovision. He is now one of the partners of SVG partners.
64. John Ryan quoted in: Barbara McCarthy, The Successful Irish Entrepreneurs.
65. Hannah Kuchler. 2014. Irish Start-Ups Stand Out from the Crowd in Silicon Valley. *The Financial Times*, 21 October.
66. Naoimh Reilly, New Irish Tech Companies Are Taking on Silicon Valley.
67. John Hartnett quoted in: John Kennedy, Irish Tech Start-Ups.
68. Olivier Ezratty. 2015. Les leçons entrepreneuriales du Web Summit, 8 November. https://www.oezratty.net/wordpress/2015/lecons-entrepreneuriales-web-summit/. Accessed 6 June 2025. Ulrich Rozier. 2015. Web Summit: the smell of scam and the flavour of success, 5 November. http://www.numerama.com/tech/129759-web-summit-lodeur-de-larnaque- flavour-success.html. Note: This link is no longer active.
69. John Collison quoted in: Adrian Weckler, Denise Calnan. 2014. Forget Silicon Valley - Look at Ireland Summit Told Irish Independent. *Irish Independent*, 7 November.
70. Barbara McCarthy, The Successful Irish Entrepreneurs.
71. John Kennedy. 2013. Silicon Valley Leaders Tell Irish Start-Ups Seeking Investment to 'Come and Get It'", 17 July. https://www.siliconrepublic.com/start-ups/silicon-valley-leaders-tell-irish-start-ups-seeking-investment-to-come-and-get-it. Accessed 6 June 2025.
72. Innovation Capital. 2013. Business & Finance, 10 July.
73. Atlantic Bridge, https://abven.com/portfolio/. Accessed 6 June 2025.

74. Peter Bodkin. 2014. "Another 450 Tech Jobs Could Come to Ireland with Transatlantic Cash Injection", 6 October. https://www.thejournal.ie/smartinvest-ireland-jobs-1708121-Oct2014/. Accessed 6 June 2025.
75. Peter Bodkin. 2014. Now There's €40 m Up for Grabs if Software's Your Bag, 4 September. https://www.thejournal.ie/irish-venture-capital-for-tech-startups-1653625-Sep2014/?utm_source=businessetc. Accessed 6 June 2025.
76. Government of Ireland, Department of Jobs, Enterprise and Innovation, Strengthening the Startup Community, 42–46.
77. Michael Hennigan. 2014. The Innovation Slowdown at the US Tech Giants, 2 July. http://www.finfacts.ie/irishfinancenews/article_1027891.shtml. Note: This webpage no longer exists.
78. Ciarán Hancock. 2015. Sales of Tech Firms since 2000 Create 300 Millionaires. *The Irish Times*, 4 August.
79. Barry O'Halloran. 2013. Worldirish Shareholders to Discuss Options Following Merger with Rival Irishcentral. *The Irish Times*, 3 September.
80. Michael Hennigan. 2011. WorldIrish.com a Useful Service but €20 m Annual Profit is ÜberOptimistic", 10 October. http://www.finfacts-blog.com/2011/10/worldirishcom-useful-service-but-20m.html. This webpage no longer exists.
81. Nick Webb. 2011. Riverdance Boss Eyes €20 m Worldirish.com Profit. *Irish Independent*, 9 October.
82. Barry O'Halloran, Worldirish Shareholders to Discuss Options.
83. Michael Hennigan, WorldIrish.com a Useful Service.
84. John Spain. 2011. Irish Diaspora Websites Clash. *Irish Independent*, 13 October.
85. Simon Carswell. 2016. Niall O'Dowd Sells IrishCentral Website for €2.7 m. *The Irish Times*, 23 May.
86. Michael Hennigan, WorldIrish.com a Useful Service.
87. Simon Carswell, Niall O'Dowd.
88. Neville Isdell, a native of County Down, Northern Ireland, emigrated to the United States in the 1950s.
89. Ciara Kenny. 2016. Epic Ireland Digital Museum to Tell Story of Irish Diaspora", *The Irish Times*, 29 April.
90. The sum was paid by the state two years after a job had been created. A Smart Approach. 2013. Business & Finance, 31 May.
91. David Monagan. 2013. Pssst! Cash on the Barrelhead for Moving Jobs to Ireland, 4 March. https://www.forbes.com/sites/davidmonagan/2013/03/04/hey-buddy-move-five-jobs-to-ireland-and-make-me-ten-grand/. Accessed 6 June 2025.
92. Government of Ireland, Department of Foreign Affairs, "Global Irish, Ireland's Diaspora Policy", Dublin, March 2015, 47.

93. Gavin McLoughlin. 2016. Clune's Connect Ireland on Course for €1.6bn-€1.8bn to Irish GDP by 2020. *Irish Independent*, 2016.
94. ConnectIreland website, https://www.connectireland.com. Accessed May 23 2019. This website no longer exists.
95. Joanna Murphy quoted in: Ciara Kenny. 2015. Business and the Diaspora: "We Are All in a Battle for the Brains". *The Irish Times*, 20 November.
96. Ciara Kenny, Business and the Diaspora.

CHAPTER 13

Diaspora Business Elites: An Overly Pervasive Presence?

In the 2010s, the contribution of diaspora businesspeople went beyond investment in Irish start-ups and business creation. From the late 2000s, their willingness to influence Irish domestic politics grew steadily. As Ireland sank into crisis, the national and international press took aim at the Irish leadership. Two articles in particular caused a stir. One, which appeared on the front page of the *Wall Street Journal*, questioned the solvency of the Irish economy.[1] The other, by economist Morgan Kelly, was published in *The Irish Times*.[2]

In the days that followed, at a GIN meeting attended by representatives of the Irish government and sixty high-profile Irish-Americans, some of whom were entrusted with raising the country's profile abroad, threatened to give up. They took the opportunity to air their grievances[3] and accused the Irish authorities of deliberately underestimating the scale of the crisis. It is evident from the remarks of an unnamed member of GIN, a Wall Street financier, that the diaspora businessmen were not fooled:

> You have a huge credibility problem. We don't believe you. When you predict rosy growth rates for three years, we know you are just picking those numbers out of the sky. [...] So front up with us.[4]

They voiced their frustration once more when Ireland, facing dire circumstances, had to turn to the European Union's rescue package. Denis

A. Groutel, *The Two Irelands and the Diaspora*,
https://doi.org/10.1007/978-3-032-12355-8_13

P. Kelleher, President of Wall Street Access, emphasised that the Irish government needed to take decisive action:

> The Irish government needs to accept some real pain, cut out the idiotic socialist spending, the excessive giveaways like the minimum wage and tax breaks to institutions to promote development, which led to ghost towns.[5]

There are undoubtedly advantages to leveraging the goodwill of the diaspora entrepreneurial elite. The downside is that, to the extent that some of its members collaborate with the Irish authorities to enhance the Irish economy, they feel entitled to voice their opinions and publicly criticise government policies. Kelleher's statements indicate that they do not believe the Irish economic model is sufficiently liberal yet. However, diaspora businessmen appear to wield notable influence in several important sectors of the national economy, often shaping its direction and playing a role in informing government policies.

13.1 An Influence on Ireland's Economic Policies

As mentioned earlier, Chuck Feeney's substantial financial contribution was of paramount importance to the development of Irish higher education institutions, including the University of Limerick. While this source of funding dried up, the institution continued to enjoy the attentions of some Irish-American millionaires through the University of Limerick Foundation. In the 2010s, Loretta Brennan Glucksman, who took over from her late husband, Lewis L. Glucksman, a well-known Irish-American philanthropist, was the chairman of the board. So was Frank Ryan, a member of the ITLG. The latter was a director of the foundation and John Hartnett was a Director Emeritus. Hartnett, a native of Limerick, told a conference organised by the network in Limerick in 2014: "This is a homecoming not only for me, but for many members of the ITLG delegation".[6]

In the 2010s, this network worked to strengthen links between Limerick, the Shannon region, and Silicon Valley. In 2010, it organised the visit of a group of Silicon Valley businessmen to the region. The University of Galway and Shannon Development, the economic development agency for the region, were also partners in this initiative. A series of conferences and meetings with entrepreneurs were held. A Silicon Valley Mentorship Programme was launched at the University of Limerick with the aim of fostering an entrepreneurial spirit within the Irish education system, a goal established by the 2009 GIEF participants. The ITLG, in partnership with Silicon Valley Bank, initiated this programme to cultivate the next generation of Irish entrepreneurs. The initiative involved students interning at Silicon Valley companies and receiving guidance from prominent business leaders.

In 2011, Hartnett opened the Hartnett Enterprise Acceleration Centre at the Limerick Institute of Technology (LIT). This incubator serves as a kind of antechamber to Silicon Valley's Innovation Centre for Irish start-ups.[7] In 2012, the ITLG partnered with the prestigious Kauffman Foundation to deliver entrepreneurship training to early-stage Irish companies based at LIT.[8] Then, in January 2014, the ITLG held its annual forum in Limerick, an event opened by President Michael D. Higgins. It provided an opportunity for Irish entrepreneurs to engage with senior executives from Dell, Disney, Intel, AOL, and Google. At the event, a memorandum of understanding was signed between the ITLG, Limerick City and County Council, LIT, the University of Limerick, Shannon Airport, and the Limerick Chamber of Commerce. The formalisation of these links between Silicon Valley and Limerick and the surrounding area was expected to foster the exchange of ideas and collaboration in education, innovation, technology, and entrepreneurship and to promote trade, investment, and job creation. As part of this agreement, Limerick and Santa Clara (California) also signed a memorandum of understanding, the result of Hartnett's seven-year effort to bring the two cities together.[9]

All of this was undoubtedly very positive for Limerick, which could be proud of having influential support in business circles in the United States. However, one might question why this city was selected independently of government regional development policies. This raises the issue of whether other cities in Ireland might have benefited more from this type of promotion than Limerick.

In the field of transport, certain diaspora figures played a decisive role during the 2010s. Aer Lingus' direct service between Dublin and Silicon Valley had been cancelled in 2009—collateral damage from the 2007–2008 financial crisis. Hartnett was among those who campaigned for its reinstatement.[10] One can easily imagine his satisfaction when, having been appointed to the Aer Lingus board in January 2014, the airline announced the return of the direct route between the two cities starting in April that same year.

By the end of the 2000s, Ireland had become significantly more accessible by air.[11] Etihad Airways played a role in this transformation. Then led by James Hogan, an Australian of Irish descent, the airline launched a Dublin–Abu Dhabi route in 2007—despite limited apparent commercial potential. Unexpectedly, by 2013, it had become one of Etihad's ten busiest routes.[12]

One of the pledges of the Fine Gael-Labour coalition's joint programme in the context of the 2011 general election[13] was to abolish the airline ticket tax introduced in 2009 by the Fianna Fáil administration, on the condition that airlines agreed to reopen routes that had been cancelled. The negotiations were successful and the Irish government announced that the tax would be removed from April 2014. Furthermore, in January 2014, Etihad announced that it was doubling the number of flights between Dublin and Abu Dhabi. From July 2014, this airline provided twenty flights a week, with almost nine thousand seats and eight hundred connections to forty-five destinations in the Middle East, Africa, and Asia. It thus became possible to travel from Dublin to Beijing, Singapore, Sydney, Tokyo, Kuala Lumpur, etc., with just one stopover.[14] However, Hogan stepped down as CEO in 2017. Etihad subsequently reduced the number of weekly flights between Dublin and Abu Dhabi.

These new routes were clearly a huge asset to the Irish economy. Firstly, they could help to promote leisure tourism from emerging countries, a market with great potential. In addition, they could facilitate business tourism and trade links with these countries.[15] Irish exports of goods and services to Arab countries, however, grew rapidly to 5.3 billion in 2015, when Dublin hosted the first business forum to promote relations between Ireland and Arab countries.[16] However, the airline industry has since suffered, first as a result of the Covid-19 health crisis and then from the increase in the price of kerosene due to the war in Ukraine and the resulting instability in global energy markets.

It should also be noted that, in the 2010s, Etihad was committed to promoting Irish culture, sport, and art. The national film industry benefited, notably through the screening of Irish films on board Etihad aircraft. The airline also sponsored painting exhibitions and the GAA hurling championship and invested in a tourist attraction, the Etihad Airways Skyline, a fourteen-storey building in Croke Park, from the top of which the visitor has a panoramic view of the Irish capital.

The influence of big names in the diaspora on the country's economic policies should also be seen against the backdrop of the 2009 report of the

Special Group on Public Service Numbers and Expenditure Programmes,[17] a group charged with examining where the state budget needed to be cut in the wake of the 2007–2008 financial crisis. The report was uncompromising and proposed budget cuts of up to €5.3 billion. Virtually all ministries and departments were to be affected, but some of the proposed measures were more drastic than others. For example, the existence of the Department of Arts, Sport and Tourism was threatened because its functions could be transferred to other departments. The Arts Council and other cultural programmes, the Irish Film Board, the tourism agency (Fáilte Ireland), and the Sports Council were also in line for significant budget cuts or, in the worst cases, doomed to disappear.[18]

But, the importance of these sectors to the Irish economy had been highlighted by businesspeople in the diaspora at the 2009 Global Irish Economic Forum (GIEF). It is thus interesting to note that, while the Irish government presented a list of drastic budget cuts that included almost $7 billion in savings over three years, it did not follow the recommendations of the Special Group on Public Service Numbers and Expenditure Programmes to the letter. The Department of Arts, Sport and Tourism was indeed spared. The government also went against the advice of the Special Group, which had expressed reservations about the return on investment of funds allocated to science, technology, and innovation. The report called for rationalisation and reorganisation of the allocation of these funds, which were to be cut by 15%, or €100 million.[19] Yet, The National Recovery Plan 2011–2014[20] reaffirmed the primacy of these sectors in making Ireland a global centre of innovation and the government's commitment to concentrating research funding in areas where Ireland could expect the greatest return on investment, including the "green economy",[21] another strong theme of the 2009 GIEF. The importance of the agri-food sector as a sector of the future was also highlighted. Interestingly, the budget of the Ministry of Agriculture was less affected by cuts than expected.

In contrast, the Departments of Social Protection, Health and Children, Defence, and Justice were stretched beyond what had been recommended by the Special Group.[22] While there is no evidence that influential diaspora figures personally lobbied to influence government decisions in the direction of the 2009 GIEF, it is obvious that some of the recommendations of "An Bord Snip Nua",[23] which ran counter to GIEF recommendations, were discarded.

The early 2010s appear to have marked a turning point in the relationship between the Irish authorities and the diaspora's entrepreneurial elite, whose influence on both economic policy and the broader economy was becoming increasingly visible. John Hartnett, in particular, emerged as a key figure. In addition to serving on numerous boards, he chaired the advisory board of the *Inspiring Ireland* project, launched in 2014 to promote Ireland's cultural heritage through digital platforms. The board's mission is to support the initiative by raising funds, increasing awareness among the Irish diaspora, and helping to guide its strategic direction.[24]

Hartnett is also a member of the Global Irish Network Advisory Group, a select circle of prominent diaspora figures who serve as a bridge between the Global Irish Network and the Irish government. He remains highly active in the American Ireland Fund—an effort publicly acknowledged by then US Secretary of State John Kerry in March 2014.[25]

From 2009 to 2011, Hartnett was a member of the Northern Ireland Working Committee, which brought him into close contact with the Obama administration and then Secretary of State Hillary Clinton. He was later appointed to lead the Global Diaspora Innovation Initiative—a joint project between the US State Department and the UK government aimed at strengthening multilateral collaboration between academic institutions in the field of cutting-edge scientific research.

Hartnett was also one of the people behind the Diaspora 2016 project. At the 2011 GIEF, it was proposed to bring together 100 diaspora businesspeople who would offer their services to the Irish government on a pro bono basis. Some of them were willing to serve for a period of three years on State boards.[26] This prospect was met with a cool reception in Ireland.[27] Maura Quinn, Director of the Institute of Directors (Ireland), publicly opposed the offer,[28] arguing that skills should take precedence over connections to the diaspora. Moreover, although new communication technologies made it possible to hold meetings online, there was no substitute for physical presence. Finally, asking for help from outsiders would send a negative signal, as it would project an image of Ireland that lacked managerial skills and confidence. There were people in the country who were perfectly capable of sitting on State boards and who had not even been approached by the authorities. Diaspora businesspeople could play an advisory role, albeit informally, but they should not be involved in decision-making.[29] The Irish government, too, gave the proposal a very lukewarm reception, so much so that a few days after Maura Quinn's letter was published, the ITLG considered withdrawing its offer.[30]

The reaction of some diaspora businessmen, offended by this rebuff, was swift. Tom Farrell, Vice President of Middle East Nokia Corporation, responded to Maura Quinn in a letter that was published in *The Irish Times*.[31] He set out to demonstrate, point by point, the weakness of her arguments and concluded:

> Finally, it is disturbing to read that 'the institute does not accept that seeking fresh overseas talent with experience of business in foreign markets is necessary, or even advisable'. I suggest the Institute of Directors reflect on the 'optics'[32] of this statement towards potential overseas customers, partners and investors in Irish companies seeking international growth.[33]

Tom McEnery, a businessman and former mayor of San Jose, also responded to Maura Quinn. His lengthy letter to *The Irish Times*[34] exemplifies the use of emotion in discourse, a technique commonly employed by Irish politicians but demonstrated here by an Irish-American. He begins his letter with a memory of an old man named Michael McDonnell who worked for his father in Silicon Valley. McDonnell "was a sound employee but a troubled man".[35] As a young man he had fought alongside Michael Collins and was forced to flee his native Ireland "[…] never again contributing to its progress. He was one of the millions who have been eliminated from giving their best for Ireland".[36] The rejection of the diaspora business leaders' offer had brought back memories of this old man, he said, because "Many of us in the Irish diaspora value the land of our grandparents and mourn her recent difficulties".[37]

However, the occasionally maudlin tone alternates between paternalistic and incisive. McEnery did not shy away from criticising the Irish authorities, questioning their governance and lamenting what he saw as a short memory when it came to acknowledging the invaluable support diaspora businesspeople had provided to Ireland:

> After years of politicians and bureaucrats catering to their own selfish agendas and thoughtless policies, Ireland is suffering. I know of other times. I was present during heady events such as the Intel ground breaking [sic] and the initiation of the Apple project. I was there when San Jose provided free offices for the IDA to proselytise the merits of Ireland throughout Silicon Valley. Such help was not the reason for the successes of the Irish tech sector - the energy and entrepreneurial spirit of the Irish did that deed - but it certainly gave it a mighty push.[38]

He also recalled that Irish businesses benefited greatly from the services of the ITLG. But the plans of some in the diaspora went much further. They wanted to make Ireland "evolve" because, according to McEnery:

> Now it is no longer Saxon perfidy that bedevils that island, no longer the old enemies of Collins and his generation, but a paralysing fear of change. [...] We only wish to help with the skills we believe are pertinent to the current economic and political dilemma.[39]

Given the Irish government's reluctance to accept the proposal, it seems likely that they deemed it necessary to prevent diaspora tycoons from exerting excessive influence over state affairs. McEnery's remarks left no doubt that some of them aimed to redraw boundaries and spur reform:

> In the area of political reform, changes such as term limits in the Dáil and revolving-door restrictions for elected and appointed public officials as well as transparency in political money, have already been suggested by me and others. [...] Let our ideas on economic and political ideas be vetted and discussed, not cavalierly deflected.[40]

Although constitutional reforms and the moralisation of political life in Ireland were among Fine Gael's main campaign themes in the 2011 elections, giving excessive leeway to members of the diaspora was evidently not the intention of the party's leaders upon assuming power.

13.2 A Desire to Make Irish Politics More Ethical

In the past, some prominent members of the diaspora attempted to extend their influence beyond the economic sphere. This was the case with Chuck Feeney, whose foundation, The Atlantic Philanthropies, provided generous financial support[41] to the Centre for Public Inquiry, established in January 2005. The organisation was chaired by Fergus Flood,[42] a retired High Court judge known for presiding over a tribunal of inquiry in the late 1990s that investigated allegations of corruption involving Irish politicians. Modelled after the Center for Public Integrity in the United States,[43] this centre aimed to improve transparency in Irish politics by probing potential corruption in both the public and private sectors. Its members hoped to work with the media and human rights organisations. The Centre also intended to promote whistleblower protection measures.

Frank Connolly, an investigative journalist who is well known in Ireland for exposing corruption scandals, was to head the organisation.[44] The arrival of the centre was obviously not to everyone's liking, and some Irish politicians were on the alert. Jim Minihan of the Progressive Democrats questioned the need for a privately funded centre that would duplicate the work of state institutions and agencies. Senate President Mary O'Rourke and other politicians harbored suspicions about the organisation's intentions.[45] They questioned whether this center might function like a private court, funded by foreign sources, operating independently of government oversight, selecting its own investigative targets, and regularly publishing reports to inform the public of its findings. Concerns were also raised about the potential for individuals involved to be libeled. Feeney replied that the funds came from the sale of his real estate in Ireland. Members of the Centre also argued that Ireland was one of the few countries in Europe without such an independent watchdog. Somewhat surprisingly, the organisation failed to garner full support among journalists. John Waters, a journalist with *The Irish Times*, wrote:

> As a matter of fact, I would welcome the closure of the Centre for Public Inquiry. The idea of a foreign 'philanthropist' sticking his nose and his dollars into the affairs of a sovereign nation, as Chuck Feeney has done in funding the centre, is to my mind deeply unhealthy.[46]

However, the centre was quickly neutralised. In December 2005, the Minister for Justice, Michael McDowell, revealed suspicions of connections of Frank Connolly, known for his strong Republican views,[47] and a case involving his brother from several years prior. After being questioned by the Irish police at the time, Connolly was cleared of any wrongdoing.[48] Intriguingly, the case resurfaced conveniently. Although Connolly denied all allegations and denounced what he believed to be a witch-hunt aimed at tarnishing his reputation and, indirectly, that of the Centre for Public Inquiry, following a meeting with Bertie Ahern and Michael McDowell, Feeney decided to suspend his funding of the Centre as long as Connolly remained director.[49] A few weeks later, Judge Flood announced its closure after just over a year of operation and the publication of two reports.[50] According to Paul Cullen of *The Irish Times*, it was not so much the two reports as the potential threat it posed in the run-up to the elections[51] that caused tremors in Irish political circles.

A group of leading figures from academia and the voluntary sector came to the organisation's defence in the name of the public's right to be informed and denounced a conspiracy against Connolly. In a letter published in *The Irish Times*, they addressed the Tánaiste, Mary Harney, directly:

> Her misgivings about the source of funding do not extend apparently to Mr Feeney's gifting an estimated €600 million to Irish universities over two decades, or to political donations to Government parties by multinational corporations.[52]

Indeed, the contribution of Irish-American businessmen in the economic sphere had never been, until then, a problem for the Irish leadership, which had also agreed to let some of them have some influence on the country's economic policy. Feeney's initiative, however, was of a different nature and threatened to cross a red line, which was unacceptable to some. Ireland has an invaluable resource in its diaspora, and its leaders have understood this. However, while senior Irish-American businessmen had the capacity to help the country out of the 2008 financial crisis, they were not easily manipulated. They made it clear that they were not willing to risk their reputations by vouching for a system whose integrity was in doubt. Indeed, during the first GIEF, some participants were quick to point to the responsibility of successive Fianna Fáil governments for the financial crisis in Ireland:

> It was noted that some elements of the crisis appeared to be home-grown due to an inadequate financial regulatory system and perceived 'self-indulgence' on some issues. [...] a further negative noted was the perception in some quarters of inadequate ethical standards in public office and the banking sector.[53]

The diaspora businessmen therefore implicitly called on the authorities to remedy the problem, for while they were willing to assist the Irish leadership, they wanted their comments and suggestions to be acted upon.[54] Denis P. Kelleher was even more direct: "The bankers were crooks, they gamed the system [...]. They got away with it for too long - where was the oversight?"[55] Mike Hemingway, another prominent diaspora figure, advised the Cowen government to resign. An early general election was indeed called and lost by Fianna Fáil in February 2011, after which it was forced to make way for the opposition.

The joint programme of the Fine Gael-Labour coalition that took office in March 2011 envisaged the creation of a "constitutional convention" to discuss possible changes to governance. Indeed, one of the main themes of the Fine Gael campaign was the need to reform the Irish political system.[56]

Feeney persisted, though in the aftermath of the election. But he opted for a less controversial initiative. He provided financial support, through The Atlantic Philanthropies, to We the Citizens, an organisation whose aim was to put pressure on the Irish authorities to keep their promises and encourage participatory democracy.[57] This objective was only partially realised. Indeed, the Constitutional Convention did come into being—but, in the end, the mountain gave birth to a mouse.[58]

13.3 When a Diaspora Personality Runs for the Presidency of the Republic

While Feeney worked discreetly through The Atlantic Philanthropies to promote more ethical political governance in Ireland, writer and journalist Niall O'Dowd sought a more direct role in the country's political scene. On 6 June 2011, readers of *The Irish Times*[59] learned that, according to a source close to the journalist and businessman, he was considering running for president of Ireland in the October 2011 election. According to the newspaper, during Barack Obama's visit to Ireland a few weeks earlier, he had been approached by a group of Irish and Irish-American politicians of different political persuasions who had urged him to run. O'Dowd confirmed the information a few days later,[60] but refused to reveal the names of the individuals in question.[61] He reported the arguments presented to him in the following terms:

> These people laid out a compelling case. I said I would consider their request. They sketched out the importance of the role, of job creation, of the US, and how a president could be a business president. The US is where Ireland needs to be. This generation has had its future stolen from them [...]. They see that the Diaspora, when it comes to tourism and direct investment, are deeply important for the future of Ireland. They feel that the

> past leadership in Ireland has utterly failed the country and that the answer these days lies far more in Boston than Berlin. I wholeheartedly agree.[62]

One cannot but wonder why O'Dowd chose to emphasise the fact that he represented a group of important people, whose names he did not reveal. Furthermore, he expressed his firm intention to make the voice of the Irish Diaspora heard: "The time for lip service to that Diaspora is over. It is time to make that voice for 40 million Irish Americans heard loud and clear […]".[63] Criticism soon followed in the Irish press. Walter Ellis[64] was particularly scathing. He noted, firstly, that O'Dowd was the first candidate for President to regard Ireland as a "brand" rather than a nation. Secondly, he criticised O'Dowd for being nostalgic for a bygone era, for being out of touch with today's Ireland, and for continuing to convey values or opinions to the Irish-American community that no longer truly reflect what the country has become. But through his criticism of O'Dowd, Ellis also openly expressed his contempt for Irish-Americans in general:

> He laments the passing of the era dominated (in Irish eyes) by the Kennedys, Tip O'Neill and Daniel Moynihan,[65] and clings to those who at least aspire to some Irishness. […] St Patrick's Day is the highlight of his year. […] In my view, he is irretrievably a citizen not alone of the US, to which he has, of course, given his pledge of allegiance, but of that mythical and parallel world known to its misty-eyed adherents as Glocca Morra… I mean, Irish America, where blood and ancestry are all. Niall O'Dowd may be kidding himself that, with his return ticket to New York booked and paid for, he can lead us all to a new tomorrow, but he will not kid the Irish people.[66]

He also criticised O'Dowd, who made no secret of his sympathy for the Republican cause, for being too close to Gerry Adams.[67] Indeed, O'Dowd was instrumental in getting the latter a visa to the United States during the peace process negotiations in the 1990s. According to Ellis, O'Dowd believed that the Nobel Peace Prize should have been awarded to Adams.

Although the Northern Ireland question had not been fully resolved—despite the signing of the Good Friday Agreement—by the early 2010s, tensions had eased and the political relationship between Ireland and the United Kingdom was gradually normalising. But it was not lost on anyone, least of all Ellis, that O'Dowd continued to display his contempt for the British people and the Royal Family in an unsubtle, even crude, manner.[68]

Bruce Morrison, a former US Congressman, responded to Ellis in *The Irish Times*.[69] He praised O'Dowd, his friend of twenty years, and took the opportunity to recall the generous contribution of prominent members of the diaspora to the peace process and to the Irish economy—an Irish America, on which Ireland could rely in all circumstances, unlike Europe, he said. However, this was not enough to silence the critics both in the press[70] and on the Internet as these selected excerpts show:

> 'When I read Morrison's article one would think that Mr O'Dowd is seeking to become primus inter pares of an enclave rather than Head of State in a sophisticated nation. [...] the Office requires [...] someone whose presence inspires awe and admiration rather than explanations and skepticism. [...] had Mr Morrison provided some rich and colourful insights into the competency, skills and sophistication of Mr O'Dowd to enable him become [sic] a statesman, rather than influence peddler in one large jurisdiction, the readers might be more enlightened. But he has left them with nothing interesting to cling to. [...] The Office requires the incumbent to be the President of the entire nation not segment(s) of it, whether at home or abroad. It requires a statesman, not a salesman.[71]

While Morrison and O'Dowd considered that American business experience and contacts were a major asset for the office of President of the Republic, it is clear that this argument worked against O'Dowd in Ireland. Apart from the question of O'Dowd's suitability as head of state, the criticism may seem somewhat misplaced when one considers that, for decades, the Irish authorities have actively sought to build networks of influence across the Atlantic—both in political and business circles—and how much the Irish economy owes to these overseas "segments" of the Irish nation. In any case, O'Dowd dropped out of the Irish presidential race less than a month after entering it. He admitted that he had realised that running such a campaign as an independent candidate was too much of a challenge, both logistically and financially.[72] Perhaps O'Dowd had hoped that Sinn Féin would sponsor him?[73] But, the party chose another personality for candidate.[74]

One wonders about the underlying reasons for the media's hostility towards candidate O'Dowd. Was it simply a manifestation of the refusal of the "emigrant" to play a role in national politics, a right he had implicitly renounced by leaving Ireland? This was the sentiment expressed in hindsight by O'Dowd, who was bitter and hurt at being seen as less Irish than others simply because he had left the country. For him, the diaspora was frightening because it threatened to disrupt the *status quo*. He denounced the attitude of Irish leaders who had never shown tangible signs of recognition for the services the diaspora, at least its businessmen, had rendered to Ireland. He noted, for example, the absence of a senator representing the Irish abroad and, of course, the refusal to grant them the right to vote. O'Dowd argued that if the Irish authorities were to recognise the rights of the diaspora it would be an admission of failure.[75] Noreen Bowden[76] contended that the Irish have a "[…] complex, deeply individual and often contradictory"[77] attitude towards emigration and shared O'Dowd's bitterness:

> By now the idea of 'harnessing the diaspora' is so widespread in Ireland that it makes the occasional student protests against 'brain drain' sound strangely old-fashioned. We don't do brain drain anymore. It's called brain circulation now, and it rests on the notion that our most qualified emigrants will either return or make their foreign-gained experience available for Ireland's benefit. […] There seems to be no limit to what we can ask of our loyal foot soldiers abroad. […] O'Dowd was willing to be the good Irishman abroad as president, acting as a travelling salesman for the country. […] Article 2 of our constitution may grant O'Dowd full entitlement to membership in the Irish Nation as an Irish citizen, but the court of popular opinion in Ireland won't. Once you go, your money, your contacts, and your expertise are welcome. Your presence in the political system is not.[78]

Bowden indirectly pointed to the problem that now faced the Irish government. In the 1990s, it relied heavily on the Irish-American entrepreneurial elite to contribute to the Irish economy through charity and/or investment, or by promoting Ireland to foreign investors. Some of its members got satisfaction from doing a good deed, others from investing wisely, the one often going hand in hand with the other. With the advent of the Internet and other technologies, it has become possible for the diaspora as a whole to contribute to Ireland's economic development, a diaspora that is tempted to claim rights in return for its assistance. The use of the diaspora thus seems to be increasingly becoming a double-edged sword.[79]

13.4 Recognising the Irish Diaspora Link: Symbolism, Stakes, and Limits

> The men and women of our diaspora represent not simply a series of departures and losses. They remain, even while absent, a precious reflection of our own growth and change, a precious reminder of the many strands of identity which compose our story. They have come [...] from Derry and Dublin and Cork and Belfast. They know the names of our townlands and villages. They remember our landscape or they have heard of it. They look to us anxiously to include them in our sense of ourselves and not to forget their contribution while we make our own. [...] I know this Oireachtas will agree with me that the truest way of cherishing our diaspora is to offer them, at all times, the reality of this island as a place of peace where the many diverse traditions [...] are bound together in tolerance and understanding.[80]

Mary Robinson's call for her fellow citizens to welcome the diaspora with open arms implicitly acknowledged the lack of warmth[81] the Irish had shown towards their diaspora until then. At the time, her speech was met with some mockery in certain quarters.[82]

However, in 1998, in accordance with the terms of the Good Friday Agreement, the Irish people approved in a referendum the amendment of Article 2 of the Irish Constitution which now includes recognition of the emotional bond between Ireland and its diaspora:

> It is the entitlement and birthright of every person born in the island of Ireland, which includes its islands and seas, to be part of the Irish Nation. That is also the entitlement of all persons otherwise qualified in accordance with law to be citizens of Ireland. Furthermore, the Irish nation cherishes its special affinity with people of Irish ancestry living abroad who share its cultural identity and heritage.[83]

The Presidential Distinguished Service Award for the Irish Abroad was announced at the second GIEF in October 2011. It is an award given annually to ten individuals who have, for at least five years, worked for Ireland or the Irish community abroad or promoted its reputation. Only Irish nationals, those eligible for Irish nationality, or individuals of Irish origin residing abroad are eligible to receive the award.[84] Among the personalities who have received this distinction are Dan Rooney, Chuck Feeney, and Donald Keough, who were members of the Ireland-America

Economic Advisory Board (IAEAB).[85] Craig Barrett, the current president of the ITLG, also received this mark of recognition.[86] Ireland owes it to him for the establishment of Intel in 1989, a company that has invested thirty billion euros in this country and employs 4900 people there. Perhaps more surprising was the choice to award the actor Gabriel Byrne, in 2015, who had created controversy by publicly criticising the Gathering.

Interestingly, the Irish Department of Foreign Affairs' webpage on the award clearly states that it does not entitle the recipient to an allowance or to Irish citizenship. The Irish government has thus set certain limits on what it is prepared to concede to the diaspora, regardless of the services it has rendered to the nation. However, in July 2014, Dublin finally decided to make a gesture towards the diaspora by creating the position of Minister for the Diaspora. In March 2015, the first government's diaspora strategy was published. It opens with these words:

> This is the first clear statement of Government of Ireland policy on the diaspora which recognises that Ireland has a unique and important relationship with its diaspora that must be nurtured and developed.[87]

These developments were certainly welcome. But did this initial strategy live up to expectations? In reality, it amounted more to a survey of existing initiatives than a bold new roadmap. While the document was filled with aspirations, it lacked truly innovative measures or ambitious objectives. Its value, therefore, appears to have been largely symbolic.

In late December 2015, however, Enda Kenny announced his intention to hold a referendum on granting Irish citizens living abroad—and residents of Northern Ireland—the right to vote in presidential elections. The vote was initially planned for 2019 but, as of December 2024, had yet to take place. If approved, the measure was expected to expand the Irish electorate by as many as three million people.[88]

The outcome of such a referendum is difficult to predict, but in any case, the political stakes would remain limited, given that the President of Ireland holds no executive powers. Once again, the gesture seems largely symbolic. Time will tell whether it will be enough to defuse frustrations and enable the Irish authorities to continue drawing on the support of the wider diaspora. As for the business elite, it is likely they will maintain their connection to Ireland—at least for as long as it serves their interests.

Notes

1. Charles Forelle, David Enrich. 2010. Ireland's Fate Tied to Doomed Banks. *The Wall Street Journal*, 10 November.
2. Morgan Kelly. 2010. If You Thought that the Bank Bailout Was Bad, Wait until the Mortgage Defaults Hit Home. *The Irish Times*, 8 November.
3. Kate Hickey. 2010. Diaspora Wants Answers on Ireland's Collapse", 17 November. https://www.irishcentral.com/news/diaspora-wants-answers-on-irelandscollapse-108641569-237364221. Accessed 6 June 2025; Dara Kelly. 2010. Irish Diaspora Leaders Question Ireland's Fiscal Policy, 14 November. https://www.irishcentral.com/news/irishdiaspora-leaders-question-irelands-fiscal-policy-107931254-237363671. Note: this link is no longer active; Lara Marlowe. 2010. Fiscal Policy Questioned by Irish Americans. *The Irish Times*, 13 November.
4. Cited in: Lara Marlowe, Fiscal Policy Questioned.
5. Denis P. Kelleher quoted in: Amy Feran. 2010. Irish Diaspora Speaks Out on IMF Bailout, 1 December. https://www.irishcentral.com/news/irish-diaspora-speaks-out-on-imf-bailout-111103349-237728881. Accessed 6 June 2025.
6. John Hartnett quoted in: John Kennedy. 2014. ITLG Forum to Focus on Limerick and Shannon Region as European Gateway for US, 8 January. https://www.siliconrepublic.com/business/itlg-forum-to-focus-on-limerick-and-shannon-region-as-european-gateway-for-us. Accessed 6 June 2025.
7. John Kennedy. 2011. How the Irish Can Become the Giants of Silicon Valley", 1 July. https://www.siliconrepublic.com/start-ups/how-the-irish-can-become-the-giants-of-silicon-valley. Accessed 6 June 2025.
8. John Kennedy. 2012. ITLG Brings Kauffman Entrepreneurship Programme to LIT", 5 October, https://www.siliconrepublic.com/start-ups/itlg-brings-kauffman-entrepreneurship-programme-to-lit. Accessed 6 June 2025.
9. Limerick Signs Memorandum of Understanding with ITLG. 2014. Business & Finance, 28 January; Limerick City and City Council. 2014. Limerick and Santa Clara Begin Sister City Relationship. Press release, 6 August. https://www.limerick.ie/council/newsroom/news/limerick-and-santa-clara-begin-sister-city-relationship. Accessed 6 June 2025.
10. Karlin Lillington. 2010. Direct Silicon Valley Route Vital for Irish Business. *The Irish Times*, 10 September.
11. Ryanair and other low-cost airlines, which operate between the island and various European cities, have also helped to promote tourism.
12. In 2013, 240,000 passengers used the route. How Dubai Is Helping Ireland's Economic Push. 2014. Arabian Business, 25 July.

13. Government of Ireland, Department of the Taoiseach, "Programme For Government 2011–2016", Dublin, 6 March 2011, 12.
14. How Dubai Is Helping Ireland's Economic Push.
15. Anne Groutel. 2017. Irish Exporting Companies: Looking East, Looking South but Still Going West. In Revisiting the UK and Ireland's Transatlantic Economic Relationship with the United States in the Twenty-First Century: Beyond Sentimental Rhetoric, Anne Groutel, Marie-Christine Pauwels, and Valérie Peyronel, eds. 205–226. London, Palgrave Macmillan. doi.org/10.1057/978-1-137-58550-9_10
16. Teddy Murphy. 2016. Business Lessons from the Gulf. Irish Examiner, 26 March.
17. Government of Ireland, Department of Finance, "Report of the Special Group on Public Service Numbers and Expenditure Programmes", Prn. A9/0987, Dublin, Stationery Office, 2009, 2 vols.
18. Government of Ireland, Report of the Special Group, vol. I, 33–34.
19. Government of Ireland, Report of the Special Group, vol. I, 14–15.
20. Government of Ireland, Department of the Taoiseach, "The National Recovery Plan 2011–2014", Prn. A10/1705, Dublin, Stationery Office, 2010, p. 115, https://www.europeansources.info/record/the-national-recovery-plan-2011-2014/. Accessed 6 June 2025.
21. Government of Ireland, The National Recovery Plan 2011–2014, 42–44.
22. Government of Ireland, Report of the Special Group, vol. I, 30–76.
23. The Expenditure Review Committee set up in 1987 by the Irish government to examine ways of reducing government budgets was humorously dubbed An Bord Snip. The term is a mixture of English (snip: "to cut") and Irish (an bord: "council" or "committee"). The Special Group on Public Service Numbers and Expenditure Programmes, which was given the same task, was therefore nicknamed An Bord Snip Nua (nua: "new").
24. https://dri.ie/inspiring-ireland/homepage, accessed on 6 June 2025.
25. John Kerry. 2014. "US State Department, Secretary of State, John Kerry on American Ireland Fund and Honoring John Hartnett for His Efforts and Contribution for Global Partnerships between Ireland and the US", 8 March. https://www.youtube.com/watch?v=ECQSgM1FveU. Accessed 6 June 2025.
26. John Collins. 2011. More Expats Agree to Sit on State Boards. *The Irish Times*, 17 October; Bosses Offer to Help Run Public Sector. 2011. *The Irish Times*, 7 October.
27. Breda Gray. 2013. Towards the Neo-Institutionalization of Irish State-Diaspora Relations in the Twenty-First Century. In Emigration Nations: Policies and Ideologies of Emigrant Engagement, ed. Michael Collyer: 115–116. London: Palgrave Macmillan.

28. It was based on a survey conducted between 20 February and 9 March 2012, among forty-five of its members who sat on state boards. Seventy-four per cent of them felt that the appointment process in these bodies was neither fair nor transparent. In addition, almost half of the sample felt that the members of their boards did not have the necessary skills to carry out the policy that the company needed to implement. Indeed, 40% admitted that the issue of skills had not been addressed at the time of their appointment. Institute of Directors. 2012. State Boards in Ireland 2012. Challenges for the Future. https://www.iodireland.ie/resources-media/research-publications/research-reports/state-boards-in-ireland-2012-challenges-for-the-future. Accessed 6 June 2025.
29. Caroline Madden. 2012. Institute of Directors Says Appointing Diaspora to State Boards a Flawed Idea. *The Irish Times*, 7 April; Breda Gray, Towards the Neo-
    Institutionalization, 115–117.
30. Eoin Reynolds. 2012. Plan for Diaspora Seats on State Boards May Be Shelved. *The Irish Times*, 10 April.
31. Tom Farrell. 2012. Appointing Diaspora to State Boards", *The Irish Times*, 12 April.
32. Farrell uses Maura Quinn's term "optics" here.
33. Tom Farrell, Appointing Diaspora to State Boards.
34. Tom McEnery. 2012. Sincere Offer of Help as Irish Abroad Watch Ireland Suffer. *The Irish Times*, 23 April.
35. McEnery, Sincere Offer.
36. McEnery, Sincere Offer.
37. McEnery, Sincere Offer.
38. McEnery, Sincere Offer.
39. McEnery, Sincere Offer.
40. McEnery, Sincere Offer.
41. According to *The Irish Times*, Feeney contributed €800,000 a year to the centre's operations. Martin Wall. 2005. The Private Investigator. *The Irish Times*, 5 February.
42. Carol Coulter. 2005. Flood to Chair New Body on Public Standards. *The Irish Times*, 1 February.
43. This non-profit organisation, created in 1989, is located in Washington. It is made up of about fifty investigative journalists who aim to improve political life in the United States.
44. Paul Cullen. 2005. Watching the Watchdog. *The Irish Times*, 10 December.
45. Martin Wall, The Private Investigator.
46. John Waters. 2006. Subversion of Connolly Affair. *The Irish Times*, 2 January.

47. According to McDowell, Connolly travelled to Colombia in April 2001 with false papers in the company of his brother, Niall. The latter along with two other suspected IRA members was arrested the following August by the Colombian authorities. The group, known as the "Colombia Three", were suspected of having travelled to Colombia to train FARC (Revolutionary Armed Forces of Colombia) fighters in the use of explosives. Liam Reid. 2006. Centre for Public Inquiry Has Ceased Its Work. *The Irish Times*, 10 April. 48.
48. Paul Cullen, Watching the Watchdog.
49. Paul Anderson. 2005. Feeney Withdraws Funding from Centre for Public Enquiry. *The Irish Times*, 7 December; Ireland, parliamentary debates, Houses of the Oireachtas, Dáil Éireann (hereafter Dáil Éireann debates), 13 December 2005, 612, 2.
50. Liam Reid, Centre for Public Enquiry Has Ceased Its Work.
51. Paul Cullen, Watching the Watchdog; for further details about this topic see: Anne Groutel. 2024. Irish Diaspora Business Elite Philanthropy: boon or bane? Revue Lisa/Lisa e-journal, 22, 57. https://doi.org/10.4000/lisa.15866
52. Future of the Centre for Public Inquiry. 2025. *The Irish Times*, 19 December.
53. Government of Ireland, Department of Foreign Affairs, "Global Irish Economic Forum Report", Dublin, 2009, 17.
54. Government of Ireland, Global Irish Economic Forum, 27.
55. Denis P. Kelleher quoted in: Amy Feran, Irish Diaspora Speaks Out on IMF Bailout.
56. Anne Groutel. 2015. Une nouvelle gouvernance: une condition nécessaire à la reprise économique en Irlande? Revue LISA / LISA e-journal 13, 2. Martine Azuelos (ed.). special issue: Anglo-Saxon Capitalism and the Anglophone World(s). https://doi.org/10.4000/lisa.8396
57. Mary Minihan. 2011. Chuck Feeney Charity Funds Citizens' Assembly Idea. *The Irish Times*, 13 April; Mary Minihan. 2011. Citizens' Group Backs Property and Water Levies. *The Irish Times*, 13 December.
58. Fintan O'Toole. 2015. How Hopes Raised by the Constitutional Convention Were Dashed. *The Irish Times*, 3 March.
59. Harry McGee. 2011. Cox Seeks to Join FG and Run as Party Presidential Candidate. *The Irish Times*, 6 June.
60. Niall O'Dowd. 2011. Why I May Run for Irish President Because It Is Time for the Irish Abroad to Speak Up. 5 June https://www.irishcentral.com/opinion/niallodowd/why-i-may-run-for-irish-president-because-it-is-time-for-the-irish-abroad-to-speak-up-123202308-238087551. Accessed 6 June 2025.

61. O'Dowd and Feeney are old acquaintances, having been part of the group involved in the Northern Ireland peace process in the early 1990s. It is possible that the latter was among those who encouraged the journalist to enter the Irish presidential race.
62. Niall O'Dowd, Why I May Run for Irish President.
63. Niall O'Dowd, Why I May Run for Irish President.
64. Walter Ellis is a former diplomatic correspondent of *The Irish Times* in Brussels and Paris.
65. Thomas Phillip O'Neill, Jr. known as Tip O'Neill (1912–1994) was an Irish-American politician. A member of the Democratic Party, he was an influential figure in the United States Congress. He was Speaker of the House of Representatives from 1977 to 1987. O'Neill, Hugh Carey, the Governor of New York, and Senators Ted Kennedy (1932–2009) and Daniel Patrick Moynihan (1927–2003), known as the "Four Horsemen", participated in the Northern Ireland peace talks that led to the St Patrick's Day Declaration in 1977. O'Neill, Kennedy, and Moynihan founded the Friends of Ireland in 1981, a group of elected members of the US Congress that works for peace in Northern Ireland.
66. Walter Ellis. 2011. O'Dowd Too Much of an Irish-American for the Áras. *The Irish Times*, 15 June.
67. Ellis, O'Dowd
68. Ellis, O'Dowd
69. Bruce Morrison. 2011. O'Dowd Can Tap Valuable Support of Irish Americans. *The Irish Times*, 23 June.
70. See, for example, an article in the *Sunday Independent* which argued that O'Dowd's Anglophobia, republican beliefs, and close relationship with Adams were real problems for a presidential bid. J. P. McCarthy. 2011. O'Dowd's Green Prism Distorts His Vision of the Áras. Sunday Independent, 26 June.
71. Myles Duffy. 2011. How Critical Is Irish-American Support to a President of Ireland? 23 June https://crimson-observer.blogspot.com/search?q=How+Critical+Is+Irish-American+Support+. Accessed 6 June 2025.
72. Niall O'Dowd. 2011. Why I Am Not Running for Irish President - A Tough Decision to Pull Out of Context, 30 June. https://www.irishcentral.com/opinion/niallodowd/why-im-not-running-for-irish-president-a-tough-decision-to-pull-out-of-contest-124830109-238091401. Accessed 6 June 2025.
73. "Niall O'Trump". 2011. The Broken Elbow.com, 1 July. https://thebrokenelbow.com/2011/07/. Accessed 6 June 2025.
74. It was Martin McGuinness, one of the former IRA cadres who was instrumental in the process that led to the Northern Ireland Peace Agreement

and later became Deputy First Minister of Northern Ireland, who received the party's endorsement.

75. Niall O'Dowd. 2011. Why the Irish Abroad Threaten the Status Quo. Thejournal.ie, 11 July. https://www.thejournal.ie/readme/column-why-the-irish-abroad-threaten-the-status-quo-174286-Jul2011/. Accessed 6 June 2025.
76. A former director of the Emigrant Advice Network, Noreen Bowden was also editor of the now-defunct globalirish.ie website.
77. Noreen Bowden. 2011. "Emigrants Give Plenty Back to Ireland, So Why Can't We Vote?" Thejournal.ie, 4 July. online: https://www.thejournal.ie/readme/column-emigrants-give-plentyback-to-ireland-so-why-cant-we-vote-163087-Jul2011/. Accessed 6 June 2025.
78. Bowden, Emigrants.
79. See also: Anne Groutel. 2015. Engaging the Irish Diaspora in Ireland's Economic Development: A Double-Edged Sword? In Irish Studies in Europe Series, 5, Scott Brewster and Werner Uber, eds. 119–130, special issue: Ireland: Arrivals and Departures.
80. Ireland. Houses of the Oireachtas parliamentary debates Dáil Éireann, 2 February 1995, 448–5 (Mary Robinson).
81. Piaras Mac Éinrí, Brian Lambkin. 2002. Whose Diaspora? Whose Migration? Whose Identity? Some Current Issues in Migration Studies. *The Irish Journal of Psychology*, 23, 3–4:136.
82. Paul Byrne. 1995. Emigration: The Great Non-Issue. The Furrow, 46, 4: 224–231.
83. Constitution of Ireland of 1 July 1937, Article 2. https://www.irishstatutebook.ie/eli/cons/en/html. Accessed 6 June 2025.
84. They must have distinguished themselves in fields as varied as education or business, art, culture, sport, science or technology and innovation, and peace and reconciliation, or through the work of a charitable organisation.
85. This council seems to have been dissolved in 2011.
86. John Kennedy. 2013. Former Intel CEO Awarded Certificate of Irish Heritage, 17 May https://www.siliconrepublic.com/business/former-intel-ceo-awarded-certificate-of-irish-heritage. Accessed 6 June 2025; John Kennedy. 2013. Former Intel CEO Craig Barrett Receives Irish Presidential Distinguished Service Award, 28 November. https://www.siliconrepublic.com/business/former-intel-ceo-craig-barrett-receives-irish-presidential-distinguished-service-award. Accessed 6 June 2025.
87. Government of Ireland, Department of Foreign Affairs, "Global Irish, Ireland's Diaspora Policy", Dublin, March 2015.
88. Time to Give Our Disenfranchised Emigrants a Real Say in Our Affairs. 2015. *Irish Independent*, 29 December.

CHAPTER 14

Conclusion

In the 1960s, the Northern Ireland authorities succeeded in creating a small network of Northern Irish businessmen in the United States who helped them to attract American investment. However, unlike Ireland, this was not the most successful formula at the time. It was not until the nationalist parties came to power in a multi-party executive under the Good Friday Agreement that contacts were made at the initiative of the City of Belfast, which established a network in the United States of businessmen, whose ancestors originated from the island of Ireland.

Some Irish-American millionaires played a central role in the secret negotiations that led to the IRA ceasefire in 1994 and in the subsequent peace process. They have also been responsible for bringing in investment, in areas ranging from finance to high technology, which the province needs to develop its economy, its private sector in particular, and, by extension, to guarantee peacekeeping. These investments help renew and expand the local economic fabric. As was the case with Ireland in the 1960s, some major companies led by Irish-American figures, such as Citigroup, the New York Stock Exchange, or Cybersource, have been pioneers.

In the aftermath of the financial crisis (2007–2008), which hit Ireland harder than Northern Ireland, the Northern Ireland Executive believed it could position itself as a more attractive destination for foreign investors than its southern neighbour. Recent years have indeed witnessed the emergence of a dynamic pool of small, innovative companies specialising

A. Groutel, *The Two Irelands and the Diaspora*,
https://doi.org/10.1007/978-3-032-12355-8_14

in new technologies. It would be desirable for these businesses to grow within Northern Ireland and serve as models for others. However, there remains a risk that the most promising of these companies may be acquired by multinational corporations, as has often been the case south of the border.

Foreign Investors value the ability to engage with high-level authorities, as is common south of the border, where they can influence economic policies in their favour. However, Northern Ireland's limited decision-making power may hinder its ability to attract investors.

Furthermore, over the past two decades, Northern Ireland's devolved political institutions were suspended several times,[1] leading to prolonged periods of uncertainty. An agreement was eventually reached, resulting in the resumption of the Northern Ireland Executive. On 3 February 2024, Sinn Féin's Michelle O'Neill was appointed First Minister, becoming the first Irish nationalist to hold the position, with the DUP's Emma Little Pengelly as Deputy First Minister. With the Northern Ireland Executive once again operational, the region is in a position to exercise a power granted in 2015: the authority to set its own corporation tax rate at a level equivalent to that of the Republic of Ireland. If implemented, this fiscal lever could act as a catalyst for reshaping Northern Ireland's economic and social landscape.[2] The case for a reduced corporation tax rate remains as compelling today as it was a decade ago. It offers a means to rebalance the regional economy, boost the competitiveness of Northern Ireland's investment proposition, and encourage leading indigenous firms to continue investing and reinvesting locally. Nevertheless, long-standing concerns remain about the long-term viability of its economy even if the predominance of the public sector has so far somewhat protected it from the worst effects of international economic crises. Brexit has also had far-reaching consequences for Northern Ireland both on the political and economic front. But a new Brexit deal for Northern Ireland was formally adopted by the United Kingdom and European Union at the end of March 2023.[3]

From the 1930s to the late 1950s, Ireland remained a relatively isolated and inward-looking country on the periphery of Europe, characterised by a conservative stance in both economic and social spheres—a trend that, though somewhat softened, persisted into the 1960s.

However, a shift occurred in the early 1960s, when members of the Irish-American business elite began to support the Irish authorities in their efforts to transition from a protectionist economic model to a more open, market-oriented economy—a development that largely went unnoticed by the broader public. These business figures played a crucial role in facilitating early US investment, laying the groundwork for Ireland's accession to the European Common Market in 1973. By the time of its entry, Ireland had already gained a reputation as a stable and attractive destination for foreign capital, encouraging a growing influx of American multinationals.

In the decades that followed, cooperation between Irish-American business leaders and Irish policymakers continued to develop. During the 1990s in particular, Irish authorities demonstrated a notable openness to the advice and influence of these powerful actors, thereby involving them—albeit indirectly—in the formulation of economic policy. The influence of these actors has grown in parallel with the increasing scale of their investments in Ireland. It is therefore not entirely unexpected that some have sought to exert greater influence over economic policymaking and, in certain cases, over the country's internal affairs, including efforts to promote one of their own for the office of President of the Republic.

At the outset of this book, we set out to explore the nature of the relationship between diaspora tycoons and Irish political leaders, their respective motivations, and how Dublin managed to secure the active support of the former.

In the decades following partition, the solicitude that the diaspora had shown towards Ireland, for lack of attention, waned. Nevertheless, the Irish political class never lost sight of the huge market it represented in the United States. Some statements by Irish leaders might suggest that ethnic Irish people living abroad were seen not so much as brothers, sisters, cousins, but as potential buyers of Irish linen, whiskey drinkers, or tourists who had the advantage of not being total strangers. These people, it was thought, could be persuaded to buy Irish goods if a little nostalgia for the country of their ancestors and a hint of a guilty conscience were aroused.

Yet by the 1950s, the ethnic Irish population abroad, according to Irish diplomats, no longer seemed to have much of an interest in the distant island that they or their ancestors had left. However, it had not escaped the notice of some of these diplomats that the attitude of Irish-Americans could change if they saw financial benefits or there was an opportunity to improve their image within the diasporic group.

These impressions corroborate some of the hypotheses put forward by Tjai M. Nielsen and Liesl Riddle,[4] i.e. in addition to financial interest, the need for social recognition within the group could also explain, in part, why members of a diaspora invest or more simply work for the good of their homeland. However, in this case it is noted that the moral obligation to do a "good deed",[5] such as buying Irish products, did not come naturally to communities whose ties to Ireland had weakened over time. As a result, during their travels across the Atlantic, Lemass and Norton had to remind the Irish abroad what they could do for the homeland.

In the latter part of the 1950s, both north and south of the border, leaders sought to use the influence of the entrepreneurial elite of the Northern Irish and Irish diaspora to attract urgently needed investment to both economies. Some of its members responded to the call of the Dublin authorities who were able to flatter them, create a network, and highlight both the financial interest and the image and prestige within the diaspora community that they would enjoy if they invested in Ireland. In Nielsen and Riddle's work, the importance of government action does not appear to be paramount. Yet it has been decisive in the Irish context. On the other hand, it is not clear that moral obligation, even if some of these figures in the discourse relished in recalling how much they owed to Ireland, was really a determining factor during this period. In any event, there was something in it for each party.

The visceral reaction of some Irish-Americans to the violent imagery emerging from Northern Ireland in the late 1970s indicates that their sense of identity had not entirely dissipated. By the 1990s, the Irish lobby in the United States remained highly influential, successfully persuading President Clinton to engage directly in the search for a resolution to the Northern Irish conflict. The active participation of prominent diaspora figures in the peace process, along with the achievements of The Ireland Funds—an organisation that has positioned itself as the philanthropic home of influential Irish and Northern Irish expatriates—suggests that for many Irish-American tycoons, ties to their ancestral homeland transcend mere business interests.Whether their involvement stems from a genuine sense of moral responsibility towards their ancestral homeland and its people, the emotional gratification of contributing to the cause of peace and national development, or the desire for public recognition within both the diaspora community and in Ireland itself remains open to interpretation. For some, visible engagement in philanthropic or peace-building efforts enhances their reputation as benefactors of the homeland, reinforcing their standing among fellow Irish-Americans while also earning symbolic prestige in Ireland. The American Ireland Fund has conveniently created a space in which members of the diaspora can convene, network, and spotlight their contributions to Ireland's progress in a way that resonates across both sides of the Atlantic.

In the early 2010s, the Irish government launched the Global Irish Network, an initiative designed to connect high-level business leaders across the globe with one another and with Dublin via modern communication technologies. To continue harnessing this "diasporic spirit"—a sentiment rooted in a perceived duty to support Ireland—the Irish authorities must remain proactive in cultivating and sustaining these connections, particularly as the newer generations of the diaspora appear less inclined to settle permanently abroad.[6]

14.1 Final Thoughts and Questions in Light of Recent Developments

At the end of August 2017, the first Trump administration (2017–2021) announced its decision to abolish the post of Special Envoy for Economic Affairs to Northern Ireland.[7] In contrast, its successor, Joe Biden, reversed this decision. He made no secret of his affection for Ireland, the land of his ancestors, during his four-day official visit to the two Irelands to commemorate the 25th anniversary of the Good Friday Agreement in April 2023. Soon after, in September 2023, Northern Ireland took a significant step in bolstering its Life & Health Sciences sector by launching a new US Advisory Board.[8] This initiative, supported by Joe Kennedy III, the US Special Envoy to Northern Ireland for Economic Affairs, aims to strengthen trade and investment opportunities between Northern Ireland and the United States. The board, comprising influential professionals from the Northern Irish diaspora, is designed to leverage their expertise and connections to drive sector growth. This move highlighted the importance of the US market for Northern Ireland's Life & Health Sciences companies and underscored the potential for mutually beneficial economic relationships.[9]

However, the political landscape shifted with the return of Donald Trump to the White House in January 2025, raising concerns about the future of US investment in Northern Ireland. The bipartisan Friends of Ireland caucus has stressed the importance of a US envoy to advocate for greater American investment and support Northern Ireland's economic development. In March 2025, leading Irish-American members of Congress urged Trump to appoint a special envoy to Northern Ireland to address growing anxieties over trade tensions. Congressmen Richard Neal[10] and Mike Kelly[11] emphasised the need for a representative to protect US interests and provide certainty for American companies investing in the region. Their letter to Trump highlighted the historical role of US envoys in supporting peace and economic development in Northern Ireland, a tradition that had continued since the Clinton administration.[12]

The call for a new special envoy comes at a critical time, as Northern Ireland still faces challenges related to post-Brexit trading rules. Despite significant US investment over the past decade, the anticipated economic boom has not yet materialised, and the region's access to both the UK and EU markets is still under strain.

While the launch of the US Advisory Board in 2023 set a positive trajectory for the Life & Health Sciences sector, the political uncertainties introduced by Trump's election pose new challenges. The outcome of these developments would significantly influence Northern Ireland's ability to attract and retain US investment, shaping its economic landscape in the years to come.

A convergence of favourable economic conditions and a proactive policy of incentives made Ireland increasingly attractive to international investors. By 2002, it had earned recognition as one of the most globalised economies in the world.[13] From its position as one of the poorest members of the European Economic Community, Ireland experienced a remarkable improvement in living standards during the Celtic Tiger years.

Yet, with the benefit of hindsight, the influence of Irish-American business elites on Ireland's economic development appears more ambivalent than uniformly positive. While it is true that their efforts facilitated the arrival of major American banks in the 1960s, and helped position Ireland as an attractive destination for foreign capital, the broader economic model they promoted warrants critical reflection.

Much of the industrial investment they helped attract through the 1960s to the late 1980s took the form of manufacturing plants reliant on low-skilled, low-cost labour. However, the type of industrial investment they helped to attract to Ireland during this period and until the late 1980s did not have all the positive effects one might have expected. In the first place, these were mainly production units employing low-skilled, low-cost labour. In addition, the latest wave of globalisation from the late 1990s onwards increased the mobility of capital and investment across the globe, and many jobs created became less sustainable.[14] Moreover, these foreign-owned facilities often operated in isolation from the domestic economy. Their supply chains were largely external, drawing on other subsidiaries within the same corporate networks rather than sourcing locally. As a result, Irish firms missed out on the expected diffusion of technology and managerial expertise. That said, a number of indigenous companies have successfully grown into multinationals themselves, but in traditional sectors of the Irish economy such as agri-food and construction materials. It is also notable that Ireland's outward direct investment has steadily increased over time, signalling a gradual maturation of its own global economic footprint.[15]

In parallel, the Irish economy has become increasingly dependent[16] on the presence of foreign multinationals to help maintain employment levels. Indeed, for a long time, the official discourse emphasised the importance of continuing to offer the most advantageous conditions possible to foreign investors—implicitly discouraging demands for wage increases—or risk the departure of these multinationals. It is probably less the case nowadays as foreign direct investment (FDI), facilitated by the "smart"[17] economic policies of the Irish government, has undeniably made a substantial positive contribution to the economy of the Republic. This impact is primarily evident through several key areas: job creation, particularly in high-growth sectors such as technology, pharmaceuticals, and financial services; significant growth in the exports of goods and services; the implementation of advanced technologies and innovation; and a notable increase in government tax revenue. These factors have collectively enhanced the economic landscape, fostering a dynamic environment for sustained growth and development. Over the past decade, Ireland has indeed witnessed the rise of numerous innovative, homegrown technology firms, fuelling hopes that this emerging sector could eventually serve as a key driver of national economic growth. Yet, as experience has shown, many of these start-ups are ultimately acquired by multinational corporations and relocate their operations to Silicon Valley in pursuit of greater scale and global market access.

Despite the success of the Irish economy, some questions remain about the long-term viability of its model, whose foundations, despite appearances, are fragile. Indeed, Brussels has the power to end Ireland's main competitive advantage, its advantageous taxation of multinationals, by imposing tax harmonisation within the European Union. But the most serious and imminent danger comes from the new administration in Washington. The first Trump administration enticed multinationals to repatriate their investments to the United States, by offering tax incentives. The Biden administration did not change track. However, with Trump's return to the presidency, the foundations of the relationship between Ireland and the United States face unprecedented scrutiny and potential disruption. Ireland now finds itself navigating a precarious economic and political moment.[18] At the heart of the issue are the substantial economic ties between Ireland and the United States, particularly in the pharmaceutical sector, where American multinationals have long found a haven in Ireland's favourable tax regime and strategic location.

At the start of 2025, Trump threatened to impose sweeping tariffs of up to 25% on EU goods—including key Irish exports such as whiskey; while this threat was not fully carried out, European products have nonetheless been subjected to a 10% tariff in the United States. Even more severe threats specifically targeting pharmaceuticals also pose a direct risk to Ireland's export-driven economy. In 2024 alone, Ireland exported €72 billion worth of goods to the United States, the vast majority of which were pharmaceuticals and chemicals.[19] These exports have not only underpinned corporate profits but have also been central to Ireland's job market, tax revenues, and public spending. Towns like Westport, which hosts a major facility producing the world's Botox supply, exemplify the transformative local impact of US investment over several decades. Yet these very communities now face the spectre of strategic disinvestment, not because of poor performance, but because of US political volatility.[20]

While pharmaceutical products have so far been granted a temporary exemption from Trump's broader tariff regime, offering short-term relief for the sector, this measure remains subject to future revision. As trade policy evolves in response to economic and political pressures, this exemption could easily be rescinded, reinforcing the broader atmosphere of uncertainty.[21]

Trump's rhetoric makes clear that Ireland's success is viewed in his administration as a symptom of past American failure. In his own words, Ireland "took our pharmaceutical companies away from presidents that didn't know what they were doing". While Trump has expressed admiration for the Irish-American community—acknowledging their electoral support and hailing their cultural contributions[22]—he has also signalled a willingness to reframe this historic relationship through a transactional lens. Ireland, once celebrated as a bridge between the United States and the European Union, may now be seen as a competitor in need of disciplining.[23]

Beyond the immediate threat of tariffs, the deeper risk lies in a structural shift: a redirection of pharmaceutical investment and intellectual property back to the United States. The tax changes initiated by Trump in 2017 inadvertently accelerated Ireland's economic boom by encouraging American firms to transfer intellectual property to Irish subsidiaries. This windfall led to extraordinary corporate tax revenues. But that success now appears fragile, as Trump floats policies aimed at reversing those flows.[24]

In response, the Irish government is taking steps to mitigate potential fallout. A new Strategic Economic Advisory Panel[25] has been set up to bolster Irish-American trade relations and offer high-level guidance on dealing with adverse U.S. policies. Composed of influential Irish business leaders based in the United States, the panel is intended as a key resource in shaping economic diplomacy. However, the government has so far withheld details on the panel's membership and influence, raising concerns about transparency and the democratic accountability of those potentially steering national trade strategy behind closed doors.[26]

In parallel, Minister for Enterprise Simon Harris is advocating for the creation of a Consultative Group on International Trade Policy to provide further expert oversight and support. Ireland's diplomatic strategy now emphasises not only safeguarding US ties, but also broadening engagement with other major economies such as Canada and China. The Irish Exporters Association has warned domestic firms not to assume Trump's threats will remain hypothetical, urging them to reassess supply chains and prepare for possible disruptions.[27]

These initiatives reflect a broader recognition that the era of unquestioned economic alignment with the United States may be drawing to a close. Even without immediate plant closures, the chilling effect on future investment could gradually erode the pillars of Ireland's economic model. Trump's unpredictability injects a level of volatility that threatens long-term planning and deters the very kind of investment on which Ireland has come to depend.

In sum, Trump's revived economic nationalism confronts Ireland with stark questions about its dependency on US multinationals, the sustainability of its current tax base, and its place within an increasingly adversarial transatlantic trade environment. The role of Irish-American business and political elites will once again be crucial. Ireland needs congressmen and senators of Daniel Patrick Moynihan's calibre—figures who, in their time, ardently defended Ireland's economic and political interests.[28] The Irish-American bond, once a geopolitical asset, may now require delicate recalibration. Ireland must now balance diplomacy with diversification, prudence with resilience, to secure its place in an increasingly uncertain global economy.

Notes

1. Following revelations of alleged IRA spying in the Northern Ireland Assembly, the Assembly was suspended between 2002 and 2007, during which time London's direct rule of the province was restored. The Saint Andrews Agreement (2006) led to the reestablishment of the Northern Assembly which resumed operations in May 2007. In January 2017, the then deputy First Minister Martin McGuinness resigned in protest over the Renewable Heat Incentive scandal and the Northern Ireland Executive consequently collapsed. The parties signed the New Decade, New Approach agreement and an Executive was subsequently established. Years later, on 3 February 2022, Democratic Unionist Party First Minister Paul Givan resigned in line with his party's protest over the Northern Ireland Protocol in the post-Brexit period and withdrew from the NI Executive which consequently collapsed.
2. KPMG. 2025. UK Spring Statement 2025, 26 March. https://kpmg.com/ie/en/home/insights/2025/03/uk-spring-statement-2025-tax.html. Accessed 6 June 2025.
3. Her Majesty's Government, The Windsor Framework: a new way forward, presented to Parliament by the Prime Minister and Minister for the Union by Command of His Majesty, CP 806, February 2023. https://assets.publishing.service.gov.uk/government/uploads/system/uploads/attachment_data/file/1138989/The_Windsor_Framework_a_new_way_forward.pdf. Accessed 6 June 2025.
4. Tjai M. Nielsen, Liesl Riddle. 2007. Why Diasporas Invest in the Homeland: A Conceptual Model of Motivation. https://doi.org/10.2139/ssrn.987725
5. Nielsen, Riddle, Why Diasporas, 8–16.
6. Feargal Cochrane. 2008. Mediating the Diaspora Space: Charting the Changing Nature of Irish-America in an Age of Globalisation. Global Migration and Transnational Politics, George Mason University, Working Paper 2, 5.
7. Adrian Rutherford. 2017. Trump Administration to Abolish Special Envoy to Northern Ireland. Belfast Telegraph, 31 August.
8. I thank my friend Ian Gourley, MD, Vice President of Clinical Development at Immunovant (US) for bringing this information to my attention.
9. Invest NI. 2023. New US Advisory Board launched to support NI's Life & Health Sciences Sector. 26 September. https://www.investni.com/

media-centre/news/new-us-advisory-board-launched-support-nis-life-health-sciences-sector. Accessed 6 June 2025.

10. Congressman Neal (democrat) holds the position of dean for both the Massachusetts Delegation and the New England Congressional Delegation, and he serves as an At-Large Whip for the House Democrats. Additionally, he leads the Friends of Ireland Caucus as the Democratic Leader, where he champions the preservation of robust relations between the United States and Ireland. He was instrumental in facilitating the Good Friday Agreement, which concluded the longest period of conflict in Irish history. Furthermore, he has been pivotal in upholding the principles of this agreement and preventing the reinstatement of a hard border.
11. George Joseph "Mike" Kelly Jr. is an American politician and businessman who has been a US representative since 2011, currently representing Pennsylvania's 16th congressional district. A member of the Republican Party, Kelly is known for his support of Donald Trump. He is a member of the Friends of Ireland Caucus.
12. Myles McCormick and Jude Webber. 2025. Donald Trump urged to appoint N Ireland envoy amid US investment 'concern'. *The Financial Times*, March 10.
13. Globalization's Last Hurrah? January/February 2002. *Foreign Policy Magazine*, 128: 38. https://doi.org/10.2307/3183355
14. Teeling demonstrated that in the early 1970s, a period when labour costs were rising in Ireland, the proportion of investors expanding their facilities in the country was greater than those divesting part or all of their Irish interests. John J. Teeling, "The Evolution of Offshore Investment". DBA Thesis, Harvard University, 1975, 132.
15. Irish stocks of direct investment abroad increased to €1248 billion at the end of 2023, up from €1211 billion at the end of 2022.The €37.3bn increase was seen primarily in Europe (€71.9bn) and was partially offset by decreases in North America (–€57.5bn). Central Statistics Office, Foreign Direct Investment Annual 2023. Central Statistics Office (Ireland). https://www.cso.ie/en/releasesandpublications/ep/p-fdia/foreigndirectinvestmentannual2023/. Accessed 6 June 2025
16. The US State Department estimates that US foreign direct investment in Ireland was $557 billion in 2021. There are currently approximately 950 US subsidiaries in Ireland, employing approximately 209,000 people and indirectly supporting the employment of another 167,000 people (more than 10% of Ireland's total workforce). Center for City Development Policy. 2025. Ireland's FDI Success Story: A Policy Framework Analysis, 3 February. https://www.cdp.center/post/irelands-fdi-success-story-a-policy-framework-analysis. Accessed 6 June 2025.
17. This term refers to the promotion of a "smart" economy.

18. Kieran McQuinn, Conor O'Toole, Dónal O'Shea. Spring 2025. Quarterly Economic Commentary, Dublin: The Economic and Social Research Institute. https://doi.org/10.26504/QEC2025SPR
19. Grainne Glynn. 2025. Trump's Tariffs Can and Will Affect Ireland, 10 March. Universityobserver.ie. https://universityobserver.ie/trumps-tariffs-can-and-will-affect-ireland/
20. Michela Tindera and Jude Webber. 2025. Transcript: How Trump's tariffs threaten Ireland's pharma fortune. *The Financial Times*, 21 May.
21. Lisa O'Carroll. 2025. Trump hints at tariff reprieve for pharma companies that bring operations back to US. *The Guardian*, 1 May. https://www.theguardian.com/business/2025/may/01/trump-tariffs-pharma-firms-us-manufacturing?utm_source=chatgpt.com. Accessed 6 June 2025.
22. It is worth pointing out that unlike his predecessors, Donald Trump, during his first mandate showed absolutely no interest in Ireland to the extent of leaving the position of US Ambassador to Ireland vacant for two and a half years.
23. Eoghan Dalton, 2025. 'They voted for me so I like them': Trump declares Irish American Heritage Month, 6 March. https://www.thejournal.ie/trump-irish-america-6642088-Mar2025/?utm. Accessed 6 June 2025.
24. Tindera, Webber, Transcript.
25. Glynn, Trump's Tariffs.
26. Niall Sargent. 2025. Nothing Seaping in: US trade advisory panel vital but opacity a concern, 29 April. https://thecurrency.news/articles/187722/nothing-seaping-through-new-us-business-advisory-panel-vital-but-opacity-a-concern/. Accessed 6 June 2025.
27. Glynn, Trump's Tariffs.
28. In August 1993, Ireland secured a $500 million tax deferral for U.S. companies operating abroad, largely due to the efforts of Senator Daniel Patrick Moynihan, who had recently become chairman of the Senate Finance Committee. Moynihan's amendment to the 1994 tax legislation preserved tax incentives for U.S. companies to operate in Ireland, effectively overriding a provision in Clinton's original budget that aimed to curb tax avoidance by multinational corporations. This move reduced the anticipated federal tax revenue by half a billion dollars, raising concerns among U.S. officials. Critics within the State Department suggested that Moynihan's stance was influenced by a private meeting with the Irish ambassador, arguing that his support of Ireland came at the expense of addressing economic distress in his own state of New York. Moynihan's staff, however, defended the move, dismissing criticism as ethnically motivated and asserting that the senator had full authority to act independently. Irish trade representatives made no apologies for lobbying to protect these advantages, viewing tax deferral as crucial for attracting foreign invest-

ment. Intel, for example, praised Moynihan's actions as instrumental in maintaining the viability of its Irish operations. The episode underscored the complex intersection of national policy, economic strategy, and ethnic politics in shaping international corporate behavior. Jack Anderson, Michael Binsteing. 1994. U.S. Taxpayers' gift to Ireland. *The Washington Post*, 7 March.

Appendix

A Selection of Biographical Profiles of Notable Irish-American Diaspora Figures Mentioned in This Book

Craig R. Barrett (b. 1939) is a distinguished American business executive and engineer, best known for his leadership at Intel Corporation, where he served as Chief Executive Officer (1998–2005) and subsequently as Chairman of the Board until his retirement in May 2009. His tenure at Intel coincided with some of the company's most challenging and transformative periods, including the aftermath of the dot-com bubble and global economic turbulence.

Barrett pursued his higher education from Stanford University, where he received a PhD in Materials Science in 1964. He went on to serve on the faculty of Stanford's Department of Materials Science and Engineering until 1974, when he joined Intel as a manager. Rapidly ascending through the ranks, he became Vice President in 1984, Executive Vice President in 1990, Chief Operating Officer in 1993, and President in 1997. A year later, he was appointed CEO, becoming the fourth person to hold this title in the company's history.

As CEO, Barrett steered Intel through an era of intense competition, technological disruption, and rapid globalisation. He played a pivotal role

A. Groutel, *The Two Irelands and the Diaspora*,
https://doi.org/10.1007/978-3-032-12355-8

in expanding Intel's global manufacturing and R&D footprint, while also reinforcing the company's leadership in semiconductor innovation. He was appointed Chairman of the Board in 2005, a role he held until stepping down in 2009.

Following his retirement from Intel, Barrett transitioned into academia and policy advisory roles. He joined the faculty of the Thunderbird School of Global Management in Phoenix, Arizona, and became an advocate for education, technological innovation, and international competitiveness. In 2000, he and his wife Barbara endowed Barrett, The Honors College at Arizona State University, with a $10 million gift, reflecting their longstanding commitment to higher education.

Barrett has been recognised internationally for his contributions to industry and education. Among his accolades is an honorary doctorate from Trinity College Dublin, awarded in 2014, underscoring his transatlantic influence and engagement in global knowledge networks.

Source: Wikipedia. Craig Barrett. https://en.wikipedia.org/wiki/Craig_Barrett_(chief_executive). Accessed 21 June 2025.

Loretta Brennan Glucksman (b. 1938) has dedicated her life to strengthening the cultural, educational, and philanthropic ties between the United States and Ireland. Raised in an Irish neighbourhood in Allentown, Pennsylvania, she is the granddaughter of four Irish immigrants. Her maternal grandfather, a miner from County Leitrim, was active in early unionisation efforts, while her father worked on the railroad during World War II before joining the Civil Service.

An early academic achiever, Loretta received a scholarship to Chestnut Hill College, where her aunt served as mother superior. She married Jack Cooney, and began her professional life in education, teaching at Trenton State College (now The College of New Jersey) while raising their three children.

Loretta Brennan's career took a new direction in the 1970s when she transitioned to public television, first launching a book-focused programme at a new Trenton-based station, and later producing and hosting *The Thursday Report*, a weekly public affairs programme she led for over a decade. She later moved into public relations.

In 1984, Loretta met Lewis Glucksman, then Chairman of the investment bank Lehman Brothers. The two shared a deep appreciation for Ireland, and in 1987 she made her first visit to the country, which she described as both "overwhelming and mesmerizing". They eventually purchased a home near Cobh, County Cork, and together made significant philanthropic contributions to Ireland until Lew's passing in 2006.

Among their most enduring legacies is Glucksman Ireland House at New York University, established in 1993 as a centre for Irish and Irish-American studies. Loretta continues to serve as co-chair of its advisory board. She also chairs The American Ireland Fund, an organisation that has raised over $250 million to support peace and reconciliation, education, and culture across the island. Her contributions include funding integrated schools in Northern Ireland that educate Catholic and Protestant children together—an effort she believes is crucial for breaking down sectarian barriers.

Loretta Brennan serves on the boards of several of Ireland's leading institutions, including the National Gallery of Ireland, Trinity College Dublin, University College Cork, and the Royal Irish Academy.

In every endeavour, Loretta Brennan Glucksman remains a steadfast champion of Ireland—promoting its history and culture, fostering U.S.–Ireland relations, and advancing the cause of peace and education on the island. Her advocacy and leadership continue to shape the Irish-American story in profound and lasting ways.

Source: *Irish America* Magazine. Loretta Brennan Glucksman.

https://www.irishamerica.com/honoree/loretta-brennan-glucksman-2/ Accessed 21 June 2025.

John Cullinane is a pioneering American software entrepreneur and philanthropist whose career has left a lasting imprint on both the U.S. technology sector and economic development efforts in Northern Ireland. A graduate of Northeastern University, Cullinane founded Cullinane Corporation, later known as Cullinet Software, which became one of the first software companies to go public in 1977. Its success positioned Cullinet as a leading force in the early enterprise software industry. The company was acquired in 1989, marking a pivotal transition in Cullinane's professional life.

A first-generation Irish-American, Cullinane was deeply shaped by his heritage. His mother, Margaret Cullinane, was a native Irish speaker from Dunmore East, County Waterford, who emigrated to the United States in 1929. In the late 1980s, John Cullinane was invited to contribute to peacebuilding and economic renewal in Northern Ireland, a region emerging from decades of conflict. Drawing on his entrepreneurial expertise, he recognised the region's untapped technological potential and committed himself to fostering cross-community economic development.

Cullinane played a central role in the formation of the Friends of Belfast, a strategic initiative aimed at encouraging U.S. investment, entrepreneurship, and job creation in Northern Ireland. Through mentorship, transatlantic networking, and the promotion of high-tech innovation, he helped attract American business interest and supported local start-ups in their efforts to compete globally. A key principle of his approach was inclusive economic opportunity: creating conditions for both Protestant and Catholic communities to engage in shared growth and reconciliation.

John Cullinane's efforts represent a model of diaspora engagement and economic diplomacy, demonstrating how private sector leadership can contribute to post-conflict development. His legacy in Northern Ireland is not only economic but also social—supporting peace through prosperity.

Source: Irish American Partnership. 21 May 2024. Software Pioneer John Cullinane on Creating Opportunity in Ireland. https://irishap.org/software-pioneer-john-cullinane-on-creating-opportunity-in-ireland/ Accessed 21 June 2025.

Charles Francis (Chuck) Feeney (1931–2023) was an Irish-American entrepreneur and philanthropist, best known for co-founding Duty Free Shoppers (DFS) and for anonymously donating the vast majority of his wealth—more than $8 billion—through his charitable foundation, the Atlantic Philanthropies. Often referred to as the "James Bond of philanthropy", Feeney championed the principle of "giving while living", deliberately giving away his fortune during his lifetime.

Born in 1931 in Elizabeth, New Jersey, to Irish-American parents with ancestral roots in County Fermanagh, Feeney served as a radio operator in the U.S. Air Force during the Korean War before achieving a degree in hotel administration from Cornell University in 1956. He began his business career selling duty-free liquor to U.S. naval personnel in Asia and, in 1960, co-founded DFS with fellow Cornell alumnus Robert Warren Miller. The company grew into the world's largest travel retailer, pioneering duty-free sales to Japanese tourists and eventually expanding across Asia, Europe, and North America.

In 1982, Feeney quietly transferred his entire 38.75% stake in DFS to the Atlantic Philanthropies, effectively separating himself from the wealth that had made him one of the richest men in the world. For over a decade, the foundation operated in secret, funding causes in education, health, human rights, and peacebuilding. Major beneficiaries included Cornell University, which received nearly $1 billion in funding; Irish higher education, particularly the University of Limerick and Dublin City University;

and Queens University Belfast, which received support for capital projects and medical research.

Feeney also made transformative investments in public health, including funding for AIDS clinics in South Africa, health reform in Vietnam, and the UCSF Medical Center in San Francisco. His support for integrated education in Northern Ireland and his donation to Sinn Féin following the IRA ceasefire in 1994 reflected his commitment to social and political reconciliation.

Atlantic Philanthropies formally concluded its activities in 2020, having fulfilled Feeney's goal of giving away its assets during his lifetime. He received numerous honours, including the Presidential Distinguished Service Award for the Irish Abroad (2012); Honorary Doctorates from institutions in Ireland, Australia, and the United States; and accolades from Cornell University, which renamed two campus thoroughfares "Feeney Way" in his honour. In 2014, Warren Buffett described him as "[his] hero and Bill Gates' hero. He should be everybody's hero".

Feeney died in October 2023 at the age of 92. He is remembered as one of the most impactful and self-effacing philanthropists of the modern era.

Source. Wikipedia. Chuck Feeney. https://simple.wikipedia.org/wiki/Chuck_Feeney. Accessed 21 June 2025.

Irial Finan (b. 1956) is an Irish business leader and seasoned executive in the global beverage industry. He currently serves as Chairman of Smurfit Westrock plc (formerly Smurfit Kappa Group), one of the world's leading sustainable packaging companies. He also sits on the boards of Coca-Cola FEMSA, Coca-Cola HBC, Coca-Cola Bottlers Japan, Coca-Cola Europacific Partners, and Fortune Brands Innovations, Inc. In addition, he is a non-executive director of Co-operation Ireland and the NUI Galway Foundation, demonstrating his continued commitment to Irish civic and educational life.

Finan spent over three decades in The Coca-Cola System, culminating in his role as Executive Vice President of The Coca-Cola Company and President of Bottling Investments Group (BIG), overseeing operations across five continents. Before joining the corporate ranks in Atlanta in 2004, he served as CEO of Coca-Cola HBC and held key leadership roles in Ireland and Northern Ireland, including as Finance Director of Coca-Cola Bottlers Ireland and Managing Director of Coca-Cola Bottlers Ulster.

A native of County Roscommon, Finan holds a Bachelor of Commerce from the National University of Ireland, Galway (NUI Galway), and is a

Fellow of the Chartered Institute of Management Accountants. In recognition of his professional achievements and service to the Irish diaspora, he was awarded an Honorary Doctor of Laws by NUI Galway in 2012.

Deeply connected to Ireland, Finan is actively involved in promoting cross-border co-operation and educational advancement through his work with Co-operation Ireland and NUI Galway. He is also a past honouree of the Irish America Stars of the South and a recipient of the Leslie C. Quick Jr Leadership Award.

Sources: Global Business & Management Experts. Irial Finan biography. https://biography.omicsonline.org/brazil/coca-cola/irial-finan-1253693?utm_. Accessed 24 June 2025.

William J. Flynn (1926–2018) was a prominent American businessman and a leading Irish-American advocate for peace in Northern Ireland. Born on 6 September 1926 in Manhattan to Irish immigrant parents with roots in County Down and County Mayo, Flynn trained for the priesthood before receiving a Degree in Economics from Fordham University. He rose to become President, CEO, and Chairman of Mutual of America, transforming the organisation into a major provider of pension plans for over 15,000 nonprofit institutions across the United States.

Flynn leveraged his business acumen and influence to support the Northern Ireland peace process during the 1980s and 1990s. As chairman of the National Committee on American Foreign Policy, he organised and hosted key conferences and high-level meetings that brought together leaders from across the political and sectarian spectrum, including those from Loyalist and Republican communities. He was a founding figure in the Irish-American group "Americans for a New Irish Agenda" and played a pivotal role in securing U.S. political support for peace efforts, notably arranging the 1994 conference that led to Gerry Adams receiving a U.S. visa—an essential moment in facilitating dialogue.

Flynn travelled frequently to Ireland, forging connections with both Unionist and Nationalist leaders, and his contributions were widely credited with helping to create the conditions for the IRA's ceasefire in 1994. He was a board member of Co-operation Ireland and a dedicated supporter of various humanitarian and civil society causes in both Ireland and the United States.

In 1996, Flynn served as Grand Marshal of the New York City St Patrick's Day Parade, further solidifying his stature within the Irish-American community. A man of vision, integrity, and persistence, William

J. Flynn remained deeply committed to the cause of peace in Ireland throughout his life.

Source: Ray O'Hanlon. 4 June 2018. Death of William J. "Bill" Flynn, 91. *The Irish Echo*. https://www.irishecho.com/2018/6/death-of-william-j-bill-flynn-91. Accessed 21 June 2025.

Peter Grace Jr. (1913–1995) was an American industrialist and corporate leader who served as President and CEO of W.R. Grace & Co. for nearly five decades, making him one of the longest-serving chief executives in American business history. Born in Manhasset, New York, on 25 May 1913, he was the grandson of **William R. Grace,** the founder of the family company and the first Roman Catholic elected mayor of New York City.

Grace was educated at St. Paul's School in New Hampshire and later at Yale University. He joined the family business in 1936, starting in the mailroom, and became President and CEO in 1945 at the age of 32, following his father's stroke and subsequent retirement. Under his leadership, W.R. Grace underwent a dramatic transformation, shifting from its historic focus on Latin America to becoming one of the largest diversified chemical producers in the United States.

During Grace's tenure, the company reduced its dependency on Latin American revenues—from 60% of sales in the 1950s to 19% by 1962—and significantly expanded its operations in chemicals, which grew to account for over half of corporate revenue by the late 1970s. Grace pursued an aggressive diversification strategy, acquiring companies in the restaurant, sporting goods, and automotive sectors, making W.R. Grace a model of mid-century American conglomeration.

Grace was also active in public affairs. During the Kennedy administration, he chaired the Commerce Department Committee on the Alliance for Progress, a key U.S. initiative to foster economic co-operation with Latin America during the Cold War. A devout Catholic and philanthropist, he received the Laetare Medal from the University of Notre Dame in 1967, the highest honour awarded to American Catholics.

Known for his longevity in leadership and for modernising a family-run enterprise into a multinational corporation, Joseph P. Grace Jr. left a significant legacy in American industrial history. He died on 19 April 1995.

Source: Wikipedia. J. Peter Grace. https://en.wikipedia.org/wiki/J._Peter_Grace. Accessed 21 June 2025.rooeny.

John Hartnett is a seasoned entrepreneur, CEO, and investor with over 25 years of executive and board leadership experience across the technology, airline, and agrifood sectors. As the Founder and CEO of SVG Ventures | THRIVE, he has built the world's leading agrifood innovation platform, with over 80 start-up investments to date. He also founded the Forbes AgTech Summit, a joint initiative with Forbes Media, and collaborates with the USDA on its National Innovation Imperative.

Previously, Hartnett held executive roles at Palm, Inc., where as EVP Global Markets he led worldwide smartphone operations to over $3.5 billion in revenue, and at Metacreations, overseeing its international growth. His early career included senior positions at Claris (Apple), AT&T/Teradata, and Digital Equipment Corporation.

He has served on numerous public and private boards, notably Aer Lingus, where he was appointed an Independent Non-Executive Director in January 2014. From 2009 to 2017, he was Chairman of SiSaf Ltd., a UK-based drug delivery company thenetwork.com, and he also served as a director of Mcor Technologies, a specialist in 3D printing systems. Hartnett founded the Irish Technology Leadership Group (ITLG) in 2007 and served on the U.S. Secretary of State's Northern Ireland Economic Working Committee in 2009. He holds a postgraduate diploma in accounting and finance, is a graduate of the Marketing Institute of Ireland, and completed executive education programmes at Stanford University and Harvard University.

Source: Thrive. John Hartnett. https://thriveagrifood.com/team/john-hartnett/. Accessed 21 June 2025.

Denis P. Kelleher (1939–2019) was founder and CEO of Wall Street Access, a diversified financial services organisation with expertise in money management and trading for institutions and hedge funds. Billions of dollars are processed through Wall Street Access annually and it is a member of the New York Stock Exchange.

Kelleher began his career in 1958 as a messenger with Merrill Lynch, where through dynamic financial talent he rose dramatically through the company ranks until 1980 when he used his acquired knowledge and experience to found Wall Street Access.

Kelleher was a native of County Kerry, Ireland, with a degree from St. John's University. He was a member of both the Independence Community Bank and The New Ireland Fund, and was proud to be recognised with the Ellis Island Medal of Honor in 1995. In 2005, he was Grand Marshal of the Saint Patrick's Day parade in New York City.

Source: *Irish America* Magazine. Denis P. Kelleher. https://www.irishamerica.com/honoree/denis-kelleher/. Accessed 21 June 2025.

Edmund F. Kelly (b. 1946) is a prominent Irish-American business executive, best known for his leadership of Liberty Mutual Group, where he served as President, Chief Executive Officer, and eventually Chairman. Born in Ireland in 1946, Kelly pursued a distinguished academic path, receiving a bachelor's degree from Queen's University Belfast and a PhD from the Massachusetts Institute of Technology (MIT). He began his career in academia as Assistant Professor of Mathematics at the University of New Brunswick and the University of Missouri at St. Louis, before transitioning to the insurance sector in the mid-1970s.

In 1974, Kelly joined Aetna Life and Casualty, where he rapidly rose through the ranks thanks to his analytical rigour and readiness to undertake complex strategic challenges. As President of Aetna's employee benefits division, he was credited with substantial improvements in cost control, marketing, and product innovation, resulting in significant growth in both pension assets and earnings. His reputation for decisive leadership and performance-based management ultimately led to his recruitment by Liberty Mutual in 1992.

As President and Chief Operating Officer of Liberty Mutual, and later as CEO (1998) and Chairman (2000), Kelly undertook an ambitious programme of restructuring and international expansion. He introduced a customer-centric model that integrated multiple points of access—digital, telephone, and in-person—ensuring what he termed "channel neutrality". Under his leadership, Liberty Mutual's international premiums grew from $190 million to $4 billion between 1994 and 2004, and operations were launched in diverse markets including China, Argentina, France, Japan, and Brazil.

One of Kelly's most consequential moves was the reorganisation of Liberty Mutual into a mutual-holding company, a complex transformation that required regulatory approval and was aimed at enhancing the firm's flexibility and competitiveness in global markets. His vision not only ensured the company's profitability but also positioned Liberty Mutual as a leader in international insurance.

A dual figure in transatlantic business and Irish-American heritage, Edmund Kelly embodies the role of the modern diaspora executive: intellectually rigorous, globally minded, and deeply influential in both economic and institutional spheres.

Source. Reference for Business. Edmund F. Kelly. https://www.referenceforbusiness.com/biography/F-L/Kelly-Edmund-F-1946.html#google_vignette. Accessed 21 June 2025.

Donald R. Keough (1926–2015) was a prominent American business executive and philanthropist, best known for his longstanding leadership roles at The Coca-Cola Company and his influence in U.S.–Irish business and cultural relations. Born in Maurice, Iowa, in 1926, Keough began his career with Coca-Cola in 1950 and rose through the ranks to become President and Chief Operating Officer from 1981 until his retirement in 1993. He also served as Chairman of Coca-Cola Enterprises, the company's global bottling division, and briefly as **Chairman of Columbia Pictures** prior to its acquisition by Sony.

Keough played a significant role in one of the most controversial marketing episodes in American business history—the 1985 launch of "New Coke"—and was instrumental in the swift return of the original formula following intense consumer backlash. His crisis leadership during this period is often cited in business case studies on brand management and customer loyalty.

Following his retirement from Coca-Cola, Keough became Chairman of Allen & Company, a New York-based investment bank, where he continued to exert influence across multiple sectors. He held board positions at major U.S. corporations, including Berkshire Hathaway, McDonald's, The Washington Post Company, Home Depot, and IAC/InterActiveCorp.

Deeply connected to his Irish heritage, Keough received multiple honours from both the United States and Ireland. He was awarded honorary doctorates from Creighton University, the University of Notre Dame, Emory University, Trinity College Dublin, and Clark University. In 1993, he received the Laetare Medal, Notre Dame's highest honour, and was named *Irish America* magazine's first Irish-American of the Year. He was granted honorary Irish citizenship in 2007 and received the Presidential Distinguished Service Award for the Irish Abroad in 2013 from President Michael D. Higgins.

A Life Trustee and Chairman Emeritus of the Board of Trustees at the University of Notre Dame, Keough was also inducted into the American Academy of Arts & Sciences and the Junior Achievement National Business Hall of Fame. In 2010, he became the first inductee into the Irish America Hall of Fame. The Keough–Naughton Institute for Irish Studies and Keough School of Global Affairs at Notre Dame, as well as Keough Hall, named in honour of his wife Marilyn, reflect the family's lasting legacy in higher education and international engagement.

Source: Niall O'Dowd. October/November 2005. Donald Keough. *Irish America* Magazine. https://www.irishamerica.com/2025/02/donald-keough/. Accessed 21 June 2025.

John Francis Mitchell (1928–2009) was a pioneering engineer and inventor whose work helped lay the foundations for modern mobile telecommunications. Born in 1928 in Chicago, Illinois, he was the son of Irish Catholic immigrants—his father William Mitchell hailed from County Sligo and his mother Bridget Keane from Listowel, County Kerry. This Irish heritage remained a meaningful part of his identity throughout his life.

Mitchell's technical and leadership achievements are most prominently associated with Motorola, where he became Chief Engineer of Mobile Communication Products in 1960. Under his leadership, the company developed the world's first transistorised pager and, later, advanced the technology that made handheld cellular telephony possible. Working alongside Martin Cooper, Mitchell played a key role in the design and development of the first commercial portable cell phone—the DynaTAC 8000X, launched in 1983. Dubbed "the Boot" for its size, this device revolutionised how people communicate.

Beyond his technical contributions, Mitchell played a significant role in public service and industry leadership. In 1983, he was appointed to U.S. President Ronald Reagan's National Security Telecommunications Advisory Committee. He also held senior roles in organisations such as the Electronic Industries Alliance, the National Association of Manufacturers, and served on numerous boards including Bell & Howell Company.

Mitchell maintained deep connections to education and philanthropy. He served as a trustee of the Illinois Institute of Technology, where he established multiple endowed scholarships, and was active in the American Lung Association and Easter Seals Campaign. Notably, he also served as a trustee for two leading Irish institutions: Dublin City University and the University of Limerick Foundation. Alongside figures such as Chuck Feeney, Mitchell was instrumental in the transformative expansion of the University of Limerick during the 1990s and 2000s. His philanthropy helped shape the modern university landscape in Ireland.

He received numerous honours during his lifetime, including honorary doctorates from the Illinois Institute of Technology (1995), Iowa Wesleyan College (1985), and Dublin City University (1996). In 2003, he was awarded the Chicago Innovation Award, and in 2010, received a posthumous Lifetime Achievement Award from the IIT Alumni Association.

John F. Mitchell's legacy is one of innovation, public service, and global impact. Deeply rooted in his Irish heritage, he remained a committed supporter of Irish education and development while transforming how the world communicates.

Source: Wikipedia. John Francis Mitchell. https://en.wikipedia.org/wiki/John_Francis_Mitchell. Accessed 21 June 2025.

John A. ("Jack") Mulcahy (1906–1994) was an Irish-born American industrialist, entrepreneur, and philanthropist, widely recognised for his contributions to Irish economic development, tourism, and the bloodstock industry in the second half of the twentieth century. Born in Dungarvan, Co. Waterford, in 1906, Mulcahy emigrated to the United States at the age of 17 after participating in Ireland's revolutionary struggles. He settled in New York, studied accountancy at City University of New York, and began a career in industry with U.S. Rubber before joining Quigley Co., Inc., where he rose from treasurer in 1932 to President and CEO by 1952.

Mulcahy's influence extended far beyond business. A staunch Republican and close ally of Richard Nixon, he was a vocal opponent of the Kennedy family's immigration policies and played an advisory role in Irish-American relations during the Nixon era. Under his leadership, Quigley expanded internationally, and in 1963 he became the first Irish-American industrialist to invest substantially in Ireland, opening production plants in Cork and his native Dungarvan. He later facilitated Pfizer's entry into Ireland, laying the foundation for the country's pharmaceutical sector.

Deeply committed to the Irish economy and heritage, Mulcahy established Mulcon Ltd to manage diverse development projects, including the celebrated Waterville Golf Links and the restoration of Ashford Castle into a luxury hotel. His vision helped brand Ireland as a premier destination for high-end tourism. As a key figure in the revitalisation of Irish horse racing and breeding, he partnered with famed trainer Vincent O'Brien, supporting the repatriation of elite bloodstock and co-founding connections that would later define Irish equine excellence.

Though a naturalised American—he famously declared himself "an American citizen first, last, and all the time"—Mulcahy retained strong personal and philanthropic ties to Ireland. He funded multiple educational, historical, and sporting initiatives, including substantial donations to the Waterford GAA, New History of Ireland project, and various Irish universities. He was awarded honorary degrees by Fordham University, Iona College, and the National University of Ireland, among others. In 1971, he received the Gold Medal of the American Irish Historical Association for his contributions to Irish-American heritage.

Source: Murphy, Maureen. Mulcahy, John Augustine ('Jack'). *Dictionary of Irish Biography*. https://www.dib.ie/biography/mulcahy-john-augustine-jack-a6027. Accessed 21 June 2025.

Niall O'Dowd (b. 1953) is an Irish-born American journalist, author, and diaspora activist known for his instrumental role in fostering Irish-American engagement with the Northern Ireland peace process. Born in Thurles, County Tipperary, and raised in Drogheda, he studied at University College Dublin, graduating with a BA in 1977 before emigrating to the United States in 1978.

O'Dowd began his journalistic career in San Francisco, where he founded *The Irishman*, the first Irish newspaper in California in over half a century. In 1985, he relocated to New York and launched *Irish America* magazine, followed by the *Irish Voice* newspaper in 1987—both of which became key platforms for the Irish-American community. In 2009, he created *IrishCentral*, a digital news outlet connecting the global Irish diaspora.

A committed advocate for Irish unity and peace, O'Dowd was a central figure in the Irish-American campaign to support Bill Clinton's presidential bid in 1991. He later acted as an intermediary between Sinn Féin and the Clinton administration, notably playing a pivotal role in securing a U.S. visa for Gerry Adams in 1994—a symbolic and practical breakthrough in the lead-up to the Good Friday Agreement. His contribution to the peace process was documented in Conor O'Clery's *Daring Diplomacy* and in the RTÉ-PBS documentary *An Irish Voice*.

Beyond journalism, O'Dowd has been active in fostering diaspora influence in both business and politics. He established a number of high-profile Irish-American business networks, such as the Wall Street 50 and Business 100, and helped initiate the U.S.–Ireland Forum, a precursor to the Irish government's Global Irish Economic Forum. He also co-founded the Irish Lobby for Immigration Reform in 2005, aimed at regularising the status of undocumented Irish immigrants in the United States.

His publications include *Fire in the Morning* (2002), a bestselling account of Irish victims of 9/11; *An Irish Voice* (2010), his autobiography; *Lincoln and the Irish* (2017), exploring Irish-American contributions to the Union cause in the U.S. Civil War; and *A New Ireland* (2020), a reflection on Ireland's transformation into a socially liberal state.

O'Dowd has written for *The New York Times*, *The Guardian*, and *The Irish Times*, and has spoken internationally on diaspora engagement in peacebuilding, including at the U.S. State Department's Global Diaspora Conference in 2011. In recognition of his contributions, he was awarded an honorary doctorate by University College Dublin in 2004 and received the Irish government's Presidential Distinguished Service Award in 2014.

In 2011, O'Dowd briefly considered a bid for the Irish presidency as a diaspora candidate, describing himself as a voice for global Irish communities. Although he ultimately withdrew from the race, his candidacy sparked public debate on the political role of the diaspora in Ireland's future.

Source: Wikipedia. Niall O'Dowd. https://en.wikipedia.org/wiki/Niall_O%27Dowd. Accessed 21 June 2025.

Sir Anthony (Tony) **O'Reilly** (1936–2024) was an Irish businessman, international rugby union player, and prominent figure in transatlantic economic and philanthropic circles. Born in Dublin in 1936, he rose to global prominence both as a sporting legend and as a corporate leader. He was best known as the long-time chairman and CEO of the H.J. Heinz Company, a leading shareholder in Independent News & Media (INM), and a co-founder of The Ireland Funds. He held dual Irish and British citizenship and was knighted in the United Kingdom for services to Northern Ireland.

Educated at Belvedere College and later University College Dublin, where he studied law, O'Reilly was also enrolled as a solicitor, though he never practised. He later obtained a PhD in Agricultural Marketing from the University of Bradford. A precocious rugby talent, he made his debut for the Irish national team at 18 and went on to earn 29 international caps. He also toured with the British and Irish Lions, scoring a record number of tries, and played for the Barbarians. His contribution to rugby was recognised by his induction into both the International Rugby Hall of Fame and the IRB Hall of Fame.

In the corporate world, O'Reilly began his business career in the Irish semi-state sector, notably at An Bord Bainne and the Irish Sugar Company, before joining H.J. Heinz in 1969. He became the first non-family CEO and later chairman, transforming the company into a global player. Simultaneously, he invested heavily in media and manufacturing, serving as chairman of Waterford Wedgwood and INM. His media empire expanded internationally across Ireland, the United Kingdom, South Africa, Australia, and New Zealand.

Despite his earlier financial success—at one point being one of Ireland's few billionaires—O'Reilly's later years were marked by significant losses, particularly linked to the collapse of Waterford Wedgwood and a failed battle for control of INM. In 2014, he faced legal proceedings over debts exceeding €20 million. His property in the Bahamas was sold under bankruptcy terms, and he later resided in France and Ireland.

O'Reilly was also an influential philanthropist. He supported a wide range of educational, cultural, and civic projects in Ireland and abroad through the O'Reilly Foundation, which provided major scholarships and funded academic infrastructure at institutions such as University College Dublin (UCD), Trinity College Dublin, Dublin City University, and Queen's University Belfast. He financed the construction of multiple theatres and libraries that bear his family's name.

Notably, O'Reilly co-founded The Ireland Funds with Dan Rooney in 1976, creating a global philanthropic network that has raised over $600 million to support Irish cultural, educational, and peacebuilding initiatives, particularly during the Troubles.

Source: Wikipedia. Tony O'Reilly. https://en.wikipedia.org/wiki/Tony_O%27Reilly. Accessed 21 June 2025.

Daniel M. Rooney (1932–2017) was a distinguished American businessman, sports executive, and diplomat, best known as Chairman and former President of the Pittsburgh Steelers, one of the most successful franchises in the history of the National Football League (NFL). Born on 20 July 1932 in Pittsburgh, Pennsylvania, he was the son of Steelers founder Art Rooney and played a central role in the team's development from the 1960s onwards. During his tenure, the Steelers secured 6 Super Bowl titles, 15 division championships, and 8 AFC championships. Rooney is widely credited with establishing the "Rooney Rule", a policy mandating that NFL teams interview minority candidates for head coaching and executive positions—an initiative that has had significant influence across professional sports and beyond.

Rooney's leadership style was characterised by pragmatism, integrity, and inclusion, and he was known for his loyalty to staff and long-term vision. He oversaw the hiring of three head coaches over nearly four decades, each of whom brought the franchise sustained success. His decision-making in player recruitment and management was similarly long-sighted, including the 2004 drafting of quarterback Ben Roethlisberger, a pivotal moment in the team's modern history.

In addition to his sporting achievements, Rooney served as US Ambassador to Ireland from 2009 to 2012 under President Barack Obama. A committed Irish-American with deep ancestral ties to Ireland, Rooney was also co-founder of The Ireland Funds, a philanthropic organisation that has raised hundreds of millions of dollars to support education, peace and reconciliation, and community development across the island of Ireland. His ambassadorial term coincided with a sensitive post-crisis period, and he was noted for his efforts to deepen transatlantic ties and support cross-border initiatives in Northern Ireland.

Throughout his life, Rooney was committed to public service, bipartisan dialogue, and Irish-American engagement. He received numerous honours, including induction into the Pro Football Hall of Fame in 2000, and was widely respected across political and cultural spheres. Rooney passed away in Pittsburgh on 13 April 2017, leaving behind a legacy that straddled sport, diplomacy, and philanthropy.

Source: Wikipedia. Dan M. Rooney. https://en.wikipedia.org/wiki/Dan_M._Rooney. Accessed 21 June 2025.

Daniel P. Tully (1932–2016) was born in Queens, New York. He graduated from St. John's University in 1953 with a Bachelor's Degree in Business Administration, after which he served honourably in the U.S. Army from 1953 to 1955. Upon completing his service, Dan Tully began what would become a remarkable 42-year career at Merrill Lynch, Pierce, Fenner & Smith. Rising from the role of accounting trainee to Chairman and Chief Executive Officer, he retired in 1997, having led the firm during a period of unprecedented global expansion. Under his leadership, Merrill Lynch became the world's largest securities firm, employing 50,000 people and operating in 45 countries.

Dan Tully's tenure was guided by a deeply principled approach to leadership, rooted in the five core values of Merrill Lynch: client focus, respect for the individual, teamwork, responsible citizenship, and integrity. His influence extended far beyond Merrill Lynch. Throughout his career, Dan Tully played a prominent leadership role in the financial services industry, serving as Vice Chairman of the American Stock Exchange, the Securities Industry Association, and the New York Stock Exchange, as well as Chairman of the National Association of Securities Dealers.

At the invitation of the U.S. Securities and Exchange Commission, Dan Tully chaired the Tully Commission, a group of respected business leaders tasked with establishing ethical principles for compensation and investment advice across the securities industry.

In addition to his professional achievements, Dan Tully dedicated himself to civic and philanthropic endeavours. He chaired the Central Park Conservancy's "Wonders of New York" campaign, which played a vital role in the restoration of Central Park in the 1990s. In 2008, he helped found Fieldpoint Private Bank and Trust, a private banking and advisory firm that has since received numerous industry accolades and serves prominent families across the United States and internationally.

Dan Tully also maintained a lifelong connection to his Irish heritage. He served as President of the Ireland–U.S. Council for Commerce and Industry and as a Commissioner for the National Pensions Reserve Fund of Ireland. He found great joy in travelling through Ireland, especially playing golf at Waterville Golf Links and spending time in the surrounding village, where he formed deep and lasting bonds.

Source: Irishcentral.com. Death of Dan Tully—Woodside boy 1st of the Irish Americans to reach the top on Wall Street. https://www.irishcentral.com/news/community/death-dan-tully-woodside-boy-1st-irish-americans-wall-street. Accessed 21 June 2025.

Index[1]

[1] Note: Page numbers followed by 'n' refer to notes.

A. Groutel, *The Two Irelands and the Diaspora*, https://doi.org/10.1007/978-3-032-12355-8

FSC
www.fsc.org
MIX
Papier | Fördert gute Waldnutzung
FSC® C083411

Kolibri 360 GmbH
Ferdinand-Jühlke-Straße 7
99095 Erfurt, Deutschland
produktsicherheit@kolibri360.de